REGIONAL ECO

Regional Economics

MARION TEMPLE
Senior Lecturer in Economics
School of Real Estate Management
Oxford Brookes University

M
St. Martin's Press

© Marion Temple 1994

All rights reserved. No reproduction, copy or transmission of
this publication may be made without written permission.

No paragraph of this publication may be reproduced, copied or
transmitted save with written permission or in accordance with
the provisions of the Copyright, Designs and Patents Act 1988,
or under the terms of any licence permitting limited copying
issued by the Copyright Licensing Agency, 90 Tottenham Court
Road, London W1P 9HE.

Any person who does any unauthorised act in relation to this
publication may be liable to criminal prosecution and civil
claims for damages.

First published in Great Britain 1994 by
THE MACMILLAN PRESS LTD
Houndmills, Basingstoke, Hampshire RG21 2XS
and London
Companies and representatives
throughout the world

A catalogue record for this book is available
from the British Library.

ISBN 0-333-57364-1 hardcover
ISBN 0-333-57365-X paperback

Printed in Great Britain by
Mackays of Chatham PLC
Chatham, Kent

First published in the United States of America 1994 by
Scholarly and Reference Division,
ST. MARTIN'S PRESS, INC.,
175 Fifth Avenue,
New York, N.Y. 10010

ISBN 0-312-12225-X

Library of Congress Cataloging-in-Publication Data applied for

Contents

List of Tables and Figures ix
Acknowledgements xii

Introduction xv

1 The Region and Regional Economics 1

   THE REGIONAL FRAMEWORK 1
      Regional Economics 1
      The Place of the Region 2
      The European Context 3
   THE REGION 4
      The Concept of a Region 5
      Administrative and Political Structures 8
      Cultural Influences 9
   THE REGIONAL PATTERN OF ECONOMIC ACTIVITY 9
      The Pattern of Output 9
      The Pattern of Employment 14
      Patterns of Leisure Activity 16
   REGIONAL ISSUES 18
      Contemporary Regional Issues 19
      Problem Regions and Regional Problems 19
      A Problem Region and Some Regional Issues 20
   THE STRUCTURE OF THE BOOK 21

2 Capital, Labour and Land in the Region 26

   REGIONAL OUTPUT AND EMPLOYMENT 26
      Deindustrialisation and the Regional Economy 26
      The Structure of Employment 29
      Regional Unemployment: An Introduction 34
      Shifts in the Structure of the Regional Economy 35
   REGIONAL MARKETS FOR THE FACTORS OF PRODUCTION 38
      Capital: Regional Dependence and External Sourcing 38
      Labour 46
      Land 65

3 Expenditure, Prices and Exchange 71

REGIONAL EXPENDITURE 71
   Income and Expenditure Patterns 71
   Consumption and Expenditure 79
   The Regional Multiplier 84
REGIONAL IMPORT–EXPORT RELATIONSHIPS 85
   Regional Input–Output Models 85
   The Imbalance of Regional Payments 90
PRICES AND REGIONAL ECONOMIC WELFARE 93
   The Operation of the Price System 93
   The Limitations of the Market 95
   Externalities: Social Costs and Benefits 98
   Welfare Economics 101

4 The Region in the National Economy 103

REGIONAL ECONOMIC GROWTH 103
   Regional Growth Within the National Economy 104
   What Influences the Economic Growth of a Region? 106
CYCLICAL FLUCTUATIONS AND THE REGIONAL ECONOMY 111
   What is an Economic Cycle? 111
   Why do Cyclical Fluctuations Occur? 114
REGIONAL UNEMPLOYMENT 118
   Characteristics of those Unemployed in the Regional Economy 122
   Why is there Regional Unemployment? 124
   Disequilibrium and Adjustment in the Regional Labour Market 127
THE REGIONAL IMPACT OF INFLATION 134

5 The Regional Location of Economic Activity 137

LOCATION THEORY 137
   The Framework for Location Theory 137
   Efficiency and Equity in Regional Location 142
THE REGIONAL LOCATION OF ECONOMIC ACTIVITY 145
   Manufacturing Location 145
   Office Location 146
   Retail Location 149
MANAGEMENT AND THE LOCATION DECISION 151
   The Location Decision and the Economic Environment 151
   Location and Property-Portfolio Strategies 152
   Property Management and the Location Decision 154
THE REGIONAL LOCATION OF PUBLIC-SECTOR ACTIVITY 155

6 Regional Growth — 157

THE SPATIAL PATTERN OF GROWTH — 157
- Interregional Trading Linkages — 159
- Regional Growth and the Terms of Trade — 163

CONVERGENCE AND DIVERGENCE — 165
- Core and Periphery in the EC Regions — 165
- Regional Convergence — 166
- Regional Divergence — 169
- Growth Zones and the Periphery — 173

GROWTH AND THE REGIONAL LABOUR MARKET — 177
- Labour Mobility — 177
- Migration and the Housing Market — 181

7 Urban Policies — 192

TAXATION IN THE LOCAL AND REGIONAL ECONOMY — 193
- The Local Tax Base — 193
- Property Taxes and their Regional Impact — 195

URBAN POLICIES — 198
- The Need for Urban Policy — 199
- The Evolution of Urban Policies — 202
- Urban Regeneration: Public/Private Partnership — 208
- Future Directions for Urban Policy — 212

APPENDIX: URBAN POLICY IN THE UK, 1969–93 — 218

8 Regional Economic Policy — 225

AN INTRODUCTION TO REGIONAL POLICY — 225
- Regional Policy Aims and Objectives — 225
- The Policy Framework — 226

POLICY INSTRUMENTS — 227
- Macroeconomic and Regional Policy Instruments — 227
- Regional Policy Incentives and Constraints — 229

REGIONAL POLICY MEASURES — 230
- The Evolution of UK Regional Policy — 230
- The Regional Impact of Public-Sector Location — 239

REGIONAL POLICY AND THE EUROPEAN COMMUNITY — 245
- The Policy Framework — 245
- Assistance to the EC Periphery — 247
- EC Regional Policy in the 1990s — 248

APPENDIX: REGIONAL POLICY IN THE UK, 1972–93 — 249

9 An Effective Regional Policy? — 261

THE IMPLEMENTATION OF REGIONAL POLICY — 261
  The Targeting of Policy Measures — 261
  Policy Implementation — 264
THE MEASUREMENT OF THE EFFECTS OF REGIONAL POLICY — 266
  The Costs and Benefits of Regional Policy — 266
  Some Problems of Measurement — 270
AN EVALUATION OF REGIONAL POLICY — 276
  The Private Sector, the Public Sector and the Welfare of the Region — 276
  Competition or Complementarity? — 277
  The Need for Subsidiarity — 278
  The Effects of Deindustrialisation — 279
AN EFFECTIVE REGIONAL POLICY? — 280
  The Need for Regional Policy — 280
  Conditions for an Effective Regional Policy — 281

Conclusion — 285

Select Bibliography — 289

Index — 294

List of Tables and Figures

Tables

2.1	The distribution of male and female employment by sector in the UK, June 1992	32
2.2	Regional economic activity rates, March–May 1992	50
2.3	Occupational distribution of the labour force, March–May 1992	61
3.1	Regional distribution of household income by source, 1990–1	74
3.2	A simple input–output model	87
3.3	Regional distribution of income-tax liability and of the main social security benefits, 1990–1	92
4.1	Regional distribution of net capital expenditure and gross value in manufacturing industry, 1981 and 1990	108
4.2	Regional unemployment, 1981–June 1993	119
4.3	Unemployment rate and disposable income, selected subregions	121
5.1	Main considerations in retail location	150
7.1	Urban Development Corporations in England	219
7.2	Enterprise zones in the UK	222
7.3	City Grants, May 1988–November 1992	223
9.1	Main social costs and benefits of regional policy	267

Figures

1.1	A spatial economic hierarchy	2
1.2	The EC regions, 1993	6
1.3	The UK regions, 1993	7
1.4	GDP in the UK regions, 1982–91	10
1.5	Sectoral employment in the EC economies, 1990	15
1.6	Sectoral distribution of employment in the UK regions, 1990	17
2.1	Manufacturing output as a share of GDP, 1960–88	27
2.2	Changes in the sectoral distribution of employment in the UK regions, 1981–92	31
2.3	Unemployment rates, selected EC member economies, 1980–8	34
2.4	The supply of capital to the region	44
2.5	The supply of capital to the EC	45
2.6	Regional annual growth rates of population, 1961–91	49
2.7	The supply of labour to the firm	51

2.8	The marginal and average input cost of labour	51
2.9	The firm's demand for labour	52
2.10	The marginal revenue product and value of marginal product of labour	53
2.11	The supply of labour in a perfectly competitive market	54
2.12	Equilibrium in the regional labour market	56
2.13	Regional wage differences reflecting employer preferences	57
2.14	Regional wage differences reflecting labour immobility	58
2.15	Qualifications of the workforce in the UK regions, 1992	60
2.16	Underemployment of labour in the regional economy	63
2.17	The short-term supply of land	65
2.18	The equilibrium level of rent	66
2.19	The determination of rent in the long term	68
2.20	Bilateral monopoly in the regional land market	68
3.1	Regional distribution of per capita personal disposable income, 1991	71
3.2	Subregional distribution of household disposable income, 1990	72
3.3	The extent of intraregional variation in average household disposable income, 1990	73
3.4	Regional distribution of the main social security benefits, 1990–1	77
3.5	The consumption function	80
3.6	The aggregate expenditure function	82
3.7	Equilibrium income and output in the regional economy	83
3.8	Full employment equilibrium in the region	83
3.9	Financial flows into and out of the region	86
3.10	Market equilibrium	94
3.11	Positive consumption externalities	99
3.12	Pollution as a negative production externality	100
4.1	Growth and cycles	103
4.2	GDP in the UK regions, 1982–91	105
4.3	A long-term increase in aggregate supply	106
4.4	Stages of the cycle	112
4.5	UK GDP, 1978–86	113
4.6	Changes in aggregate demand	115
4.7	Duration of unemployment by gender, January 1993	120
4.8	Classical unemployment	126
4.9	Keynesian unemployment	127
4.10	Unemployment due to an increase in the regional labour supply	128
4.11	Regional unemployment due to below-average labour productivity	130

4.12	Interregional labour-market adjustment	132
6.1	GDP per capita, EC economies, 1990	158
6.2	Characteristic market conditions for a primary product	163
6.3	Peripheral regions in receipt of EC Objective Funding, 1993	167
6.4	The supply-side adjustment process	168
6.5	Investment-led expansion in the attractive region	171
6.6	La Dorsale	175
6.7	East–West growth zones	175
6.8	Regional distribution of owner-occupied and rented housing, 1981–91	183
6.9	The housing trap	187
6.10	Regional variations in house prices, 1981–92	188
7.1	The positive externalities of infrastructure provision	216
7.2	UDCs, Inner City Task Forces and City Action Teams, England, 1993	220
8.1	Government expenditure on regional preferential assistance to industry in the assisted areas, 1984–5 to 1991–2	235
8.2	New locations and relocations of government departments and agencies from the South East since March 1988	243
8.3	Regions eligible for Objective 1 Funding, 1989–93	250
8.4	EC regions eligible for Objective 1 Funding, 1993	251
8.5	Assisted areas, UK, 1972–7	256
8.6	Assisted areas, UK, 1977–82	257
8.7	Assisted areas, UK, 1984–93	258
8.8	Assisted areas, UK, 1993	259

Acknowledgements

When Stephen Rutt heard that I had returned to a previous field of interest and begun lecturing in spatial economics again, he was kind enough to suggest that I think about writing a text on the subject. This book is the result of his suggestion, and his subsequent encouragement and constructive advice are greatly appreciated. If at least some of its readers enjoy reading the book as much as I have enjoyed writing it, the time taken in its authorship will have been well spent.

Academics deal in the currency of ideas. The compilation of those ideas into a text designed to enhance their accessibility to potential readers is no exception. In the process of compilation, the existing pool of knowledge is drawn upon extensively – both consciously and subconsciously – by the author. The present author's debt to academic colleagues who are interested in, and/or have written about, issues pertinent to regional economics is accordingly gratefully acknowledged.

As noted above, the initial writing of this book coincided with the preparation of lectures used for my own teaching. Students in the past two academic years have acted as a sounding board for some of the material. Their responses, questions and ideas have helped provide me with some interesting thoughts, both about regional economics and about some of the continuing gaps in our understanding of the regional economy.

Economists are well aware of the opportunity cost of the use of their time. Working within a comparatively small university department such as the School of Real Estate Management at Oxford Brookes University, the opportunity cost of undertaking a project on the scale of this book is tangible. Apologies are therefore due to all my colleagues there for that work not undertaken during the preparation of this book, accompanied by thanks for their patience.

Such considerations have also affected my family, whose patience and encouragement are greatly appreciated. Particular thanks are due to my son, Martin, who assisted with the calculations and accuracy of the tables and pointed out some overly opaque sections in the text.

I am also grateful to the anonymous referee whose comments on an earlier version of the text were very useful and helpful. Remaining errors and omissions are solely the fault of the author.

MARION TEMPLE

Acknowledgements

The author and publishers are grateful to the Central Statistical Office for permission to reproduce copyright tables and extracts of tables from *Regional Trends*, and to the Department of the Environment for permission to reproduce the material in Figure 7.2.

Introduction

Regional economics is an area of specialism of relevance to students studying a variety of courses. An understanding of the spatial dimension of the economy is relevant to economists if they are to appreciate fully the operation of economic mechanisms. Regional economics is relevant to students studying many courses relating to the built environment, such as planning and real-estate management. Knowledge of the regional economy is essential to students of economic geography.

While this book centres primarily upon the economics of the regional economy, the subject matter will be of interest to planners, geographers and real-estate managers too. The text has been written to provide a bridge between introductory economics and the advanced material to be found in relevant academic journals and texts aimed at final-year/postgraduate students.

The economic analysis contained in the book draws upon tools such as demand and supply, with which students who have undertaken introductory courses in economics at undergraduate level should be familiar. While knowledge of this economic analysis will help the reader, most of the argument should also be accessible to those who are less familiar with formal economic theory.

This book looks at the economics of the region in the context of the spatial economic hierarchy. The influence of subregional and local urban economies upon the regional economy is recognised. The dependence of the regional economy upon the wider national and supranational economic framework is considered.

The influence of the European Community is seen to be particularly important. The single-internal-market provisions adopted in 1993, the likely European Economic Area, embracing the European Free Trade Area and the EC economies, and the potential further extension of EC membership, all point towards greater spatial interaction and economic competition among regions in Europe in the late 1990s.

The book begins by looking at the constituent parts of the regional economy, which to a considerable degree are common to most regions in Europe. The supply conditions of production-process inputs of capital, labour and land are considered. The main influences upon demand are then explained as a prelude to considering the operation of prices and markets in the regional economy, and interregional trading relationships.

The middle chapters discuss the location of economic activity and the effects on the regional economy of changing patterns of growth and location. Later chapters draw upon the earlier content to discuss the main spatial policy issues. The increased role of urban policy as a tool of regional policy is recognised, as is that of the European Community, in addition to discussion of longer-established regional policy issues.

As explained above, regional economics is an area in which people from different subject disciplines, such as economists, geographers and planners, all have an interest. For this reason the potentially relevant academic literature is extensive. This book does not seek to be encyclopaedic in its coverage of currently available academic research. To ensure that the arguments presented in the text are not unduly interrupted, reference to research is deliberately selective. The objective of such referencing is to interest the reader in further investigation and to provide pointers towards more detailed literature.

For this reason, at the end of each chapter a limited number of references are made to particularly relevant journal articles and literature on the subject. The bibliography at the end of the book offers a fuller indication of the scope of relevant literature that may be of interest to the reader wishing to find out more about regional economics.

A comparable approach is taken with the coverage of EC regions outside the UK, which centres on selected brief case studies. These are utilised to illuminate topics of interest in the text, and are not designed to offer an extensive coverage of EC regions outside the UK, which would be beyond the scope of this book.

The book raises many questions about the operation of the regional economy; the disparities in the recent economic growth and development experience of different regions of the UK and the EC; and the nature of political policy responses to regional issues. For the most part, answers to these questions are not to be found in this book. Rather than offering definitive answers the objective of this book is to raise questions and help provide readers with necessary information and ideas that will enable them to pursue their own analysis, and to stimulate debate on the questions.

MARION TEMPLE

1 The Region and Regional Economics

THE REGIONAL FRAMEWORK

Regional Economics

Economics is often defined as being about the *allocation* of scarce resources between competing uses in order to *produce* goods and services, and about how those goods and services should be *distributed* among individuals.

Much theory focuses upon this in the static sense, using techniques of partial and general equilibrium analysis. When economists wish to extend their analysis in order to consider economic behaviour over a period of time in the context of a dynamic environment, they adjust their use of these analytic techniques accordingly.

Similarly, when economists wish to extend their analysis in order to consider economic behaviour over a geographical area in the context of the spatial environment, they take analytic techniques with which students are familiar from introductory courses in economics and extend their use in a way that is appropriate to that field of enquiry.

For the study of economics within the context of the region to be worthwhile, we must believe that this spatial dimension is intrinsic to the subject matter of economics. Further, we must believe that one of the 'spaces' relevant to our investigation corresponds to a 'region'.

The European economies are primarily driven by monetary exchange: where barter activity exists, it is on a localised scale and is small in terms of relative value. So, analysis of 'real' economic activity within the region must be paralleled by analysis of the corresponding financial flows that have an impact on the region.

Economics is a social science, and so it is concerned with the behaviour of individuals as agents within a broader structural framework. We shall therefore be looking at the individual in the role of 'economic agent', both as consumer of the output of the production process and as supplier of the factors of production necessary to that production process.

We shall also be concerned with the organisations that influence and affect the individual's economic behaviour: both employing organisations and government as it relates to the regional economy. The balance of economic activity between private and public sector and the differences among the main European economies in this regard will be discussed, as will the impact of public policy upon the regional economy.

The Place of the Region

The pattern of spatial economic activity can be simplified as a series of circles: the innermost circle representing the local economy, the next representing the regional economy, the next the national economy, the next the European economy, and the outermost representing the international economy (Figure 1.1).

The amount and the importance of economic activity both within and between the different circles will vary among different individual economies. To take the example most relevant to this book, the regional level or circle of economic activity will be stronger in some economies than in others.

This will be true of other important aspects of regional life too. In the UK there is less political administration and decison-making at regional level than in some other comparable European economies such as Germany, France and Spain. The political and administrative system of the UK has traditionally been relatively centralised and has become increasingly so during the 1980s and early 1990s. This centralisation of political control in recent years has been parallelled by the reduction of the scope of financial and political power vested with local government in the UK.

Commercial and financial activity in the individual regions of the UK are also often effectively controlled from a central national headquarters in London. However in this respect the UK's economy is less centralised than are the economies of France or the Republic of Ireland.

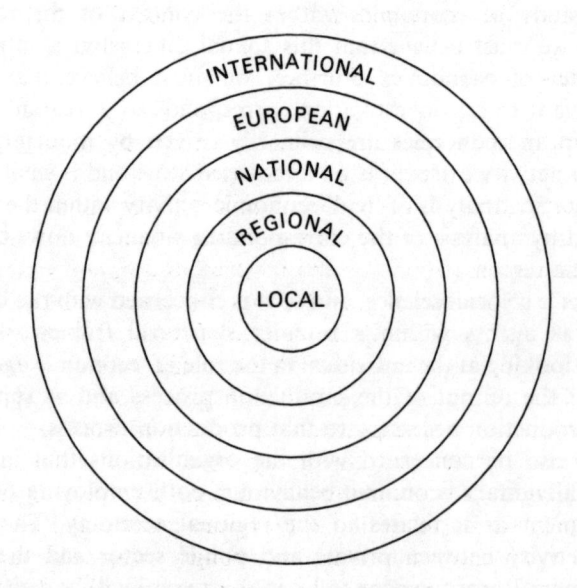

Figure 1.1 A spatial economic hierarchy

Many regional economists and commentators are concerned that the UK regions that are located furthest from London have become 'branch plant' economies. As these branch plants of larger organisations are owned and managed from outside the region, the affected region may lack effective control over its destiny. The resulting patterns of economic dependency then mirror those created by the multinational patterns of ownership of large organisations in the international economy.

So banking, finance and industry in the UK are controlled increasingly from boardrooms in London as ownership of economic assets has become increasingly concentrated at national level in recent decades. The underlying questions are whether the drift of ownership to the south east has reduced control of the economy at the local level, and whether this matters for the future of the regional economy.

The UK media are also heavily centralised. Although local and provincial newspapers continue to exist, they are less strong, for example, than their French counterparts. Of the media, it is local radio that can hope to generate and retain local interest.

Relatively low cross-country transport times compared with France or Italy also add to the effective integration of the UK economy relative to some of its mainland-European counterparts.

As result of this relatively well integrated economy, the extent of the regional disparities introduced in the next chapter are less than the extent of those between the north and south of Italy. However interregional disparities both clearly exist in the UK and are of increasing relevance in the mid-1990s as they have widened in extent since the late 1970s.

The European Context

Why is the European context important to an investigation of the regional economy?

UK, and particularly English, perceptions of the relationship between the region and the political centre may be unduly influenced by the island geography that focuses attention on the island as a nation state. Awareness on the European mainland of growth zones that transcend national political boundaries is likely to influence the pattern of regional development on the continent. Similarly regions may well develop differentially in relation to the European market to a greater extent than they do in relation to the national economy. Awareness of the potential and the problems generated by the single European market and the European context within which much growth and expansion is occurring has led regional and local economies to compete for a share in the available European growth and investment.

European policy intervention is also strongly directed at regions rather than at nation states. Scotland has direct access to some sources of European funding without always having to use London as an intermediary.

European Community regional policy therefore also plays a role in influencing the regional economy in the 1990s, as we shall see in Chapter 8.

Every economic activity within every region in Europe is now taking place within the framework of the single European market. While some aspects of European market harmonisation have been delayed, the potential economic effects of the single European market cannot be ignored.

The creation of the single market should create the market size and market flexibility needed as a prerequisite to future economic growth and expansion. While the removal of technical, physical and fiscal barriers to economic activity will not be as complete in practice as it might appear in theory, a supranational European economy will undoubtedly be created. While individual nations and individual regions are likely to retain their cultural and linguistic independence and diversity, the unified market within which they function will be a major influence upon their economic development.

The framework of the European market is important because of its economic size and potential. In terms of wealth, income and population the internal European market rivals the internal market of the USA. This means that the internal conditions for growth are present.

Eastern Europe also provides an area for potential external expansion into new markets. Expansion and trade are important because of the existing trading status of the European economies and their component regions. Traditionally their economies have been far more 'open' than for instance those of the USA and its constituent states.

For these reasons the European context and the constraints and opportunities presented by the increasing 'Europeanisation' of the regional economy will be a continuing theme of this book.

THE REGION

For administrative purposes, the larger regions in the European Community are those areas shown on Figure 1.2. As is clear from the map, there is no standard approach among the different EC countries in relation to defining their constituent regions. Neither geographical size nor population size are directly comparable, as the regional make up of the different member economies reflects the political and administrative system that has evolved in each.

Figure 1.3 illustrates the constituent 'standard regions' for the UK on a larger scale. These are:

1. North
2. North West
3. West Midlands
4. East Midlands

5. South West
6. South East
7. East Anglia
8. Yorkshire & Humberside

in England and, in addition, the three nation-regions of:

1. Wales
2. Scotland
3. Northern Ireland.

These are the administrative regions to which the detailed UK statistics quoted in this book refer. As with the European regions, the UK standard regions are not so standard: Scotland is the largest measured by geographical area while the South East is the largest in terms of population size.

With these varations in mind, the following paragraphs consider the concept of a region more closely.

The Concept of a Region

The concept of a region can sometimes appear elusive or inconsistent and therefore of dubious merit. Can a region be defined in terms of some generally acceptable straightforward quantitative measure such as population size, income or rates of internal economic activity? The answer tends to be negative: the definition of a region remains essentially complex and qualitative in many respects, influenced by convention and custom as well as by administrative convenience or even – sometimes – economic cohesion.

In relation to the UK, Scotland offers a good example of the difficulties of applying a simple definition to a 'region'. Scotland is a nation with an independent judiciary and separate education system, but it is also an administrative region of the UK. Within the Scottish economy are smaller local economies: the Highlands economy is noticeably and clearly different from that of the central Edinburgh–Glasgow belt.

The Scottish economy as a separate economic entity would not be out of place within the EC context. Scottish Gross National Product is smaller than that of Norway or Denmark but it is significantly greater than that of Greece, Ireland or Portugal, which are individual nation members of the EC. However these are identifiably the economies in the EC with the lowest income and growth. So they may not provide good evidence to support the case for an independent Scotland.

The Scottish economy clearly is not short of economic resources. The Scottish education system is good and the economy's labour force as skilled as many elsewhere in Europe. Scotland has its own natural resources, notably North-Sea oil. It could be financiallly independent of the rest of the UK in that two banks are Scottish and Edinburgh is a major international

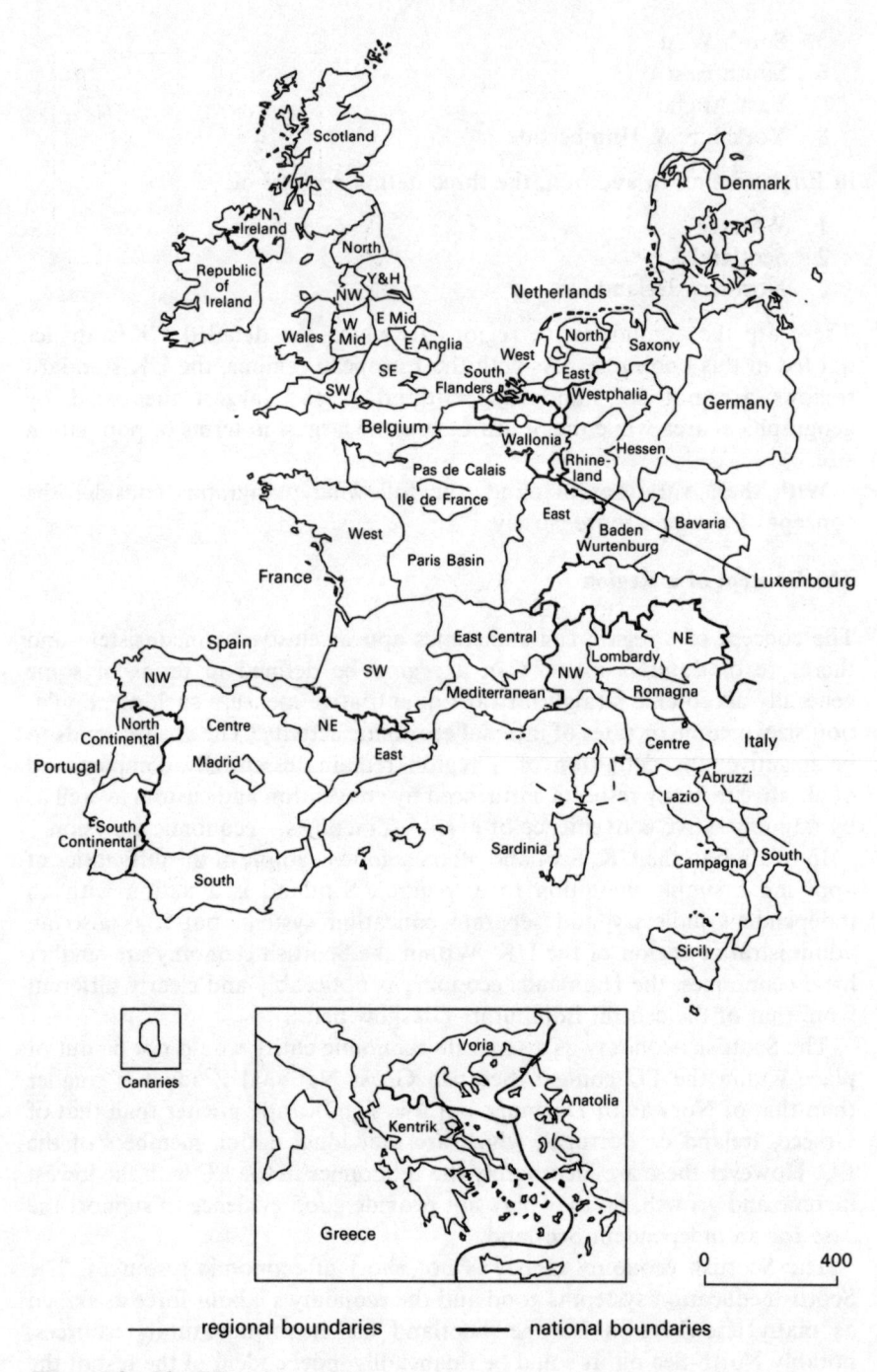

Figure 1.2 *The EC regions, 1993*

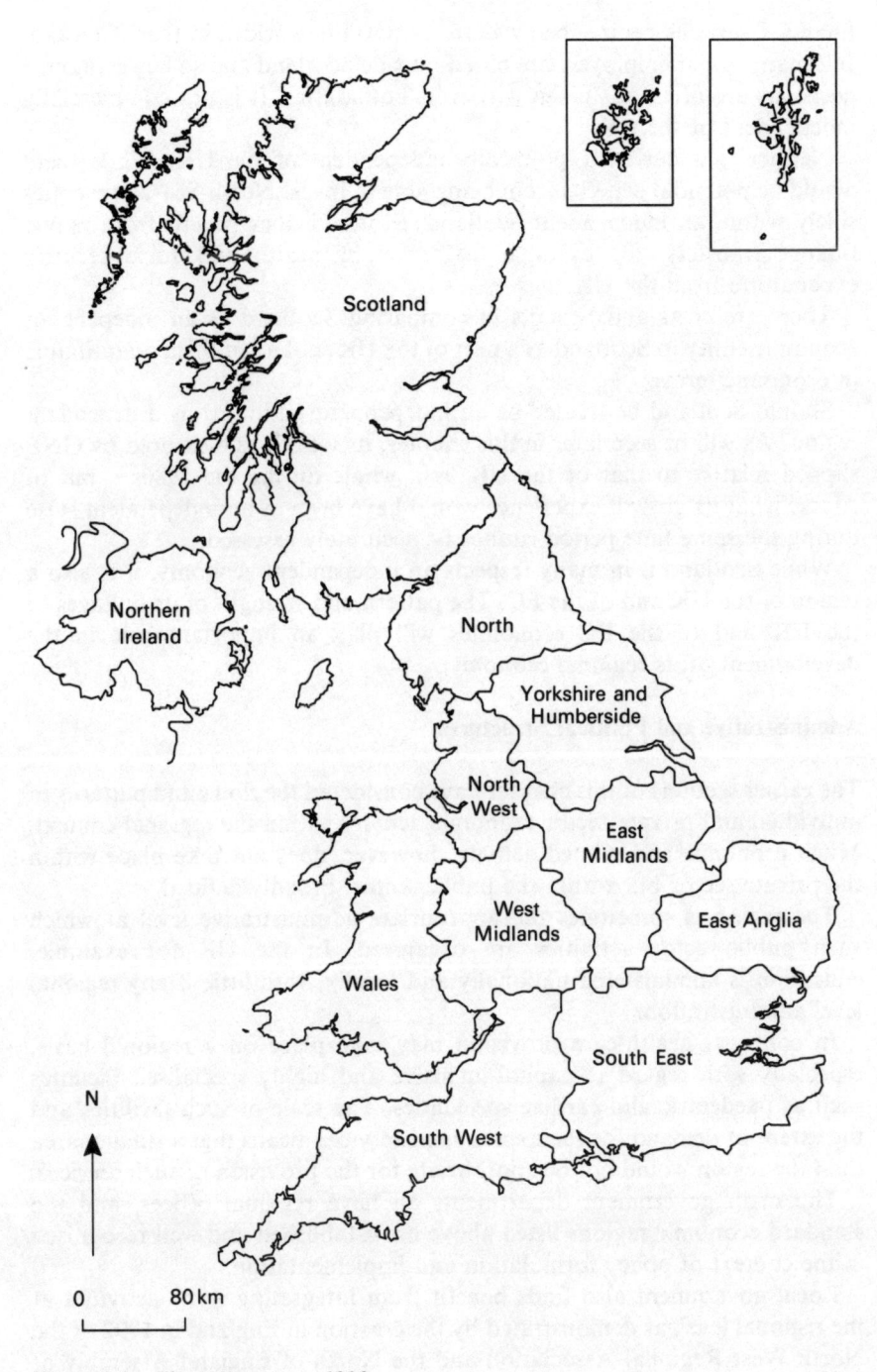

Figure 1.3 The UK regions, 1993

financial services centre, being more important worldwide than Chicago. But many major employers are based outside Scotland and so key economic decisions are often not taken within its boundaries. It is not commercially independent of the UK.

Neither is it currently politically independent of the UK. While there would be potential benefits from being able to invest North-Sea-oil revenues solely within an independent Scotland, Scotland does benefit from public finance transfers, for example, in terms of health and social-security expenditure from the UK.

There are costs and benefits in comparing Scotland as an independent economic entity to Scotland as a part of the UK, not all of them quantifiable in economic terms.

Should Scotland be treated as an independent nation or as a dependent region? As will be seen later in this chapter, its wealth as measured by GNP slipped relative to that of the UK as a whole during the 1980s – but of course what its growth experience would have been as an independent state during the same time period cannot be accurately assessed.

While Scotland is in many respects an independent economy, it is also a region of the UK and of the EC. The pattern and strength of its linkages to the UK and to the EC economies will play an important role in the development of its regional economy.

Administrative and Political Structures

The earlier sections of this chapter have considered the flows and patterns of individual and private-sector economic activity within the regional context. Much economic and related activity, however, does not take place within the private sector but within the public sector, broadly defined.

The region is sometimes the appropriate administrative level at which such public-sector activities are organised. In the UK for example, education is administered nationally and locally, with little if any regional level administration.

In contrast, health-care provision may take place on a regional basis, especially with regard to capital-intensive and highly specialised facilities such as paedeatric and cardiac specialities. The scale of such facilities and the extent of demand for their specialised services means that a smaller area than the region would not be appropriate for the provision of such services.

The main government departments all have regional offices, and the standard economic regions listed above are established and well recognised in the context of policy formulation and implementation.

Local government also finds benefit from integrating some activities at the regional level, as demonstrated by the creation in England in 1992 of the North West Regional Association and the North of England Assembly of Local Authorities.

Attitudes to planning at the regional level differ significantly from country to country. Similarly, the extent of regional political power and identity vary among different countries, as does the strength of regional administrative systems. The German regions – the *Länder* – such as the Rhineland palatinate have a much stronger regional identity and degree of effective autonomy from central government than is the case in England. The German metropolitan cities of Berlin, Bremen and Hamburg equally have greater rights as 'city states' than do their English counterparts.

The European Commission has recognised the usefulness of the region through the work of the EC Committee of the Regions. The region is administratvely rational as a point of reference between central and local government: what is more problematic is whether the region should be an appropriate level of decentralisation for political power and government in the search for effective subsidiarity inside the European Community.

Cultural Influences

Regions within the nation sometimes have their own clear cultural identities. This may be associated with linguistic, political and cultural differences between the region and the nation of which it is a part, as is the case in Catalonia in north-eastern Spain. Where the differences are significant and the benefits of being a member of the nation are not perceived as great, then pressures for independence of the region from the nation build up, as in Catalonia, or in Scotland and Northern Ireland.

Political differences and disunity can be noticeable even where cultural divergence is less obvious than in the above cases. For example the voting patterns in the UK 1992 general election showed a clear regional disparity in political support. With the exception of central London, the south of England tends to vote predominantly Conservative while the north of England, Scotland and Wales all predominantly vote Labour. The implications for political and cultural cohesion are clear. What is interesting too in the context of regional economics is whether the voting pattern and accompanying pattern of political support in the UK during the 1980s and 1990s has significantly affected central government's perception of the importance of an active regional policy within the UK economy.

THE REGIONAL PATTERN OF ECONOMIC ACTIVITY

The Pattern of Output

This section serves as a brief introduction to the more detailed exploration of the regional structure of output and of the markets for the factors of production, that is, land, labour and capital that follows in Chapter 2.

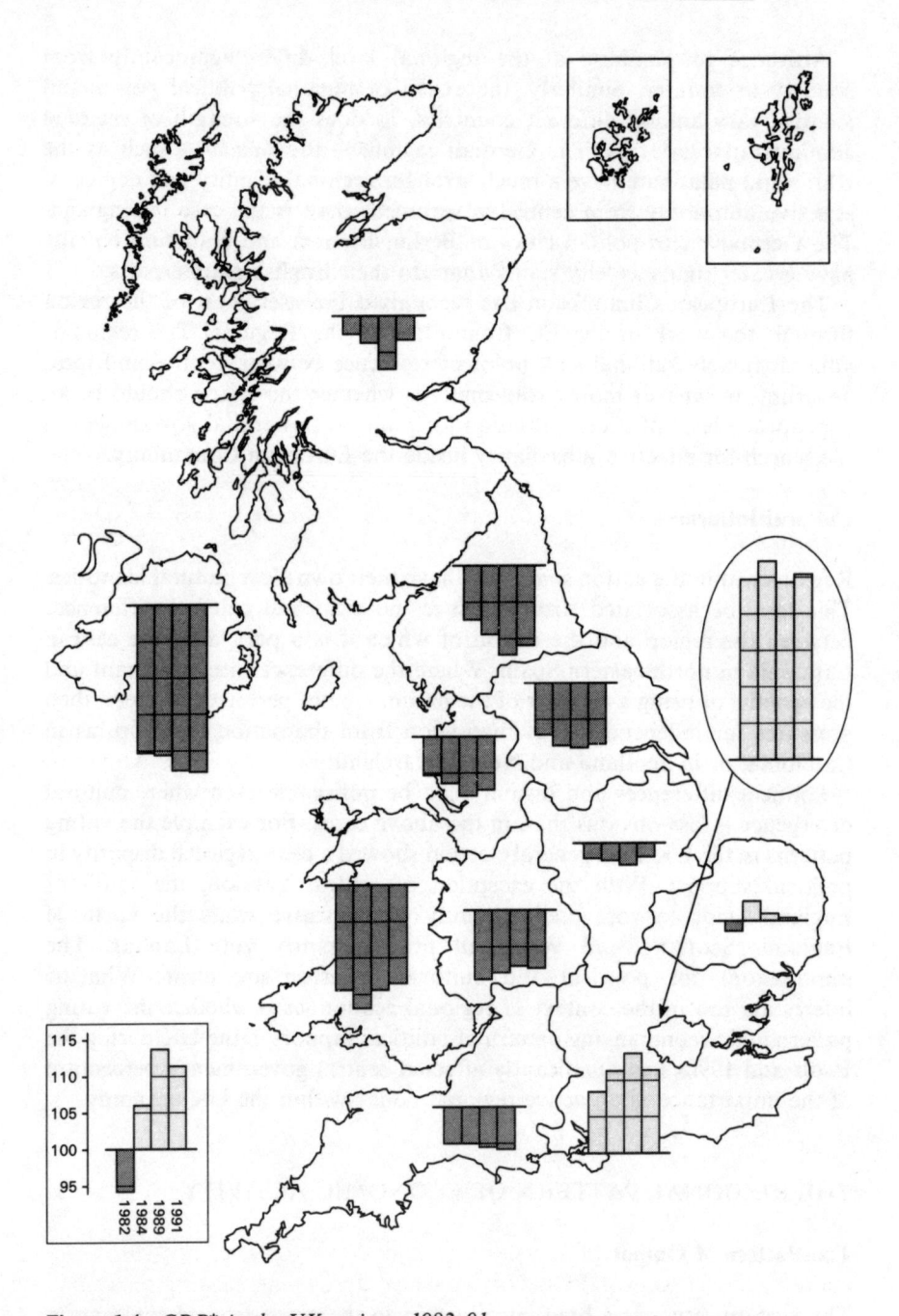

Figure 1.4 *GDP* in the UK regions, 1982–91*
* GDP per head at factor cost and current prices relative to UK index = 100.
Source of data: UK CSO, *Regional Trends*, vol. 28 (1993), table 12.1.

Figure 1.4 shows the regional distribution of per capita GDP for four years between 1982 and 1991. The UK figure is taken to be 100, so all regions with per capita GDP above 100 have per capita GDP above the national average. Figures below 100 indicate below national average regional per capita GDP.

The figures for England and the nation regions show that England as a nation has consistently enjoyed a slightly above average per capita GDP, at around 102 per cent of the UK average. In contrast Scotland, Wales and Northern Ireland are well below the average. Scotland has experienced around 92–96 per cent of the average UK per capita GDP. Wales has consistently had about 82–86 per cent of the UK average value of per capita GDP. However Northern Ireland shows the greatest deficit relative to the UK overall at 77–80 per cent.

Other aspects of this relative weakness of the 'outer regions' will become apparent during this book. For the present it is noteworthy that these indicators are not untypical of the pattern of interregional disparities in the UK economy during the 1980s.

While per capita GDP in Northern Ireland is nearly 25 per cent below the UK average, Figure 1.4 demonstrates that the Greater London area of the South East of England enjoys a figure 25 per cent above the average. The overall gap between the richest and poorest regions in the UK as measured by per capita GDP is therefore 50 per cent.

In view of some of the underlying structural changes that have taken place in the UK economy since the late 1970s, the consistency of the ranking of the regions in Figure 1.4 is almost surprising. One region that has experienced a relative deterioration in its living standards as measured by per capita GDP is the North of England, which has slipped below 90 per cent of the UK average since the mid-1980s.

The UK recession of the early 1990s diminished the extent of the interregional gap to a limited extent as the south of England was particularly adversely affected. However as the recovery also began in the South East, it appears relatively unlikely that this reduction in UK interregional disparities will be other than temporary. The extent of these interregional disparities therefore forms an important part for the rationale for policy intervention in the region discussed at the beginning of Chapter 8.

The structure of output in the economy

Output is usually categorised into three main sectors: primary, secondary and tertiary. The primary sector is made up of agriculture and energy production. The secondary sector consists mainly of manufacturing, for example, car production. The tertiary sector is services, for example, banking.

Some regions have a pattern of output dominated by economic activity within one of these sectors. In such a case the region's output is sectorally specialised. Other regions may have a more diverse sectoral structure of production, with two or three of the primary, manufacturing and tertiary sectors contributing a significant proportion to total regional output.

Within the EC, the structure of output by sector within the national economies of the individual members is very different. For example, in 1990 the sectoral shares in total output in the UK were such that agriculture represented less than 5 per cent, manufacturing about 25 per cent and services over two thirds of the total.

In this respect the UK has an unusually high proportion of output in the tertiary and an unusually low proportion in the manufacturing sector compared with similar European economies. Historically it is now accepted that economies pass through a period of sectoral structural change accompanied by a shrinking of the primary sector and expansion of the secondary – manufacturing – sector. This process of economic change is continuing in many regions of Europe, including areas of France, the Republic of Ireland and Italy.

The deindustrialisation of the UK, reflected in the shrinking of manufacturing output and employment in the 1980s, has undoubtedly had a major impact upon certain of its constituent regional economies. What is less clear is whether this is a long-term, 'inevitable' structural trend in economic development analogous to the revolution experienced in the agricultural sector, or a highly undesirable short-term experience that should be reversed as soon as possible.

The structure of output in the region

The structure of production within the individual regions of the national economy may also be expected to be very different. However it is important to note that the share of manufacturing output will typically vary by more across the regions within an economy than will the share of services. For example, within the UK economy manufacturing contributed 29 per cent of total output in the West Midlands region in 1991, but only 15 per cent in the South East (*Regional Trends* (1993), table 12.3).

One possible explanation for this observation might be that the greater spatial equality in the distribution of services in the UK arises from the role of services provided on a national basis by central government, such as health and education. If this were the case there would be implications for the location of economic activity in the region where the government enhanced or reduced its role as provider of a good or service to a national standard. However while education, health and public administration are important, having accounted for 26 per cent of service-sector output in the UK in 1989, banking and finance accounted for 22 per cent, and distribution for a further 22 per cent (UK CSO, *Blue Book*, 1990). While there will be local and regional variations, it is private-sector decisions that dominate the location of service sector activity in the UK.

Where central government takes an active interest in the location of manufacturing activity, will we see a more even distribution of manufacturing output among regions than where such decisions are left to the private entrepreneur? As we shall see later, the spatial distribution of manufacturing production in the Republic of Ireland would appear to have been effectively influenced by active regional policy measures during the 1980s. However the evidence from UK regions such as Scotland and Northern Ireland is perhaps less sanguine.

The theory underpinning location decisions with respect to secondary and tertiary output in both private and public sectors will be explained in Chapter 5. The influence and effects of local and central-government policies upon the spatial distribution of output are studied in the final chapters of this book.

Before you read further, think about the structure of output within the region where you live.

Which sector is the most important? Is it primary, secondary or tertiary? Is economic activity focused upon one sector or is there a 'spread' among the three sectors? Within the sector that is most strongly represented, is there a dominant industry, or a wide range of industries?

These are important questions to which we return and consider more fully in the regional context in Chapter 2.

Output and trade

The European economies are all relatively open economies, that is, traded exports and imports account for a relatively high proportion, typically at least a quarter of their national income. In the case of the UK economy, manufactured goods are traded relatively more than services. For example the share of manufactured goods in UK exports increased during the 1980s, from 56 per cent to 61 per cent, while the share of services in UK exports remained stable, falling slightly from 26 per cent to 25 per cent (CSO, UK Balance of Payments, 1990).

Component regional economies are also typically very open, with large-scale flows of goods and services inwards and outwards. This is to be expected: specialisation and trade are such that the imports and exports of the individual region are likely to represent a greater *percentage* of the region's total output than is the case for the national economy. In other words, the region is less self sufficient than is the economy of which it forms a constituent part. These interregional trade flows and the issues arising from them are discussed in Chapter 3.

The Pattern of Employment

As labour is a factor of production whose services are required to produce output, the pattern of employment in an economy reflects the pattern of output. Where there is a declining demand for coal and steel, there is a declining demand for coalminers and steelworkers. Where the location of coal and steel production is spatially uneven across the economy, then those regions where coal and steel are mainly located are the regions that experience an above-average decline in the demand for labour services and so are likely to experience relatively greater unemployment. This structural change in the pattern of employment is considered later in greater detail, as are the nature of both the actual and possible policy responses to it.

The sectoral changes in economic structure introduced in the section above in terms of output have also had some subtler effects on employment patterns. As economies move from an agricultural to a manufacturing base, agricultural output diminishes by less than the reduction in agricultural employment. In other words, extensive productivity gains in the agricultural sector allow the release of labour to other forms of employment.

For many of the twelve-member economies of the EC, this transfer of labour out of the agricultural sector has already taken place. As Figure 1.5 shows, less than 3 per cent of the labour force is employed in the primary sector in Belgium and the UK.

In contrast, over a fifth of Greek employment is in the primary sector, as is over 10 per cent in Spain, Portugal and Ireland.

Can you identify a common factor in the location of these four economies relative to the EC as a whole?

Greece, Ireland, Spain and Portugal are all located around the edge of the EC: they are all on the periphery of the EC. Whether such a peripheral location puts these economies at an inherent locational disadvantage relative to the EC as a whole is an important question that is considered later in the book.

The comparatively high proportion of employment in the primary sector in Greece is reflected in comparatively low proportions of employment in either manufacturing or services. In the Republic of Ireland too less than 60 per cent of employment is in the service sector and less than 30 per cent in manufacturing. This employment pattern indicates an economic structure quite different to that of, for example, Germany or the Netherlands.

In most of the richer economies of the EC the service sector is an important source of employment. As Figure 1.5 shows, over two thirds of total employment is in the service sector in the Benelux economies, Denmark and the UK.

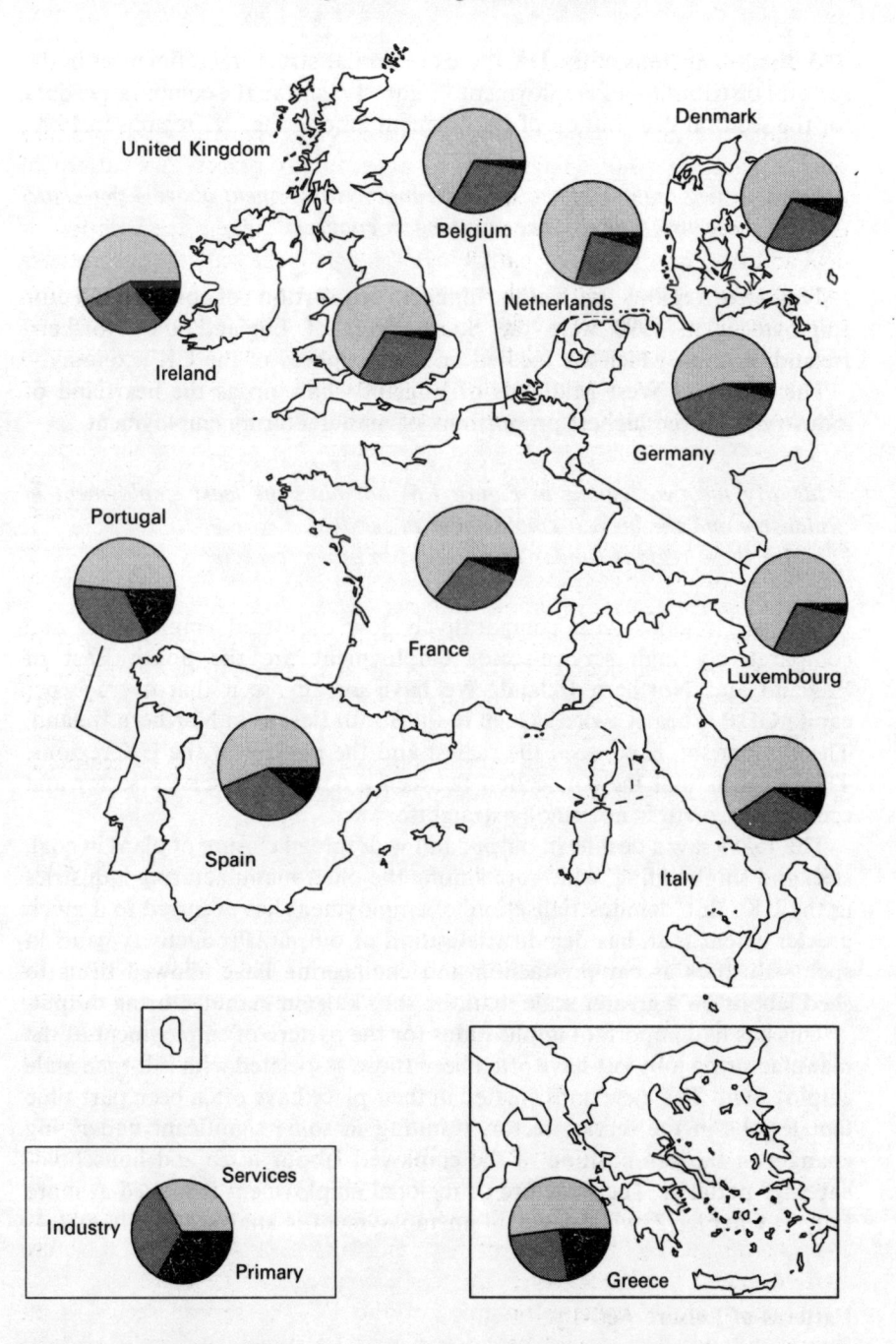

Figure 1.5 Sectoral employment in the EC economies, percentages, 1990
Source of data: UK CSO, *Regional Trends* (1993), table 2.1.

Within the regions of the UK there are similar structural differences in the sectoral distribution of employment. Figure 1.6 shows the comparative data for the sectoral distribution of employment among the UK regions in 1990.

In which two regions of the UK is primary employment above 4 per cent? Do these two regions have anything in common?

The two regions with the highest proportion of primary sector employment in 1990 were the South West of England and Northern Ireland, both of which are located on the periphery of the UK economy.

The East and West Midlands of England show up as the heartland of industry, with the highest proportions of manufacturing employment.

Identify the two regions in Figure 1.6 that have the least employment in industry and the highest employment in services.
Are these regions similar or different in other respects?

The two regions with comparatively low industrial employment and comparatively high service-sector employment are the South East of England and Northern Ireland. We have already seen that average per capita GDP is nearly twice as high in the South East as in Northern Ireland. The comparison is between the richest and the poorest of the UK regions. This suggests that the connection between a developing service sector and economic growth is not wholly straightforward.

The 1980s saw a decline in output and widespread closure of plant in coal, steel and shipbuilding, which are among the older manufacturing industries in the UK. But 'deindustrialisation' of employment has occurred to a much greater extent than has deindustrialisation of output. Productivity gains in such industries as car production and engineering have allowed firms to shed labour on a greater scale than the shrinkage in manufacturing output.

This has had important implications for the pattern of employment as the manufacturing jobs lost have often been those associated with full-time male employment. The 'new' jobs created in their place have often been part-time female jobs in the service sector, resulting in some significant underlying changes in the composition of the employed labour force and household-earnings patterns. The structure of regional employment is looked at more fully in Chapter 2, while regional unemployment is analysed in Chapter 4.

Patterns of Leisure Activity

The section above, which introduced the pattern of output, noted the inherent centralising tendencies exhibited by an economy such as the UK

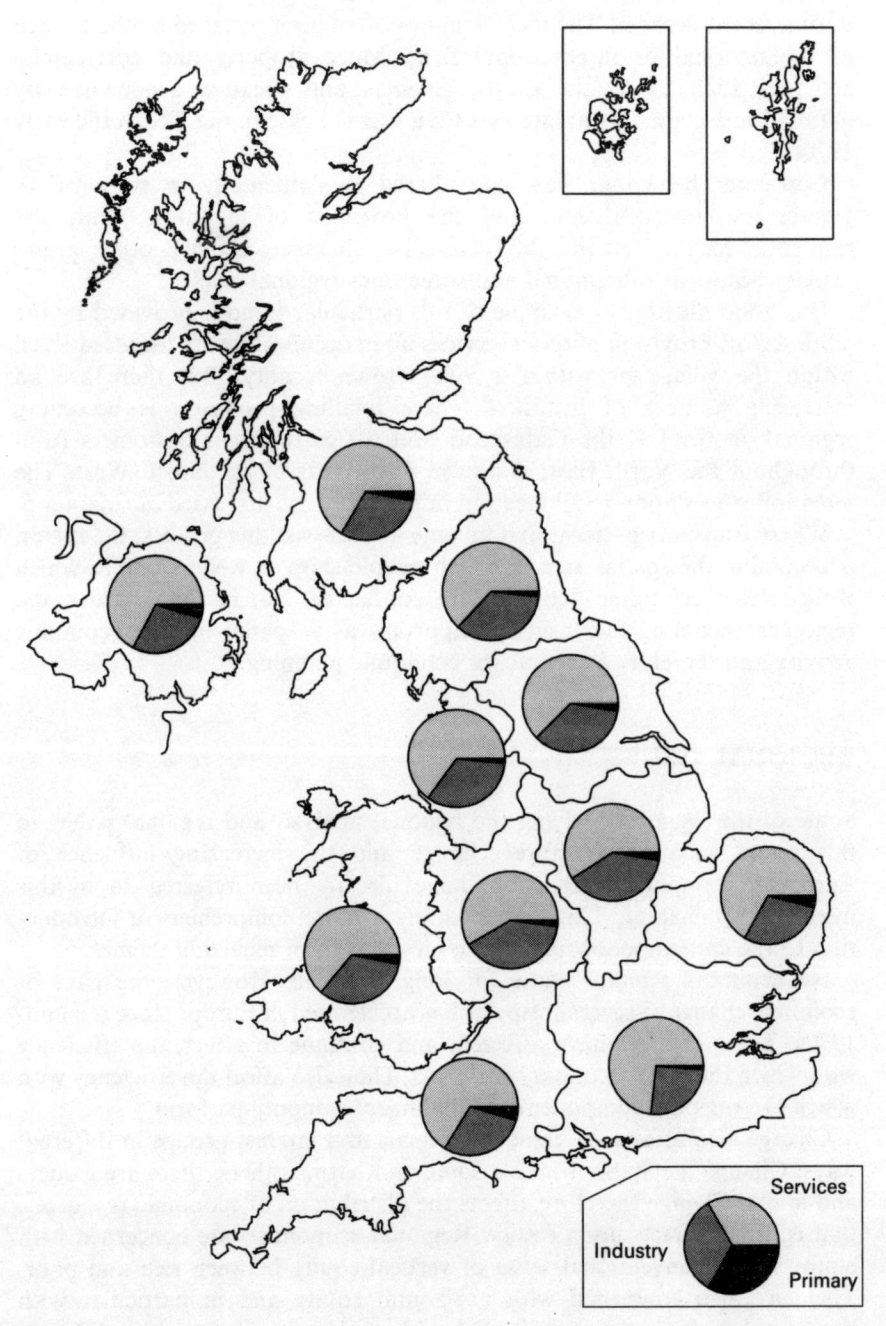

Figure 1.6 *Sectoral distribution of employment in the UK regions, percentages, 1990*
Source of data: UK CSO, *Regional Trends* (1993), table 2.1.

during recent decades. The local firm has often been replaced by the branch of the national or international firm. More property and commercial activities such as hotels, shops, cinemas and theatres are owned by national rather than local interests than was the case in the UK in the early 1970s.

Consumer behaviour has also altered fundamentally in response to greater mobility, affluence and the provision of facilities. While the residential locality remains the focus of much leisure activity, other leisure activity occurs at subregional and sometimes regional level.

One good illustrative example of this particular trend is provided by the retail sector. Provision of retail services often occurs at a very localised level: within the village or within a village/town locality. But there are an increasing number of instances where retailing provision is becoming regional: in the UK the Gateshead Metro Centre draws customers from throughout the North East, and even from parts of the North West. The main influences upon retail location in the 1990s are discussed in Chapter 5.

Where transport patterns and income levels assist this process, the region is becoming the spatial area in which people shop as well as one in which work-related economic activities are conducted. So, in this context, the region is becoming increasingly important as a spatial unit of economic activity and therefore as a unit for economic planning.

REGIONAL ISSUES

Some of the issues underlying the regional analysis and regional policy in this book, such as structural change and the increasing influence of European economic integration, have already been referred to in this introductory chapter. This section offers a more comprehensive introduction to the contemporary regional issues that form recurring themes.

No economy remains static for long, if at all. However, the pace of economic change in several respects has accelerated in Europe since the mid-1970s. These changes have affected, and continue to affect, the efficiency with which the macroeconomy performs. They also affect the efficiency with which the regional components of the macroeconomy perform.

Change also affects different individuals and interest groups in different ways. Change inevitably benefits some and harms others: there are gainers and losers. Change therefore affects the distribution of economic resources, that is, it has effects upon equity. Regional economists are concerned with equity in the conventional sense of vertical equity between rich and poor. They are also concerned with horizontal equity and in particular with horizontal equity in the context of spatial equity between groups in different regions.

Contemporary Regional Issues

Within this broad framework of regional efficiency and equity, ten regional issues can be identified that underpin much of the ensuing analysis in this book.

- The *deindustrialisation* of the economy due especially to the shrinking employment opportunities in the traditional manufacturing sector of the economy.
- The expansion of the tertiary or *service* sector of the economy in both the private and public sectors.
- Recent *technological change*, including continuing innovations in information technology and robotisation of production processes.
- The changing structure of *demand for the factors of production* – capital, labour and land, arising from these first three influences upon the structure of economic activity.
- The increasing national, European and international integration of the *markets for the factors of production* – in particular, but not exclusively, financial capital.
- The changing influences upon the *location of economic activity* both interregional and intraregional.
- Whether increasing economic integration in Europe, either formal or informal, will contribute to a greater *convergence or to greater divergence* of regional growth.
- The increasing *political centralisation* experienced in some economies with concomitant loss of political control at local and regional, and potentially national, level.
- The trend towards partnership between private enterprise and the public sector in the search for solutions to regional and urban problems, sometimes referred to as the *privatisation of regional policy*.
- The *effectiveness* of policy responses to regional problems and the conditions necessary for effective policy intervention.

Problem Regions and Regional Problems

The regional problem has many dimensions, as indicated by the multiple classification of issues indicated above. These all affect the economic development of the region for better or for worse. As suggested earlier in this chapter, this regional effect then impinges upon the economy at other levels of spatial aggregation.

While there may be disagreement over detailed measurements, there is little disagreement that regional inequalities in relation to economic activity and the distribution of economic resources have widened in the UK since the early 1980s. This interregional divergence has adversely affected the macroeconomic performance of the UK during these years.

Interestingly, interregional divergence within the UK economy has been accompanied by intraregional divergence over the same period. In other words the gaps between growth and stagnation and between rich and poor have expanded between local areas within regions as well as between regions. This divergence also impacts upon the regional economy, and hence upon the national economy.

Chapter 6 considers in some detail the likelihood of similar divergence among the growth experience of the EC regions in the absence of positive policy intervention in the spatial distribution of economic activity.

The problem regions are those experiencing levels of income and growth below the national average over a period of time. In the UK, Northern Ireland has consistently been the poorest region, and the region with the most intractable regional problems. It is also one of the poorer regions in the EC. Research has indicated that Northern Ireland's difficulties do reflect economic problems, in addition to its long-standing political uncertainties. Northern Ireland's economic problems as a region are exemplified by low growth; low per capita income, low population economic activity rates; high unemployment and high outmigration.

Its regional economy has a high degree of dependency in that much employment is either in branch plants and offices, many belonging to organisations owned outside the region, or in the public sector, especially UK-government employment. Such dependency arguably inhibits indigenous growth. The prevailing structure of output and employment also acts as a constraint upon growth, with those industries expanding at the national level such as financial services, being underrepresented in the region.

This 'problem region' became more of a problem during the 1980s as it failed to benefit from the UK economy's growth in the mid-1980s. Instead growth was limited in Northern Ireland during these years, and unemployment increased. So how does the plight of the regional economy of Northern Ireland help to illuminate the issues signalled in the section above?

A Problem Region and Some Regional Issues

Deindustrialisation of the regional economy has certainly been an integral part of the regional problem, with declining employment and output in traditional industries such as shipbuilding, engineering and textiles. New firms and plants have been established but tend to have been short-lived, so have not provided a stable foundation for the region's economy. The expansion of a service sector supplying consumer needs has been limited by low income growth, and there has been little expansion of services supplying producer organisations.

Northern Ireland has been no exception as regards the legacy left by industrial decline of both redundant labour and derelict land. The skill level of the labour force has also been affected by significant outmigration from the region, predominantly of the younger and more highly skilled members of the labour force.

There is concern that increasing European integration will increasingly marginalise the peripheral Northern Ireland economy. This may further accelerate its existing divergence from the UK average rate of growth, especially in view of the physical distances between Northern Ireland and mainland Europe.

Northern Ireland has experienced the concentration of political power to London as much if not more than other regions. It also has experience of being a 'branch-plant' economy with relatively few local regional employers of any significant size.

Where Northern Ireland is exceptional in the UK regions is that its regional development and expenditure upon regional policy has continued to be a high political priority. The perception of national government has been of a need to try to ensure that the poorest region in the UK does not become relatively poorer. The problems of evaluating regional and other spatial economic policies and their effectiveness are addressed in the later chapters of the book.

THE STRUCTURE OF THE BOOK

This book aims to provide an exposition of those aspects of economic analysis most relevant to an understanding of the contemporary issues facing the regional economy in the mid 1990s, and of the policy responses to those issues. To guide the reader, this final section of the introductory chapter offers a brief summary of the main issues raised and questions considered in the different chapters.

Chapter 2: Capital, Labour and Land in the Region

Chapter 2 discusses regional output and employment as an introduction to a more detailed consideration of regional factor endowments and markets. The later sections of the chapter look at the markets for land, labour and financial capital. The main implications for regional markets of the increasingly national and international mobility and ownership of factors of production are addressed.

Key questions are:

- How extensive has been the regional impact of deindustrialisation?
- What are the effects of the increase in tertiary employment upon traditional patterns of employment?
- How does the characteristic inelasticity of the supply of land affect the regional economy?
- To what extent does the perfect-competition model fit the regional labour market?
- How do the productivity and skill levels of labour affect regional labour markets?
- How has the internationalisation of the financial capital markets affected the supply of capital to the region?
- Does the emergence of the 'branch-plant' economy matter to those regions most affected?

Chapter 3: Expenditure, Prices and Exchange

Chapter 3 looks initially at the implications of regional employment structures for regional income. The analysis of consumption expenditure and its multiplied effects are then developed. Patterns of expenditure link into an explanation of input–output models of the regional economy. This leads into a discussion of interregional balance of payments. The final section of the chapter takes the exposition of supply in Chapter 2 and demand in Chapter 3 and brings them together to consider their interaction in the market. The market model is extended to provide an introductory explanation of externalities and welfare in the regional context.

The chapter looks at the following key questions:

- How dependent is regional prosperity upon the sources of income of its inhabitants?
- What economic variables determine the value of the multiplier effect in the regional economy?
- Can regions export their balance-of-payments difficulties?
- How useful are concepts of economic and social welfare to regional economists?

Chapter 4: The Region in the National Economy

Chapter 4 draws upon the earlier analysis of demand and supply to build up a relatively simple approach to regional growth and development. The effect of national economic growth upon the individual region is explained as are the regional implications of economic cyclical fluctuations. Regional unemployment and the adjustment processes in regional labour markets are discussed. The final section looks briefly at inflation in the regional economy.

Key questions central to the economic analysis contained in the chapter are:

- Why do rates of growth differ among different regions in the same national economy?
- What affects the sensitivity of the individual regional economy to national cyclical fluctuations in the level of economic activity?
- What causes regional unemployment?
- Are regional labour markets self-equilibrating?
- To what extent can the region isolate itself from national inflationary pressures?

Chapter 5: The Regional Location of Economic Activity

Chapter 5 focuses upon some key issues regarding the regional and spatial location of the main types of economic activity in the 1990s. Key questions are:

- Why does the spatial pattern of economic activity vary over time?
- Why are there spatial variations in economic activity, that is, why is economic activity concentrated in some locations and sparse in other locations?
- How mobile is economic activity among regions?
- Is the location of different types of economic activity affected by similar underlying considerations?
- How are location decisions made by management and how does this affect regional location?
- What are the main considerations underlying the regional location of public-sector activity?

Chapter 6: Regional Growth

Chapter 6 looks at the spatial pattern of economic growth and development and in particular at the potential for regional convergence or divergence among the regions in the EC. Consideration is given to the role of labour mobility and migration in regional growth differences.

Several key questions are discussed, including:

- Can all regions realistically expect to attain high rates of economic growth?
- Does the market mechanism doom the peripheral regions of the EC to relative economic decline?

❏ How likely is the emergence of a supranational European growth zone?
❏ Does the housing market act as a particular constraint upon regional and national economic growth in the UK relative to other comparable European economies?

Chapter 7: Urban Policies

The opening sections of Chapter 7 investigate the financing of local government and the effects of taxation upon the regional and local economy. The main part of the chapter then looks in detail at urban policies, and at the respective roles of the private and public sectors in urban regeneration. The evolution of urban policy in the UK between 1978 and 1993 is described in the Appendix to this chapter.

Key questions are:

❏ How should local and regional taxation revenues be raised?
❏ How efficient and equitable is a local property tax base?
❏ Why are local economy and/or urban policies necessary?
❏ How effective are public/private-sector partnership schemes in urban regeneration?
❏ How successful has urban policy been as a means of stimulating the local and regional economy?

Chapter 8: Regional Economic Policy

Chapter 8 discusses the aims and objectives of regional policy. The diminishing role played by 'traditional' national regional policies in the UK during the 1980s is noted. The available regional policy instruments are explained, as are the regional effects of other government policies. The direction of the main EC economic policies that affect the regional economy are considered. The evolution of UK regional policy between 1972 and 1993 is described in the Appendix to this chapter.

Regional policy is potentially an extensive area, so the chapter focuses on some selected key questions:

❏ What does regional policy seek to achieve?
❏ What instruments of regional policy are available?
❏ How does the location of the government's own activity affect the region?
❏ How do nonregional policy measures impact on the region?
❏ How has the increasing importance of EC funding affected regional policy in recent decades?

Chapter 9: An Effective Regional Policy?

Chapter 9 looks at the effectiveness and efficiency of regional policies. It assesses the targeting of policy measures, and their implementation. The measurement of policy effects and the limitations of this measurement are considered. The final section of the chapter evaluates regional policy and points to the future for policy intervention in response to the regional problem.

The central questions raised in Chapter 9 are:

❑ What are the limitations on policy implementation?
❑ How can we measure the effectiveness and efficiency of regional policy measures?
❑ How effective and efficient has regional policy been?
❑ What should be the future of regional policy?

2 Capital, Labour and Land in the Region

REGIONAL OUTPUT AND EMPLOYMENT

Deindustrialisation and the Regional Economy

In looking at the structure of output in a region we are interested in the current output pattern not only in itself but also as an indicator of the likely future pattern of development and prosperity for that region. We are especially interested in the robustness of the region's output pattern.

In looking at the output pattern of many regions within the EC we have to bear in mind the underlying trend exhibited within many of these economies during recent decades. The industrialised economies have typically seen a long-term trend decline in the contribution of both agriculture and manufacturing output as a proportion of the total; the expanding area of output has been in those industries related to the service sector of the economy.

Relative price effects

In looking at the statistics relating to the structure of output in an economy, we need to distinguish between value and volume measures of output. The *value* of output tells us the money revenue of production; the *volume* of output tells us how much is produced.

Most available national data relating to output shares is measured at current prices. Apparent changes in the share of total output accounted for by a particular industry over a given time will reflect both changes in the volume of output accounted for by that industry and changes in the relative prices of the output of that industry.

What does this mean in practical terms?

What do you think would be the effect upon the contribution of agriculture to total output in France if all agricultural prices increased by 10 per cent?

Such a policy change is likely to result in increased market prices for the sale of most agricultural produce. This would show in the statistics as an increase in the value of agricultural output in France. As a result, the share of agriculture in total output would appear to increase, even if the actual volume of agricultural production remains the same.

Similarly, any significant increase or decrease in the price of oil over a given time would affect the apparent contribution of the energy industry to the total output of an economy.

Does deindustrialisation matter?

Is a shrinking manufacturing sector a natural counterpart to an expanding service sector? Is this deindustrialisation an endemic part of economic development and so a pattern of progress to be encouraged in shaping the regional economy of the future?

Or is a manufacturing base necessary as the foundation upon which all other economic wealth is created? If so an economy or a region without a strong manufacturing base may have only limited economic strength in its position relative to the rest of the economic world.

Figure 2.1 shows that four of the European economies experienced a common trend decline in the share of manufacturing in total output in the thirty years between 1960 and 1990.

While the decline in manufacturing was relatively greater in the UK, France, Italy and West Germany shared a similar scale of deindustrialisation as measured by the proportion of manufacturing output in total production.

Deindustrialisation and the regional economy

If manufacturing is evenly distributed throughout the spatial economy, then deindustrialisation will not necessarily greatly affect the regional economy.

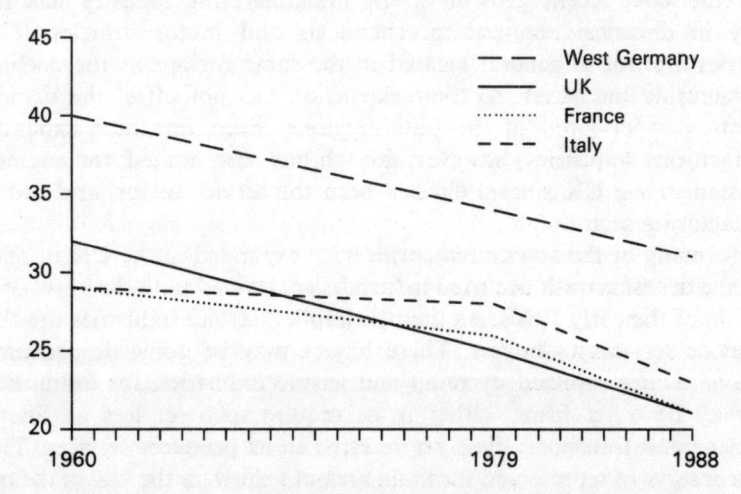

Figure 2.1 Manufacturing output as a share of GDP, 1960–88, percentages

Source of data: OECD Historical Statistics, quoted in UK Treasury, *Economic Briefing*, no. 1, December 1990

However once we begin to investigate which industries have been shrinking in terms of volume and value of production, we find that they were not spatially evenly distributed. Instead these declining manufacturing industries were concentrated in particular areas, and so those regions have been more affected as a consequence of deindustrialisation.

In the UK the declining manufacturing industries in recent years have been steel, shipbuilding, mechanical engineering and textiles. All these industries grew in the economy at a time when the manufacturing industry's location was dominated by proximity to energy and raw materials. As they have declined, so too has the coalmining industry, which historically has been their primary energy source.

Consequently both coalmining and these declining manufacturing industries were all predominantly located in South Wales, central Scotland and the North of England. Geographically, they were concentrated in the 'outer regions' of the UK economy and these regions have been worst affected by their decline.

Other regions, such as the West Midlands, were affected by the process of deindustrialisation during the 1980s. Regional specialisation in metal manufacture and engineering left the region badly exposed to the early 1980s recession which particularly affected these key industries. Regional policy in the 1960s and 1970s had been implemented upon the assumption that the West Midlands was relatively prosperous and so the region was a net donor rather than a net recipient of regional aid until the mid-1980s. The West Midlands' experience in the early 1980s provides an interesting example of how the regional map can alter relatively rapidly.

For the UK, recent growth in the manufacturing industry has been mainly in electrical engineering, chemicals and motor vehicles. These industries are not in general located in the same regions as the declining manufacturing industries, so their expansion has not offset the deindustrialisation experienced in the outer regions. Even for these expanding manufacturing industries, however, growth has been limited: the engine of expansion in the UK since 1980 has been the service sector, and not the manufacturing sector.

While many of the service industries have expanded in the UK in recent years, the fastest growth occurred in 'producer services' until the onset of the recession of the early 1990s. As the title implies, service industries are there to provide services to buyers. These buyers may be domestic consumers whose needs are supplied by retail and leisure industries, for example, or they may be other firms. Other firms require such services as finance, marketing and transport: these are referred to as producer services. These producer services represented the main area of growth in the UK in the mid-1980s, and their location tended to be heavily concentrated in London and the South East of England.

Deindustrialisation and regional inequality

In summary, deindustrialisation due to the shrinking of the manufacturing sector has not affected the UK economy evenly. All regions have been affected to some extent, but the outer regions have been particularly adversely affected. As service-sector growth did not take place in these outer regions, but predominantly in London and the South East, deindustrialisation in the UK has resulted in increased regional inequality.

This increasing interregional inequality has been exacerbated by the legacy of the decline in such industries as coalmining, steel and shipbuilding. The large-scale dereliction of land left by the demise of coalmines and shipyards has created a problem of regeneration that has absorbed significant resources, as is explained in Chapter 7.

A less tractable problem has been that of the redundant labour force left by this decline in traditional industries. The skills and experience of coalminers and shipyard workers are not the skills and experience demanded by the expanding service sector, as we shall see in the following section.

Deindustrialisation is therefore one reason why spatial inequality has increased since 1980, and one reason why the study of regional economics is crucial to an understanding of the contemporary UK and other EC economies.

The Structure of Employment

As we saw above, the structure of output in the UK economy and in other comparable European economies has altered since the 1970s. In general, economic development appears to follow a path where resources are dedicated to agricultural output; then the manufacturing sector develops and resources are released from the agricultural sector. What is less clear is whether the next stage is a similar pattern of release of resources from the manufacturing sector into the service sector.

These structural economic changes have regional effects because agriculture, manufacturing and services are not spatially evenly distributed across the economy. The changes in the structure of output outlined above will be reflected in changes in the structure of employment, which we consider in this section.

The connection between changes in output and changes in employment is complicated by productivity changes. In other words, when productivity increases in an industry, fewer employees can produce the same level of output or the same number of employees can produce more output. Changes in productivity affect the link between output changes and the resulting changes in employment in the national and regional labour markets.

Figure 2.2 shows that the biggest reduction in the share of primary-sector employment during the 1980s was experienced by the East Midlands and Wales. The smallest reductions in this sector were in the South East and Northern Ireland. In the case of the South East, this is because primary-sector employment may be at, or close to, a minimum. In Northern Ireland the figures suggest that there is potential for further shrinkage of employment in this sector.

Both the West Midlands and the South East of England experienced an above-average reduction in manufacturing employment and an above-average increase in service-sector employment in the 1980s. Scotland experienced a similarly above average rate of decrease in manufacturing employment, but this was not paralleled by the rate of expansion of service-sector employment.

The smallest reductions in manufacturing employment and the smallest increases in service-sector employment were recorded in Wales and the Yorkshire and Humberside region in England. These had the most stable sectoral employment structure of the UK regions during this decade.

For the industrialised European economies, the changes in the structure of overall employment since 1960 mirror the changes in the structure of output we considered above. Employment in the manufacturing sector has fallen, while employment in the service sector has expanded.

But there are some important differences of detail to which we must pay attention if we are to study the anatomy of the regional economy. In the UK for example, employment within the manufacturing sector has fallen by more than the fall in manufacturing output.

Before you read on, can you think of a likely explanation for this phenomenon?

This 'saving' in employment by the manufacturing sector has arisen because productivity, that is, output per employee, has increased faster in the manufacturing sector than it has for the economy as a whole. In other words the manufacturing sector within the overall UK economy has become more capital-intensive in recent decades.

At least until 1989, this saving of manufacturing-sector employment was paralleled by a relative increase in service-sector employment over and above the increase in UK service-sector output. These national trends have important implications for the regional economy.

The distribution of employment by gender

The proportions of employees in manufacturing and services also have implications for the distribution of employment between men and women, as is clear from the sectoral distribution of employees in employment in the UK in June 1992 shown in Table 2.1.

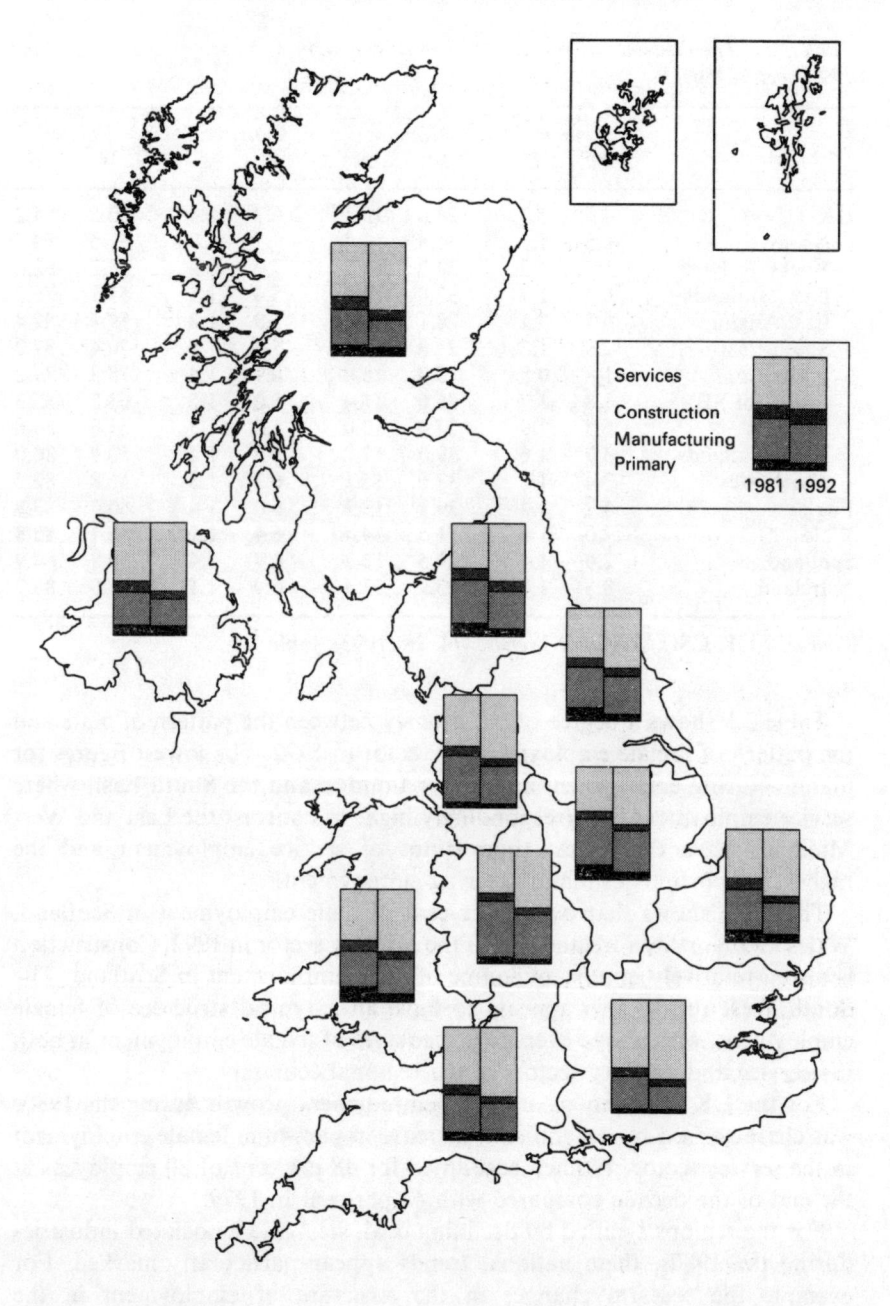

Figure 2.2 Changes in the sectoral distribution of employment in the UK regions, percentages, 1981–92

Source: Data calculated from UK CSO, *Regional Trends*, vol. 28 (1993), table 7.7.
Note: Industry is divided into manufacturing and construction in this figure.

Table 2.1 The distribution of male and female employment by sector in the UK, June 1992 (percentages)

	Primary M	Primary F	Manufact. M	Manufact. F	Construct. M	Construct. F	Services M	Services F
UK	4.7	1.5	28.6	13.1	6.3	1.4	60.5	84.2
North	6.5	1.3	31.4	13.4	8.7	1.2	51.5	84.0
Yorks. & Hum.	5.7	1.3	34.2	14.8	7.0	1.2	53.2	82.6
East Midlands	6.4	1.7	37.0	20.5	5.4	1.5	51.1	76.3
East Anglia	6.7	3.1	28.1	13.3	5.8	1.2	59.3	82.4
South East	2.8	1.3	21.3	9.9	5.5	1.5	70.4	87.2
Gtr Lon.	1.8	0.8	15.0	8.0	4.9	1.4	78.3	89.8
Rest of SE	3.8	1.7	26.6	11.4	6.0	1.5	63.5	85.3
South West	5.5	1.9	27.4	10.0	5.6	1.3	61.6	86.8
West Midlands	3.7	1.6	39.6	17.2	5.8	1.4	50.9	80.0
North West	3.4	1.2	33.6	15.1	6.2	1.3	56.8	82.5
England	4.2	1.4	29.1	13.2	6.0	1.4	60.7	83.8
Wales	7.0	1.6	31.5	14.4	6.4	1.1	55.1	82.8
Scotland	7.0	1.4	24.5	12.3	8.7	1.4	59.8	84.9
N.Ireland	8.3	1.7	23.9	13.4	6.9	1.1	61.0	83.7

Source: UK CSO, *Regional Trends*, vol. 28 (1993), table 7.7.

Table 2.1 shows a degree of consistency between the pattern of male and the pattern of female employment by sector in 1992. The lowest figures for manufacturing employment appear for London and the South East, where service employment is correspondingly high. In contrast the East and West Midlands have the lowest proportions of service employment and the highest proportions of manufacturing employment.

The table shows that over 7 per cent of male employment in Scotland, Wales and Northern Ireland was in the primary sector in 1992. Construction is also a relatively important source of male employment in Scotland. The South West region also appears to have an a typical structure of female employment, with above-average percentages of female employment in both the service and primary sectors of the regional economy.

For the UK economy as a whole, employment growth during the 1980s was characterised by a significant increase in part-time female employment in the service sector. Women accounted for 48 per cent of all employees at the end of the decade compared with 42 per cent in 1979.

For the regions typified by declining coal, steel and associated industries during the 1980s, these national trends appear particularly marked. For example the sectoral changes in the structure of employment in the Yorkshire and Humberside region in the 1980s were as follows: 66 000 jobs lost in the primary sector (mainly coal); 74 000 jobs lost in the manufacturing sector (mainly steel); 194 000 jobs gained in the service sector (Leigh and Stilwell, 1992, p. 68).

The jobs lost were predominantly full-time male jobs; those gained were predominantly part-time female jobs. This pattern was repeated during the 1980s in other regions, such as the North East and central Scotland, with a heavy dependence upon mining and traditional manufacturing industries.

The process of deindustrialisation meant that job losses in these regions were concentrated in mining, steel and shipbuilding among both unskilled and skilled male manual workers. The jobs created were typically part-time, low skill, low-wage service-sector employment predominantly filled by female employees.

Deindustrialisation and regional unemployment

One predictable consequence of this changing employment structure was a serious skill mismatch between those made redundant from manufacturing and the type of posts being created in service industries. In addition there were two less predictable consequences of the changing regional employment structure. Firstly, the early 1980s recession appears to have resulted in an increase in the level of 'hidden' unemployment in those regions and areas most affected. Secondly, those regions worst affected by the early 1980s recession were least able to benefit from the expansion in the economy, especially in the service sector, in the mid-1980s.

Hidden unemployment occurs when individuals who wish to work are not working, but are not recorded in the official statistics as being unemployed. Wales is typical of several regions where deindustrialisation in the early 1980s resulted in reduced manufacturing output, especially in long-established industries. This reduced output in manufacturing industries such as steel and engineering, resulted in an even greater reduction in manufacturing employment, as higher productivity released jobs additional to those released by the reduction in the absolute level of output.

While part of this reduced employment is reflected in higher unemployment statistics for the region, not all unemployment appears in the statistics. For example, in Wales in the 1980s the reduction in the activity rate of the male labour force exceeded the increase in recorded official unemployment, so part of the balance must reflect higher hidden – unrecorded – unemployment.

The reliability of official unemployment data is further complicated by the presence of the black economy. The black economy covers labour-market transactions that are not officially recorded. Two groups of workers are particularly involved in the black economy. First are those in regular full-time employment who take on additional part-time work elsewhere but fail to declare it to avoid income-tax liability on their extra earnings. The second group are the registered unemployed who take on casual work but fail to declare it in order to avoid compromising their entitlement to unemployment benefit. The latter group remain on the unemployment register but are receiving some, although usually only casual, employment.

The second main regional effect of deindustrialisation upon employment affected regional performance in terms of both output and employment in the UK in the 1980s. For most of the UK regions, the greater the reduction in employment experienced during the 1979–83 recession, the weaker the recovery experienced by that region's economy between 1983 and 1987. For the 1980s, 'on average an extra 1% decline in industrial employment in a region reduces service employment growth by 0.6%' (Mackay, 1992, p. 100).

The growth in service-sector output and employment of the late 1980s was greatest in those regions least affected by the process of manufacturing deindustrialisation. This effect tended to contribute to interregional divergence in the UK economy during the 1980s in respect of both unemployment and growth.

Regional Unemployment: An Introduction

As we shall see later, especially in Chapter 4, different regions within the EC economies had very different experiences as regards unemployment during the 1980s. Some very general overall trends, however, have been common to the experience of the EC as a whole. Figure 2.3 uses OECD data, as this

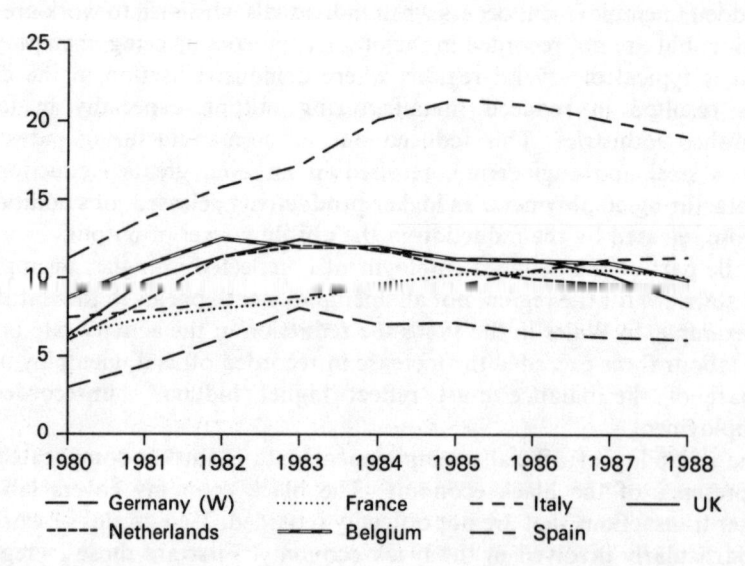

Figure 2.3 Unemployment rates, selected EC member economies, 1980–8 (annual averages in per cent)

Source of data: OECD, Main Economic Indicators and Quarterly Labour Force Statistics (1990).

standardises individual government's definitions of unemployment in relation to International Labour Office guidelines for ease of intereconomy comparison.

We can see from these figures that all these economies experienced rising unemployment between 1980 and 1982, as they were all were affected by the recession at the beginning of the 1980s. (The regional impact of this recession is considered in greater detail in Chapter 4.) Similarly, all the economies, except that of Italy, experienced reducing national unemployment rates between 1986 and 1988.

The level of national unemployment is very variable between these European economies. In West Germany the unemployment rates shown in Figure 2.3 never rise above 8 per cent, while Spanish unemployment is never below 10 per cent, and was above 15 per cent for most of the decade.

The labour-force structure of regional unemployment

Unemployment is more of a problem for both the individual and the economy the longer the period out of work. For this reason it is interesting to note that the older age groups have above-average vulnerability to unemployment and an above-average duration of unemployment. For example, in the UK in July 1989 13 per cent of unemployed males aged between 16 and 19 were continuously unemployed for more than a year; but this percentage rose to 66 per cent of unemployed males aged 50–59 years (UK CSO, *Social Trends*, 1990).

So the age structure of a region's population will have implications for the likely severity and duration of unemployment within the region. In turn this will affect the associated reductions in income levels and consumer expenditure that result from prolonged unemployment.

Shifts in the Structure of the Regional Economy

The sections above have offered a fairly brief introductory sketch to outline the changing regional structure of output and employment in the 1980s. In some economies, such as the Republic of Ireland, some regions were affected by the shift of employment away from agriculture. In others, in particular the UK, some regions were affected by the shift of employment away from manufacturing through deindustrialisation. The emphasis so far has been upon the adverse effects of the 1980s process of deindustrialisation. This section widens the picture to introduce the 'shift-share' analysis of changes in regional employment and in particular the role of the urban–rural shift in employment in the UK during the 1970s.

Shift-share analysis

Shift-share analysis is a technique for considering regional employment, but it has limitations, considered below. It is included here both because it has provided some interesting insights into the pattern of regional employment change and because it is the forerunner of the other shift analysis discussed later in this section.

Shift-share analysis divides the growth of regional employment over a period of time into three constituent parts: (1) the part that is due to the region's share in national growth, that is, if the national economy is growing the region should experience growth; (2) the part that is due to the region's specific mix of industry, that is, if the region has above average representation of growth industries it should benefit accordingly; and (3) the part that is due to residual influences not included above, that is, regional growth not explained by industrial structure.

Shift-share analysis would therefore predict that a region with a favourable mix of industry would experience higher employment growth than a region with an unfavourable mix of industry. Unfortunately economic life is more complex than this: equipping an area with a favourable mix of industry does not guarantee growth, as many regions and economies are well aware. The limitations of the basic shift-share approach arise from its tendency towards the inherent simplification of a complex problem. Its four main limitations may be summarised as:

- Its sensitivity to the level of aggregation used. For example the motor-manufacturing industry might be identified as an industry with a growth rate above the national average in the 1970s. Its location in a region would then be thought to favour that region in the 1970s. However it might be that the market for cars was expanding but the market for lorries contracting. Again, although the market for cars was expanding overall, it might be that the market for small cars was expanding rapidly but the market for luxury cars was expanding at no more than the national average rate of growth. Given this intraindustry variation, shift-share analysis applied to the motor-manufacturing industry overall would act as a poor predictor for the experience of a specific plant in a specific region.
- It is a partial approach that considers the industry in isolation from its environment, and especially in isolation from local market 'linkages', for example with local component suppliers. It also takes no account of the benefits arising from external, or agglomeration, scale economies, which we shall discuss later in this book. The presence or absence of strong linkages and external economies can significantly influence the output performance and growth of industry in a region.

❑ The third residual part referred to above may represent a relatively large part of the total change in employment, but shift-share in itself offers no explanation for these residual influences. As a result the analysis does not take account of local and regional variations in, for example, labour skills and productivity, which may be pertinent in this context.
❑ Finally, shift-share analysis must be set up carefully, as with any time-series analysis, to try to ensure that the choice of base year does not bias the result.

The urban–rural shift

Empirical studies such as that by Fothergill and Gudgin (1982) demonstrated that the residual part of regional employment change in the UK regions, especially in the 1970s, was more important than the employment effect of the regions' industrial structure. These studies accordingly sought to explain the shift-share residual, and identified an important urban–rural shift in employment structure in the UK regions. In other words employers were leaving urban centres in favour of more rural locations, rural in this context including suburban and business park locations.

The exit of manufacturing employment, in particular, from major urban centres benefited less urbanised regions such as East Anglia, the South East and the South West during the 1970s. Employers preferred being away from urban centres, but preferred to remain in the southern half of England. The urban–rural shift did not result in any significant shift towards northern rural locations.

The exit from urban centres in the 1960s and 1970s may be explained by a combination of quantitative influences such as lower rents and qualititative influences such as poor inner-city environments. (The main influences upon contemporary industrial location are discussed more fully in Chapter 5.) The result was a deterioration in economic and environmental conditions in the older inner cities, to which the 1980s urban policies adopted in such economies as the Netherlands and the UK and discussed in Chapter 7 were a response.

We have noted above that the reasons for the movement of employment away from urban centres to more rural locations may have reflected the benefits of nonlabour costs such as lower rents. The market for labour is therefore not the only factor market affected by these shifts in the spatial distribution of industrial activity. In addition to labour, capital and land are required by production processes. For this reason the following sections of this chapter investigate the regional markets for all three factors of production, with particular reference to the experience of the regional economies of Europe in the 1980s and the first half of the 1990s.

REGIONAL MARKETS FOR THE FACTORS OF PRODUCTION

This section looks at demand and supply conditions in the regional markets for the three factors of production: capital, labour and land. The operation of these markets is explained in some detail. An understanding of the way these markets work in the regions of Europe in the 1990s is essential in that it will provide a sound basis for considering both the dynamics affecting the growth experience of these regions and the relevant regional policy responses.

Capital: Regional Dependence and External Sourcing

The markets for all three factors of production – capital, labour and land – have become increasingly less localised and more centralised in the EC economies since the early 1970s. Of the three, however, it is financial capital that is in some senses least within the control of the region and is the most internationalised of the factors of production in respect of market characteristics.

There is concern that the economies, especially those of the more peripheral regions of the EC, are dominated by organisations whose capitalisation and ownership lie outside the region. The relevant economic analysis then becomes analogous to that of those aspects of international economics concerned with the 'branch-plant' national economies whose future may potentially be controlled by externally owned international and multinational organisations. In the UK, both the nation regions of Scotland and Wales have been relatively successful in attracting inward investment from overseas organisations. As a result both regional economies are increasingly dominated by 'branch plants' of overseas owned multinational corporations, with little decision-making power lying within their respective regions.

In the context of the regional economy, there is an inherently extra layer to this potential dependence as for many national organisations capitalisation and ownership are external to the individual region. For example in the North East of England in the late 1980s: 'around 80% of manufacturing employment is in externally owned and controlled companies, including about 16% in foreign owned businesses' (Robinson *et al.*, 1992, p. 91).

In the case of the contemporary Scottish economy, ownership of expanding industries such as North-Sea oil and gas, office machinery and whisky is by outside concerns. Critics accordingly feel that the Scottish region is increasingly peripherisalised and marginalised relative to both the UK and the EC economies.

In many EC economies the capitalisation and ownership of employing organisations is heavily concentrated in a small minority of regions, and especially in the region of the capital city. The French economy is dominated by Paris and the Irish economy by Dublin to a greater extent than the UK economy is dominated by London. Such centralisation is seen to create regional dependence upon the capital region and the creation of branch-plant regional economies.

Does the branch-plant economy matter?

As noted above, many of the UK regions have experienced increased externalisation of the ownership of their productive capacity in recent decades. An underlying trend towards greater industrial concentration has been reinforced by government financial incentives available to organisations establishing branch plants in 'assisted areas' in the North of England, Scotland and Wales. Other regions in Europe, especially those with below-average labour costs such as those in Spain and Greece, have experienced a similar trend.

As pointed out by Fothergill and Guy (1990), it is important to distinguish between the branch plant and the subsidiary. A large multisite organisation will often encompass both. The subsidiary is typically a unit offering a product or service to the organisation that is not available anywhere else inside the organisation. For example the organisation's marketing may be undertaken by a wholly owned subsidiary.

In contrast the individual branch plant and its activities may not be unique to the organisation. An organisation may run several production-line plants performing parallell activities. Or a branch plant may be established specifically to produce a product with a limited life span. It is this absence of a unique long-term role within the organisation that can make the branch plant particularly vulnerable to closure, as we shall see below.

It is difficult to find a single answer to the question of whether being an economy dominated by branch plants matters to the region. The following paragraphs look first at the potential benefits from branch-plant investment in the region, then consider some of the disadvantages to the receiving region.

The optimistic view stresses the benefits to be gained from technology transfer and generally for the transfer of best-practice production methods from the head-quarters centre to the branch periphery. For example Ashcroft *et al.* (1987) investigated the impact on Scotland of the external acquisition of 54 large Scottish firms between 1965 and 1980. The study concluded that the region was a net beneficiary from the acquisition process, primarily due to the resultant improvements in technology, management and access to finance. Such benefits help to generate additional income, employment and associated economies of scale in the receiving region.

The pessimistic view of the branch-plant dominated economy perceives a cumulative cycle of dependency from which the receiving regional economy would have great difficulty in escaping. In this view nonlocal ownership and capitalisation stultifies local initiative and innovation. Decision-making control lies outside the receiving region, and so the decision takers are not affected by the outcome of their decisions.

In this model all primary decisions are taken at the centre and all primary functions of the organisation are retained there. Only secondary decisions and secondary functions are delegated to the branch-plant region. The study of acquisitions in Scotland referred to above found that key functions such as research and marketing were often withdrawn from the acquired Scottish company and concentrated centrally at the owner organisation's location outside Scotland.

This typifies a tendency for pivotal organisational functions such as finance, research and marketing to be concentrated at a headquarters outside the branch-plant region. In the UK these 'high-order' functions are concentrated in London and the South East. Similar spatial concentrations of key functions occur in most other European economies, with the possible exception of the Netherlands. The outcome is a spatial dimension to the division of labour that reinforces interregional inequality in employment opportunities. In turn this adds to spatial inequity in regional incomes, as we shall see in more detail in Chapter 3.

The branch-plant regional economy therefore has the problem of exclusion from high-order organisational functions. Employment in branch plants tends to be predominantly low skilled and low paid, and accordingly yields limited multiplier benefits to the regional economy.

Branch plants are also heavily reliant upon the parent organisation for the provision of both inputs and services. Consequently limited use is made of local services and suppliers, further reducing the potential linkages between the branch plant and its local economy. In addition branch plants are highly vulnerable to redundancy and closure in periods of recession or fundamental technological or market change. Because they often serve no unique long-term role within the organisation, branch plants are more likely to be closed down in the face of cost and profit pressures upon the parent organisation.

Fothergill and Guy (1990) point out that the onset of economic recession often acts as a short-term trigger that results in branch-plant closure due to longer-term changes in technological and/or market conditions. The UK recession in the early 1980s resulted in large-scale branch-plant closures in regions such as the North and Northern Ireland. These closures contributed significantly to the widening north–south divide that characterised the UK economy in the 1980s. The policy implications of this are considered more fully in Chapter 9, where the particular case of Northern Ireland is also discussed in greater detail.

The mobility of financial capital

Having looked at the main implications of external ownership of the region's productive capacity, the following section analyses the regional availability of, and market for, financial capital in the European regional economies in the mid-1990s.

The international capital market Capital as an economic resource appears in two forms: as financial capital and as physical capital. Physical capital, that is, machinery, tends to be relatively immobile, but the key characteristic of financial capital is its spatial mobility.

The supply of financial capital available to a region is unlikely to be solely determined by its internal stock of financial capital. While the supply of land can be taken to be characteristically inelastic, especially in the short term, the supply of financial capital to the region can be taken to be relatively elastic.

The European economies typically have banking systems operating at a national rather than a regional level. There are some significant differences in the degree of centralisation of banking systems in the different economies. The UK banking system is now predominantly national, while those of France and Italy are more distinctively regional. The centralisation of the UK banking system has increased during recent decades, with earlier mergers between banks being followed in the 1980s and 1990s by mergers among other financial institutions such as building societies, to create a national rather than regional financial structure. The increasing role played by overseas banks in the London money markets has further added to the internationalisation of the capital market.

Financial capital to fund investment, for example in buildings and machinery, therefore flows between the different regions of the national economy. Increasingly in the EC economies, financial capital is flowing between the different economies within the EC, and more widely on an international scale. Capital flows and the potential sources of capital available to a region are therefore international rather than national. This has the effect of further increasing the elasticity of the supply conditions for capital faced by any individual region within the EC.

Differentials in real interest rates and in the levels of expected risk and return will affect the size and direction of international flows of financial capital. Inward investment into Europe from Japan and the Far East already represents a significant part of the total, as does inward investment from the North-American economies. The latter is important because of the size of the US capital market. For example the extent of the sums available for investment by such North American financial institutions as pension funds are so great that a relatively small percentage change in their investment will have a noticeable effect upon confidence in the capital market of the recipient economy.

Inward investment from economies such as Japan and Hong Kong to UK regions such as South Wales and the North East played an important role in the expansion of their manufacturing sectors in the early 1990s. The rationale underlying much of this investment was the gaining of a foothold in the European market. Once at least 70 per cent of the total value of the final product represents value added at a production site within the EC, the final product is deemed to have been produced within the boundaries of the EC and is not subject to trade barriers. For this reason assembly, for example of cars and television sets, has been located in regions of the UK or Spain so that the overseas organisation can export the finished product to the rest of the EC market from within EC trading boundaries.

The removal of EC exchange controls In addition to inward flows of investment from overseas, the completely free movement of financial capital among the EC economies is a relatively new phenomenon of which the member states have little previous experience. The lifting of exchange controls by the UK government in 1979 resulted in large-scale movements of capital to overseas destinations during the 1980s.

It is only in the 1990s that earlier controls upon the movement of foreign exchange and financial capital have been lifted by some of the founder members of the EC. For example neither France nor Italy completed the removal of their controls upon movements of foreign capital until July 1990. With the single internal market financial capital has become the most homogeneous and most mobile factor of production within the EC.

Capital availability

The supply of financial capital to an individual region Does a highly elastic supply of financial capital and a highly developed banking system mean that finance is readily and equally available to all regions in the EC upon demand? As so often in economics, the situation is not straightforward. The supply of financial capital in response to demand will be affected by the expected return, which will itself incorporate judgements as to the timescale of the investment and the anticipated risk associated with it. In these respects not all regions and not all locations will be viewed as homogeneous by investors. They will prefer to invest through established commercial centres such as London, Frankfurt and Rotterdam. In the European context, the relative importance of these commercial centres has shifted during the 1990s. This is the natural outcome of both the effects of the changes in the Eastern European economies and of East–West German integration. Further, the advent of the single internal market has affected the internal financial dynamics within the EC.

At the regional level these shifts in financial flows affect both the availability of financial capital and the relative importance of regional financial centres. For example the Scottish economy will be affected by the importance and flows of funds through Edinburgh relative to London; that of Catalonia by the size of the flow of funds through Barcelona relative to Madrid.

Demand for finance for a new factory, or for new machinery for an existing factory, will be met more readily in some locations than in others. We can note that this unevenness is likely to be present independent of whether the source of finance is internal to the operating company or is an external financial institution. Different regions will be perceived by potential lenders as having different attached risk factors. The expected investment returns in one region will be subject to comparison with potential returns in other regions and in other economies before capital is readily supplied.

The presence of spatial differences in rates of return on investment will also have a second complicating effect. Where rates of return are identified as high and worthwhile, financial institutions will be keen to invest. So investment in favoured locations may be supply-driven as well as responding to existing demand. In other words, supply may seek to create demand.

Where such supply-driven investment occurs we can predict a cumulative effect upon existing disparities in the availability of capital and rates of economic growth. This in turn will exacerbate inequalities among different regions of the EC and will contribute to spatial divergence rather than convergence of growth and wealth in the EC.

In the case of the UK, overseas investors favour the already affluent South East region. After the South East, Scotland and Wales are relative beneficiaries of inward overseas investment. The reasons for this are not clear, but may be related to the clear national image of these two nation regions, which helps them to project a stronger identity to potential overseas investors.

In general, however, investors in the UK have preferred the 'safe' South East as the destination for their investment finance. It is too early to judge whether this preference will have received a long-term knock from the adverse effects of the early 1990s recession upon the South East regional economy. The suspicion must be that earlier investment patterns will return in the absence of strong government policy measures to redirect them. There accordingly seems little likelihood of any major alteration of the pattern of regional investment in the UK in 1985, when only 17 per cent of available venture capital went to benefit the 40 per cent of the population in the five outer regions of the UK economy (Martin, 1989).

While in principle the centralisation and sophistication of the financial systems of the EC economies would suggest that financial capital might be readily available to individual regions, in practice this may not always be the case. There will be occasions where the needs of the investor coincide with the needs of the borrower in both time and space, but there is no reason for undue optimism regarding the smooth operation of the invisible hand in the market for financial capital. Where coincidence of the wants of the investor and the borrower fails to occur in time and space, the potential borrower, and so the region in which the borrower is located, may find that finance is not readily available.

The resulting problems of regional growth convergence and divergence, and the actual and potential public policy responses are considered in later chapters.

The supply of capital to the EC When we consider the limiting case of perfect competition in the theory of the firm, we find that the perfectly competitive firm faces a perfectly elastic, that is, horizontal, demand curve for its output. Similarly we suggested above that, in wishing to obtain capital, the individual region faces a near-perfectly elastic supply curve for this input as illustrated in Figure 2.4.

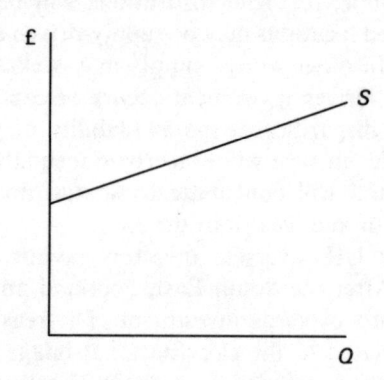

Figure 2.4 The supply of capital to the region

While the individual firm in a market characterised by perfect competition faces a perfectly elastic demand curve for its output, the industry of which it forms a part faces a downward sloping demand curve for its output.

Bearing this in mind, what shape would you expect the capital supply curve to take for the EC as a whole?

The answer is that the situation will represent the mirror image of the case of the demand for the output of a perfectly competitive industry. When we consider the supply of capital to a group of regions such as those that constitute the member economies of the EC, we find that the larger entity faces an upward sloping supply curve for capital, as shown in Figure 2.5.

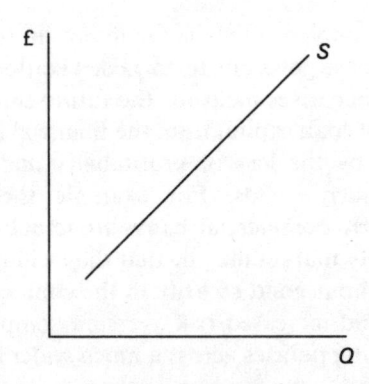

Figure 2.5 The supply of capital to the EC

What characteristics can we expect this supply curve to demonstrate during the 1990s? What will demand for financial capital be like compared with the 1980s? What effect will these conditions have upon the likely level of real interest rates? To attempt to reach an answer to some of these questions we need to look at the underlying influences in the capital market in the 1990s.

Underlying sources of capital demand in the 1990s In the 1990s there are several major sources of demand for capital that were not present to the same extent during the 1980s.

Firstly, the former East German economy and the other economies of Eastern Europe require major programmes of investment for modernisation and reconstruction and so represent potential additional demand for capital.

Secondly, the industrial and commercial expansion generated by the creation of the European single internal market implies greater demand for investment capital so that organisations can take advantage of the new potential market opportunities opened up within the EC.

Thirdly, the European economies have high aspirations relating to the improvement of the supply side of their economies through investment in major infrastructure projects. By their nature, large-scale infrastructure projects require large-scale investment and often bring few direct tangible benefits, especially in the short-term. This represents a further element adding to the demand for financial capital during the decade.

Outside Europe there is demand for capital to finance construction and development, in particular in the Middle East. And, as in earlier decades, conditions in the international financial market are affected by the need to finance the US budget deficit.

Increased demand for financial capital for the reasons outlined above is likely to push up real interest rates. Where investment is financed from the public sector, it will also bring upward pressure upon rates of taxation. The sizeable tax increases implemented in Germany in 1991 provide a good example of the need for a government to raise taxation to restrain current consumption and finance investment for the future through forced saving.

The overall supply of loan capital from the financial institutions may well be adversely affected by the loss of profitability and financial problems experienced in the early 1990s. For example the aftermath of the overexposure of the UK commercial banks to actual and potential losses in the domestic property market may be that they will be both less able and less willing to lend without good security in the coming years. This lack of availability of funds and increased risk aversion compared with the 1980s may well apply to lending policies across a much wider spectrum of markets than that for property.

To return to our earlier questions regarding the capital market facing the EC regional economies in the 1990s, we can indicate some likely general trends. There is no particular reason to expect the supply of financial capital to be more elastic or greater than in the 1980s. Demand for the available capital is likely to be greater. If the overall supply of savings is less adequate relative to the level of demand for financial capital, then the general level of real interest rates will tend to be relatively high. If such a higher level of real interest rates does occur, this could have a detrimental effect on the rates of growth of the EC economies, their constituent regions and other international economies, including those of the developing countries.

Labour

Although it is more complex than this suggests, for the sake of simplicity the regional problem is often defined in terms of an above-average regional rate of unemployment. For this reason the analysis of the regional labour market is one of the most sophisticated and well-developed areas of regional economics.

Here we look at the existing structure of regional labour markets, beginning with patterns of regional pay and then building upon the coverage of the regional market for financial capital provided in the preceding section. The main influences underlying the demand for and supply of labour in the regional market are introduced. The usefulness of the competitive model in the regional context is then considered in light of selected noncompetitive characteristics of the regional labour market.

Regional pay differences

Wage levels and labour costs The price of labour is the wage cost of employing that labour. However calculation of wage costs is more complex than the approach typified by introductory economics might imply. From the employer's viewpoint, it is not only the monetary wage paid that is important: it is the wage cost per unit of output produced. The employer also has to consider other aspects of employment costs. In the UK examples of these nonwage employment costs are National Insurance and pension contributions, holiday entitlements, the ease with which employees can or cannot be fired, and legal restrictions upon the number of hours worked per week.

When these wider institutional and legal aspects of labour costs are taken into account, the UK became a relatively low-labour-cost area within the EC in the early 1990s. For example employee-protection measures were less rigorous than in many other EC economies. The price of labour was therefore falling relative to that in some other EC economies such as France and Italy. This had a positive effect upon the demand from employers to locate in the UK. Relative German labour costs also fell in the early 1990s because of the effects of merging the former East-German low-wage labour market with the much higher-wage West-German labour market.

As the EC's single internal market applies to factors of production as well as production, in theory the single market could result in a single wage structure across the entire EC. The social provisions of the EC legislation with respect to such employment issues as minimum wage and maternity benefits aim to achieve such commonality by aligning nonwage employment costs in the different economies of the EC.

The analysis in the following sections of this chapter seeks to investigate further whether or not such a single market wage is likely to emerge across the different regions and economies of the EC.

Regional wage differences

Some regions gain a reputation as high-wage regions, while others gain a reputation as low-wage regions. The statistics relating to wages and earnings usually support these existing reputations, which have a tendency to persist over time and seem difficult to alter. (Earnings data for the UK regions are discussed in Chapter 3.)

To understand better the operation of the regional labour market, we need to ask:

- *Why* are there differences in regional wage levels?
- *Why*, once established, do these differences appear to be so persistent over time?

These two issues are addressed more fully in this section. They raise some interesting related secondary questions that are considered too, for example:

- What are the implications of the single internal market and the EC labour market's growing cohesion for the existing pattern of regional wage differences?

- Do those regions that exhibit relatively low wages experience formal labour-market discrimination in some sense? Or are there sound economic explanations other than discrimination for the differences that are observed?
- Does the variability of wage patterns among regions matter in relation to the maximisation of economic efficiency or is it solely of concern as an issue of equity?
- And what, if any, are the implications for government policy responses to the regional labour market?

This discussion focuses upon the observed differences in wages among regions. In other words, the emphasis is upon the *price* earned by labour in the regional labour market. Later in this book we extend our consideration of the regional labour market to look at the quantity of labour employed (Chapter 4) and at the likely economic effects of labour mobility between regions (Chapter 6).

Supply and demand in the regional labour market

The supply of labour The supply of labour to a particular region or to an urban centre within that region may vary markedly among different areas of the economy. Quantitatively, labour will be more readily available in some locations than in others. The main influences upon the quantity of labour available will be:

- Population density, that is, how many people live in the region.
- Demographic structure, for example, the age structure of the resident population and the percentage of working age.
- Economic activity rates, that is, the proportion of the potential working population who wish to be economically active.
- The rate of unemployment in the region.

Interregional population density is not constant over time. Figure 2.6 summarises the regional growth rate of population since the 1960s. This demonstrates that the greatest rate of population growth has been in East Anglia and the smallest increase has occurred in the North of England, London and Scotland.

The UK 1991 Census statistics provide information regarding the age structure of the population, which is relevant to the potential size of the labour supply in the region. These statistics indicate that the South East has the highest proportion of population in the 16–44 age group by region. On the other hand the South West and Wales both have a lower proportion in this age group, but a higher proportion over retirement age (UK Census, 1991).

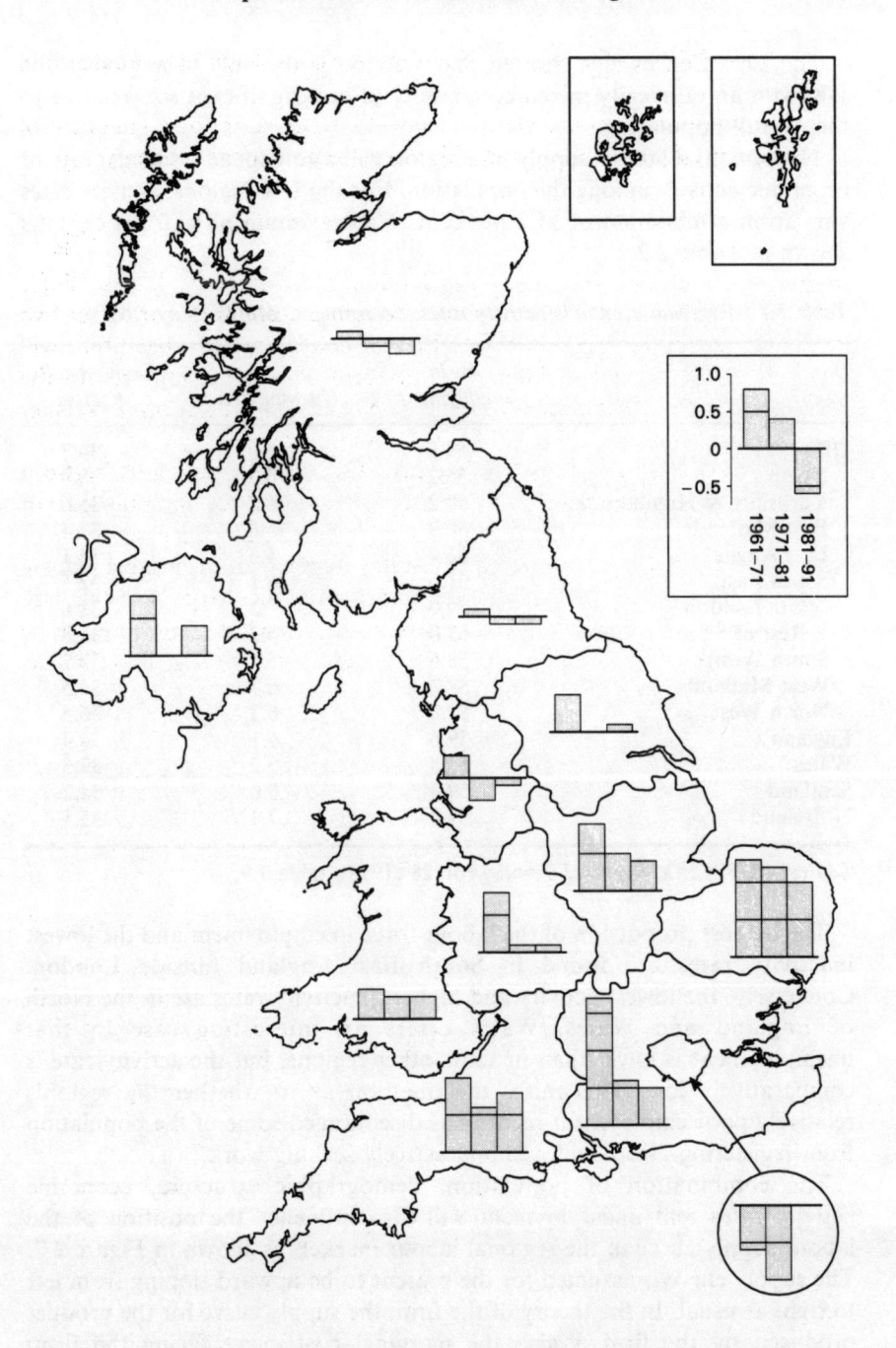

Figure 2.6 Regional annual growth rates of population, percentages, 1961–91
Source of data: UK CSO, *Regional Trends*, vol. 28 (1993), table 3.1.

The 1991 Census also showed that London is the only subregion in the UK with an ethnically mixed community of any significant size relative to the overall population.

The potential labour supply in a region will also depend upon the rate of economic activity among the population. For the UK regions, activity rates vary from a minimum of 55.2 per cent to a maximum of 63.0 per cent, as shown in Table 2.2.

Table 2.2 Regional economic activity rates, percentages, March–May 1992

	All in employment	Unemployed	Economically inactive
UK	59.3	6.0	34.7
North	55.2	6.7	38.0
Yorkshire & Humberside	58.2	6.2	35.6
East Midlands	60.9	5.6	33.5
East Anglia	61.4	4.6	34.1
South East	61.5	6.1	32.5
Gtr London	59.0	7.5	33.6
Rest of SE	63.0	5.2	31.8
South West	58.6	5.7	35.7
West Midlands	58.8	6.7	34.5
North West	57.3	6.2	36.5
England	59.6	6.1	34.4
Wales	55.3	5.2	39.5
Scotland	59.3	6.0	34.7
N. Ireland	57.7	7.3	35.1

Source: UK CSO, *Regional Trends*, vol. 28 (1993), table 7.9.

The highest proportion of the labour force in employment and the lowest inactivity rates are found in South East England outside London. Conversely, the lowest activity and highest inactivity rates are in the North of England and Wales. Wales offers an interesting case in that unemployment is lower than in some other regions, but the activity rate is comparatively low. This raises the question as to whether the region's relatively poor employment record has discouraged some of the population from registering as unemployed and actively seeking work.

The combination of population, demographic structure, economic activity rates and unemployment will also influence the position of the labour supply curve in the regional labour market, as shown in Figure 2.7. The supply curve is assumed for the present to be upward sloping from left to right as usual. In the theory of the firm, the supply curve for the product produced by the firm is also the marginal cost curve facing the firm. Analogously, the factor-supply curve facing the firm also represents the marginal input cost (MIC) to the firm, as indicated in Figure 2.7.

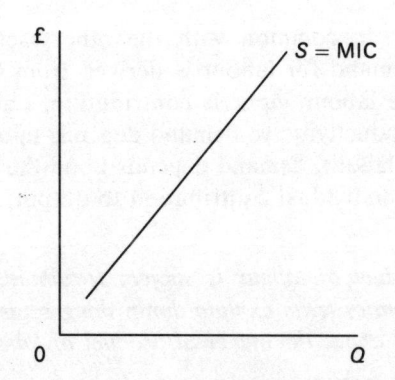

Figure 2.7 The supply of labour to the firm

We know too from the introductory theory of the firm that when average costs are increasing, marginal costs are increasing more rapidly. A similar relationship holds in the factor market: when average input costs are increasing, then marginal input costs must be increasing faster. This relationship between the average input cost (AIC) of the factor of production – in this case labour- and the associated marginal input cost is illustrated in Figure 2.8.

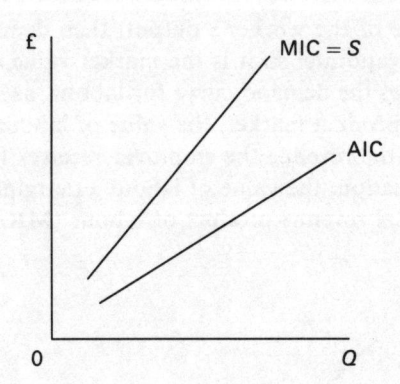

Figure 2.8 The marginal and average input cost of labour

The slope, or elasticity of the labour supply curve in the regional labour market will depend upon the responsiveness of the quantity of the relevant labour supplied to changes in the labour price, in this case the wage available in the regional labour market. The different conditions with respect to the supply elasticity of labour in competitive and uncompetitive regional labour markets are explained more fully below.

Demand for labour In common with the other factors of production, capital and land, demand for labour is derived from the demand for the output to which the labour input is contributing. Labour's contribution depends upon its productivity, so demand depends upon labour's product. For a single unit of labour, demand depends upon the physical amount of that unit of labour's individual contribution to output, that is, its marginal product.

> *The marginal product of labour is subject to diminishing returns. Most introductory economics texts explain diminishing returns: can you remember what it tells us about the marginal product of labour?*

The concept of diminishing returns tells us that, in the short-term, the amount of fixed factors of production, such as buildings and machinery, with which labour can work will after some point limit marginal product. In other words, as more people are put to work with the same amount of equipment, the quantity of output each can produce will after a certain point begin to diminish.

Texts often use examples such as agricultural workers digging a field to illustrate this point effectively. If there are ten spades available, then the marginal product of additional workers over and above ten soon begins to diminish. Another contemporary example is the typical office with limited space and computing facilities in which only a limited number of staff can be productively employed.

If there is no sale of the worker's output, then demand for their labour services will soon evaporate: so it is the market value of marginal product (VMP) that underlies the demand curve for labour, as shown in Figure 2.9.

In a competitive product market, the value of labour's marginal product will be the same as the revenue the employer receives from the sale of that product. In this situation, the value of labour's marginal product (VMP) is equal to the marginal revenue product of labour (MRP), as in Figure 2.9.

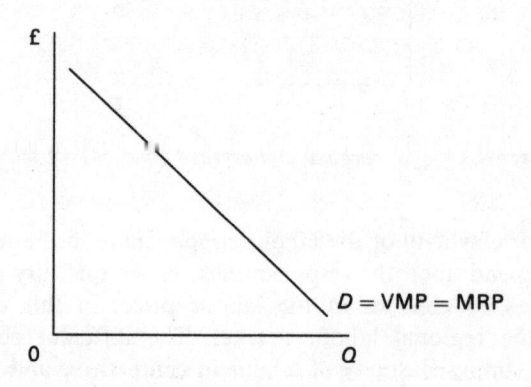

Figure 2.9 The firm's demand for labour

Where the product market is uncompetitive, the marginal revenue product will decrease faster than the value of marginal product. This is similar to imperfect competition in the theory of the firm where marginal revenue declines faster than average revenue as the firm increases its sales. As a result, the MRP curve is steeper and lies to the left of the VMP curve as shown in Figure 2.10 (We develop further the implications of this particular factor-market situation in a later section of this chapter that deals with the regional market for land as a factor of production.)

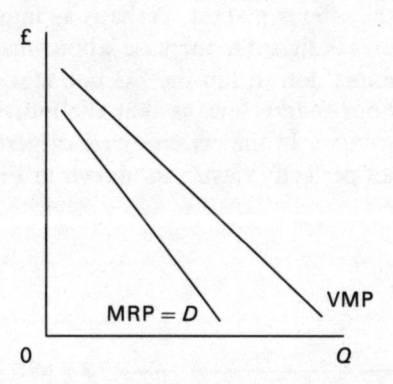

Figure 2.10 The marginal revenue product and value of marginal product of labour

The slope, or price elasticity of the derived demand for labour curve, that is, MRP, in Figures 2.9 and 2.10 above, will depend upon several considerations. Where demand for the final product is relatively price elastic, the derived demand for labour is likely to be more elastic than will be the case for labour producing a product in inelastic demand. Where labour costs represent a high proportion of the total costs associated with production, demand is likely to be more elastic than where labour costs represent only a small proportion of total costs. Where the production process is such that it is easy to substitute capital and/or land for labour, the elasticity of derived demand for labour will be greater. Also, the elasticity of derived demand for labour will increase over time, as the employer has longer to adjust to the new price of labour.

The position of the derived demand for labour curve will also depend upon a number of different influences, such as the availability of substitute factors of production and the employer's tastes and preferences. The latter point is studied more fully later in this chapter.

The perfectly competitive labour market

The main assumptions that must be satisfied for a labour market to satisfy the conditions of perfect competition are as follows:

❑ All labour is homogeneous, so we can ignore all personal characteristics, differences in levels of skill, work experience and so on;
❑ There is freedom of entry into and exit from the labour market, so potential entry barriers such as qualifications are seen as unimportant, as are costs such as pension transferability associated with job change.
❑ All labour is perfectly mobile, both among different occupations and geographically among regions.

In the UK several legislative changes in the 1980s aimed to increase the competitiveness of the labour market. Perhaps as importantly, the EC has enacted many measures designed to increase labour-market competition and lower barriers to competition within the EC boundaries.

A competitive labour market means that the individual worker faces a highly elastic supply curve. In the extreme case of perfect competition, this supply curve becomes perfectly elastic, as shown in Figure 2.11.

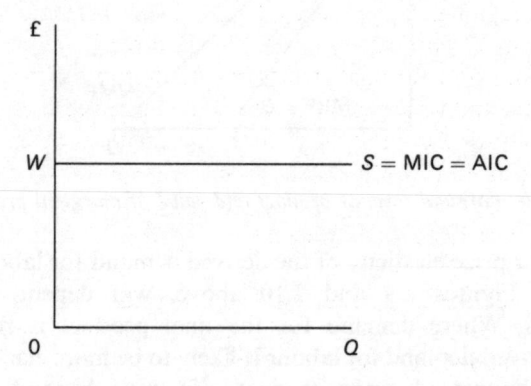

Figure 2.11 The supply of labour in a perfectly competitive market

Where the labour market is highly competitive, the individual worker becomes a price taker with respect to wage rates, the price of labour being determined by industry-wide demand and supply conditions. This situation contrasts with the highly inelastic supply curve for land discussed later in this chapter.

Why does the average worker in some regions experience low wages and poor employment prospects compared with those in other regions within the EC? Why do these established differences persist over time? Is it an indicator of differences in industrial and occupational structure, reflecting the fact that high-wage industries and occupations are more strongly represented in some regions than others? Do regional wage differences persist, even if we allow for differences in occupational and industrial structure, because regional labour markets are not competitive? Are there demand influences that affect the equilibrium wage rate obtained in the labour market of different regions?

Uncompetitive regional labour markets

There are three main reasons why regional labour markets may not correspond to the perfectly competitive market model outlined above. Both the geographic immobility of labour and the different skill attributes of the labour force in different regions will affect labour-supply conditions in the regional labour market. On the demand side of the labour market, the possible response of employers given a heterogeneous rather than homogeneous labour force are discussed.

Segregated regional labour markets

Regional differences in occupational and industrial structure were introduced earlier in this chapter, and regional differences in earnings were considered in the preceding section. Here we introduce some differences in regional wages that derive from differences in demand, where those demand differences do not always directly reflect differences in the industrial and occupational structure of different regions.

Many regional and local labour markets are characterised by *segregation*, which may take the form of segregation by occupation, by industry, by sex, by religion, age or ethnic origin. Where this segregation reflects employers' preferences for employing, or not employing, workers with particular identifiable characteristics, it is most accurately considered as a *demand-side* influence upon the labour market reflecting employers' *tastes*. Those aspects of the segregated labour market derived from these subjective employer preferences, as distinct from regional variations in industrial and occupational structure, are dealt with next.

Stigmatised regional labour markets We saw above that the demand for labour, as for any factor of production, will be derived from the final demand for the product of that labour. This labour demand is reflected in the value marginal product (VMP) of labour curve. Rational employers will choose how much labour to employ by equating labour's marginal value product with its marginal cost as an input (MIC), which reflects supply conditions. Demand and supply interact through the labour market to yield a profit-maximising and optimal outcome, at a wage of W_e (Figure 2.12).

This analysis is relevant in situations where employers behave wholly rationally in response to economic incentives. However behavioural theory indicates that employers and their organisations are not always rational in their decision making. We shall see in Chapter 5 that organisational behaviour with regard to the location of economic activity is not always wholly rational. Nor are organisations' employment decisions always wholly rational. Accordingly this section investigates the implications of one type of

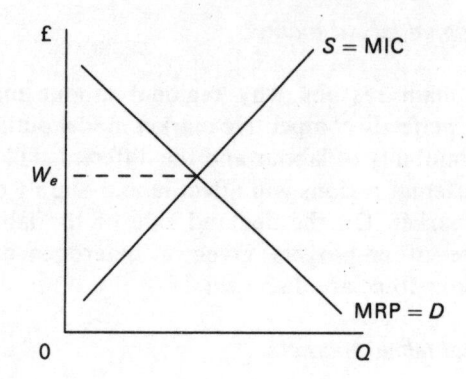

Figure 2.12 Equilibrium in the regional labour market

potentially irrational behaviour affecting employment decisions for relative regional wage levels.

The organisation's location decision may be influenced by management preferences for their area of residence. Management may also have preferences for the type, or the area of origin, of labour employed. Where these preferences are revealed as tastes, the position of the labour-demand curve will be affected.

It has been argued that some employers will prefer to employ, or not employ, male or female workers. Religious and racial prejudices also influence labour demand in a discriminatory manner. To place the analysis more specifically in the context of regional and spatial labour markets, employers may have preferences for workers from one area or locality as against another area.

These employer tastes can be shown analytically by a shift in the position of the labour demand curve. In the case of workers from the preferred area, the labour-demand curve will shift out from the origin and to the right, as shown by D_F in Figure 2.13. On the other hand, demand for the labour provided by the workforce from the disliked area will be reduced, as shown by the dotted line D_A in Figure 2.13.

Before you read on, think about how such employer preferences may affect wage levels in both the favoured and the disfavoured region compared with the level that would prevail in the absence of such employer preferences.

Unless the labour supply happens to be perfectly elastic, the employer pays for this labour-market discrimination. Figure 2.13 demonstrates that the group of employees in the preferred area are able to earn wages of W_F as against the lower rate of W_E. For this preferred area or region the costs of discrimination fall on the employer, and the workforce benefits from discrimination in their favour. The extent to which wages are pushed up,

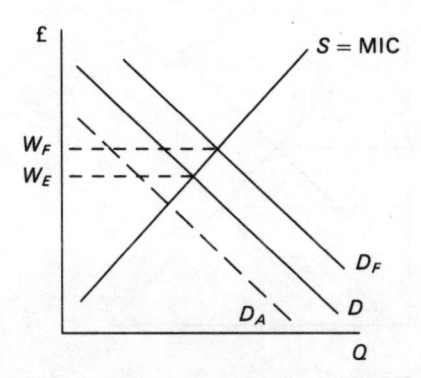

Figure 2.13 Regional wage differences reflecting employer preferences

that is, the size of the gap between W_F and W_E for a given degree of employer preference will depend upon the elasticity of the labour-supply curve.

The workforce in the area or region to which the employer is averse will be paid less, unless labour-supply conditions are perfectly elastic. For this region the workforce bears the cost of being discriminated against, so suffers a welfare loss. The extent of this loss will similarly depend upon the elasticity of the labour-supply curve.

This type of irrational employer behaviour resulting in economically irrational regional wage differences does occur. Areas with a reputation for industrial unrest or low productivity will become stigmatised as undesirable, reinforcing existing prejudices against their workforce. Equally, employers may prefer labour from areas with a 'good reputation' to an extent that outweighs any quantitatively higher productivity performance. Once established, such prejudices are hard to overcome, and the regional wage imbalances associated with them hard to erode.

Labour immobility

Even if we accept the other assumptions of a perfectly competitive labour market and assume that labour is homogeneous and there is freedom of entry into and exit from the labour market, geographic labour immobility will affect regional labour-market equilibria and so affect overall national labour-market equilibrium.

For example, where a significant number of the members of an occupation are geographically immobile, basic demand-and-supply analysis can illustrate the effects of this immobility upon relative regional wages in an otherwise free labour market. In some years in the recent past, the case of teachers in France provides a useful example (Figure 2.14).

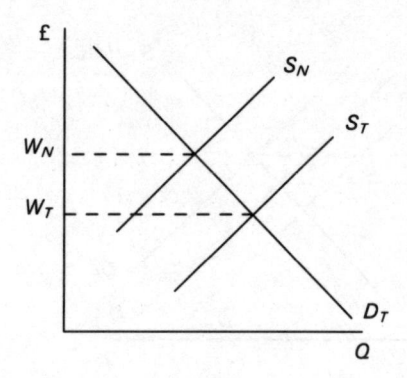

Figure 2.14 Regional wage differences reflecting labour immobility

If the total supply of teachers being trained, S_T, reflects reasonably accurately the total level of demand for teachers in the economy, but many teachers prefer not to work in Paris and the north of France, there will be an unavoidable excess supply to the south of France. Relative pay levels in the south of France could then be reduced in light of this excess supply. But in the north extra incentive payments over and above W_T are needed to attract an adequate supply of teachers.

The extra payment $W_T W_N$ represents an economic-rent element to its recipients as they are better off than they would be if teachers were spatially perfectly mobile and showed no locational preferences. The extra payment $W_T W_N$ equally represents a welfare loss to the government, which should only have needed to offer W_T as a national equilibrium wage. The size of this welfare loss will be influenced by the extent to which labour is unavailable to the north, as this will affect the position of S_N, and by the elasticity of the derived demand for labour curve, D_T.

Skills in the regional labour force

The availability of labour with different skills indicates that the labour force is heterogeneous and not homogeneous. The supply of labour available with a particular skill will be less elastic than the overall supply of labour ignoring specific skills. The skills available in the regional labour force are important because, when an organisation is making a decision with regard to a particular location, it will be interested in the *quality* as well as *quantity* of the labour force available in the vicinity. For example, an insurance company considering the relocation of a regional or head office will be interested in the potential supply of clerical staff in the local labour market. A firm relocating its research centre may have rather different priorities with regard to the local labour supply.

For these reasons the availability of skills in the labour force is important for the growth potential of the regional economy. Unskilled labour without any qualifications represents a quarter to one third of the labour force in the UK regions (Department of Employment, 1990), but the extent of interregional variation in the availability of graduate employees is much greater. As Figure 2.15 shows, graduates represent nearly 15 per cent of the workforce in the South East but only around 8 per cent in the North of England.

Why do you think these differences among UK regions in the availability of graduates in the labour force may be important?

If the labour force were homogeneous, the labour market could in principle operate as a competitive market. But labour is not homogeneous: different individuals have different skills and different amounts and types of work experience, so labour is *heterogeneous*. In the context of the regional labour market, two important considerations follow from this heterogeneity of labour.

First, as illustrated by Figure 2.15, there are differences in the skill levels and attributes of the labour supply available in the different regions of the UK. Second, economies such as those in Western Europe have experienced an underlying structural increase in the skill levels associated with employment. This has happened independently of whether employment is in the agricultural, manufacturing or service sector.

While there is not always a direct relationship between the level of qualifications and the earnings someone receives in employment, earnings are often higher for those holding higher qualifications. This means that the earning capacity of the workforce in London and the South East may be greater in this respect than that of the workforce in those regions where less than 10 per cent of the workforce are graduates. As we shall see in Chapter 3, this may affect the pattern of expenditure in the region too.

Figure 2.15 shows that over a quarter of the workforce have no qualifications in a majority of the UK regions. The unqualified represent a particularly high proportion of the contemporary workforce in the East and West Midlands and Northern Ireland.

Unskilled workers without formal qualifications are becoming increasingly disadvantaged in the labour market. Where a group of workers is made redundant, for example as the result of a factory closure, it is typically the least-skilled members of the group who are the last to find new employment. In some cases a minority may not find new employment. For them the labour market does not 'clear', because there is no demand for their labour services at any price. In the absence of effective retraining they are likely to join the long-term unemployed. In contrast the experienced and highly skilled worker is often unemployed for only a relatively short time, and is less likely to have been made redundant in the first place.

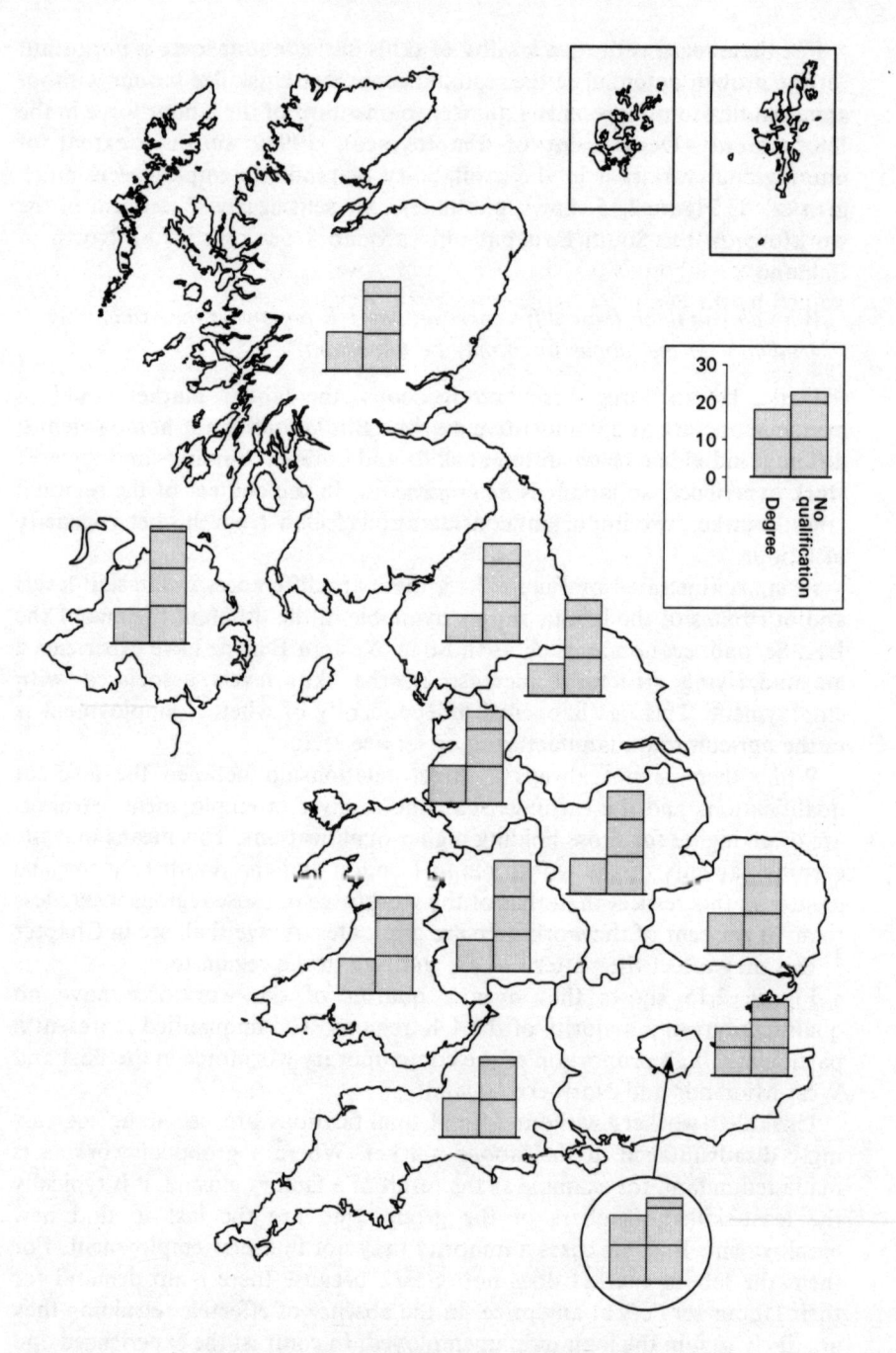

Figure 2.15 *Qualifications of the workforce in the UK regions, percentages, 1992*
Source of data: UK CSO, *Regional Trends*, vol. 28 (1993), table 7.8.

This argument suggests that the traditional view of labour as the short-term variable factor of production, while land and capital were the short-term fixed factors of production, may no longer be entirely accurate. Workers without significant skills or work experience *specific* to their employer are likely to be viewed as a variable factor of production. Unskilled and inexperienced labour will be recruited and laid off as the pressures of the market dictate.

However labour with significant skill levels and/or specific experience valued by the employer may be more realistically regarded as a fixed factor of production. In the face of recession, the employer will seek to retain the services of the more skilled and experienced members of the labour force. This is a rational decision for management seeking to maximise long-term profits. It reflects the high costs of recruiting and training new staff relative to the costs of retaining existing staff with specific attributes important to the employer.

Skilled and experienced employees, therefore, will not be made redundant except as a last resort. This helps to explain why skilled and professional workers were still being made redundant in spring 1993 in the UK, very late in the 1990s recession. When the labour market is tight, these workers will be able to bargain effectively to maintain, and possibly to increase, their real wage due to the inelasticity of the labour-supply curve presented to the employer. This effect further reduces the level of effective competition in the contemporary labour market.

Table 2.3 Occupational distribution of the labour force, percentages, March–May 1992*

	Prof. & manage.	Craft & nonman.	Services	Semi-skilled	Self employed	Total in empl.
UK	11.4	18.2	9.2	4.8	7.1	59.3
North	9.1	17.2	9.1	5.6	4.9	55.2
Yorks. & Humb.	10.1	18.3	9.3	5.9	6.1	58.2
East Midlands	11.2	19.9	8.9	5.8	6.7	60.9
East Anglia	11.2	18.9	8.7	3.8	8.6	61.4
South East	14.0	18.8	9.4	3.4	8.1	61.5
Gtr London	13.8	17.9	8.4	2.9	7.5	59.0
Rest of SE	14.1	19.3	10.0	3.7	4.1	63.0
South West	10.6	17.0	10.4	4.2	8.8	58.6
West Midlands	10.4	17.6	8.9	6.8	6.6	58.8
North West	10.8	18.4	9.0	5.3	6.4	57.3
England	11.8	18.3	9.3	4.8	7.3	59.6
Wales	8.7	15.5	9.2	5.3	7.3	55.3
Scotland	10.1	19.3	9.4	5.1	5.4	59.3
N. Ireland	8.7	16.8	7.4	4.1	7.0	57.7

* main occupational groupings only are included, so the component figures do not add up to the total percentage in employment.
Source: Calculated from UK CSO, *Regional Trends*, vol. 28 (1993), table 7.9.

There is a lot of data in this table, so you may prefer to look closely at regions and/or occupational groupings of particular interest. For example, what does the table tell you about the interregional distribution of different occupational groupings such as professional and managerial employment?

Wales and Northern Ireland are underrepresented in terms of the regional distribution of professional and managerial employment, for which the highest proportion is found in the South East of England. The South East also has the lowest proportion of semi-skilled occupational employment. A high proportion of semi-skilled employment is found in the East Midlands.

The South East, outside London, and the South West have high proportions of service-sector occupations. The South West also has an above-average percentage of the self-employed, as does East Anglia. In contrast there are relatively fewer self-employed in the North of England.

Regional differences in the skill levels and occupational and other attributes of the labour force are likely to be reflected in regional imbalances in employment opportunities. This will be partly cause and partly effect. Those organisations that seek to employ highly skilled labour will tend not to locate in areas with a more limited pool of such labour. Also, highly skilled and graduate labour will tend not to live in areas perceived to offer few or limited career opportunities.

In recent decades the outer regions of the UK economy have all experienced rates of outmigration of skilled and graduate labour above the national average. This has been especially true of Wales and Northern Ireland. Other regions such as the South West of the Republic of Ireland have been similarly affected.

In the UK, perceived and actual regional disparities in the supply of suitable labour may represent a significant disincentive to organisations employing a highly qualified workforce to locate outside the South East. This in turn may constrain the economic growth of those regions outside the South East and the growth of their main urban centres.

Where a region has a labour force characterised by skill levels below the national average and/or a high proportion of workers with redundant skills, that region has a problem of a shortage of human capital and/or of outdated human capital. Such inadequacies respecting the regional supply of human capital require a positive policy response comparable to earlier regional policies designed to rectify deficiencies in the regional supply of physical capital.

Implications for public policy

Regional wage differences mean that labour in a particular region is paid at a rate either above or below the national equilibrium wage level. Where regional wage differences mean that regional wages are above the national average, firms' costs are increased relative to the national average. Such higher costs can result in cost pressures that contribute to inflationary pressures in the affected regions. These inflationary pressures will feed through into the national economy. During a period of economic expansion and high levels of economic activity, these above-average wages contribute to potential overheating and consequent constraints upon economic growth.

In other regions, regional wage differentials result in wage rates below the national average. These lower rates of remuneration will be reflected in a lower labour supply within the low-wage region relative to that which would be forthcoming if a nationally uniform wage rate were paid. In Figure 2.16, the level of under- and unemployment of the potential labour supply that can be ascribed to the lower wage, W_A, below the national equilibrium wage, W_E is shown by the horizontal distance $Q_A Q_E$. The size of this effect will be determined by the elasticity of the labour supply curve at the relevant wage levels. The more elastic the labour supply curve between A and E, the greater the number of potential members of the workforce who will be deterred from supplying their labour at a wage below W_E.

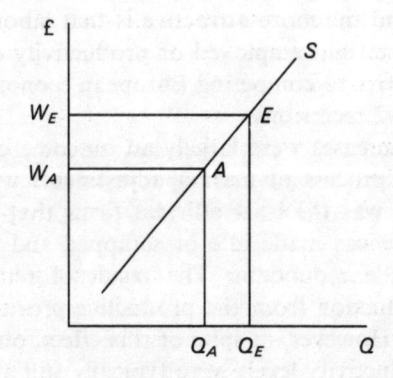

Figure 2.16 Underemployment of labour in the regional economy

The resulting underutilisation of the region's potentially available labour supply means that earnings, and therefore demand and prosperity, in the region will not be as high as would otherwise be the case. (Regional differences in earnings and incomes are discussed more fully in Chapter 3.) It also means that potential regional output is less than would be achievable at the higher wage rate. Neither the region nor the national economy are maximising productive potential, and so there may be a loss of economic efficiency.

This loss of economic efficiency is likely to be compounded by the effects of disequilibrium in the region where labour demand and wages are above the national average. Here, labour-skill bottlenecks and shortages will be reached more rapidly than would happen if wages and employment were spread more evenly across the national economy. As noted above, cost-inflationary pressures are also likely in such regions. As a result of the interregional imbalance in the national economy, neither region's labour market is in underlying equilibrium.

This failure to maximise productive potential means the economy is losing output that might otherwise have been produced. In these circumstances regional policy measures that aim to reduce regional labour-market imbalances and encourage equilibrium and the maximisation of productive potential should prove highly cost effective.

Productivity and labour

Demand for labour will, as suggested above, depend upon demand for the particular skills and expertise that the employer requires. In other words, labour is often valued for its *heterogeneity* rather than its *homogeneity*.

We saw above that labour is demanded for its contribution to the value of output, that is, its marginal value product (MVP). The more productive is labour, the higher is its marginal value product, and so the higher are potential wage levels and the more attractive is that labour to a potential employer. The output per unit employed or productivity of British labour generally improved relative to competing European economies during both the 1979–81 and 1989–92 recessions.

These productivity increases were largely an outcome of the recessions. To the extent that the process of market adjustments worked efficiently during the recession, it was the least efficient firms that closed; the least efficient machinery that was made idle or scrapped and the less efficient workers who were made redundant. The result of removing the least efficient factors of production from the productive process is that overall productivity levels rise. However, in spite of this effect, on an industry-by-industry basis UK productivity levels were typically still about 20 per cent below those of Germany in the early 1990s (NIESR, 1992).

The shakeout experienced in the 1979/81 recession meant that, on emergence from recession, the economy desperately needed investment in new production techniques and technologies. This investment in machinery would raise capital productivity. There was also a growing awareness of the need to direct investment towards the improvement of labour skills and labour productivity, increasingly seen as a bottleneck to the expansion of the UK economy. Investment was also needed in land, buildings and property to modernise production facilities and the environment within which production takes place.

The overheating of the UK economy in the late 1980s meant that the recovery in the level of investment was shortlived and was followed by the lengthy recession of the early 1990s. If labour productivity is to rise in the mid- and late 1990s to raise overall productivity in the economy then investment in capital, land and labour must occur. The earlier section of this chapter considered the market for the financial capital that is necessary to finance this investment, and concluded that it is likely to be relatively tight during the 1990s.

The impact of the labour market upon an organisation's success at its chosen location may be crucial. In principle, the availability of inputs of land, labour and capital may be critical to a region's growth potential. Studies of the organisation's location decision suggest that the decision maker in the organisation *in practice* places great emphasis upon accessibility to inputs and outputs; upon external economies of scale and personal preference (or even prejudice) in arriving at location decisions.

The regional location of economic activity will be considered in detail in Chapter 5. To conclude the present section the following is pertinent:

> The availability of resources therefore acted as a constraint on regional employment growth, with those regions which were able to provide the necessary inputs expanding the fastest. It is worth reiterating that accessibility to markets (whether input markets or output markets) was found to be of no help in explaining regional differences in employment growth (Armstrong and Taylor, 1993, pp. 161–2).

Land

Short-term conditions for the supply of land

The supply of land, both in total and for uses such as building factory space, is typically assumed to be perfectly inelastic in the short term, so that the supply curve is vertical. This means that the marginal input cost associated with the use of an additional unit of land by the user becomes the same as its average input cost (MIC = AIC), as shown in Figure 2.17.

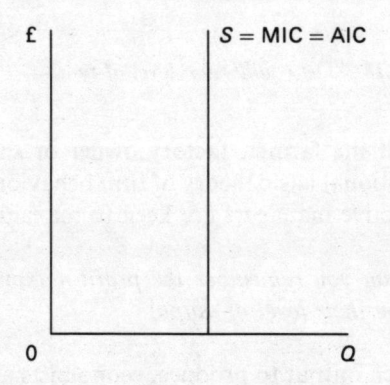

Figure 2.17 The short-term supply of land

The demand for land

Economic theory assumes that land, in common with other economic resources, is demanded not in its own right but for its contribution to the value of the user's final product. So the demand for land is a derived demand.

The farmer's demand for land on which to grow wheat is derived from the revenue expected from the sale of the wheat produced. The owner of a factory making jewellery demands the use of the factory in order to gain the revenue derived from the sale of the jewellery. The retailer demands shopfloor space to gain revenue from the sale of goods and services to the consumer.

If we assume that the farmer, the owner of the jewellery factory and the shopkeeper all sell their final product in a highly competitive market, then we have a single downward-sloping demand curve as in Figure 2.18. If we assume competition in the market then every additional unit of the final product will be sold for the same price as the preceding unit. This means, more precisely, that the value of the marginal product (VMP) is equal to the marginal revenue product derived from the sale of the final unit (MRP).

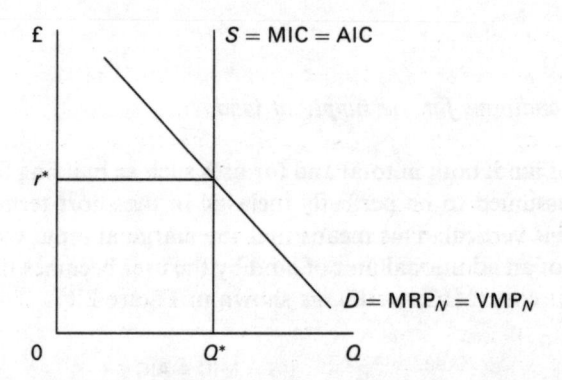

Figure 2.18 The equilibrium level of rent

How much land will the farmer, factory owner or shopkeeper wish to demand? In the conventional basic theory of firm behaviour, we assume that entrepreneurs and effective managers are keen to maximise profits.

Before reading on, can you remember the profit-maximising condition by which firms determine their level of output?

In deciding how much output to produce, economists assume that profit-maximising entrepreneurs and managers will try to maximise profit by producing output up to and including the level at which the addition to total cost, that is, the marginal cost (MC), of production associated with the final unit of output equals the addition to total revenue, that is, the marginal revenue (MR) associated with its sale.

Formally, we predict that the firm maximises profits by operating at the level of output where MC = MR. The situation is analogous with respect to the firm's level of inputs.

We assume that the entrepreneur or the manager aims to maximise profits, and that this is achieved by operating at the level of input use where the addition to total input cost associated with the hire of the last unit of the input equals the addition to total revenue product associated with its use. In other words, the profit-maximising firm will seek to equate marginal input cost (MIC) and marginal revenue product (MRP).

So, with respect to the input market, the firm maximises profits by using the level of inputs, in this case the quantity of land, such that MIC = MRP. In Figure 2.18, this means that Q^* will be demanded, yielding an equilibrium price or rent of r^*.

The long-term supply of land

In the long term the supply of land for a particular use is usually assumed to be very elastic. However this elasticity may be constrained, especially where planning restrictions are tight or suitable sites for development and economic use are limited by geographic conditions. Nineteenth-century settlers in North America may have faced a relatively elastic supply of agricultural land in some states, but at the end of the twentieth century it is difficult to think of many parallels. Rarely is the supply of land highly elastic today, at least in the European economies.

The supply of land to a particular use is also affected by the nature of the economy's land market. The land market is more or less active in different economies. In some countries the market for land is typically relatively inactive, with little substantive alteration over time in land holdings and/or ownership. In Europe there is a wide variation in the degree of activity in national land markets, with the UK probably having the most sophisticated land market in the EC.

We can therefore realistically proceed on the assumption that the long-term supply schedule for land is neither perfectly inelastic nor highly elastic. As the relevant supply curve is no longer vertical, the marginal input cost associated with additional use (MIC) exceeds the average input cost to the user (AIC), as shown on Figure 2.19.

This lack of perfect elasticity in the supply of land as an input means that the supply side of the market for land is characterised by conditions of 'monopsony' rather than competition. Where the user faces a competitive

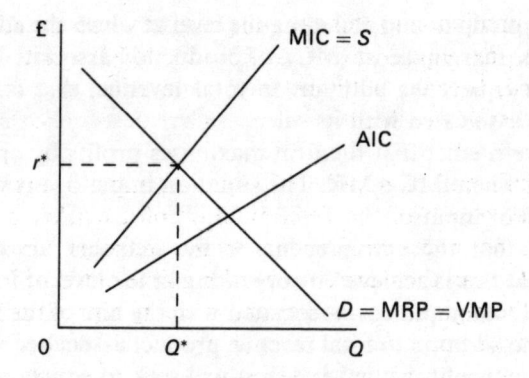

Figure 2.19 The determination of rent in the long term

market in which to sell the end product derived from the use of the land, as we discussed above, then the price determination represented in Figure 2.19 is realistic.

As before, we assume that the user of the land as an input will aim to maximise profits, and so the market equilibrium will occur where MIC = MRP, yielding an equilibrium quantity traded of Q^* and an equilibrium market rent or land price of r^*.

Bilateral monopoly

However, where the user *also* faces a degree of imperfect competition or monopoly at the point of sale of the end product for which the land is used as an input, then the market situation is characterised by monopsony/monopoly, sometimes referred to as bilateral monopoly. This situation is illustrated in Figure 2.20.

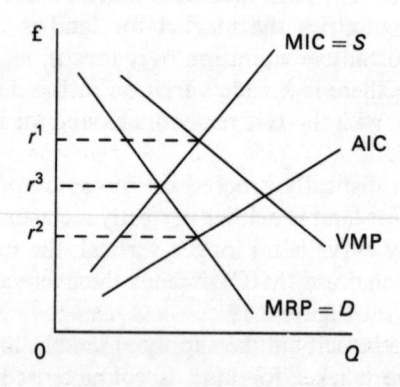

Figure 2.20 Bilateral monopoly in the regional land market

The simple prediction in this case might seem to be a market outcome at r_3, reflecting the equation of MIC and MRP. But life is not so straightforward, because both the buyer and seller in the market have a degree of market power due to their respective positions as monopolist and monopsonist.

In practice bilateral monopoly represents an important piece of economic analysis in the context of the determination of a market price or rent for land. There is no single market determined outcome for the appropriate price or rent. Instead there are a range of possible outcomes. In Figure 2.20, r_1 represents the highest attainable rent, while r_2 represents the lowest rent that we would predict.

The exact outcome in the market within this range of possibilities will depend upon the relative bargaining strengths of the buyer and seller at the time of negotiation of a rent or price for the land.

What factors do you think might influence the ability of a potential tenant to negotiate a lower rent for the use of the land, that is, a price near to r_2 rather than r_1?

There are several important considerations here, of which the following are examples:

- How use-specific is the piece of land in question?
- How keen is the potential owner/tenant to buy or to rent?
- How many other suitable sites are available?
- How many other potential offers are in the pipeline?

What do all these considerations have in common? They all reflect the relative strengths of current demand and supply for the land in question. At a time of weak demand and relatively abundant supply, we would expect a price or rent to be determined near the bottom of the range near to r_2 in Figure 2.20.

In reality bargains may be struck in these market conditions of weak demand that reduce the effective market price by other means, such as the inclusion of a rent-free period for the tenant, a period free of rent plus rates; or other similar inducements designed to buttress demand. Such inducements played an important role in rent determination in England in the recession of the early 1990s due to the general provision for 'upward-only' rent reviews, that were not always appropriate to prevailing market conditions in those years.

Conversely a market characterised by tight supply and strong demand will be reflected in a price or rent determined near to r_1, and with full costs such as rates being passed on by the land owner to the tenant or purchaser.

Rent variations do arise spatially and over time because of these bilateral negotiating conditions. And, as demand and supply for land use tend to vary cyclically by more than average, so rent and land price levels and land occupancy levels vary across the economic cycle. This phenomenon is investigated more fully in the course of this book and in particular in Chapter 4.

References and Further Reading

Armstrong, H. and J. Taylor (1993) *Regional Economics and Policy*, 2nd edn (London: Harvester Wheatsheaf).
Ashcroft, Brian *et al.* (1987) *The economic effects of the inward acquisition of Scottish manufacturing companies 1965–1980*, ESU Research Paper no 11, Scottish Office (Edinburgh: HMSO).
Department of Employment (1990) *Labour Force Survey* (London: HMSO).
Fothergill, S. and G. Gudgin (1982) *Unequal Growth* (London: Heinemann).
Fothergill, S. and N. Guy, (1990) *Retreat from the Regions* (London: Jessica Kingsley Publishers/Regional Studies Association).
HM Treasury (1990) *Economic Briefing* No. 1 (London: HM Treasury).
Leigh, C. and J. Stilwell (1992) 'Yorkshire and Humberside', in Townroe and Martin (1992).
Mackay, R. R. (1992) 'Wales', in Townroe and Martin (1992).
Martin, Ron (1989) 'The growth and geographical anatomy of venture capital in the UK', *Regional Studies*, vol. 23, no. 5, pp. 389–403.
National Institute for Economic and Social Research (1992) *Review*, February.
Office of Population Censuses and Surveys (1991, 1992) *Population Trends* (London: HMSO).
Organisation for Economic Cooperation and Development (1990) *Main Economic Indicators and Quarterly Labour Force Statistics*.
Robinson, F. (1992) 'The Northern Region', in Townroe and Martin (1992).
Townroe, P. and R. Martin (eds) (1992) *Regional Development in the 1990s* (London: Jessica Kingsley Publishers/Regional Studies Association).
United Kingdom Central Statistical Office (1990) *Social Trends* (London: HMSO).
United Kingdom Central Statistical Office (1993) *Regional Trends* (London: HMSO).

3 Expenditure, Prices and Exchange

REGIONAL EXPENDITURE

Income and Expenditure Patterns

For international and interregional comparison, real per capita gross domestic output is usually taken as the basis of comparison. While this convention has been followed in this book, there are other factors that actively contribute to the quality of life in a region.

For example, population densities, crime levels and the degree of racial and religious harmony may all influence residents' perceptions of a region. The standard of housing that is available, standards of retailing and leisure facilities may also affect views of the pleasantness of a region as a place to live. But however pleasant a region may appear to be as a place to live, there is likely to be emigration in the absence of sources of stable employment. Economic activity provides the lifeblood of the region: without economic activity the region is not likely to thrive.

Figure 3.1 shows the regional distribution of personal disposable income, that is, income after deduction of tax and national-insurance contributions, as this is a major influence upon regional consumer expenditure.

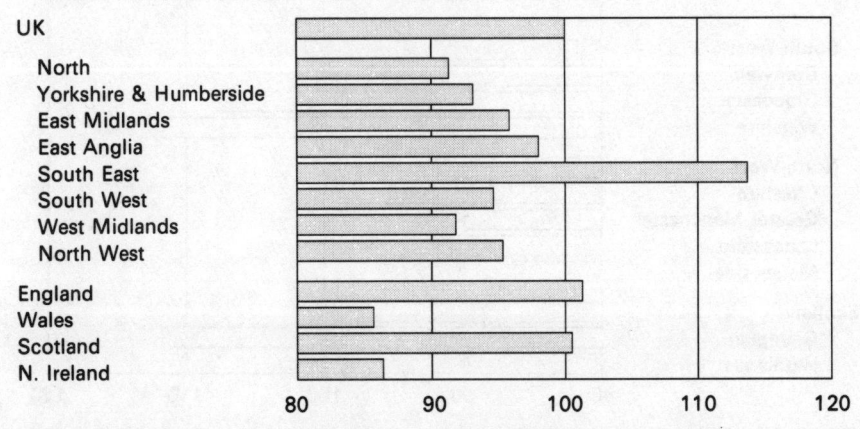

Figure 3.1 Regional distribution of per capita personal disposable income, 1991 (index: UK=100)
Source of data: UK CSO, *Regional Trends*, vol. 28 (1993), table 12.6.

72   *Regional Economics*

Figure 3.1 demonstrates that the population in the South East of England typically had 13 per cent more income to dispose of in 1991 than the average member of the UK population. Only the population in Scotland also enjoyed personal disposable incomes slightly above the UK national average. For all other regions, disposable-income levels were below the national average, significantly so in the cases of Wales and Northern Ireland.

While the Scottish regional economy performs relatively well on this indicator of economic prosperity, it is worth remembering that it performed relatively badly in terms of output which we considered in Figure 1.4. Scotland also demonstrates a high degree of *intra*regional variation in income, as we shall see below. The Scottish example therefore provides a useful reminder that the regional problem is multi-faceted: we should take care not to read too much signficance into one isolated economic indicator.

It is interesting to see that, within these regional variations, there are considerable subregional variations in household disposable income. Figure 3.2 provides detail of this with respect to selected subregions of the South West and North West of England and Scotland.

Within the South West region, Figure 3.2 shows us that households in Wiltshire, which is relatively close to the affluent South East, had an average disposable income that was 11 per cent above the national average. However households in Cornwall, on the western periphery of both the region and of the UK, had an average disposable income that was over 8 per cent below the national average. The degree of variation within the South West region is therefore about 20 per cent: one of the widest in the UK, as is clear from Figure 3.3.

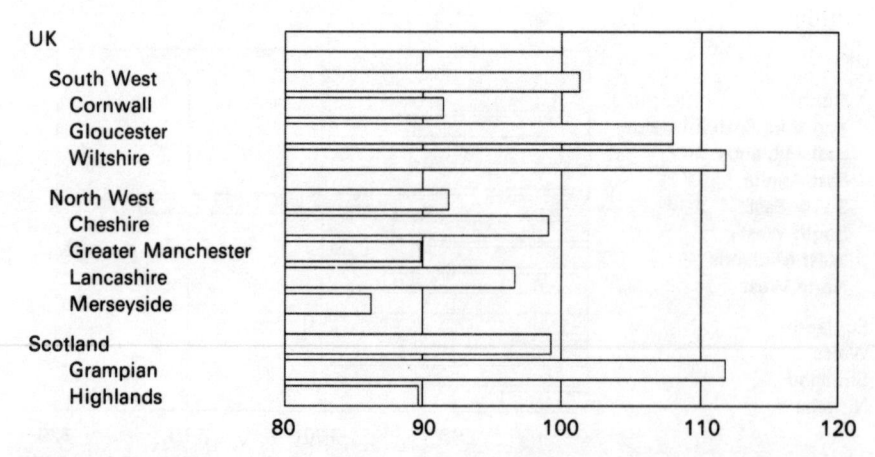

Figure 3.2 Subregional distribution of household disposable income, 1990 (index: UK=100, selected subregions only)

Source of data: UK CSO, *Regional Trends*, vol. 28 (1993), table 14.4.

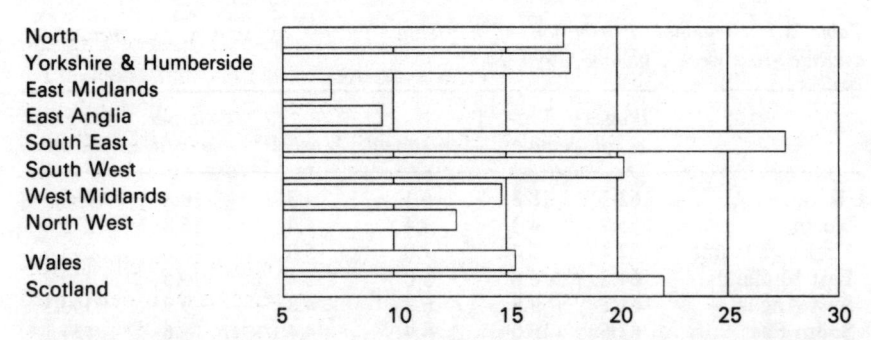

Figure 3.3 The extent of intraregional variation in average household disposable income, 1990, percentages

Source: data calculated from UK CSO, *Regional Trends*, vol. 28 (1993), table 14.4.

With intraregional variation of around 12 per cent, the North West is a more cohesive region in this respect. Merseyside is one of the poorest subregions in the UK according to this measure, the others being Durham in the North East, Mid-Glamorgan in Wales, and the subregions of Northern Ireland.

As noted above, Scotland demonstrates a relatively high degree of intraregional variation in household disposable income. There is a difference of over 22 per cent between Grampian, where incomes are typically over 10 per cent above the UK average, and the Highlands and Islands subregion, where average household disposable income was 10 per cent below the national average.

However the widest intraregional variation, as shown by Figure 3.3, is within the South East region of England. Here the typical household in Surrey is more than 27 per cent better off than the typical household in Kent or on the Isle of Wight.

Income sources

Economic activity generates the income that finances the expenditure that keeps the economy alive. The income received by individuals and households can be classified in three ways:

- Earned income generated through the provision of labour services by the individual or household.
- Unearned income generated by the ownership of land or capital, which attracts income in the form of rent and/or interest and dividend payments.
- Unearned income received as transfer payments, such as pensions, and unemployment benefit.

Table 3.1 Regional distribution of household income by source, percentages of average gross weekly income, 1990–1

	Wages & sal.	Self-employ.	Investment	Pensions*	Soc. Sec. benefit	Av. gross wk inc.
UK	62.1	8.8	6.1	4.7	10.8	350.1
North	65.9	4.3	3.4	4.4	15.8	275.8
Yorks. & Humb.	62.4	5.4	7.0	5.0	13.6	295.5
East Midlands	64.3	6.8	5.0	5.4	10.5	340.2
East Anglia	61.7	9.8	6.2	4.8	9.9	340.3
South East	63.6	10.0	6.4	4.4	7.6	434.1
Gtr London	63.6	9.7	6.6	4.4	7.7	442.5
Rest of SE	63.6	10.2	6.3	4.3	7.5	429.4
South West	58.0	11.5	7.0	6.0	9.6	355.9
West Midlands	61.2	8.9	5.3	4.1	12.4	319.7
North West	60.1	9.1	5.8	4.3	12.7	321.0
England	62.5	8.7	6.1	4.7	10.2	359.7
Wales	57.8	8.2	5.4	5.6	16.1	284.4
Scotland	61.0	7.9	7.3	4.8	13.6	306.5
N. Ireland	62.5	6.7	3.0	2.7	16.5	274.1

*Note that 'pensions' excludes those received as social security benefits, which are included in the latter category.
Source: UK CSO, *Regional Trends*, vol. 28 (1993), table 8.1.

The statistics in Table 3.1 demonstrate that there are significant interregional variations in sources of income. The characteristics of the income sources in four selected regions are considered below to highlight some of these variations and explain their effect upon average income in the regions.

What characteristics distinguish the sources of income in the North of England from the UK national average?

The information in the table shows us that households in the North of England are typically more dependent upon wages and salaries and upon social-security benefits than the national average. Income from self-employment and investment income are markedly below the national average. These factors combine to yield an average gross weekly household income of £275.80, £75 per week below the UK average.

What characteristics distinguish the sources of income in the South East of England from the UK national average?

In the South East, income from self-employment and from wages and salaries is above the UK average, while there is comparatively less income from social-security benefits and pensions. Average gross weekly household income in the South East region is £434.10, £84 above the UK national average and nearly £160 above that in the North of England.

What characteristics distinguish the sources of income in the South West of England from the UK national average?

Wages and salaries from paid employment are less important a source of income in the South West than in most other UK regions, while the South West has the highest proportion of income from self-employment of any region in the UK. The region has the highest regional income from nonearned sources, that is, investments, annuities and private pensions. The overall average weekly income in the region is very close to the national average, but its make-up is very different from the national average.

What characteristics distinguish the sources of income in Wales from the UK national average?

Like the South West of England, Wales receives a higher proportion of income from annuities and pensions than the UK average. Income from wages and salaries is the lowest for any region in the UK and income from social-security benefits is among the highest. The result is an average weekly gross household income about £65 below the UK national average.

Earned income: stability and instability As we saw in Chapter 2, levels of earnings vary across regions, due to variations in influences such as unemployment rates, age structure and industrial and occupational structure. Other things being equal, a region experiencing 10 per cent unemployment will have a lower regional level of earned income than an otherwise similar region experiencing 5 per cent unemployment.

How would you expect differences in the age structure of the population to affect earned-income levels across the different regions of an economy?

The smaller the proportion of the population who are of working age, the lower the level of earned income that is likely to accrue to the region. The proportion of dependent children in the population is subject to regional variation: the proportion of elderly people in the population is also subject to interregional variation. The latter affects regional patterns of unearned income and expenditure, as we have seen, for example, in the higher proportions of pension income in Wales and the South West of England.

Female economic activity rates and interregional differences in female earnings also affect regional differences in income and expenditure. For example, New Earnings Survey data for April 1992 show that female gross weekly earnings in London and the South East of England were typically £36 above the national average for female employees. Low pay for females was most prevalent in the East and West Midlands, where female gross weekly earnings were typically £24 below the national average earnings of female employees.

However the most potent effect upon regional earned-income differentials is generated by regional differences in occupational and industrial structure. A region in which high-earning jobs are located will benefit from significantly higher income and expenditure levels than a region in which employment is predominantly low paid. The South East of England accordingly benefits from the relatively high proportion of professional and managerial employment located in the region.

One notable effect of the 1980s process of deindustrialisation discussed in Chapter 2 has been the loss of relatively well-paid skilled manual employment in the traditional manufacturing regions of the UK. In its place has come more part-time low-paid employment, so reducing the earned income and economic vitality of the regions affected. In these circumstances it is hardly surprising that those regions that experienced the greatest deindustrialisation in the early 1980s were the least able to benefit from economic expansion later in the decade.

In contrast the South West region of England benefited from the expansion of high-technology industry in the 1980s, especially in the local areas around Bristol and Gloucester. Avon, the county area around Bristol, had the second-highest concentration of high-technology employment in England in the 1980s, yielding corresponding high earned incomes for those employed in the industry and the associated producer service industries. As a result regional earned income and regional per capita gross domestic product both improved relative to the UK national average during the 1980s, to the extent that the South West became the third-richest region in England in 1990 (the South East and East Anglia being more affluent) (Gripaios and Bishop, 1992).

These regional earnings differences affect the value of the regional economic multiplier, a concept explained later in this chapter. They also have important implications for the type of economic activity that government authorities should attract into the relatively depressed regions if their regional economies are to be effectively regenerated.

Unearned income: the effect of real interest rates While the emphasis in this book, both in this chapter and elsewhere, is primarily upon earned income and its effects upon the regional economy, unearned income is covered briefly in this section. We saw above that this source of income is especially important to the regional economy of the South West of England.

The level of income that can be received as the result of ownership of financial capital and/or land is primarily affected by current real rates of interest and by the extent to which such income is taxed. During most of the 1980s, when real rates of interest in the UK were relatively high, unearned incomes were relatively buoyant.

This meant that those regions and localities in which a relatively high proportion of the resident population were in receipt of these forms of unearned income benefited from their relative affluence and expenditure. One beneficiary region was the South West of England, with an above-average proportion of households containing pensioners in receipt of significant levels of unearned income derived from their ownership of financial investments, annuities and pensions. This situation offers a marked contrast to the 1970s, when real returns on capital in the form of income had been much lower, and so this group of income recipients had benefited less.

Unearned income: the effects of government expenditure changes The other form of unearned income is that income received through transfer payments such as unemployment benefit. This income is affected by government policy with regard to the real value of such benefits, and the extent of their coverage. The progressive shrinkage of entitlement to unemployment benefit in the UK during the 1980s reduced this source of income in those regions most affected (Figure 3.4).

The regional distribution of unearned income in the form of government benefit payments is spatially highly unequal in the UK. The regional distribution of such payments partly, but not wholly, reflects the regional distribution of unemployment. In 1991 the highest payments of unemployment benefit were made to the North, North West and Northern Ireland.

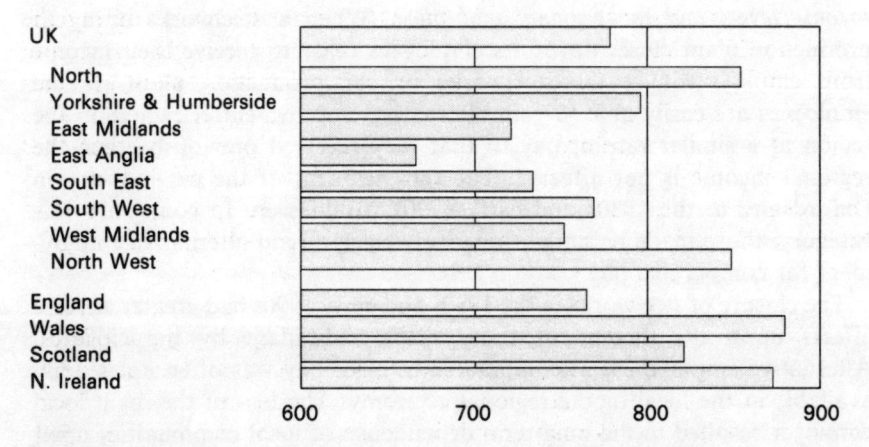

Figure 3.4 Regional distribution of the main social security benefits, 1990–1 (£ per head)

Source of data: UK CSO, *Regional Trends*, vol. 28 (1993), table 8.6.

High levels of incidence of invalidity benefit tend to follow high levels of unemployment benefit. The regional problem of low rates of economic activity and corresponding low levels of income is not confined to measured unemployment. Areas with above-average rates of unemployment tend also to be those with above-average levels of their population over fifty and in poor health. Wales and Scotland both receive more National Insurance benefits in the form of sickness and invalidity benefit than other regions in the UK. Disablement benefits are over-represented in the North and in Northern Ireland relative to the other UK regions. The consequent low income makes it more difficult for the affected regional economy to effectively generate internal indigenous economic expansion.

The regional economy of Northern Ireland, with its long-term record of high unemployment, provides a good example to illustrate this point. As Figure 3.4 shows, Northern Ireland receives more government social-security benefits per head than any other region except Wales. This is mainly in the form of retirement pensions, income support and sickness and invalidity benefits. The high level of income support paid into households in Northern Ireland is a symptom of the region's low earning capacity.

This low indigenous income and expenditure have meant that levels of expenditure generated within the regional economy are not adequate to generate growth or even to sustain existing economic activities. The result has been increasing and long-term dependence upon public-sector expenditures. By 1990, total public-sector expenditure in the region accounted for over half of total regional expenditure (Gudgin and Roper, cited in Hart and Harrison, 1992, p. 120).

Income levels and the regional multiplier When a steelworks or a car production plant closes down, its employees cease to receive their income from employment at the steelworks or car production plant. If the employees are easily able to gain alternative employment elsewhere in the region at a similar rate of pay to that they received previously, then the regional income is not affected. The retrenchment of the car industry in Oxfordshire in the 1980s and early 1990s would seem to come into this category: those made redundant relatively easily found alternative employment for comparable pay.

The closure of steelworks in the 1980s and early 1990s had greater adverse effects upon the income of those made redundant by the closures. Alternative employment at comparable rates of pay was often not readily available in the local or the regional economy. The loss of the main local employer resulted in the long-term dependence of local communities upon benefit income rather than earned income. Consequently areas affected by steelworks closure, such as South Wales and the North East of England, experienced a long-term diminution in their income-earning capacity.

This fall in income leads to a fall in expenditure in the affected region. The resulting lower expenditure means lower revenue for local traders, so reducing their incomes. Their expenditure falls in turn, and so the initial steelworks closure has an adverse *multiplier* effect upon the regional economy.

This regional multiplier effect is important to understanding the divergent experience of regional economies through the cumulative effects of economic contraction and expansion. For this reason the analysis of regional multipliers is explained more fully later in this chapter.

Consumption and Expenditure

This section focuses upon a predominantly Keynesian analytic framework. The selection of such a focus is essentially pragmatic: the Keynesian approach both assists in the development of the multiplier analysis later in the present chapter and in the framework for the analysis of regional policy intervention by government in Chapter 8.

We begin with total expenditure (E) in an economy. This has four components: consumption (C), investment (I), government expenditure (G) and net exports that is, exports minus imports ($X - Z$). In general introductory economics, this is often shown in the form of an equation, so that:

$$E = C + I + G + (X - Z)$$

The same components make up total expenditure in a regional economy. At the regional level, domestic consumption expenditure will represent a lower proportion of total expenditure than it does at national level. This is because a higher proportion of the goods and services bought by the consumer will be produced outside the region than are produced outside the national economy. Imports and exports accordingly represent a higher proportion of total expenditure for the regional than they do for the national economy. In other words, the regional economy is typically more 'open' than is the national economy. This additional dependence upon interregional trade is considered more fully in the final section of this chapter.

Government expenditure is subject to regional variation, whereas it is a single total at national level. For example, UK government defence expenditure in the 1980s benefited the South West of England as a region to a greater extent than other English regions. These regional variations in government expenditure are discussed in more detail in the later chapters of this book that look at regional policy.

Investment expenditure also varies among regions, as we saw in Chapter 2. The potential effects of this variation upon regional growth and upon cyclical instability in the regional economy are considered in more depth in later chapters.

This present section looks more closely at the consumption component of regional expenditure, and at how this affects the regional economy.

Consumption expenditure

As indicated above, domestic consumption represents the largest single element in expenditure in the national economy, accounting for about two thirds of the total. A higher proportion of consumption expenditure will leak out of the regional economy in the form of regional imports. In the regional context, therefore, domestic consumption will form a smaller proportion of the total than it does at national level.

The theory relating to consumption, however, remains analogous between the regional and the national economy. The main influence upon the level of domestic consumption in the region is personal disposable income. Some of the main reasons for interregional variations in personal disposable income were outlined earlier in this chapter, using examples from selected UK regions in the 1980s. The regional consumption function can therefore be drawn in a comparable manner to the macro-consumption function, as illustrated in Figure 3.5.

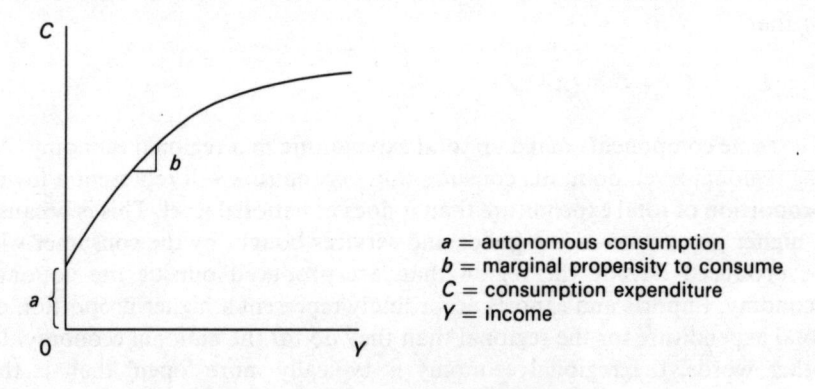

a = autonomous consumption
b = marginal propensity to consume
C = consumption expenditure
Y = income

Figure 3.5 *The consumption function*

Apart from personal disposable income, the other influences upon the individual's current consumption are usually taken to be their:

- Stock of wealth.
- Stock of outstanding debt.
- Current level of income and wealth relative to their expectations in terms of a concept of permanent income.
- Age in relation to observed life-cycle patterns of consumption.

Before reading further, see whether you can think of at least two ways in which these influences will affect interregional patterns of consumption.

There are several ways in which regional patterns of consumption are influenced by the factors that underlie consumption. Some of the more important are outlined below.

Wealth holders are not necessarily distributed evenly across the regional space of the national economy, so consumption derived from stocks of wealth may also be subject to regional variation. As we saw above, the regional economy of the South West of England appears to have benefited from the relatively high income and expenditure of this group of nonearned-income recipients during the 1980s.

Similarly the stock of outstanding debt is not necessarily spatially even. For example, in England in the early 1990s levels of mortgage debt were typically higher in London and the South East than in other regions of the economy. These high regional debt levels had the effect of depressing consumption in London and the South East in these years, so increasing the severity of the impact of the national recession in this region in the early 1990s.

The early 1990s recession also reduced current consumption due to its depressing effects upon people's perceived and actual ability to attain and retain their target levels of permanent income. Unemployment, fear of unemployment, and lack of bonus and overtime payments to the employed all depressed income levels during the recession years. Those whose normal or permanent income levels were adversely affected accordingly felt unwilling to commit themselves to major consumption expenditure until their incomes were higher and/or perceived to be more secure.

Individuals' consumption level is also typically affected by their age: for example the young tend to spend in excess of their current income while the middle aged tend to spend less and save to finance the expenditure of their retirement years. A region or local area with a population untypical of the country overall in terms of age structure may accordingly exhibit above- or below-average patterns of current consumption expenditure. Coastal localities with significantly high levels of retired inhabitants demonstrate such expenditure patterns in the local economy.

The marginal propensity to consume (mpc) measures the proportion of each additional pound of disposable income that the individual wishes to spend. It is illustrated by the slope of the consumption function, shown as *b* in Figure 3.5. (Note that there is also a degree of autonomous consumption, shown by *a*, which is independent of the level of income.) Typically, the slope of the consumption function, that is, the marginal propensity to consume, is not constant. Instead it is typically higher at low levels of income and reduces at higher levels of income. This, too, will affect regional patterns of consumption expenditure in relation to interregional variations in income.

Total expenditure

Introductory books explaining the workings of the macroeconomy usually assume that the components of expenditure other than consumption – that is, investment, government expenditure and net exports – are primarily independent of the level of income. This means that the overall expenditure function for the macroeconomy lies above and parallell to the consumption function (see Figure 3.6). As these other lines are parallel to the consumption function, the slope of this expenditure function still reflects the value of the marginal propensity to consume.

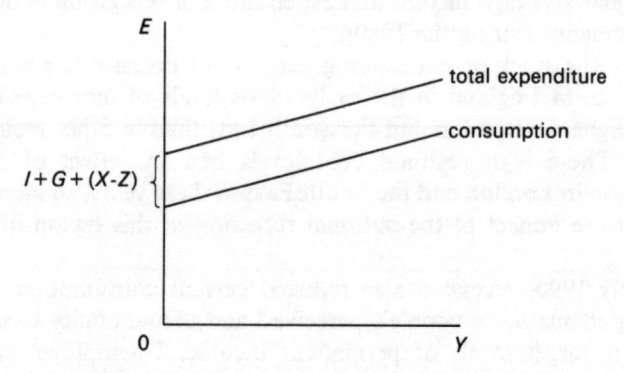

Figure 3.6 The aggregate expenditure function

To what extent is this a reasonable assumption to make for the regional economy? While the amount of incoming investment received in a region will be influenced by the income of that region, this influence will be secondary to considerations such as the degree of business confidence in both the regional and the associated national economy, and national interest rates. For this level of analysis, investment expenditure can realistically be assumed to be independent of income.

The same assumption is reasonable in the case of government expenditure in the regional economy. While an element of government expenditure received in the region, such as unemployment benefit, will be directly related to the level of income, most items of incoming government expenditure will not be directly income-related. Defence, education and infrastructure expenditures, for example, will not be income-determined. Regional health expenditure will not be primarily determined by income levels, although income may be a secondary determinant.

It was argued above that the regional economy will necessarily be more open than the national economy of which it forms a part. For this reason income may affect imports to a greater extent than is the case at national level. This must be remembered when using basic macroeconomic analyis in the regional context.

Equilibrium income and output

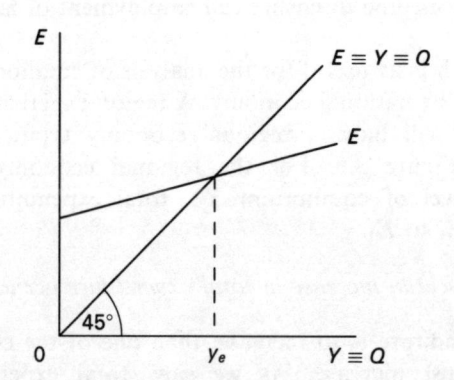

Figure 3.7 Equilibrium income and output in the regional economy

The 45° line on Figure 3.7 shows all the points where the total level of expenditure within the economy could equal total income and total output. However only one of these potential equilibrium points can be the actual point of equilibrium for the economy at any one time. This unique equilibrium will occur where the expenditure function intersects the 45° line shown as Y_e on Figure 3.7.

This is a conventional illustration of basic Keynesian analysis. A central feature of Keynes' theory was that there is no inherent reason to expect Y_e to equal the level of income necessary to generate the full employment of all available resources in the economy, shown as Y_{fe} on Figure 3.8.

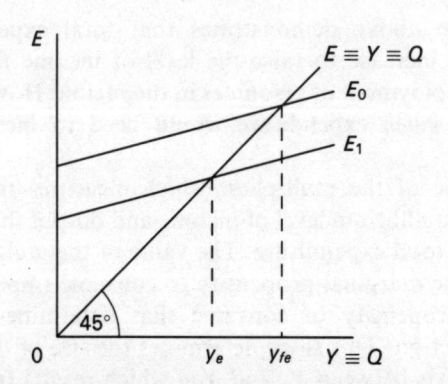

Figure 3.8 Full employment equilibrium in the region

In the Keynesian view there is no built-in mechanism in the economy that ensures that the actual total level of expenditure will generate just enough demand for labour to guarantee employment for all who wish to work.

Figure 3.8 shows a situation where expenditure does *not* generate a high enough level of income to ensure full employment of labour (or of land or capital).

This approach is as useful for the analysis of equilibrium in the regional economy as in the national economy. A region experiencing above-average unemployment will have a regional economy typified by the situation illustrated in Figure 3.8. For the regional economy to reach its full employment level of equilibrium Y_{fe}, total expenditure would have to increase from E_1 to E_0.

How could such an increase in total expenditure occur?

If total expenditure is to increase, then one of the components of total expenditure must increase. As we saw, total expenditure consists of $C + I + G + (X - Z)$ so an increase in any of these is required.

A basic tenet of Keynesian analysis is that the government has direct control over its own expenditure and therefore this component can be manipulated directly to ensure full employment. Inflationary pressure will only be avoided once the extra expenditure and demand created by such a direct increase in government expenditure goes mainly towards the reemployment of unemployed resources, and not towards creating excess demand for resources already employed to full capacity. This argument is directly pertinent to the analysis of government's role in regional policy, discussed in Chapters 8 and 9.

The Regional Multiplier

The explanation above demonstrates that total expenditure within the region needs to increase to raise the level of income from Y_e to Y_{fe} and establish full employment of resources in the region. However it does not yet tell us *by how much* expenditure would need to increase to reach this objective.

It is the value of the multiplier, which measures the size of the final increase in the equilibrium level of income and output that will result from a given change in total expenditure. The value of the multiplier is determined by the size of the marginal propensity to consume (mpc). It is the value of the marginal propensity to consume that determines the slope of the expenditure function. This slope determines the size of the movement along the horizontal axis between Y_e and Y_{fe}, which results from a given shift in the expenditure function. If we simplify the explanation by concentrating upon the consumption and investment/savings components of the economy, then the multiplier (k) is measured as:

$$1/(1 - mpc) = 1/mps = k$$

This is because all income received by the consumer must be spent or saved, the proportions depending upon the relative values of mpc and mps. For example, if the consumer receives an additional £100, it may be that £70 is spent and £30 is saved. So:

$$mpc + mps = 1$$

If we extend this simple version of the multiplier to include the effects of taxation (t) and imports (z), then the multiplier becomes:

$$1/(1 - mpc) = 1/(mps + mpt + mpz) = k$$

The higher the rates of saving and taxation and the higher the proportion of consumption spent on imports, the lower the value of the multiplier in the economy.

We have already noted that regional economies are typically more open to imports and exports than are the national economies of which they form a part. As a result, regional multipliers are typically lower in value than the multiplier for the corresponding national economy.

REGIONAL IMPORT–EXPORT RELATIONSHIPS

Regional Input–Output Models

Originally developed in the 1930s, input–output models and derivative models are useful today as contemporary computer technology facilitates the specification and operation of relatively detailed economic models. We have seen in this book that the factors of production – capital, labour and land – are supplied as inputs into the production process. The owners of the factors of production are paid an income in return for this supply of inputs. This income provides the means whereby demand is generated and output may be sold.

With regard to the regional economy, models demonstrating the nature of the economic linkages between these inputs and outputs and the corresponding financial flows are useful for two reasons. Firstly, they illustrate the economic structure of the region and the direction and size of the flows of economic activity, both within the region and externally. Secondly, they illustrate the extent to which the corresponding financial flows remain internal to the region and the extent to which money flows into and out of the region. Input–output models therefore demonstrate the economic interdependence both within the region and between the different regions in the economy.

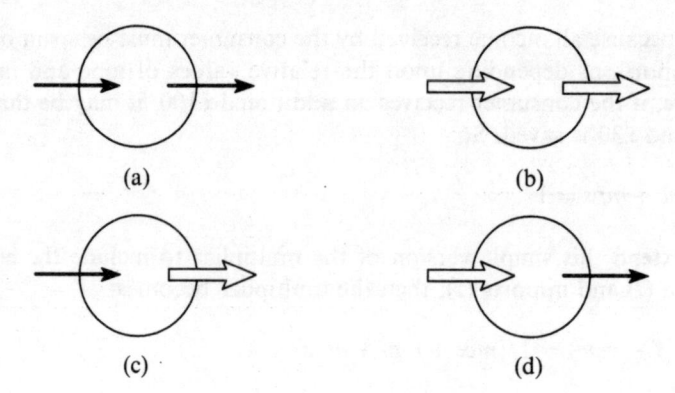

Figure 3.9 Financial flows into and out of the region

The input–output model can formally show us how open or closed is the region's economy. In Figure 3.9(a), the size of the financial flows into and out of the region are relatively small, and so the region is relatively closed. In contrast, Figure 3.9(b) shows a more open regional economy characterised by more extensive flows both into and out of the region.

In Figure 3.9(c) the financial flows into the region are less than the financial flows out of the region. Such a region would experience a net loss of income and internal demand for its output. Some regions suspect that their economic situation is as illustrated by Figure 3.9(c), so they find difficulty in generating the resource base from which to grow and expand. In contrast Figure 3.9(d) illustrates the case of a region benefiting from a net inflow of income and internal demand. This is a schematic outline of input–output relationships, which we now consider in more detail.

A simplified input–output model

Input–output models can be developed for the subregional or the urban economy as well as the regional economy. They demonstrate the component parts of the economy from the perspective of both inputs and outputs. However, in principle, the total value of the inputs must, in the accounting sense, equal the total value of the outputs. This accounting equation is demonstrated in Table 3.2 where total input value equals the value of total domestic output.

Table 3.2 illustrates a very simple version of an input–output model to demonstrate the basic principles. The *supply* side of the economy is shown by the entries in the left-hand vertical column, mainly sales from the different sectors of industry and sales of imported products in the region. The horizontal headings across the top of the table demonstrate the *demand* side of the economy: the purchases by industry, private- and public-sector demand and export demand.

There are alternative ways of presenting and formulating input–output models, but this simple version is useful for consistency as it builds upon the components of the economy introduced so far.

Table 3.2 A simple input–output model

| Sales by | Purchases by ||||||| Total dom. output |
	Primary	Manufact.	Construct.	Service	Consumpt.	Govt expend.	Exports	
Primary	20	75	5	30	10	5	15	160
Manufacturing	15	65	10	10	70	5	330	505
Construction	–	5	5	5	10	5	20	50
Services	5	20	5	150	5	5	60	250
Imports	20	120	10	5	110	5	5	275
Income from employment	20	250	210	400	–	–	–	880
Total input	80	535	245	600	205	25	430	2120

What are some of the main features of the hypothetical regional economy illustrated in Table 3.2?

The simple input–output model gives us several interesting pieces of information about the regional economy. For example:

❑ Total exports (430) exceed total imports (275) so the region has a balance-of-payments surplus.
❑ Part of this balance-of-payments surplus is due to the strength of net exports from the manufacturing sector (330). Although the region's manufacturing sector is a major importer, the value of its finished exports is much greater than the value of imported inputs such as raw materials.
❑ Compared with the manufacturing sector, the service sector of the regional economy is relatively closed with little importing or exporting. This assumption is realistic, and has implications for the relative openness of regional economies in the real world.

In addition to providing information as to the present structure of the regional economy, input–output models allow economists to predict the effects of change upon the economy. The more detailed the model, in principle the more detailed the path along which the effects of the change can be plotted. In practice the level of detail is usually constrained by both the limited availability and the costs of data.

In the simple model above, we could assume that cars are one of the region's main manufacturing exports and that there is a 10 per cent increase in the export demand for cars in a particular time period. The effects of this increase can be followed through. The increase in demand for cars will require increased inputs by the manufacturing sector. Imported parts will increase, as will intraregional supplies of component parts. There will be greater demand for the services of labour to produce the cars, reflected in increased income from employment.

Input–output linkages and regional growth

The earlier schematic diagrams demonstrating the possible size of financial flows into and out of the region can be used to discuss the intraregional growth potential of industries in a region. Where an industry has a growth rate above the national average, its location within a region may contribute to the growth potential of that region.

Whether this growth potential may benefit the region or not depends crucially upon the pattern of the industry's input–output linkages. Where these linkages are strong within the region, the region will benefit. Where the linkages are such that the benefits of the value-added within the region leak to the outside, the benefit to the region is diminished.

Government policies that locate expanding industries in relatively depressed regions will not necessarily result in higher growth in the region concerned. The success of the policy may depend critically upon the input–output linkages associated with the industry.

This was recognised by Francois Perroux in relation to his concept of *poles de croissance* or 'growth poles'. A *pole de croissance* is an industry, or group of related industries, that have growth rates above the national average *and* the capacity to generate growth through the impact of strong input–output linkages. Where such industries are spatially concentrated, as was the case with steel and engineering, the concept of a growth pole takes on an additional spatial context. If the growth-pole concept is to be translated into an effective interventionist instrument of regional policy, both the nature of industry's input–output linkages and the potential size of the stimulus, or multiplier effects, associated with the industry need to be examined.

Input–output linkages and the multiplier

How great will be the increase in the level of economic activity as the result of a change in the economic make-up of the region?

This will depend upon the value of the relevant multipliers in the region. The concept of the multiplier was introduced earlier in this chapter: now we can see more closely how it operates in practice. The value of the multiplier will be larger the smaller are the leakages out of the region and the higher the proportion of the increase in economic activity that remains within the region.

The overall final value of the multiplier will be larger the higher the proportion of the *initial* increase in expenditure and income that remains within the region. This may suggest that, in general, government policy expenditure into the region should be directed at those sectors that are closed within the region, such as services and construction rather than manufacturing, which is characteristically more open.

The regional economy is multidimensional: the input–output table reduces it to two dimensions. Even this simple model indicates that a given change can affect the regional economy in a number of ways. There will therefore be a corresponding number of potential multiplier effects. In practice economists usually look at three regional multipliers: the output, employment and income multipliers.

The output multiplier measures the extent of the final increase in regional output that results from the initial change. In the example above, if car manufacture represented 10 per cent of regional manufacturing, a 10 per cent initial increase in demand for cars would be a 1 per cent initial increase in manufacturing demand. If the higher car output stimulates a greater output of other goods and services on the region, and then an even greater output of cars and other goods and services, the final increase in manufacturing output might be about twice the initial increase, yielding a regional output multiplier of 2.

The employment multiplier can be measured similarly. The initial stimulus to the regional economy will create some jobs: however more jobs will eventually be created as the effects of the initial increased demand for cars work through the regional economy.

Both the output and employment multipliers assume that there is spare capacity in the regional economy so that this process of expansion is not constrained. In the case of the output multiplier, the spare capacity must exist in production capacity. In the case of the employment multiplier, there must be less than full employment in the regional economy.

A third multiplier is the household-income multiplier, which measures the final benefit to household incomes from the initial income expansion that results from the change. Household income and consumption patterns vary, as explained in the opening sections of this chapter.

The final value of the household-income multiplier will depend upon the income level of those who benefit from the initial economic expansion: are they well-paid professional workers or unskilled workers? Household composition will also affect the income multiplier as, for example, households with dependent children tend to spend more and save less than other households. Households with a high level of indebtedness may save increased income rather than spend it. Some households may spend a higher proportion of any increase in income on imported products than others.

Overall, regional multipliers will tend to be smaller than comparable national multipliers because the regional economy will tend to be more open than the national economy. If input–output models and/or regional multipliers are used at a more local economic level, the values of the multipliers will shrink further as the degree of openness of the economy increases.

The Imbalance of Regional Payments

Regions are in general relatively open economies with a high proportion of external trade. Although these are rarely statistically measured, regions therefore have external financial-trading balances analogous to a national economy's balance of payments.

If the region's external balance of payments is initially in equilibrium, the processes of dynamic economic change can bring disequilibrium over a period of time. Such a disequilibrium could in principle be met by policies comparable to those applied to national-economy balance-of-payments' disequilibria. Policies designed to rectify national balance-of-payments' disequilibria fall into two categories: those designed to alter or 'switch' the pattern of internal and external expenditure; and those designed to alter the amount of aggregate expenditure available in the economy.

Under a system of floating exchange rates, the existence of its separate currency allows an economy to choose its rate of inflation relative to other economies. A regional economy has no separate currency, so it cannot choose its rate of inflation in this way. More generally, a regional economy, unlike a national economy, cannot effectively isolate itself from any of the economic shocks generated by other regions within its shared currency area.

This is clear from experience within federal economies such as the US. For instance, Texas would have benefited from the freedom of a separate currency enabling devaluation of its currency relative to the rest of the USA when the fall in the oil price devastated its oil-dependent state economy in 1986. A separate currency would have allowed Texas slowly to devalue its currency so as to alter the internal relative price structure and encourage the economy to move gradually away from its dependence upon oil.

Expenditure-switching policies

Currency devaluation under a fixed-exchange-rate regime (or depreciation under a floating rate regime) and revaluation (appreciation) are *expenditure-switching* policies, which encourage economic adjustment to correct balance-of-payments' disequilibria through the change in the value of the domestic currency relative to foreign currencies. A currency devaluation has the effect of reducing the price of exports to external purchasers, while correspondingly raising the price of imports to internal purchasers. As a result, demand for exports will increase yielding increased export revenue. Demand for imports will correspondingly decrease, resulting in lower import expenditure. The size of these changes in relative demand for imports and exports will depend upon the relevant elasticities of demand. Once the elasticities are positive, these effects should combine to help correct the payments imbalance.

A separate currency can accordingly allow devaluation or revaluation as appropriate so that the economy can fully, or at least partially, offset a rise in domestic costs or a fall in domestic revenue and help restore the balance-of-payments equilibrium.

The more open the economy, the higher is likely to be its dependence upon imports, and so the less elastic the price response to currency devaluation. In this case there is less potential for a significant economic gain from devaluation. This means that regions with lower trading links to the rest of their national economies may gain the most from a separate regional currency; those with the greatest trading links may gain the least. This argument may help to explain why it is the smallest members of the EC, such as Belgium and the Netherlands, that are the keenest to adopt a common European currency.

Expenditure-changing policies

When, as in the case of the regional economy, there is a common currency so that expenditure-switching policies are not a practical means of correcting payments imbalances, then *expenditure reducing* or *expenditure increasing* policies are required to facilitate economic adjustment in the light of external payments imbalances. If there is a balance-of-payments deficit, expenditure-reducing policies would be appropriate. These would reduce aggregate expenditure in the economy, so that there was less demand for imports. There would also be less demand for goods and services within the economy, and so producers would have a greater incentive to seek export markets. The combination of these effects should be lower imports and higher exports, so helping to correct the imbalance of payments.

The necessary change in the overall level of expenditure could be achieved through public-finance transfers, that is, through the raising of tax revenue and through central-government expenditure, which is not equal across the regions that form the national economy. In the earlier example the adjustment the Texan economy needed to make in the late 1980s due to reduced oil revenue would have been assisted by the extent of net public-finance transfers from the northern states of the USA.

Regions can suffer a relatively sudden loss of income following a fall in the market price of an exported raw material or the decline of a staple industry. There is little doubt that when this happens the built-in stabilisers of central-government public finance play an important equilibrating role in the regional economy. Lower income and sales receipts in the region affected mean that the region's inhabitants pay less in taxes, including National Insurance contributions and their equivalent, to central government. Incoming flows of government expenditure into the region, especially in the form of unemployment and related benefits, will also increase.

The interregional distribution of benefits discussed earlier is repeated here for comparison with the size of interregional differences in income-tax liability. Greater than average benefit payments are received in the North, North West, Wales, Scotland and Northern Ireland (Table 3.3).

Table 3.3 *Regional distribution of income-tax liability and of the main social security benefits, £ per head, 1990–1*

	Social-security benefits	Tax paid in excess of base rate (those liable only)	Average income tax payable
UK	778.5	2580	2490
North	854.4	1869	2130
Yorkshire & Humberside	796.2	2306	2150
East Midlands	720.9	2230	2150
E. Anglia	666.0	2227	2440
South East	733.6	9686	3140
South West	768.9	2247	2250
West Midlands	751.6	2519	2240
North West	848.7	2443	2160
England	764.7	2640	2570
Wales	879.7	1979	1940
Scotland	821.5	2059	2170
N. Ireland	872.6	2357	2050

Source: UK CSO, *Regional Trends*, vol. 28 (1993), tables 8.6, 8.8, and calculations from 8.8.

The South East of England is the only region where income-tax payments are higher than the UK average. This pattern is repeated in relation to payment of higher-rate income tax (shown in the middle column of Table 3.3) where the average payment made by the higher-rate taxpayer in the South East is nearly four times higher than that made in the West Midlands, the region with the next highest payment in this category. This demonstrates the concentration of high-income-earning capacity in the South East, and the importance of a progressive income-tax system if interregional differences in income are to be evened out across the spatial economy.

The stabilising effects of public financial flows help to cushion a regional economy from the more severe effects of structural change, as we shall see more fully later, especially in Chapter 8 which deals with regional policy. As the EC plays an increasing role in both industrial and regional policy, so its public-finance role should be enhanced to allow for the expenditure-adjusting policies that will be increasingly necessary to absorb the shocks of structural change within the regions of the EC.

One important conclusion is that the more effective the single internal market of the EC becomes and the more integrated its economy and currency, the more important will be the role of expenditure-adjusting policies conducted at the EC level. Public-finance transfers across the EC from the well-off to the less well-off regional and national economies will be essential if economic adjustments are be achieved reasonably smoothly in a more integrated economic area.

PRICES AND REGIONAL ECONOMIC WELFARE

Chapter 2 focused primarily upon conditions of supply to the regional economy. This chapter focuses upon price determination and demand conditions at both the micro- and macroeconomic level. This section draws upon demand- and supply analysis to investigate the role of the market and the price system. In particular, the efficiency of the allocation of resources in the regional economy is of interest. This analysis in addition provides part of the framework within which issues of public-sector involvement and policy intervention in the region are discussed later in the book.

The Operation of the Price System

In a market economy with flexible prices, the price system independently coordinates buyers' and suppliers' intentions and actions in a decentralised manner. Introductory demand-and-supply analysis demonstrates the mechanism through which the market achieves this coordinating role.

For example, assume that the housing market in a particular region or city is initially in equilibrium at P_0, Q_0 as shown on Figure 3.10. Then the average incomes of the population increase. As the income elasticity of demand for housing is typically positive in contemporary European economies, the result is likely to be an increase in demand for housing. This is shown by a rightward shift of the demand curve for housing to D_1. The extent of the shift in the demand curve from D_0 to D_1 will reflect the size of the income elasticity of demand for housing at the relevant levels of income.

There is now excess demand for housing at the original price of P_0, so demand exceeds supply and prices are pushed upwards. These higher prices act as an incentive to encourage builders to build more houses in the area.

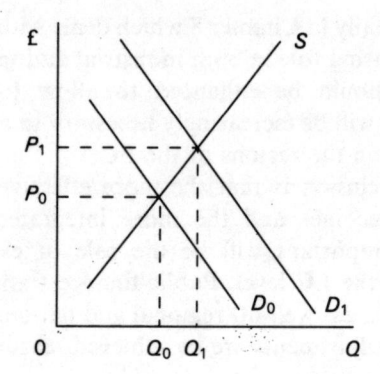

Figure 3.10 Market equilibrium

As a result there will be an increase in supply. The new equilibrium in the regional housing market is established at P_1, Q_1.

The flexibility of prices in the market acts both as a signal to producers and as an incentive to consumers. First, the increase in the price of houses in the above example signals builders to supply more houses. Second, the increase in the price of houses will result in some consumers withdrawing their potential demand for housing. The interaction of both acts to bring the market to its new equilibrium.

> Before reading on, you can check your understanding of the above paragraph by thinking through the effects of a fall in the price of housing upon (i) the quantity of supply and (ii) the quantity demanded in the housing market.

The central function of the price system is therefore to serve as a means of communication of information. This information is communicated among numerous different individuals, both buyers and sellers. Prices act as the means of communication and coordination between these numerous buyers and sellers. In this way the price system acts as a means of organising economic activity without the need for central control. It helps to attain market equilibrium in a rational manner at little cost. The eighteenth-century economist Adam Smith used the concept of the price system as an 'invisible hand', an analogy that remains useful today.

The price system and welfare economics

The discussion above provided a simple illustration of how the price system operates so as to restore equilibrium to the market. The explanation of the operation of the price system can now be taken a stage further to illustrate how it *may* act as a means of organising economic activity so that social welfare is maximised.

In economics, social welfare is maximised when everyone in society is as well off as is possible given the constraint of finite economic resources. For this maximisation to be possible, the structure of relative prices in the economy must be such that the ratio of the market price of goods a and b must equal the ratio of their marginal utilities to the consumer. This in turn must equal the ratio of their marginal costs of production. In equation form, this is shown as:

pa = marginal utility a = marginal cost a
pb = marginal utility b = marginal cost b

Once this set of equal ratios can be extended from a case of two goods, a and b to all goods and services traded in the market, then social welfare is maximised. This condition for welfare maximisation is known as a Pareto optimum. However it can only be satisfied under highly restrictive conditions. All economic behaviour by buyers and sellers in the market must be rational and subject to perfect information. All factor and product markets must be perfectly competitive.

Chapter 2 provided some examples of factor markets that are not always characterised by perfect competition. For example, the supply of financial capital is largely controlled by a relatively small number of banks. Labour is frequently heterogeneous in the eyes of the employer, different types of skill and degrees of age and experience serving to differentiate members of the labour force and reduce the usefulness of the perfect competition model in the labour market. The next section of this chapter looks more generally at some of the limitations of the market as a means for ensuring the efficient allocation of economic resources.

The Limitations of the Market

The section above demonstrated that the market may provide a medium within which demand and supply interact to generate a system of relative prices, which ensures the efficient allocation of limited economic resources among competing uses. However the result of efficient allocation is subject to restrictive conditions with respect to competitive markets, which is explained above.

As these restrictive market conditions are not always met, we cannot assume that the market is always the best means of allocating resources. The resulting role of the public sector in the regional and local economy is therefore considered in detail in the later chapters of this book. To set the scene for those later chapters, these sections of the present chapter draw together the main theoretical background to the role of public-sector intervention in the operation of the economy. This section brings together and summarises the main features that serve to limit market efficiency in the allocation of economic resources.

The market is limited where any one, or a combination, of the following features are present.

Externalities

Positive or negative externalities can arise in association with either production or consumption, and are explained in more detail later in this section. It is a matter for debate whether the market can be adapted to cater for these externalities, or whether the market should be replaced where they are present.

Limited information

Neither consumers of products nor employers of factors of production normally have perfect information regarding their actual or potential market transactions. The information available in the market is therefore limited rather than perfect.

It is again a subject of debate in terms of economic theory as to whether the market can adapt or be adapted to take account of this imperfect information surrounding consumption and employment decisions. This issue is further complicated by an apparently universal positive time preference, which means nearly everyone prefers benefits now to less-certain future benefits.

In other words, decision taking in the private sector is skewed towards short-term advantage potentially at the expense of greater long-term benefit. As we shall see in Chapter 8 when we consider regional policy initiatives, it is questionable whether the public-sector's record indicates a longer decision-making horizon or a similarly short-term perspective coloured by the need for electoral popularity.

Monopoly

The theory of monopoly is covered in detail in other books relating to the theory of the firm. Here the main points are summarised only briefly.

Economic theory predicts that in a static context, that is, looking at a snapshot picture of the economy, monopoly will result in inefficiency due to three features of monopolistic market equilibrium. First, profits earned by the monopolist are in excess of the normal profit or transfer earnings required to retain the monopolist in production, and these extra profits continue to accrue into the long-term. Second, prices exceed the marginal costs of production, so negating the conditions for Pareto optimality outlined earlier. Third, the monopolist's profit-maximising level of output will be less than would occur if the same firm was producing in a perfectly competitive market.

However, if we consider the dynamic context, looking at what may happen to the monopolist over a period of time a different picture may emerge. If the monopolistic firm uses its extra profits to finance greater research and development or greater investment, then costs may be reduced and efficiency increased. If these investments do occur and result in lower costs and lower prices to the consumer, then the efficiency arguments against monopoly become much less clearcut.

Public goods

A pure public good, such as defence, is a good for which the benefits to be gained from consumption are nonrival and nonexcludable. They are nonrival because one person's consumption does not directly affect the availability of defence to another consumer. Most goods are rival: if one person eats an apple, that apple is no longer available to anyone else. They are nonexcludable because no-one can be excluded from receiving their benefits. Nonexcludability creates a free-rider problem, free riders being those who benefit from provision of the good without contributing to the cost of that provision.

Few goods are 'pure' public goods: there are more examples of 'impure' or quasi-public goods, such as education and health. These are partly, but not wholly, excludable and partly rival in consumption.

The spatial distribution of these public goods is not necessarily uniform among the different regions of an economy. In the UK, education expenditure tends to be higher in more affluent regions. Defence is notable in a regional context because employment in industries providing defence and defence equipment is subject to wide regional variation.

Where the government intervenes to provide public goods, such provision must be financed, usually through taxation. The financing of provision then raises further questions regarding the efficient allocation of economic resources in society, although those are, for the most part, outside the scope of this book.

If none of these limitations are present in the market, then the market may be the most efficient means of allocating resources. However, one important question that must be asked is: The market may be efficient . . . but is it fair?

The market operates efficiently when it is not subject to the limitations outlined above and the Pareto optimal conditions are met. But when it operates efficiently, society may not be very happy with the fairness of the outcome. The market may leave some people very rich and others very poor. Economists refer to fairness as 'equity': the market may be efficient, but it is not necessarily equitable.

Equity or fairness is central to regional economics. The key to the regional problem is perceived inequity in the spatial or interregional allocation and distribution of economic resources. Chapter 2 introduced some of the reasons why such regional inequalities may result from the operation of the market and the following chapters will illuminate other inherent economic mechanisms generating regional disparities. It is therefore inequity as well as inefficiency in the inter- and intraregional allocation and distribution of resources that public-sector intervention should seek to alleviate.

The role of the government in the economy is important as it accounts for about 40 per cent of National Income in an economy such as the UK. Some of this role derives from the limitations of the market explained in this section, such as industry and competition policies. Public-sector policy towards industry has a significant regional impact, as is explained in Chapter 8. In addition, the government intervenes so as to manage the overall performance of the national economy with respect to objectives such as full employment and price stability. These policies, which are not regionally explicit, also have a regional impact, as we shall see.

Externalities: Social Costs and Benefits

Externalities arise where one person's welfare is affected by the consumption or production activity of another person and this effect is not reflected in the pattern of relative prices. Externalities may arise either from production (in which case they affect supply) or from consumption (in which case they affect demand).

Externalities may be positive, for example, the marginal social benefit (MSB) of consumption may exceed the marginal private benefit (MPB). In this case the socially desirable demand curve will lie above and to the right of the private-market demand curve. Or externalities may be negative, for example, the marginal social benefit of consumption may be less than the marginal private benefit. In this case the socially desirable demand curve would lie below and to the left of the private market demand curve.

Figure 3.11 assumes a situation with no production externalities and positive consumption externalities.

The inclusion of social benefits, shown by the MSB curve, indicates that the equilibrium market quantity should be OQ_s. But if demand reflects only the private and not the social benefits of consumption, as shown by the MPB curve, then OQ_p will be bought and sold.

In this case where only OQ_p is produced, society is said to suffer a welfare loss equivalent to the area of the triangle ABC.

If a subsidy is given to encourage private consumption and is equal to the value of the social benefit of consumption, then equilibrium production would increase to OQ_s. The subsidy has had the effect of internalising the

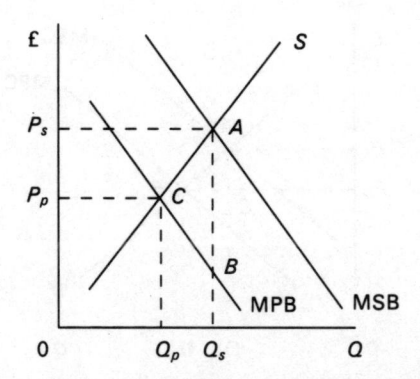

Figure 3.11 Positive consumption externalities

externalities within the price mechanism. Where the subsidy enhances consumption so that OQ_s is bought and sold, social welfare is improved.

The greater the extent of the externalities in a market, the greater the likely divergence of private and social benefits, the greater the size of the welfare loss, and so the greater the case for intervening in the operation of the market so as to internalise the externalities.

Pollution is an example of a common negative production externality. Think about its effects and see if you can draw a diagram to illustrate the effects of a pollutant – for example, the effects of acid rain generated from a power station in Yorkshire upon forests in Scotland – upon the market for electricity in the UK.

Your diagram should look similar to Figure 3.12. In this example there are no consumption externalities so the demand curve remains unaltered. Pollution is a negative production externality and so has the effect of making the marginal social cost of production (MSC) greater than the marginal private cost of production (MPC).

The welfare loss born by those adversely affected by the effects of acid rain upon Scottish woodland is shown by the triangle ABC. Where a tax upon the electricity producers in Yorkshire whose sulphur emissions cause the acid rain in Scotland has the effect of reducing electricity production from OQ_p to OQ_s, the negative externality would be internalised through the price system.

Externalities, property rights and public intervention

As explained above, externalities exist when the production or consumption of a good imposes a cost or yields a benefit that is not reflected in the

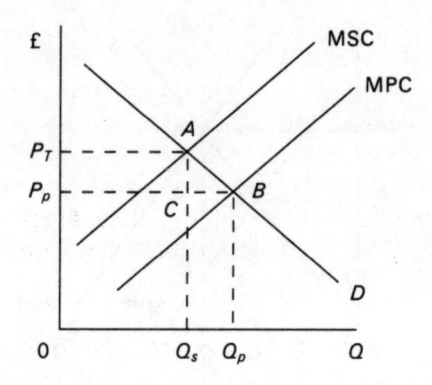

Figure 3.12 Pollution as a negative production externality

existing pattern of market prices. As everyone becomes more keen to be seen to be 'green', externalities, or the social costs and benefits resulting from economic activity, are perceived as increasingly important.

Some externalities may have direct implications for the spatial location of economic activity. For example, in 1991 people living near the Docklands development site in London brought a lawsuit against the London Docklands Development Corporation and the private developers. The grounds of the residents' complaint were: excessive dust; noise, due to increased traffic plus twenty-four hour maintenance work on the Docklands Light Railway; interference to their TV reception; and, adverse effects on their health, for example, an increased incidence of asthma.

In this case these organisations against whom the lawsuit was to be brought were identifiable. The culprit in the earlier acid-rain example may be identifiable, although perhaps less clearly so. But against whom could a lawsuit be brought for identifiable costs resulting from the climatic results of the greenhouse effect?

In the example of the Docklands development, individual property rights could be ascertained and this helps the process of progressing action designed to deal with negative externalities. Property rights occur at three levels.

Individual property rights Where the beneficiary or the imposer of social costs can be identified, the pattern of relative prices can be used to internalise externalities, for example, through the imposition of taxes. As a result, the private decision makers will adjust their individual decisions so that the socially optimal rate of production and consumption may be achieved. However this approach is only feasible where individual property rights can be identified.

Social property rights An economist called Pigou highlighted the situation where there are no identifiable individual property rights but society has rights that the price system should reflect. In this case, general taxes and subsidies can be used to correct market failures associated with externalities with the aim of improving social welfare.

To the extent that the presence of interregional disparities can be identified as the consequence of market failure, Pigou's argument provides the theoretical basis for the government policy intervention discussed in Chapter 8.

Universal property rights Solutions are less easily found, and policy measures less easily implemented, where externalities have effects that cross national boundaries and so affect universal property rights. A topical example is provided by the climate changes associated with the greenhouse effect.

Welfare Economics

The sections above have briefly introduced some of the principles of welfare economics as a background to some of the regional policy analysis of later chapters. Welfare economics offers an analytic framework within which we can try to assess the effects of changes in economic conditions upon the welfare (or well being) of individual members of society. It guides decision making with regard to the allocation and distribution of economic resources in circumstances when the price mechanism may not be appropriate due to the limitations introduced above.

The concept of Pareto optimality explained earlier is reflected in the Pareto criterion. The Pareto criterion states that an economic change will result in an overall improvement in social welfare only if at least one individual's welfare increases as a result of the change while no-one else's decreases.

The example above of a tax on acid rain fails this test. The imposition of the tax may have resulted in improved welfare for those in Scotland suffering the adverse effects of acid rain. However it decreased the welfare of the electricity producers, and of electricity consumers who may bear part of the burden of the tax to the extent that the tax would be passed on in higher electricity prices.

Some economists believe that this is too restrictive a set of conditions for the analysis of economic welfare. The Hicks–Kaldor criterion suggests that a *potential* welfare improvement occurs once the gainers could compensate the losers and still remain better off. In terms of our acid rain example, if the amount of gain to those disadvantaged by acid rain as a result of the imposition of the tax *exceeds* the loss born by electricity producers and consumers as a result of the tax, then social welfare is improved by the imposition of the tax. This Hicks–Kaldor framework may therefore provide a more fruitful basis for the analysis of the welfare implications of issues in regional economics than does the more restrictive Pareto criterion.

References and Further Reading

Armstrong, Harvey and J. Taylor (1993) *Regional Economics and Policy*, 2nd edn (London: Harvester Wheatsheaf).
Gripaios, P. and P. Bishop (1992) 'The South West', in Townroe and Martin (1992).
Gudgin, G. and S. Roper (1990) *The Northern Ireland Economy* (Belfast: NIERC).
Hart, M. and R. T. Harrison (1992) 'Northern Ireland', in Townroe and Martin (1992).
Townroe, P. and R. Martin (eds) (1992) *Regional Development in the 1990s* (London: Jessica Kingsley Publishers/Regional Studies Association).
United Kingdom Central Statistical Office (1993) *Regional Trends* (London: HMSO).

For a fuller discussion of welfare economics, the reader is recommended to a standard intermediate microeconomics book such as D. Laidler and S. Estrin, *Introduction to Microeconomics*, 3rd edn (Philip Allan, 1989).

4 The Region in the National Economy

REGIONAL ECONOMIC GROWTH

This section discusses the main reasons underlying differences in the growth experience of different regions relative to the national economy of which they form a part. For example, investment decisions taken by organisations incorporate some judgement regarding the spatial location at which that investment of their resources occurs. In part, this judgment depends upon the recent, current and expected future prosperity (or lack of prosperity) of the region in which the organisation is considering making its investment. Before considering in Chapter 5 the more specific factors underlying the organisation's location decision, this chapter investigates the region's economic growth, building upon the material developed in Chapters 2 and 3.

Economic growth is usually defined as an increase in real per-capita gross domestic product to allow for changes in population size and the rate of inflation. The UK's growth rate in recent decades has been high by historical standards, but less impressive by international standards. It is important to regional economics that this growth has not been evenly distributed throughout the different regions of the economy. Instead some regions gained from the process of growth and other regions lost.

Economic growth does not occur smoothly over time, as is shown schematically by Figure 4.1. The long-term trend expansion of the output of the economy is shown by *GG*. But there are periods, such as *A*, when short-

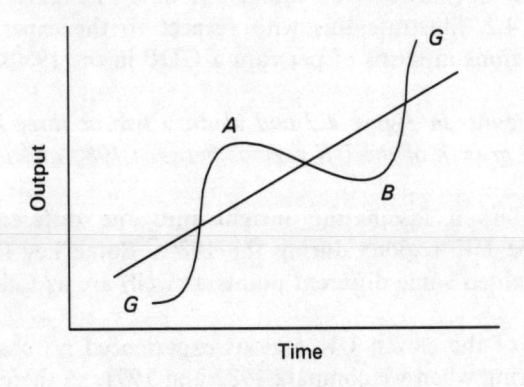

Figure 4.1 *Growth and cycles*

term economic expansion is above this long-term average trend rate of growth and periods when the economy is operating below trend, such as *B*. In this section we look at the processes underlying growth: the cyclical path around the long-term growth trend and cyclical impacts upon the regional economy are considered later in this chapter.

Regional Growth Within the National Economy

National economies within the European Community

Official EC gross domestic product (GDP) statistics for the EC economies at the end of the 1980s show wide variation. Five countries had GDP levels significantly higher than their neighbours, that is, France, Italy, Luxembourg, the UK and West Germany. At the end of the decade the latter was by far the wealthiest of the EC economies. German unification had an immediate short-term impact upon this situation, leaving the unified German economy behind those of France, Italy and Benelux in terms of per capita GDP.

The variation in member economies' per capita GDP led to the emergence of the concept of a supranational growth zone, or 'spine', in the late 1980s and early 1990s. This EC growth spine runs from the UK in the north of the EC through Germany and France to Italy in the south. This, and related growth-zone concepts, are investigated more fully in Chapter 6.

Regional economies within the nation

How does the level and rate of growth of an economy's GDP affect the growth of its constituent regions?

Other things being equal, we might expect that the regional economy will grow more readily within the framework of a growing national economy. Other things may not however be equal. The data in Figure 1.4, repeated here as Figure 4.2, illustrate this with respect to the experience of the standard UK regions in terms of per capita GDP in the 1980s.

Look at the figures in Figure 4.2 and identify two or three key points in relation to the growth of the UK regions between 1980 and 1991.

This data offers a fascinating insight into the differential growth experience of the UK regions during the 1980s. Some key features (you may have highlighted some different points as well) are as follows:

❑ Eight out of the eleven UK regions experienced no change in their rank ordering when we compare 1982 and 1991, so there was general stability in terms of a regional league table.

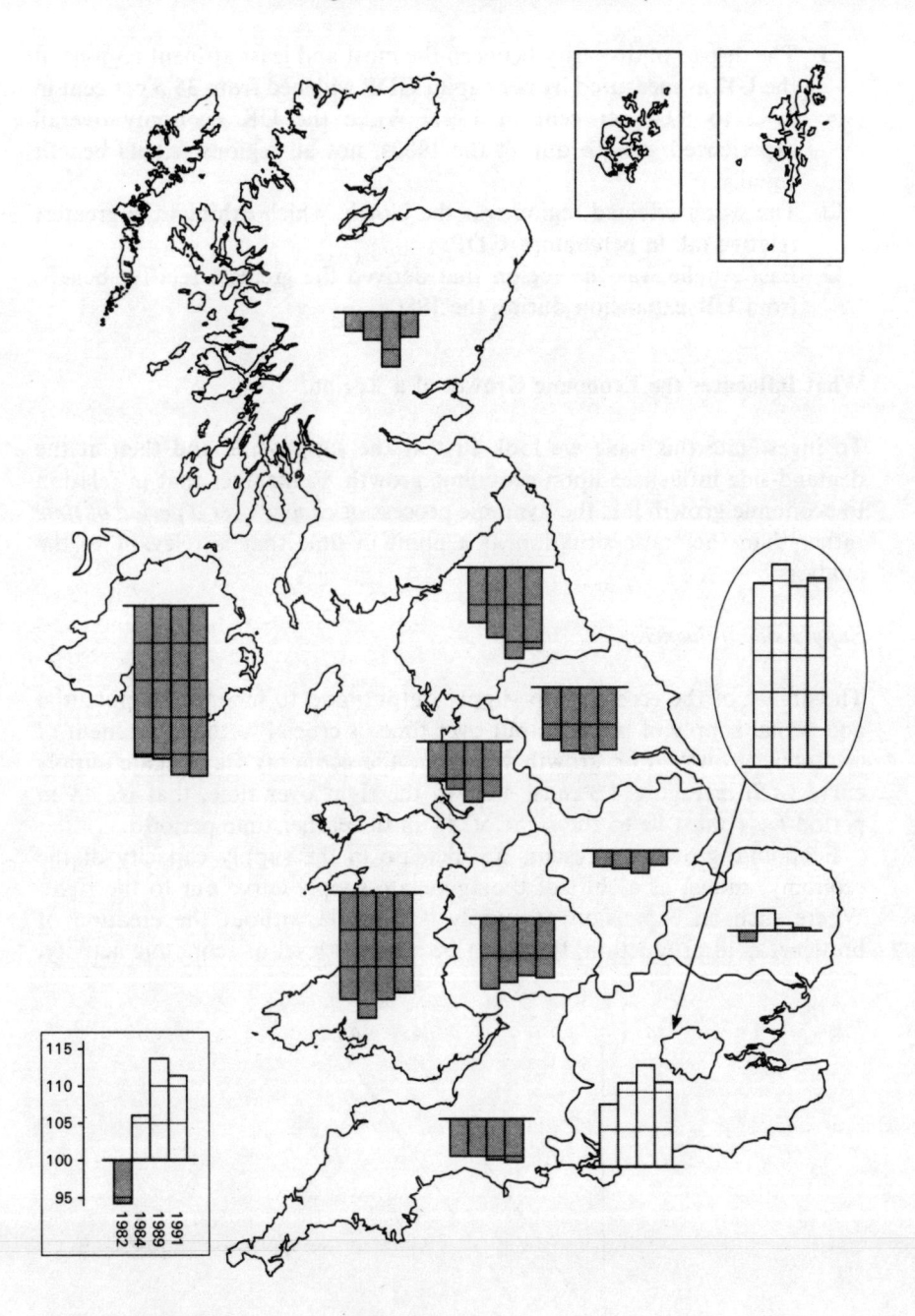

Figure 4.2 GDP* in the UK regions, 1982–91

* GDP per head at factor cost and current prices.
Source: UK CSO, *Regional Trends*, vol. 28 (1993), table 12.1.

- ❑ The degree of disparity between the most and least affluent regions of the UK as measured by per capita GDP widened from 35.5 per cent in 1982 to 39.4 per cent in 1991. While the UK economy overall experienced growth during the 1980s, not all regions felt its benefit equally.
- ❑ The worst affected region was the North, which exhibits the greatest relative fall in percentage GDP.
- ❑ East Anglia was the region that derived the greatest relative benefit from UK expansion during the 1980s.

What Influences the Economic Growth of a Region?

To investigate this issue we look first at the supply-side and then at the demand-side influences upon economic growth. Remember that in relation to economic growth it is the dynamic process of *change over a period of time* rather than the static situation at a point in time that is relevant to the analysis.

Supply-side influences

The ability of the economy to supply output, and to increase its potential and actual supply of more output over time, is crucial to the attainment of economic growth. For growth to occur, the economy's aggregate supply curve (AS) in Figure 4.3 must shift to the right over time, that is, AS in period $t+1$ must lie to the right of AS in the earlier time period t.

Economic growth represents an increase in the supply capacity of the economy, shown as a shift of the aggregate supply curve out to the right. Where such an expansion of supply is possible without the creation of bottlenecks in production, there can be a higher level of economic activity.

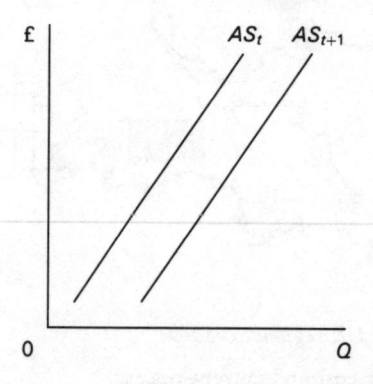

Figure 4.3 A long-term increase in aggregate supply

The extent to which the economy can expand without undue pressure upon the overall price level will be shown by the elasticity of aggregate supply.

Why may the attainment of such a supply-side expansion be important to regions of the UK such as the South East in the mid-1990s?

In the South East of England the regional economy began to overheat more quickly in the boom years of the late 1980s than was the case in other comparable regional economies. It is therefore desirable that such a situation be avoided as the regional economy expands after the recession of the early 1990s.

The ability of the economy to supply output depends upon several considerations. First is the quantity and quality of the available inputs of the factors of production – labour, land and capital – to the production process. Second is the technology with which these inputs can be combined to produce output. Third is the availability of economies of scale – both internal and external – in relation to the production process. Fourth is the way in which the production process and related processes are organised.

The availability of factors of production

The main influences underlying the quantity and quality of labour, land and capital available to the regional economy's production and related processes were discussed in detail in Chapter 2 so are only briefly recapitulated in this section.

The supply of land In the short term the supply of land, especially for example for industrial or building use, is usually assumed to be highly inelastic and this convention is accepted here. In the long term, supply for such use may be assumed to be highly elastic. However this elasticity may be limited, especially where planning restrictions are tight or suitable sites for development and economic use are limited by geographic conditions.

The supply of labour The quantity and quality of labour available to a particular region or urban centre may vary markedly among different areas of the economy. The main influences upon the quantity of labour available may be summarised as population density, demographic structure, economic activity rates and the rate of unemployment.

As we saw in Chapter 2, the quality of the labour supply as measured by the stock of human capital is not evenly distributed around the economy. The degree and type of skills and work experience differ spatially over the different regions of the economy. This unevenness in the spatial distribution of human capital is likely to contribute to uneven growth potential among and within different regions.

The quantity of labour available in a region will be influenced by central-government policies such as those relating to the structure of income tax. For example, a reduction in marginal rates of income tax *may* increase the labour supply through its effect on participation rates, once the substitution effect exceeds the income effect.

The occupational mobility of labour may be improved through training and education measures which increase the quality of the labour force. This qualitative aspect of labour supply may be affected by regional and local policy initiatives, examples of which are considered in the discussion of policy later in this book. Greater geographical labour mobility will also improve the availability of labour in the regional labour market.

The supply of capital 'Capital', as a factor of production, may refer to either financial capital and/or physical capital. In Chapter 2 we contrasted the relative immobility of capital in its physical form with the relative mobility of financial capital in the contemporary European economy. The supply of financial capital to a region is likely to be relatively elastic, reflecting regional differentials in perceived risk and expected returns.

While central-government policy influences such variables as the general level of interest rates, the implementation of regional and urban policies by government also results in the creation of tax advantages for selected locations, such as enterprise zones (which are studied more fully in Chapter 7) and assisted areas in the UK (see Chapter 8). The data in Table 4.1 suggest no simple relationship between such financial help to assisted areas and the interregional distribution of manufacturing investment.

Table 4.1 Regional distribution of net capital expenditure and gross value in manufacturing industry, percentages of UK total, 1981 and 1990

	Net capital expenditure 1981	1990	Gross value added 1981	1990
UK	100.0	100.0	100.0	100.0
North	6.5	6.5	6.2	5.5
Yorks. & Humberside	8.3	9.2	8.8	9.2
East Midlands	7.2	7.3	7.5	8.4
East Anglia	3.0	3.2	3.2	3.7
South East	24.7	22.3	28.3	26.2
South West	6.2	5.8	6.7	6.8
West Midlands	9.7	10.6	11.3	12.0
North West	14.0	15.7	13.5	13.0
England	79.6	80.7	85.6	84.7
Wales	6.8	8.0	3.8	5.2
Scotland	11.2	9.0	8.8	8.1
N. Ireland	2.4	2.3	1.8	2.0

Source: UK CSO, *Regional Trends*, vol. 28 (1993), table 13.1.

The two left-hand columns of Table 4.1 show the regional distribution of net capital expenditure in manufacturing in 1981 and 1990. The distribution changes during the decade, partly reflecting the pattern of the shift away from manufacturing in the structure of the economy.

Although net capital expenditure in the South East was a smaller proportion of the UK total in 1990 than at the beginning of the decade, it remained over 20 per cent of the total. The South East correspondingly has the highest share in value added in the manufacturing sector.

In spite of the long-term government assistance towards the costs of investment in manufacturing industry in regions such as the North of England and Northern Ireland, value-added remains proportionally higher in the South East of England. This suggests that manufacturing industry in the South East is producing higher value-added products and/or utilising more effective production techniques. In 1990 the manufacturing value-added per person employed in the South East on average was over £25 400. In the North, the comparable figure was £22 800, and in Northern Ireland only £19 700 (UK CSO, 1993, table 13.1).

Economies of scale

Economies of scale occur when an expansion of the number of inputs results in a more than proportional expansion of output, so benefiting the producer by reducing the average unit costs of production. The realisation of scale economies in the production process, whether internal or external, reduces the average costs of expanding output and so contributes to economic growth.

Internal economies of scale Internal economies of scale are reductions in unit cost that accrue to the organisation as a result of internal change. Examples are the use of larger-scale equipment, the benefits from bulk-buying and bulk sales and marketing, and the financial and managerial benefits of larger size.

As the economy grows the individual organisations that comprise that economy find it easier to grow within a framework of expansion, and so to benefit from the realisation of internal economies of scale. Much of the interest and excitement generated by the prospect of the EC's single market after the beginning of 1993 derived from the prospective realisation of internal scale economies as a result of firms' access to a wider and growing market.

External economies of scale External economies of scale are cost advantages derived from sources external to the organisation. Improved industry-wide research, training and technical support can yield significant mutual benefits for all firms. Chapters 7 and 8 look at some of the policy and industry initiatives that have been taken with the aim of accelerating the realisation of external economies of scale. Improved infrastructure provision, in areas such as transport and energy, offers a further example of an important source of external-scale economies to the individual organisation.

It is often argued that external economies of scale played a vital role in the nineteenth-century growth of the UK economy. Similarly their importance in the context of the EC, the UK and their component regional economies during the 1990s should not be underestimated.

The organisation of the production process

Another major contributing influence to the economy's growth potential is the organisation of production and related processes. In the nineteenth century the change in organisation from home and small-workshop production to factory production was fundamental to economic growth.

Two important contemporary examples of ways in which altered production organisation may contribute to productive potential stem from communications technology and from the continuing development of specialist services. Faxes and computers have revolutionised communication and made a significant contribution to lowering production costs for many organisations. Services required by the organisation in the fields of marketing, communications and finance have developed as management specialisms in recent years. These are now often provided by specialists either within the organisation or through the employment of specialists external to the organisation. Provision of these, often high-value, specialist producer services often appears as a characteristic of the dynamic regional economy of the 1990s.

Aggregate demand and regional economic growth

Investment is a key component of aggregate demand in relation to economic growth, with regard to both quantity and quality of investment. Investment in physical capital must be financed from financial capital. Savings are therefore crucial as the source of finance for investment. Savings must be channelled into financing productive investment if economic growth is to be stimulated. This also means that, to achieve economic growth, resources must be diverted from consumption into investment/saving. Consumption is essentially present consumption and use of resources: investment/saving involves restraint from current consumption to facilitate a higher level of future consumption.

This relationship can be formally demonstrated through the Harrod–Domar growth equation, which in its simple form states that:

$$g = s/v$$

where g = the rate of growth of the economy; s = the rate of saving in the economy; v = the economy's capital/output ratio that is, the amount of capital required to generate extra units of output. The more capital-intensive the production process, the higher the capital/output ratio and the more savings and investment are necessary to achieve a given rate of growth.

In Chapter 3 aggregate demand analysis was introduced in the static Keynesian framework. The Harrod–Domar approach to economic growth develops this primarily static framework to investigate the dynamics of the economy. We saw in Chapter 3 that income can either be spent or saved so:

$$y = c + s$$

This means that, like the multiplier, the Harrod–Domar equation can also be expressed in relation to current consumption in the form of:

$$g = (1 - c)/v$$

If this seems a little difficult, a worded summary of the central hypothesis may be helpful. In essence, the theory suggests that the higher the saving, the higher the potential level of investment and potential increase in output, and therefore the potential rate of growth of the economy.

CYCLICAL FLUCTUATIONS AND THE REGIONAL ECONOMY

What is an Economic Cycle?

Economic cycles are recurrent fluctuations in the level of economic activity. Statistically they are deviations from the long-term underlying trend of economic growth. As noted in the above section concerned with regional economic growth, such economic growth does not occur smoothly: there are short-term cycles around the long-term trend rate of growth (see Figure 4.1).

Cyclical fluctuations in the level of economic activity typically have four identifiable stages, as shown in Figure 4.4.

These four stages in a typical economic cycle are:

❑ Recession, during which economic activity falls back from the peak of the boom period.
❑ Slump, during which unemployment increases and economic activity runs below its long-term trend level.

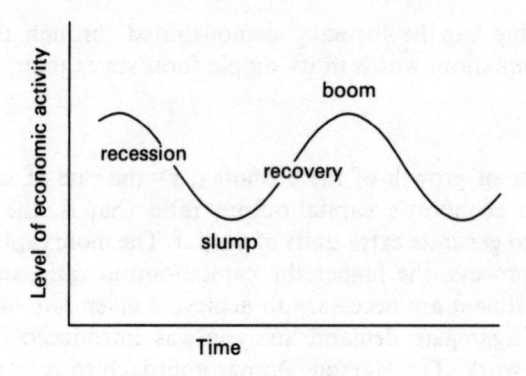

Figure 4.4 Stages of the cycle

❑ Recovery, during which firms receive more orders and economic activity increases back towards the long-term trend.
❑ Boom, during which expansion continues until it becomes unsustainable and recession is triggered.

While economic cycles are irregular rather than regular, they do appear to be endemic in industrialised economies, independent of the particular characteristics of their political and institutional structure.

The change in GDP in the UK economy between 1978 and 1986 provides a good example with which to illustrate the national economic cycle and its potential regional impact. The recession in the level of economic activity in the UK in the early 1980s shows up in the statistics for output in Figure 4.5 which dip significantly in 1979–81 before recovering in 1982–3. Economic recovery led to continued expansion, which then resulted in the boom of 1987–8, before a further period of recession set in again in 1989. The UK economy then experienced a prolonged period of recession until 1992, followed by a slow recovery.

The data in Figure 4.5 are indexed at 1985 = 100, as 1985 was a year when the economy was on or near to its long term trend path, rather than in the depths of recession or at the height of a boom. The table demonstrates three key features of the recession of the early 1980s in the UK.

Can you identify two or three features of the recession from the data in the table?

Three features worth emphasising are:

❑ The dip in GDP in 1981 at 89.0. Note too that the 1979 level of GDP is not regained until 1983.
❑ The size of the recessionary impact upon the manufacturing sector between 1980 and 1981. Note that it is 1984 before the 1980 level of

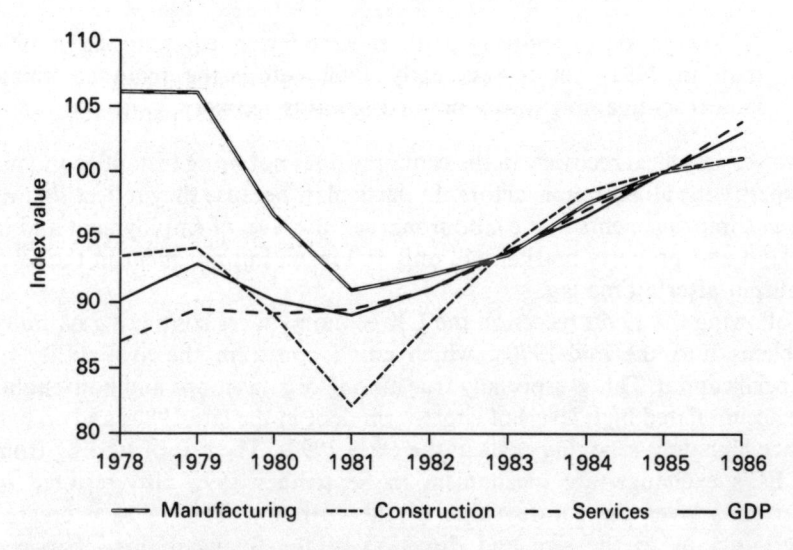

Figure 4.5 UK GDP, by output, 1978-86
Source of data: UK CSO, National Accounts, *Blue Book* (1989), table 1.5.

manufacturing output is regained for the UK economy as a whole. The differential regional impact of this period of recession in the manufacturing industry was introduced earlier and its effects upon individual regional economies are considered in more detail in Chapter 6.

❑ The relatively minor impact of this recession upon the service sector of the economy, indicated by the slight dip in the value of service-sector output in 1980. This relative insulation of service-oriented regional economies such as the South East of England from the early 1980s recession would appear to have provided the base for their expansion (and arguably their over-expansion) later in the decade.

In comparison the 1989-92 cyclical downturn in the UK economy had the following characteristics:

❑ A smaller overall fall in the value of GDP and manufacturing output than in 1979-81, but of a longer duration. In other words the early 1990s recession in the manufacturing sector was shallower but longer than that of the early 1980s.

❑ A much larger fall in service-sector output than in 1979-81, so that this recession had a much greater impact in London and the South East of England than had been the case in 1979-81.

❑ A larger fall in the value of output, and of a much longer duration, of the construction industry than in 1979-81.

❑ A slow period of recovery as there were fewer redundancies in 1992 than in 1991, yet it was early 1993 before the main economic indicators unambiguously pointed towards recovery.

However a cyclical recovery in the economy does not bring instant economic prosperity for all economic actors. In particular, because they reflect *derived demand*, improvements in the labour market, the level of employment and in the land and property market will only follow an improvement in the level of output after a time lag.

Following the 1990s recession the UK economy faces continuing liquidity problems into the mid-1990s, which could constrain the availability of financial capital. This is especially true among organisations and households that accumulated high levels of short-term debt in the late 1980s and so had to face high debt-servicing costs in the early 1990s. The exit of sterling from the EC's exchange-rate mechanism in September 1992 also resulted in uncertainty over the future value of the currency. This in turn created uncertainty as to the size and direction of the financial flows between overseas investment by UK institutions and organisations, and inward investment to the UK and its constituent regions by overseas organisations.

Why do Cyclical Fluctuations Occur?

This section utilises some of the economic ideas already covered in this book to summarise briefly the main economic mechanisms underpining the tendency of the level of economic activity to fluctuate over time in industrialised economies and their component regions. The impact of these mechanisms and of regional economic cycles upon regional patterns of growth is then developed further in Chapter 6.

Here a number of economic concepts are drawn upon to indicate the way in which cyclical fluctuations in the overall level of economic activity are generated. They also help to explain why the movement of cyclical fluctuations tends to be cumulative once the direction of the economic cycle has changed.

Changes in aggregate expenditure

As we saw in Chapter 3, total or aggregate expenditure in the economy is composed of consumption (C), investment (I), government expenditure (G) and net exports ($X - Z$) so that:

$$E = C + I + G + (X - Z)$$

In the UK in the 1960s the main causes of cyclical fluctuations in the overall level of economic activity were changes in the investment and government-

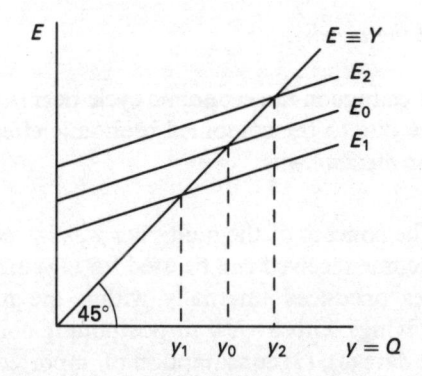

Figure 4.6 *Changes in aggregate demand*

expenditure elements of aggregate expenditure. In the 1980s investment and consumption became the least stable components of aggregate expenditure.

This change mainly occurred for two reasons. First, a higher proportion of consumption began to be financed by credit rather than from current income. As a result consumption began to behave more like investment, for example, being more directly influenced by real interest rates. Second, in the UK in the 1980s the predominant government philosophy was in favour of reducing active interventionist expenditure and so government expenditure may have had less direct effect upon the overall economy.

Changes in total potential output

Cyclical changes may be brought about by alterations in supply-side conditions in the economy that significantly affect its underlying productive potential. There are two main ways in which such underlying changes in supply-side conditions may occur.

First, sudden increases or decreases in the price and/or availability of primary commodities such as oil or foodstuffs. One notable example in this context is provided by the recessionary impact of the 1970s oil-price increases upon the European oil-importing economies.

Second, fundamental or basic technological innovation can have significant effects upon the level of economic activity and upon both the economy's cycle and growth paths. Historically, changes in energy sources such as the adoption of electricity, and changes in modes of transport such as the adoption of rail and then road transport offer useful examples. All these examples represent new technologies applied across a wide range of applications in the production process within a relatively short time scale. Their effect upon the ability of the economy to produce more and to produce it more efficiently was therefore fundamental.

The multiplier and the accelerator

Once a directional change in the economic cycle begins, its effect is likely to become cumulative due to the combined economic effects of the multiplier and the accelerator mechanisms.

The Multiplier The concept of the multiplier was introduced in Chapter 3. We assume that income received can be used for (1) current consumption of goods and services produced internally within the national or regional economy (c); (2) savings with a view to postponing consumption from the present to a future date (s); (3) consumption of imported goods and services (z); or (4) the payment of taxes (t).

In the form of an equation, income can be shown as:

$$y = c + s + z + t$$

The corresponding multiplier may be shown by:

$$k = 1/(1 - mpc) \quad \text{or} \quad 1/(mps + mpz + mpt)$$

As we saw in Chapter 3, the value of the multiplier for the national or the regional economy is determined by the value of the marginal propensity to consume. The larger the value of the multiplier, the greater the effect upon the level of output shown in Figure 4.6 that results from any given change in aggregate expenditure. The multiplier means any change in expenditure – whether an increase or a decrease – will yield a multiplied effect upon output and so contribute to the extent of cyclical increases and decreases in the overall level of economic activity in the national or the regional economy.

The Accelerator The accelerator indicates that an accelerating growth of output is necessary if the amount of investment is to increase. Otherwise investment is only likely to be enough to make good the effects of depreciation of physical capital such as machinery. In a recession, investment is likely to be so low that the overall capital stock of the affected economy is reduced. This is because the rate of replacement of physical capital as it wears out is inadequate to offset the effects of depreciation upon the capital stock.

In formal terms the accelerator effect can be shown as an equation for investment in the following form:

$$I_t = vY_t + dK_{t-1}$$

where I = investment; K = the capital stock; Y = national income; v = capital/output ratio; d = replacement investment; t = the current time period; and $t - 1$ = the preceding time period.

Put in words, this equation yields the commonsense result that the higher the capital/output ratio, the more investment the economy must generate if it is to be able to expand. This is important, as the capital/output ratio varies considerably among different industries. A regional or national economy dominated by industries with a high capital/output ratio, such as steel or chemicals, will therefore have a relatively high capital requirement. An economy predominantly made up of industries with a lower capital/output ratio, such as textiles, is likely to need to generate a lower level of investment to achieve expansion.

Built-in stabilisers

Some aspects of government fiscal policy act as 'built-in stabilisers', damping down the amplitude of the cycle in the national and regional economy. Key examples of these are income tax and unemployment benefit.

As the economy moves into the recession phase of the economic cycle, some people will lose their jobs and so stop paying income tax. Others will find that bonus and overtime payments are reduced, also reducing their incomes and so reducing their income-tax liability. The outflow of income-tax payments from the region affected by the recession to central government will therefore fall.

The recession will bring higher unemployment, and so the government will need to pay out more unemployment benefit. The inflow of funds from central government to the affected region will accordingly increase. Combined with the reduced tax payments explained above, this increased government payment of benefits will automatically increase net public expenditure in the region and in the overall economy in response to the loss of income caused by the recession. Because this change in public funding and tax receipts occurs automatically in response to the changed level of economic activity, these are referred to as built-in stabilisers. Their effect upon the economy is both automatic and countercyclical and so they help to offset the amplitude of cyclical fluctuations in the level of economic activity.

Explain how these built-in stabilisers would operate when the regional economy is in the recovery phase of a cycle.

As the economy expands, unemployment will diminish and so will the government's expenditure upon unemployment benefit. Similarly, more economic activity will imply both more people in work and more income in the form of overtime and bonus payments. Incomes will therefore increase, as will income-tax payments. In this phase of the economic cycle the government's net expenditure in the economy will fall automatically.

The early 1980s recession in the manufacturing sector of UK industry was regionally uneven in its spatial impact. Those regions worst affected, such as

South Wales, found it hardest to recover from their recessionary experience and so gained least advantage from the expansionary period of the late 1980s.

The early 1990s recession affected different sectors, and therefore had a different regional economic impact. In this recession producer services and construction were affected more adversely than in the previous recession. It will be interesting to see the regional implications of this different impact upon the spatial and sectoral distribution of any sustained economic expansion that may follow in the UK later in the 1990s.

This and the preceding section of this chapter have looked at economic growth and cyclical fluctuations around the trend growth path of the economy. We have seen that recessions and slumps in economic activity result in unemployment of the factors of production. Indeed zero growth of output could lead to increasing unemployment in the regional economy. It has been suggested that 'a region's GDP has to grow at an annual rate of over 3 per cent just to maintain employment at a constant level ... for employment to grow by 1 per cent per annum, output growth has to reach 5%' (Armstrong and Taylor, 1993, p. 140).

The next section of this chapter accordingly builds up the explanation of the unemployment of labour in the regional labour market.

REGIONAL UNEMPLOYMENT

In early 1986 the number of registered unemployed in the UK peaked at 3.5 million as a result of the recession of the early 1980s. This figure represented about 14.2 per cent of the labour force. Since 1986 the rate of unemployment has been measured in relation to the *working population* rather than the labour force. The working population is the labour force plus the self-employed and military personnel. This change in the measurement of the unemployed had the effect of reducing statistical unemployment nationally by about 2 per cent, for example from 14 per cent to 12 per cent. As there are more self-employed members of the labour force in the South East than in the North East, this change had a differential regional effect upon the unemployment statistics. Similarly the regional distribution of military personnel is uneven and so this amendment too had an effect upon the statistical measurement of regional unemployment.

From 1986 the number unemployed nationally in the UK reduced steadily to 5.6 per cent in March 1990, after which the effects of the early 1990s recession led to a steady increase to around 10.5 per cent in January 1993 (see Table 4.2). The figures for mid-1993 in Table 4.2 indicate that the downturn in national unemployment associated with the mid-1990s recovery in economic activity is being achieved more rapidly than after the 1980s recession.

Table 4.2 Regional unemployment, percentages, 1981–June 1993

	1981	1985	1988	1991	Jan 1993	June 1993
UK	8.1	10.9	8.1	8.1	10.6	10.4
North	11.7	15.4	11.9	10.4	12.1	12.2
Yorks. & Humb.	8.8	12.0	9.3	8.7	10.6	10.3
East Midlands	7.4	9.8	7.1	7.2	9.7	9.5
East Anglia	6.3	8.1	5.2	5.8	8.6	8.4
South East	5.5	8.1	5.3	7.0	10.5	10.9
Gtr London	5.5	8.8	6.6	8.2	11.7	11.6
Rest of SE	5.5	7.4	4.2	6.0	9.5	10.2
South West	6.8	9.3	6.2	7.1	10.0	9.8
West Midlands	10.0	12.8	8.9	8.6	11.5	11.0
North West	10.2	13.7	10.4	9.4	10.9	10.8
England	7.7	10.4	7.4	7.8	10.6	10.5
Wales	10.4	13.6	9.9	8.7	10.3	10.2
Scotland	9.9	12.9	11.3	8.7	9.9	9.6
N. Ireland	12.7	15.9	15.6	13.8	14.7	14.4

Sources: UK CSO, *Regional Trends*, vol. 28 (1993), table 7.15; Department of Employment data.

In the first half of 1993 the measured rate of unemployment fell in all regions except the North and the South East of England. This shorter time lag between the beginning of economic recovery and the beginning of an increase in employment may reflect the different industrial and spatial impact of the two recessions.

The 1980s recession was concentrated in the manufacturing sector, resulting in large-scale redundancies of skilled manual workers whose skills were often not in demand elsewhere in the economy. We have noted earlier that this process of deindustrialisation appears to have fundamentally weakened those regional economies worst affected.

Consequently their economies were not able to regenerate growth and employment indigenously in the aftermath of the recession. In these regions, therefore, unemployment dragged on into the longer term. Since 1981 unemployment has rarely fallen below 10 per cent in the north, having only briefly been below 10 per cent in 1989–90. Unemployment in Northern Ireland has not fallen below 10 per cent since 1981.

In contrast the 1990s recession had a greater impact upon the service industries and in regions such as the South East of England. While this recession was of longer duration it was not so deep. As a result those made redundant from the service sector in general had skills that made them reemployable within alternative service employment.

It also appears likely that the damage to the regional economy of, for example, the South East caused by the 1990s recession was less severe than that caused to other regional economies by the 1980s recession.

Consequently recovery of the regional economy could take place more rapidly and employment increase in response.

The incidence of unemployment in itself is not necessarily the most significant indicator of the severity of the economic difficulties faced by a regional economy. If people are out of work for two or three months then find equally well-paid alternative employment, the loss to themsleves and the economy is limited. Unemployment is a greater problem where reemployment becomes difficult. For this reason, Figure 4.7 provides data showing the regional pattern of unemployment by duration and gender as at January 1993.

Figure 4.7 indicates the above-average incidence of unemployment lasting between six months and three years in the West Midlands and Greater London. In other words, those who became unemployed between January 1990 and June 1992 had particular difficulty in obtaining new employment in these regions. More significant, however, is the incidence of periods of unemployment lasting over three years and over five years in the North and North West of England and in Northern Ireland. The unemployed represented here were unable to obtain reemployment when national unemployment reached its *minimum* between the 1980s and 1990s recessions.

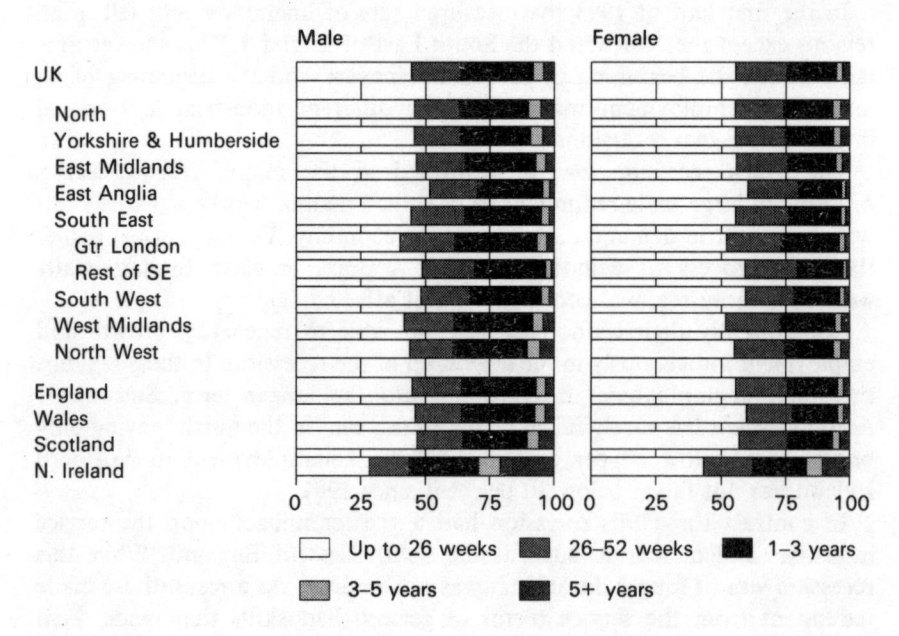

Figure 4.7 Duration of unemployment by gender, percentages, January 1993

Source: data calculated from UK CSO, *Regional Trends*, vol. 28 (1993), tables 14.3, 14.4.

As has been suggested earlier, the regional incidence of unemployment is revealing, but does not tell the whole story. For this reason subregional unemployment figures for January 1993 for selected regions are shown in Table 4.3.

Table 4.3 Unemployment rate and disposable income, selected subregions

	Unemployment rate* (%) Jan. 1993	Disposable income (£ per head) 1990
UK	10.8	100.0
South West	10.4	102.3
Cornwall	14.0	91.5
Gloucester	8.6	108.0
Wiltshire	8.7	111.8
North West	11.2	91.9
Cheshire	8.8	99.1
Gtr Manchester	10.9	89.9
Lancashire	9.3	96.7
Merseyside	15.5	86.3
Scotland	10.3	99.3
Grampian	5.5	111.8
Highlands	11.9	89.7
Strathclyde	12.2	93.1

* Not seasonally adjusted, hence the difference from Table 4.2.
Source: UK CSO, *Regional Trends*, vol. 28 (1993), tables 14.3, 14.4.

The differences in subregional rates of unemployment follow the subregional pattern of variations in disposable income discussed in Chapter 3. Within the South West region, with its regional unemployment rate below the UK national average, Cornwall on the western periphery has an above-average rate of unemployment.

We noted above that the North West region exhibits an above-average incidence of unemployment and long-term unemployment. Table 4.3 demonstrates that a relatively high proportion of this unemployment is concentrated into the cities of Manchester, and more especially, Liverpool and Merseyside.

The subregions of Scotland again reflect this pattern. Low income and high unemployment are concentrated in the peripheral subregion of the Highlands and Islands and in the urban subregion of Strathclyde.

This more detailed picture of the spatial pattern of low income and high unemployment helps explain the concentration of public-policy measures upon particular urban centres, subregions and travel-to-work areas, which are discussed in the later chapters of this book.

Characteristics of Those Unemployed in the Regional Economy

All people are not equally likely to be affected by unemployment during their working life: individuals' chances of unemployment are affected by their labour-market characteristics. In particular the following characteristics are most likely to affect individuals' chances of becoming unemployed.

1. *Skill levels*: the least skilled are the most likely to be out of work. As the overall skill levels of the working population rise over time, and as jobs become more highly skilled, this becomes increasingly true. As we have seen, the regional distribution of the unskilled is not spatially even. Regions such as the South East contain a lower proportion of the unskilled in their workforce; regions such as the North West contain a higher proportion of unskilled workers than the national average. This differential in the regional incidence of unskilled workers will feed through into the incidence of regional unemployment.

2. *Skill types*: those with outdated skills are more likely to become unemployed. We saw in Chapter 2 that labour is demanded for its specific skill contribution to the production process. When labour is made redundant, this may also reflect the redundancy of its inherent skills. Pertinent contemporary examples in the UK and comparable European economies relate to those skills needed in such employment as coal mining, shipyards and heavy engineering.

The fall in demand for the output of these European industries has been accompanied by a fall in the derived demand for the skilled labour that was employed by them. The regional distribution of these industries and their employees was not even, so this change in industrial structure has fed through unevenly into the regional incidence of unemployment in the European economies.

3. *Industry differences*: the industry in which people usually work will affect their chances of becoming unemployed. This partly reflects the preceding point, for example if coal mining is a declining industry, then miners are more likely to be made redundant than the 'average worker'.

However it also reflects different cyclical employment patterns in different industries. Some industries are more likely to shed labour than others during a recession. A notable example in this context is the construction industry. Particularly in the UK, traditional working practices are such that labour is made redundant fairly rapidly in response to a downturn in orders in the industry.

4. *Age and health*: in the UK the 50–59 age group represents two thirds of those males experiencing periods of unemployment lasting over six months. Those with poor health are similarly over-represented among the unemployed. In January 1993 males aged under 20 years experienced an unemployment rate below the UK average in all regions, while females aged under 20 years had above-UK average unemployment rates in all regions

except the South East. However those most likely to become unemployed are between 20 and 30 years old, whether male or female (Department of Employment statistics).

Why do you think the under-30-year-old age group may have above-average vulnerability to unemployment?

Due to their lack of experience and the costs to the employer of their training, the costs of employing a young member of staff may appear high relative to their productivity. Unless the wage structure reflects age-related differences in productivity, the younger age groups may therefore be more likely to experience redundancy.

5. *Discrimination*: while overt discriminatory employment practices are illegal in all the EC economies, the disabled, members of ethnic minority groups, and females experience an above-average incidence of unemployment.

The combination of the above features of the workforce means that those living and working in some regions are more likely to become unemployed than people in other regions. Therefore the regional disparities in unemployment that are observed partly reflect these spatial disparities in the structure of the labour force.

It is not only the incidence of unemployment that indicates the extent to which unemployment is a problem of the regional economy: the duration of that unemployment is also important. Unemployment is classified as long-term if the period of unemployment continues for longer than six months.

The duration of unemployment is important because people continually out of work for a long period of time lose their skills and lose the habit of working. Their skills become rusty in the same way as a machine left idle for a long time will rust. For this reason, the longer the duration of unemployment the more difficult it becomes to gain new employment in the absence of special public-policy incentives for employers.

In the North West of England during the 1980s recession over 50 per cent of those unemployed experienced long-term unemployment of over six months. Of these, over 10 per cent remained continually unemployed for over five years (Clarke, Gibbs, Brime and Law, 1992, p. 83). This pattern of acute long-term unemployment during the 1980s was repeated in several of the other UK regions. Those regions lost employment, income and prosperity over a sustained time. The consequent loss to the national economy of human-capital skills and experience and productive potential was of considerable significance.

In the case of the North West, the proportion of long-term unemployed under the age of 50 years was above the regional average in the 1980s recession. In other words, those 'losing' their skills were not only the older age groups but also a significant number of workers aged 25–45 years. The incidence of long-term redundancy among these age groups highlights the need for retraining programmes to counter such long-term unemployment.

Why is there Regional Unemployment?

As with any other market, the labour market will be in equilibrium when demand equals supply at the market-clearing real wage. In static labour-market equilibrium, unemployment will be greater than zero, as there is always some residual unemployment due to the dynamics of the labour market, with people in the process of changing employment.

In terms of basic market theory, unemployment represents an excess of the labour supply relative to demand at the prevailing real wage. In principle, then, unemployment could be due to one or a combination of:

- Excess supply of labour.
- Lack of demand for labour.
- Too high a real wage.

To understand regional unemployment more fully it is necessary to flesh out this skeletal summary. To do so the taxonomy of structural, classical and Keynesian unemployment is used to analyse the operation of the regional labour market. This will help explain the incidence and depth of regional unemployment, and so help investigate the question of what *does* cause unemployment in the regional labour market.

Frictional unemployment

At any one time, some people will be out of work because they are in the process of changing jobs. This is an inherent feature of a dynamic labour market. As long as the time taken in the process of changing jobs is not too lengthy, frictional unemployment does not represent a problem in the labour market.

Structural unemployment

In a regional economy with a perfectly competitive labour market characterised by homogeneous and perfectly mobile labour, there would be little or no structural unemployment. Structural unemployment arises from the heterogeneity of labour introduced in Chapter 2. It is then reinforced by the occupational and geographical immobility of labour, which make it more difficult for those subject to structural unemployment to find alternative employment. Structural unemployment therefore reflects problems relating to the skill characteristics, or the *quality*, rather than the *quantity* of labour available in the regional labour market.

The structurally unemployed often have skills for which there is no longer any significant labour-market demand. Where this is the case, their existing skills are no longer useful so one means of alleviating structural unemployment lies in their retraining, replacing redundant skills with new skills. In extreme cases, those with redundant skills may not obtain work by reducing the cost of their labour: there may be no demand for their redundant skills at any wage rate.

All economies and their constituent regional economies experience changing patterns of employment over time. Many of the European economies are experiencing declining agricultural employment, while in the UK there was a decline in manufacturing industry employment throughout the 1980s. In addition to these long-term secular trends, changes in technology and in the organisation of production continually reduce demand for labour with old skills and create demand for labour with new skills.

The sooner those with redundant skills can be retrained, the sooner they become reemployable. Without adequate facilities and programmes for retraining, structural unemployment can become long term. The relatively high proportions of the total number registered as out of work in the UK in the aftermath of the 1980s recession was the subject of comment earlier in this section. Typically, half of the unemployed were out of work for over six months, a fifth for over three years, and around a tenth continuously for more than five years.

Unemployment with this long-term duration makes it increasingly difficult for those affected to relearn work patterns and learn new skills. The increased provision of both flexible and new skills to the labour force is therefore an important element of supply-oriented regional policies. Such policies are needed to raise the regional economy's productive potential and reduce both the amount and duration of structural unemployment.

Classical unemployment

Classical unemployment occurs where the labour market behaves in the same way as if it were a product market. Classical unemployment is a symptom of the excess supply of labour relative to demand. For example, in Figure 4.8 the quantity of labour supplied at the real wage w_{r1} is q_{s1}, but at this wage only q_{d1} units of labour are demanded. As is clear from the figure, supply exceeds demand and so $q_{d1}q_{s1}$ units of labour will be unemployed at the real wage w_{r1}.

If the real wage falls to w_r0, then demand for labour will equal the quantity of labour supplied at this new lower real wage. In this model the solution to unemployment is for the real wage to fall in order to 'clear' the market. This solution is internal to, so lies *within*, the labour market. For this reason, classical unemployment is often referred to as 'voluntary' in the

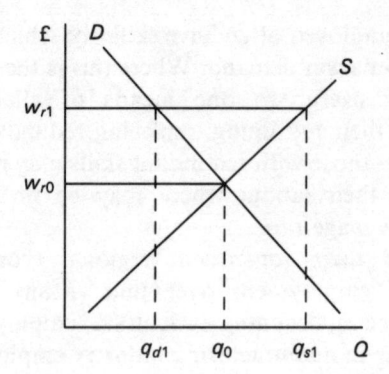

Figure 4.8 Classical unemployment

sense that it can be solved by the unemployed accepting work at a lower real wage.

In the classical view, labour markets, including regional labour markets, will adjust more effectively the more competitive they are. The policy implication is that barriers to competition in the labour market should be removed. This was the philosophy underlying the four UK Employment Acts of the 1980s, which aimed to reduce the influence of the trades unions upon the process of wage determination. Wages should as a result have become more flexible and so more responsive to changes in demand and supply. Similarly, moves towards removing barriers and restrictions between labour markets in the EC reflect the same market philosophy. The resulting adjustment processes are explained more fully later in this section, after the Keynesian approach to the labour market has been introduced.

Keynesian unemployment

In contrast to the classical view introduced above, Keynes' basic hypothesis was that the level of unemployment could not be reduced as the result of action taken within the labour market. Keynesian analysis emphasises the interdependence of the labour and the product markets in the economy. Because the derived demand for labour is dependent upon the existence of final demand in the product market, disequilibrium in the labour market is linked to disequilibrium in the markets for products. Keynesian unemployment is therefore 'involuntary' in the sense that its solution lies outside the labour market: the individual unemployed worker cannot as an individual take action that will ensure reemployment.

In the Keynesian view, unemployment in a region may arise as the result of an inadequate level of one of the components of aggregate expenditure, such as investment or exports relative to the level of expenditure necessary to generate full employment of the region's economic resources.

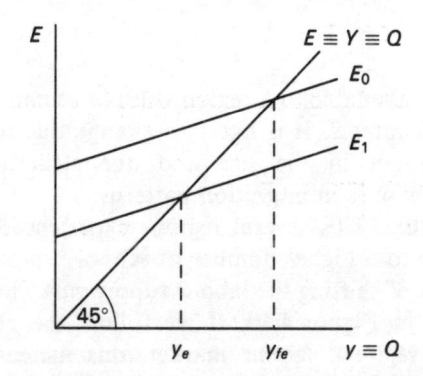

Figure 4.9   Keynesian unemployment

Figure 4.9 repeats Figure 3.8 to illustrate this point. In the figure, total current expenditure in the region is at E_1, yielding an equilibrium level of income and output at Y_e. This is not high enough to sustain full employment, shown by Y_{fe}, as explained in Chapter 3. The distance $Y_e Y_{fe}$ along the horizontal axis represents the extent of Keynesian unemployment in the regional economy.

This inadequate current level of expenditure may be specific to the region, or it may reflect a more general lack of total expenditure in the national economy, as might occur during a cyclical recession. Because the demand for labour is a derived demand, the level of employment in the regional economy will only tend to increase following an increase in the overall level of expenditure after a time lag. This increase in expenditure may need to be generated through public sector policy intervention: the Keynesian economy has no inherent tendency towards full employment equilibrium.

Disequilibrium and Adjustment in the Regional Labour Market

There have been examples of regional labour markets adjusting to altered economic circumstances in the 1980s and 1990s, and selected examples are considered in more depth in this section. This fuller coverage will facilitate a greater understanding of the workings of the regional labour market and the implications for regional unemployment. As regional unemployment is often viewed as a prime indicator of regional economic problems, such an understanding is important to the study of regional economics. We shall continue to build upon the analytic framework of the regional labour market, looking first at an example of adjustment to a change in supply conditions, and then at the case of a change in demand conditions in the regional labour market.

Labour supply

The labour supply available to a region will not remain constant over time, as explained in Chapter 2. It is likely to change due to such influences as demographic changes in the size and age structure of the resident population, and changes in migration patterns.

In the UK in the 1980s several regions experienced an increase in the labour supply due to a higher number of school leavers in the population. This had the effect of shifting the labour supply curve to the right, as shown by SL_0 and SL_1 in Figure 4.10. If we follow the classical view of the operation of the regional labour market, this increase in supply would require a reduction in the market real wage rate to avoid increasing unemployment among this group of the population. In Figure 4.10, the equilibrium real wage would have needed to fall, for example from w_0 to w_1.

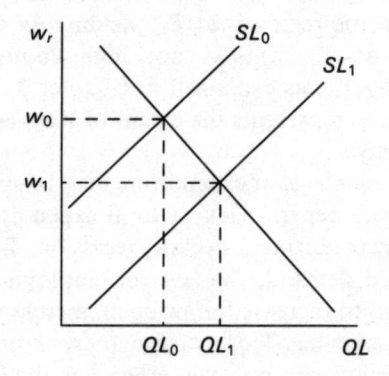

Figure 4.10 *Unemployment due to an increase in the regional labour supply*

Demographic forecasts for the 1990s indicate a reduction in the number of school leavers in many regions of the UK economy. In the absence of other influences upon the labour market, what effect would you expect such a decrease in the number of school leavers to have upon equilibrium real wage rates?

The effect shown in Figure 4.10 would occur in reverse, leading to upward pressure upon real wage rates in those regions where school leavers were in short supply. If these upward pressures upon wage rates due to labour-supply conditions occur, wage costs may also exert upward pressure upon price levels.

An analogous change in labour-market supply conditions was experienced by the regional economies of East and West Germany upon unification. In terms of Figure 4.10, the effect of German unification was to increase the labour supply available to the former West German economy by bringing in the East German labour supply. Therefore, following the classical view of the labour market, the equilibrium level of real wages in the unified German economy would have to fall to reduce the likelihood of rising unemployment.

The demand for labour and labour productivity

In Chapter 2 we saw that the demand for labour was derived from the demand for that labour's expected contribution to the employer's activity. In other words, labour is demanded for the *value of the marginal product* it contributes to the employer. This has two components: the financial contribution to the employer's revenue derived from the employment of the labour; and the physical amount the labour produces, that is, labour productivity.

The productivity of labour in a region is affected, among other things, by the amount of investment taking place in that region. In this way, as explained below, lack of investment can result in lower wages in a region and/or higher regional unemployment.

Low investment in a region can occur for a variety of reasons, not wholly independent. A cyclical downturn in the level of activity in the national economy will result in lower investment, which may affect some regions more than others. Changes in the industrial structure of the economy will lead to disinvestment in declining industries. As explained earlier, the outer regions of the UK economy were significantly affected by such structural disinvestment in traditional manufacturing industries in the 1980s. As explained in Chapter 2, investors may also have preferences and aversions regarding the spatial distribution of investment which exacerbates the scale of disinvestment in some regional economies.

Low investment and net disinvestment in some UK regions during the 1980s affected regional unemployment and regional labour markets in two ways. First, firm closures result directly in unemployment for those made redundant, and indirectly in under- and unemployment for those in the region economically dependent upon the closed firms. Second, firms that continue to operate with a rundown stock of capital due to disinvestment will experience reduced capital productivity.

This lower capital productivity will adversely affect the productivity of the labour employed to work with this rundown capital stock. Labour working with state-of-the-art technology is likely to be more productive than labour working with outdated technology and machines subject to faults and breakdown.

The economic effect of the lower labour productivity experienced by labour employed in rundown production processes can be shown diagrammatically by a leftward shift of the marginal value product of labour (MVPL) curve, as in Figure 4.11. The graph assumes a normal

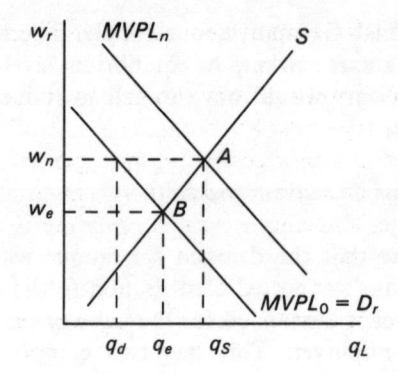

Figure 4.11 Regional unemployment due to below-average labour productivity

upward-sloping labour-supply curve for the region. The demand for labour in the region experiencing low and under-investment is shown by D_r.

This demand-for-labour curve reflects the marginal value product of labour using outdated technologies and old equipment ($MVPL_0$). The potential marginal value of the product of this labour, were it equipped with new, best practice technology and equipment, is shown as $MVPL_n$.

The regional labour market equilibrium is shown by $w_e q_e$ at point B. If real wages are above w_e, for example due to nationally negotiated wage rates, w_n based upon the use of best-practice production processes, the region may experience unemployment of $q_s q_d$ due to the excess supply of labour to the market at this higher wage rate.

Figure 4.11 demonstrates the failure of the region to realise its potential income and employment levels due to inadequate regional investment. At the regional labour-market equilibrium point B, employment at q_e is below the potential q_s attainable at the national equilibrium point A. The regional equilibrium wage rate w_e is similarly less than w_n. These effects combine to yield a loss of potential income to the regional labour market, shown by the area $w_n A B w_e$ in Figure 4.11. The extent of this regional loss of potential income will depend upon the size of the productivity gap between the region and national best practice, and upon the elasticity of the region's labour supply curve at the relevant real wage rates.

There are two general policy implications arising from this analysis. The first is that labour is over-priced at w_n and so regional wages should reflect regional labour productivity more closely at we. This would eliminate regional unemployment due to the imposition of national wages on a regional labour market where they result in classical unemployment due to pricing labour out of work. However, at this lower wage equilibrium point B, the potential labour supply $q_e q_s$ is not employed. Unless the relevant section of the labour-supply curve is totally inelastic (and therefore vertical), this equilibrium is not a full employment equilibrium for the regional labour market.

The alternative policy approach is to implement measures designed to raise investment in the region, so encouraging a shift of the MPVL curve to the right. Increasing labour productivity in the region helps make it possible to move towards a higher income and employment equilibrium rather than reinforcing a low-wage, low-employment equilibrium in the regional labour market.

Adjustment to structural imbalance in more than one region

The previous section considered some of the effects upon equilbrium in the regional labour market where disinvestment resulted in regional labour productivity typically below the national average. This section develops the same approach to consider more fully the potential dynamics of adjustment in the regional labour market in the face of a major structural change resulting in disequilibrium.

The emphasis is again upon demand conditions in the regional labour market. For the present we continue to assume that the mobility of labour is limited to avoid overcomplicating the exposition. This assumption of relative labour immobility is relaxed in Chapter 6, where the alternative possibility – that labour mobility may make a significant contribution to correcting regional labour-market imbalances – is discussed.

Initial labour-market equilibrium The attempt to rapidly equalise real wage levels between East and West Germany following unification offers a good recent example of some of the problems that may result from attempts to integrate two labour markets, or to try to rapidly correct a major structural imbalance between interregional labour markets. The example is especially pertinent given the increasing pace of economic integration, whether formal or informal, within the regional and national economies of the EC during the 1990s.

For the purpose of this exposition, it is assumed that both the East and West German labour markets were independently in equilibrium at the time of unification. In this initial equilibrium, the real wage rate in the West German labour market was OF, as shown in Figure 4.12(a), and the marginal value of product-of-labour curve $MVPL_w$.

In East Germany, the initial equilibrium real wage facing employers was OE, reflecting the $MVPL_E$ curve in Figure 4.12(b). This reflects the lower overall marginal value of the product of labour in the East German regional labour market in comparison with that of the West German regional labour market. This discrepancy between the values of labour's marginal product reflects differences in the general levels of investment, technology and

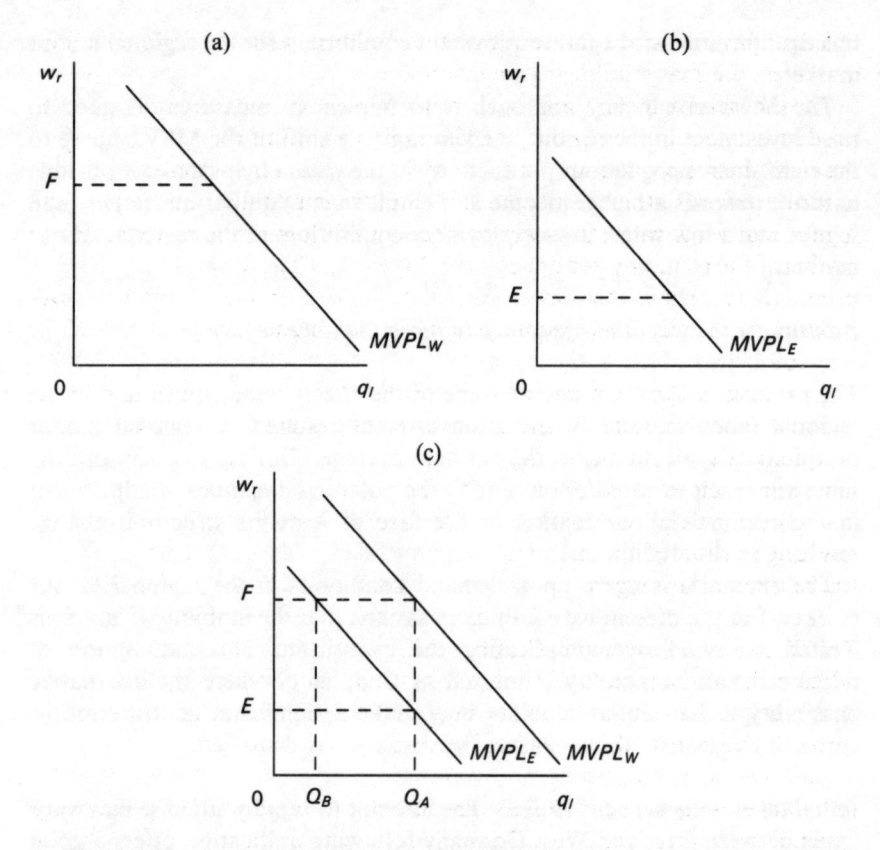

Figure 4.12 Interregional labour-market adjustment

organisation of production in the two areas at the time of German unification.

As we saw in the last section, the equilibrium real wage for a region with lower labour productivity is likely to be lower than that for a regional labour market where there is a higher overall level of labour productivity.

The initial effects of disequilibrium Figure 4.12(c) shows the result when a national higher real product wage is derived from the high-productivity sector of the economy and applied throughout regional and sectoral labour markets. This may occur as the result of the imposition of nationally negotiated wage rates across regions with differing average levels of labour productivity, as was considered in the previous section. The statutory imposition of EC wide real wage rates would have a similar effect. Alternatively it may be the result of government policy measures intended to equalise pay across disparate regional economies, as was the case of East and West Germany following unification.

At the national uniform real wage OF, the workers in the high-productivity sector or region of the economy continue in employment because their productivity, and so the marginal value product of their contribution to output, justifies this level of wage remuneration. But at this higher real wage rate OF, fewer workers in the low-productivity sector or region of the economy continue in employment. Their lower overall level of productivity means that fewer can offer a high enough marginal value product to justify their employment at the higher wage OF, and so unemployment of $Q_A - Q_B$ results.

As Figure 4.12(c) demonstrates, the extent of this regional unemployment is likely to be greater: (1) the greater the initial discrepancy between the marginal value of product of labour in the two (or more) regional or sectoral labour markets affected, shown by the vertical distance EF on the diagram; and (2) the greater the elasticity of the derived demand for labour over the relevant portion of the marginal value product-of-labour curve, shown by the horizontal distance $Q_A - Q_B$.

The process of adjustment The above discussion indicates that the *primary* adjustment to the structural change in regional labour-market conditions in this example falls upon the sector or region with lower labour productivity through the increased incidence of unemployment among its workforce.

The *secondary* adjustment to this interregional structural labour-market imbalance will occur through the mechanisms that affect aggregate expenditure, introduced in Chapter 3. Increased unemployment in the lower-labour-productivity region, such as Eastern Germany, Southern Italy or Northern Ireland, results in increased financial transfers into that region, for example through the payment of unemployment benefits. These transfer payments will help to stimulate demand in the less-well-off region. These payments will be financed at least in part through tax receipts from the better off region. Demand in the better-off region is therefore reduced or dampened in favour of greater demand in the less-well-off region. In relation to the example used here of German unification, the political impact of such an attempted transfer of resources from the more prosperous former West Germany to the less prosperous former East Germany has not been overwhelmingly favourable. The West has demonstrated some reluctance to experience any rapid reduction in its real living standards in favour of a more rapid assimilation of the East German economy.

The *speed* of adjustment to a new overall labour market equilibrium between the two, or more, regional labour markets then depends upon the politically and economically feasible extent and timing of the resource transfer necessary for the accomplishment of that new equilibrium. Where the gap to be bridged between the regional labour markets is extensive, the size of transfers of funds from the better off to the less-well-off region may well influence the speed of change that is realistically attainable. A relatively fast rate of adjustment may be attractive as a means of quickly restoring overall labour-market equilibrium, but it may be a risky strategy in political terms as the example of post-unification Germany indicates.

Faster adjustment requires relatively high rates of taxation to fund higher transfers from the more to the less prosperous region. However these higher rates of taxation may be resisted by taxpayers in the better-off region. This resistance may take the form of political unpopularity for the existing government. Alternatively it may take the form of pressure for higher nominal wage rates to compensate for the effect of higher taxation upon real wages. The latter may contribute to inflationary pressures, so exacerbating the existing macroeconomic management difficulties facing the government.

Existing workers in the high-productivity region or sector are highly likely to resist any reduction in their living standards. Any such perceived reduction in living standards is likely to lead them to press for higher nominal wage rates, with consequent inflationary pressures upon the economy.

Regional policy measures seeking to facilitate the adjustment of regional labour markets to underlying structural change should therefore be designed to cushion the effect upon the real wage received by existing workers in the more prosperous region. This consideration affects many of the regional policy instruments discussed in Chapter 8. One implication of this approach to analysing the regional labour market may therefore be that major or sudden structural imbalances between interregional or intersectoral labour markets are not easily absorbed. Regional disparities in the rate of unemployment therefore may be overcome, but their solution may require a relatively consistent long-term policy strategy as short-term alleviative measures may prove politically unfeasible. An analogous argument would apply to significant structural imbalances in the interregional markets for the other factors of production, land and capital.

THE REGIONAL IMPACT OF INFLATION

We have seen earlier that the regional economy does not have monetary independence from the national economy. The regional economy cannot separate its currency or its price level from that of the national economy: it has no independent monetary policy nor an independent exchange-rate policy. For these reasons it may be argued that regional inflation cannot occur, at least in the longer term. Instead the regional price level will mirror the national price level.

However there are several reasons for looking briefly at inflation in the regional context. It has been argued in this book that regional factor markets are not all characterised by perfect competition or near-perfect competition. In the absence of such competition the market adjustment necessary to even out short-term disequilibria will take longer and be a more problematic process. In the process of adjustment, or its absence, different prices in different regional markets may contribute towards different overall regional price levels and so to regional differentials in inflation.

Some regional differentials may persist into the long term, for example some labour costs. Many wage rates are determined nationally, so are not subject to significant regional differences. For example, with the exception of the additional London weighting to reflect higher living costs in London, civil servants have traditionally been paid on the same scales regardless of their regional location in the UK.

However the same national standardisation does not apply to all services provided by the private sector, and especially those provided by the self-employed. In the UK there have been consistent and persistent interregional differences in the cost of services such as plumbers and hairdressers. These are reflected in regional differences in the cost of living between, for example, the South East and the North East of England, differences that have not been eliminated over time.

Similarly, as we shall see in greater detail in Chapter 6, house prices have been subject to persistent interregional variation in the UK throughout the past thirty years at least. The size of the gap between the price of a house in the relatively expensive South East of England and its counterpart in the less-expensive regions of the UK has varied over time, but the gap has not been eliminated by market forces.

In the UK, labour and property costs above the national average contributed to above-average inflation in the South East region in 1987–8. This tendency for inflation to generate in the South East region to a greater extent than in the other UK regions is problematic for the economy as a whole and therefore cannot be ignored.

When inflation increases in the South East of England and then ripples out to other regions, the outcome is an increase in inflation for the economy as a whole. The greater the economic inequality among the regions of the economy, the more rapidly will the prosperous region(s) run into potential inflationary constraints in times of economic expansion.

In light of this consideration, it is perhaps ironic that the UK government downgraded regional policy in the 1980s at the same time as concentrating macroeconomic policy measures on the control of inflation. Interregional disparities in inflation and the level of resource utilisation mean that macroeconomic policies designed to contain inflation in an expanding region such as the South East of England may have an unduly restrictive impact upon less prosperous regions seeking to overcome present unemployment. Immobility of labour and land, combined with the heterogeneity of the factors of production, mean that regional markets do not adjust rapidly to even out interregional price variations. Some of these, such as the interregional variation in UK house prices, become embedded in the national price structure. For these reasons interregional differences in inflation and in employment should be minimised if the economy as a whole is to benefit in the longer term.

References and Further Reading

Armstrong, H. and J. Taylor (1993) *Regional Economics and Policy*, 2nd edn (London: Harvester Wheatsheaf).
Balchin, P. N., J. L. Kieve and G. H. Bull (1988) *Urban Land Economics and Public Policy*, 4th edn (London: Macmillan).
Campbell, Mike (1991) 'Trends and prospects in the regional labour market', *The Regional Review*, vol. 1, no. 2, pp. 16, 17.
Clarke, M., D. Gibbs, E. K. Brime and C. M. Law (1992) 'The North West' in Townroe and Martin (1992).
Department of Employment (1990, 1992, 1993) *Gazette* (London: HMSO).
Smith, David (1989) *North and South* (Harmondsworth: Penguin).
Townroe, P. and R. Martin (eds) (1992) *Regional Development in the 1990s* (London: Jessica Kingsley Publishers/Regional Studies Association).
United Kingdom Central Statistical Office (1989) *National Accounts* (London: HMSO).
United Kingdom Central Statistical Office (1993) *Regional Trends* (London: HMSO).

5 The Regional Location of Economic Activity

LOCATION THEORY

The Framework for Location Theory

Chapter 2 highlighted the uneven spatial distribution of economic activity across the regions of the economy. This chapter investigates the reasons underlying the location of this economic activity that contribute to this spatial unevenness. The chapter opens with a brief look at the main location models. This is followed by a consideration of location in the wider context of the overall goals of economic efficiency and equity that were explained in Chapter 3.

The next section considers whether the location of different types of economic activity is affected by similar or different underlying considerations. For example, are shopping centres located with regard to the same or different considerations as manufacturing plants?

We then discuss the role of management in the decisions taken by the organisation with respect to the regional location of its activities. As we saw in Chapter 2, economic activities take place at a location that normally involves the use of buildings and land. The influence of property management upon the location decision is therefore explained.

The final section of the chapter considers the influences underlying the regional location of public-sector activities. The public sector is such a large actor in the economies of the EC that it is important to consider whether the location of its activities depend upon the same or upon different considerations as the location of private-sector activity.

Traditional location theory

Today, in economies such as the UK, where the property market and the processes associated with the development of land for commercial and industrial use are relatively sophisticated, the provision of factory and office space often takes place in response to an expectation of *future demand* for these buildings, not in response to a *current existing demand*. This means that the location of much large-scale economic activity today is influenced by rather different considerations than were predominant a century ago, when location usually depended upon the decision and preferences of the individual entrepreneur.

Traditional theories of industrial location viewed the firm as optimising its location in relation to the dictates of the production process. The process of production entails the bringing together of inputs of labour, land and capital, the factors of production, to facilitate their combination in order to yield an output. This output, or product, then has to be distributed to the buyer in the market. This production process can be summarised as:

$$\text{Inputs} \longrightarrow \text{Process} \longrightarrow \text{Output} \longrightarrow \text{Market}$$

Where inputs of labour, land or capital represent the major proportion of the total cost of production, or are highly immobile, production is located near to the source of inputs. For these reasons much of the traditional industrial production that grew up in the UK during the nineteenth century was located close to the source of energy in the coalfields. The spatial location of some manufacturing production is determined by ease of access to, for example, the skilled labour required for the processing of those inputs.

Such considerations tend to reinforce established spatial patterns of location. The presence of shipyards on the Tyne and the Clyde resulted in the development of local labour forces with skills appropriate to the needs of the shipbuilding industry. Local colleges responded to the needs of local industry by providing further training and qualifications tailored to the needs of the local industrial employers.

The availability of a highly skilled local labour force therefore becomes established and serves to attract other employers with similar labour force requirements into the local ecoomy. The degree of specialisation develops, to the benefit of the local economy, until the growth of the industry turns to decline and the high level of local specialisation becomes a liability to the local economy rather than an asset.

Both historically and today, many firms locate close to the market for their output so as to minimise their distribution costs. Traditionally this consideration contributed to the continued development of centres of population and to the concentration of activity. As we shall see in more detail below, today the result may in some cases be the dispersal rather than the concentration of the location of economic activity.

Whether the organisation sites its activities in relation to inputs or output, the outcome of this type of industrial-location model is one in which location reflects the outcome of a rational decision-making process by the firm. The firm uses its location to further its general aim of cost minimisation to achieve technical efficiency and profit maximisation.

The contribution of management theory

In the 1960s developments in management theory drew attention to the irrational aspects often present in organisational behaviour. Management was seen to take suboptimising decisions, partly due to the effects of uncertainty and imperfect knowledge upon decison making. For example, decisions to locate and to relocate are typically taken irregularly by the organisation, and so, at any single given time, current locations are unlikely to be optimal. The search for a new location may also be limited and imprecise due to the costs of searching for the 'perfect' site. This approach yields a more complex set of models than the simpler cost-minimising form outlined above.

The management organisational hierarchy highlighted by management theory may be paralleled by a locational hierarchy. As organisations grow and become more concentrated over time in terms of ownership, so location may become more concentrated in certain locations. The increasing degree of national and/or international as distinct from local or regional ownership may therefore be reflected in increasing centralisation of location decisions away from the local and regional economy. The result may be similar to that shown schematically below:

Head Office —— high-order functions —— main urban centre

Branch plants —— lower-order functions —— smaller urban centres

For example, London is the main urban centre in England, so retains more than its fair share of high-order economic activity. Daniels argues that it exerts a 'shadow effect' upon development and location within a sixty-mile radius, so that location tends to be either within London, or at least sixty miles away (Daniels, 1979, p. 12). When firms with head offices in London do locate beyond the London shadow, their subordinate location is often within easy travelling distance of the capital, leading to the 1980s expansion along the M4 corridor. Similar considerations underly the concern of the outer regions of both the UK and comparable Western European economies that they are, or are becoming, branch-plant economies with inferior economic growth prospects.

To be effective, intervention in location, such as the government policy initiatives discussed in the later chapters of this book, should take account of the vertical structure of organisations and the corresponding vertical hierarchy in their locational choice.

Catchment areas and the location of economic activity

The idea of locational hierarchies has underpinned a number of theoretical models that have sought to explain the spatial distribution of population and activity across the economy. The detail of these models is the province of economic geography rather than regional economics. The underlying concept is, however, explained here both as a useful part of the framework for the discussion of location that follows in the later sections of the present chapter, and because of the importance of contemporary urban policy as an integral part of regional policy in several of the European economies.

The ideas of W. Christaller, published in Germany in the early 1930s, represent a crucial contribution to this approach to location theory. Christaller's 'central-place' theory of location postulated a spatial hierarchy of population settlements, from the small village to the town to the city that is central to its region. The emergence of the spatial pattern of this vertical hierarchy of settlements within a region was postulated as the consequence of the economic relationships between the village, town and city.

In contemporary language, Christaller's hypothesis emphasises the role of the catchment area needed to support a particular economic activity. A village population may support a general store, but not a cinema or a taxi service. A town's population may support a grocery supermarket but not a large department store or a theatre. The village resident therefore looks to the town for the nearest cinema and to the city for the nearest theatre.

The city becomes the focus for regional provision of those goods and services requiring a regional catchment area. The town becomes the focus for provision of goods and services requiring a smaller catchment area. The catchment area has two aspects: the geographic area or market range over which the good or service is provided, and the economic threshhold of the purchasing power, or income, needed to support the activity. We shall see below that contemporary models of retail location continue to draw upon developments from Christaller's approach.

This catchment-area approach to location yields two potential short-term outcomes: the noncompeting and the competing. In the noncompeting outcome, an entrepreneur seeking to establish a business will look for a gap in the market. For example, an entrepreneur wishing to retail computer software will look for a location with a catchment area where there is no established supplier. Such an approach to location will result in a series of computer software retailers equally spaced across the catchment areas of the region. The market is divided between them, with possibly limited competition. Each retail outlet in the regional market has its own sphere of influence. These spheres of influence are adjacent rather than overlapping: only where they overlap will competition appear.

The alternative short-term outcome encourages locational competition. In this case an entrepreneur seeking to establish a new business will set up in direct competition with an existing supplier. The new entrepreneur aims to capture market share from the existing entrepreneur through competition, usually based on price competition. In the longer term the market will only support one of the competitors. Therefore the long-term equilibrium outcome will be represented by a number of firms reasonably equally spaced across the market.

This model is useful in respect of market conditions that approximate to competition, with limited potential for the realisation of economies of scale.

Where there are economies of scale, especially external economies of scale, the model is not so useful. External, or agglomeration, economies of scale will encourage clustering rather than distancing in the location of economic activity.

An apt example is provided by many of the producer service industries, such as financial services and advertising. In these industries real or perceived external economies of agglomeration are high and so firms tend to locate spatially close together, usually within a city. The locational pattern resulting from such clustering is very different from that envisaged by Christaller's approach. It is important therefore to consider the main underlying influences that affect the location of different types of economic activity, and this question is addressed later in this chapter.

Local and international perspectives

The increasing internationalisation of the European capital market was noted in Chapter 2. This has implications for the location of economic activity in the recent past and into the future. For example, a significant part of the development of offices in Brussels in the early 1970s was initiated and financed from the UK (Bateman, 1985). Since then London's role as a financial centre has meant a continuing involvement by British firms in the development of industrial and commercial activity in Western Europe, a trend accelerated by the lack of market opportunities in the UK economy during the 1990-2 recession.

Paris and Frankfurt have also acted as centres from where financial and managerial control have influenced the evolution of the pattern of economic activity in the main European economies. Their sphere of economic influence was considerably enlarged with the fall of the 'iron curtain' at the beginning of the 1990s. While German organisations were quick to try to take advantage of the market opportunities opened up by German unification, the French were quick to invest in some of the other East European economies, such as the Czech Republic, Slovakia and Hungary, in the early 1990s.

The EC economies have also benefited from inward flows of overseas financial investment. Several multinational organisations have chosen to locate in EC countries. This has been a strategic location decision designed to gain a foothold in the EC market. For example, there has been extensive investment in the UK car manufacturing industry by Nissan, Toyota and Honda to provide these Japanese producers with access to the profitable European car market. This has meant the establishment of production plants – in regions such as the North East of England – designed primarily to manufacture goods for export, both from the region and from the national economy.

What should be the main benefits to the receiving region of this type of inward investment?

In relation to aggregate expenditure in the regional economy, as these products are intended for export they will add to total expenditure and boost the income received by the producing region. In the case of car manufacture, the benefits to the region should continue into the medium and longer term, as demand for the final product is characterised by buoyant income elasticity.

The industry employs skilled labour at commensurate rates of pay, so the income effects upon the regional economy will be beneficial, as explained in Chapter 3. The region may also benefit from the introduction of modern technology and modern management and financial strategies.

However, as noted in our discussion of branch plants in Chapter 2, there are potential disadvantages to the receiving region in terms of lack of local management control and limited economic linkages to the region if little use is made of local suppliers and services.

Efficiency and Equity in Regional Location

A theoretical framework for the analysis of the location of economic activity is outlined in this section. While not being any more difficult to understand than the material relating to prices and welfare in Chapter 3, this section draws upon those ideas to explain the implications of location for economic efficiency and equity. These fundamental economic tenets are relevant to the discussion of location later in this chapter regarding both the private and the public sectors of the economy. The analysis in this section also provides a foundation for discussion of the implications of the issues raised for government regional policy on location in Chapters 8 and 9.

Technical efficiency

Technical efficiency is maximised when the organisation minimises its production costs. The analysis of the spatial supply conditions regarding the inputs into the production process in Chapter 2 demonstrated that spatial variation in cost is likely to be greater for labour than for financial capital. In focusing upon location, we are also interested in spatial variations in the cost of land, that is, the costs associated with the site and property occupied by the production process.

Property, like labour but in contrast with financial capital, is a heterogeneous and not a homogeneous factor of production. Some properties have specific characteristics better suited to the needs of the user organisation than do other properties. A good fit between property specification and user requirement should yield higher productivity from utilisation of the property than will otherwise be attainable. The small firm trying to operate from unsuitable premises because it cannot afford more suitable premises may not operate as efficiently as the firm that has obtained better premises.

Technological change is highly relevant to property. A building constructed in 1994 is not the same as a building constructed in 1894. A building constructed in 1894 and modernised in 1994 is still not identical to a contemporary building. Current best-practice technology in building construction is, sometimes literally, embedded in the building specification. Newly built, or well refurbished, office or factory space incorporates characteristics that enable modern systems for computing and heating to be operated more efficiently than in buildings reflecting the best practice of previous years. This potential for the use of more efficient techniques reduces minimum attainable operational costs, so increasing technical efficiency.

Location decisions taken by organisations should maximise technical efficiency. There appears to be no obvious reason why organisations' ability to maximise technical efficiency in property utilisation should be subject to significant spatial variation. Of the factors of production used in production, the cost of labour would appear to be the most sensitive to spatial variation across the economy.

Allocative efficiency

Private-sector organisations may seek to maximise profits over varying time scales, using varying strategies and with varying degrees of success: but it is generally accepted that their overall behaviour is directed towards profit maximisation. In contrast public-sector organisations may be charged with minimising costs, but not necessarily with maximising profits. Compared with their private-sector counterparts, most have multiple objectives encompassing social as well as economic objectives. This multiplication of objectives raises the likelihood of conflict between those objectives. Such conflict is inherently likely to lower the attainable level of overall efficiency in the public-sector organisation.

One strategy for minimising this conflict, and aiming to raise efficiency, adopted in the public sector in recent years has been the separation of financial management and control from the 'professional', that is, inherently unprofitable aspects of public-sector activities. This strategy of making economic subsidies explicit was exemplified by the 1991 reorganisation of the National Health Service in the UK.

Strategies can also be devised that try to reduce, or at least make explicit, these potential conflicts through the use of common measures for the disparate elements in the public sector equation. Financial cost-effectiveness evaluation, like that underpinning the UK's National Audit Office approach, can be broadened to wider cost-benefit evaluation.

Estimated shadow prices may in principle measure nonquantitative social costs and benefits in terms of a financial common denominator. Shadow-pricing techniques may counter the distortionary effects of an organisation's monopsonistic and/or monopolistic market roles. Shadow prices seek to replace the actual market price with an estimate of what the market price would be if markets were perfectly competitive. In other words, the Pareto-optimal price equal to marginal cost, discussed in Chapter 3, is used as the basis for decision making rather than the observed market price. While the presence of social costs and benefits and monopsony/monopoly in the market hampers the identification of an optimally allocatively efficient set of shadow prices, their use may add to the rationality of the decision-making process. Shadow prices allow decisions to be made on an 'as if there were perfect competition' basis, even where perfect competition is clearly absent from the market.

With respect to decisions concerning the location of economic activity, the limitations on decision making in relation to welfare economics and the establishment of an optimal set of market prices are exacerbated by the time scale over which the decison is effective. The location of the organisation's activities is typically a long-term decision: however property prices typically alter over the long term. The behaviour of the key variables in the UK property market over the past seven years has raised, rather than reduced, economists' uncertainty as to their expected future behaviour in the next seven years. For example the rental value of property in London was much higher than that in the rest of the UK in 1989. However by 1993 this gap had narrowed significantly in a way not predicted in 1989. The resulting level of uncertainty in the property market in respect of variables such as future regional differences in rent values makes difficult the task of rational current decision taking with respect to location. These difficulties are shared by public and private sector alike and so impact upon the allocative efficiency of all location decisions in the economy.

Equity

The extreme case in which all economic activity is spatially equally distributed among the regions of the economy is so far from reality as to be discounted for the present in the case of the EC economies. Economic activity in the UK is to some extent centralised in London and the South East. Centralisation is greater in both the French and the Republic of Ireland economies.

At the other extreme, all activity could be located in the capital city and the economy's most prosperous region. In the case of the UK, if all economic activities were located in London and the South East the outcome would be viewed as inequitable. But why should this be so?

First, such a degree of centralisation is seen as unhealthy to the functioning of a democratic state. If all opportunity for economic gain is seen to be in privileged regions, the population of the unprivileged region(s) are likely to be discontent.

Second, in more overtly economic terms, such centralisation would deprive large groups of the population of employment on grounds of inaccessibility. The opportunity for certain categories of employment would be restricted to, or highly concentrated in, certain regions. This limitation of equality of opportunity is again likely to feed through into political and social division in the country affected.

In practice these concerns regarding equity and fairness are aired. However, the current degree of centralisation of economic activity in selected regions of the EC-member economies implies that such equity considerations are not high on the list of priorities with respect the location of economic activity.

Equity is difficult to include explicitly in the modelling and analyis of location. Awareness of the equity effects of regional location should however underpin the regional policies towards the location of economic activity discussed in Chapters 8 and 9.

THE REGIONAL LOCATION OF ECONOMIC ACTIVITY

Manufacturing Location

The changing economic structure of the UK means manufacturing output and employment are diminishing in overall importance, with manufacturing employment now representing less than a quarter of total employment. This process of deindustrialisation in the UK was introduced in Chapter 2, and its effects upon regional growth are considered more fully in Chapter 6.

The technology of manufacturing production has also altered. Many manufacturing organisations find traditional locations inappropriate to the needs of modern techniques of production. These may be more capital-intensive and space-extensive than those used forty years ago. The desire for larger more expansive sites for manufacturing processes has led to the movement of manufacturing production away from established urban areas. Many manufacturing firms have relocated process plants to greenfield sites with easy access. Conurbations have lost manufacturing employment, while areas such as the M4 corridor through the Thames valley in England have gained manufacturing employment.

An example of such a move by manufacturing industry would be the car maker Rover's move of production facilities from its established site at

Cowley in Oxford to a new site at Swindon with easy access to the M4. The policy implications of this movement of manufacturing location for traditional urban areas are investigated in Chapters 7 and 8.

The change in the regional distribution of manufacturing industry from the traditional industrial areas such as the North of England and South Wales to the Southern and Midland regions of England has continued in spite of government regional policy initiatives to retain and attract industry to regions such as the North.

Why do you think the influences changing the distribution of manufacturing activity towards the South of England are so strong?

In fairly general terms, this altered distribution is the outcome of any one or a combination of the following influences:

- The shrinking of 'old' industries, such as steel and engineering, which was explained in Chapter 2.
- The growth of 'new' industries on greenfield sites with good access to infrastructure such as the motorway network.
- The continuing loss of local control of the ownership of manufacturing activity in recent decades. The continuing concentration of ownership of productive activity has resulted in the closure of branch plants in regions that are perceived to be outlying by those managers responsible for decision making in the organisation's head office.
- The availability of such producer services as marketing and finance is perceived as being greater in regions such as the South compared with the North of England. As a result the external economies generated from these services are seen to be greater in the South.
- The management responsible for taking location decisions often perceive their own career opportunities to be superior in the South of England, so have a locational preference for that and neighbouring regions.

Office Location

To consider the regional and spatial location of offices, it is useful to categorise different types of office activity. One useful classification identifies the following three distinct types of office activity:

- The head office of an organisation.
- A unit primarily functioning as an office, such as the finance department of a manufacturing firm when it is located in an office separate from the manufacturing plant.

❏ Office functions that are physically attached to the firm's main activity. An example would be the finance department office located in the same building as the firm's manufacturing process.

The expansion of service-sector employment experienced by most of the EC economies during recent decades is reflected in the expansion of office-based occupations. Office functions have been growing in importance as a set of activities carried out in these economies. As a result offices have increasingly become physically detached from the organisation's main processes. This is especially true of such office functions as accounting, advertising and marketing.

These office-based activities then generate their own external economies of scale. For this reason, financial and marketing offices are often located in a cluster in the same area of a city. These external economies then generate their own momentum and act as an important determinant of office location.

The tendency for such producer service activities to locate together rather than close to the organisation to which they provide a service is enhanced by the increasing tendency for organisations to 'hive off' such activities in the 1990s. Where organisations buy in producer services such as finance from outside consultants rather than maintaining such services internally, the traditional influences upon manufacturing location become even less important in determining office location.

External, or agglomeration, economies of scale combined with the clustering of head-office activities in major conurbations have left some European economies with highly centralised office markets. Until the 1980s the French office market was dominated by Paris to the virtual exclusion of other cities. In England, London was the dominant office location. Many organisations are attracted to the capital city for their office headquarters' location in order to be in close proximity to political contacts and the national media.

These patterns of locational preference for the capital city resulted in high rent differentials in the office market between the capital and other cities in several European economies. In contrast, the Netherlands office market has traditionally been less centralised. While Amsterdam has been important as an office location, so too have The Hague, Rotterdam and Utrecht.

In France, decentralisation from Paris has been encouraged through office development in other major cities, such as Lyon and Marseille. In England, high costs in London encouraged development in cities such as Bristol. However a new centralising tendency may be occurring in that selected cities, such as Frankfurt, London and Paris, are now viewed as preferred locations in the context of the European rather than the national office market.

For many organisations office costs are not a significant element in total operating costs. For these organisations the costs of their office location is not crucial in terms of overall cost minimisation. This is one reason why the approach to office location put forward by, for example, Bateman may be realistic for some organisations:

> It would be simplistic to offer an explanation for office development in classical bid-rent theory terms, since utility maximisation by an occupier may be a secondary consideration for development to profit maximisation for the financial institutions (Bateman, 1985, p. 3).

In Bateman's view the location of much office development is the outcome of an investment decision taken by the property developer. This investment decision aims to maximise the return on the investor's financial investment. While the financial investor undoubtedly seeks to maximise profits through the financing of office development, the time scale is likely to be long term rather than short term.

Much office development occurs on a speculative basis, a notable example being the new offices built in London Docklands at the beginning of the 1990s. Such offices may be built in response to the locational preferences of the *suppliers* of financial capital to those undertaking the office development rather than in response to existing *demand* for office accommodation at the chosen location. In these circumstances supply is provided in anticipation of future demand. Where the future demand fails to materialise, as in the case of the market for office space in London in the early 1990s, the result is over-supply and financial loss for the speculative developers.

The conditions for short-term profit maximisation as understood in economic theory play little part in this approach to the analysis of the firm's office location. The speculative developer will be keen to select a location that is perceived to be 'safe' in that there is likely to be market demand for the office space at the expected time of completion of the office development. The location of these office developments will therefore be influenced by the wish to minimise risk.

Because offices often represent a low proportion of the organisation's total costs, office location is often 'footloose'. This explains why a market situation in which demand responds to available and potentially available supply can exist in the market for office accommodation. The organisation will often move office activities to existing vacant premises, rather than demanding individual construction and an individual location precisely tailored to their specific requirements. If government policy is to be effective in influencing the interregional location of office activities, these factors underlying office location must be taken into account in the formulation of policy measures.

Retail Location

The spatial location of retail activity has also altered during recent decades in the UK and in comparable EC economies. Increased affluence has meant more shopping is undertaken by consumers; increased mobility has meant that more shopping is undertaken at locations a distance away from the consumer's place of residence. The pattern of retailing has altered, in particular in two ways. First, the scale of retail organisations has increased so that, in addition to small family-owned businesses, there are more national and multinational retailers. Second, in addition to established town-centre retail provision, out-of-town retailing has expanded.

The latter trend has especially important implications for the regional and subregional economy. A proportion of consumer-shopping activity is now being undertaken on a regional and subregional, and not on a local, basis. It can no longer be taken for granted that consumers will make small purchases at their local shop and travel to the nearest city for larger shopping purchases. The cities in a region, or even in adjacent regions, may now be competing for shoppers to a greater extent than in the past.

For example, surveys conducted of shoppers in both the South East and North West of England in 1992 and 1993 indicated that a proportion of shopping trips were undertaken on a regional or interregional basis. About half of a sample of shoppers questioned in Carlisle in the North West of England in December 1992 undertook their main Christmas shopping in the Metrocentre in the North East over fifty miles away. A similar trend was identified in the South East, where shoppers in east Kent travel to Canterbury for major shopping trips (School of Real Estate Management, 1993).

Typically the destinations of these long-distance shopping trips are out-of-town shopping centres. Many of these serve a subregional, and some a regional, catchment area. In England some out-of-town shopping centres have developed at the expense of nearby city centres. For example concern has been expressed over the future of shopping in Sheffield city centre due to nearby Meadowhall centre attracting shoppers away from Sheffield. However the Metrocentre near Newcastle appears to be expanding at the same rate as shopping provision in Newcastle city centre. In drawing shoppers from a fifty-mile, or wider, catchment area regional and subregional out-of-town retailing casts a shadow effect upon other urban areas. For example, in the Newcastle area the Metrocentre at Gateshead has successfully attracted relocating stores from established market towns up to 30–40 miles away (Ibid).

Large stores and out-of-town shopping centres are typically subject to active property management. The general role of property management in organisations' location decisions is considered in the following sections of this chapter. Here we look briefly at the particular application to retail location. As a sector of economic activity, retailing was one of the pioneers of detailed location management. Multistore retailers use sophisticated models to monitor the relative performance of their different stores and establish guidelines for store location.

The details of these models are beyond the scope of this book, but an overview of the general approach is summarised in Table 5.1. This suggests that the factors underlying retail location decisions may be categorised as population; accessibility, competition and costs.

Table 5.1 Main considerations in retail location

Population	Accessibility	Competition	Costs
Size	Pedestrian flow	Direct competition	Purchase price
Age structure	Public transport	Anchor stores	Lease terms
Household size	Car ownership	Compatibility	Building
Income level	Road conditions	Turnover estimates	Planning gain
Occupations	Parking	Design/age	Rates
Employers	Staff access	Parking	Refurbishment
Unemployment	Delivery access	Saturation	Maintenance
Housing type	Visibility	Competitive	Security
Ethnic mix		Potential	Staff
			Turnover loss

Source: adapted from McGoldrick, 1990, p. 161.

The size and structure of the population of the store's potential catchment area is important as it affects demand for the store's range of goods and services.

Suggest one or two ways in which you would expect the size and structure of the population to affect the demand faced by a retailer.

The influence of size is direct: other things being equal, the larger the population located within the store's catchment area the greater the demand. Income levels will affect the nature of demand: a discount store will fare better in an area with relatively low incomes; a store retailing expensive merchandise will fare better in a wealthy catchment area.

Accessibility affects the flow of customers to the store and affects costs, for instance good access will reduce delivery costs. The right-hand column in Table 5.1 identifies some of the main component costs considered by the retailer, primarily relating to the building and to staffing. Finally, the presence of actual and potential competitors will affect the retailer's location decision.

Increasing scale, increasing regionalisation and the increasing professionalisation of retail management have therefore all affected the pattern of retail location emerging in the EC economies in the 1990s. This final point, concerning the management of location, is developed further in the following section.

MANAGEMENT AND THE LOCATION DECISION

This section aims to clarify and explain the role of management in the location and relocation of economic activity. This will help provide an understanding of the framework for the economic analysis of the role of property in respect of management's role in the location decision.

This discussion of the role of management in the location decision is pertinent to the location of economic activity in both the private and the public sectors of the economy. The location of public-sector activity is introduced in the final section of this chapter. The implications of the analysis for the relevant aspects of government regional and location policies are considered in Chapter 8.

The Location Decision and the Economic Environment

Location decisions in larger organisations are generally important enough to be taken at board level on the basis of research information supplied by the research or property department. This is because of the effects of the location decision upon the balance sheet: for example an industrial company's costs will be affected by its location, so the object of the exercise is to minimise these costs.

For multisite organisations where property represents an important element of total costs and/or asset values, the objective may also be to maximise revenue: for example, for retail and office users the value of property held will often be an important element in total assets. In the case of some of the major retailers, the net book value of their property assets is almost as high as the value of their annual turnover.

An organisation relocating in spring 1992 may have taken the decision to relocate in spring 1989. The economic environment that inspired its decision in 1989 would have been very different from that faced in 1992. The two differences in the economic environment between these two years that are most relevant to the organisation's location are relative property costs at the two different times; and the relative cost and availability of labour at the two different times.

For example, an organisation that sought to escape from the rising cost pressures brought on by high property and labour costs in London in the late 1980s might find that it could as easily remain in London or the South East in the early 1990s. Rising unemployment in the area slackened demand in the labour market in 1990–3. The fall in property costs in the region meant that, for example, London Docklands property was available at rents no higher than those in Manchester, Nottingham or Bristol.

While the property market may remain slack until the mid-1990s, not everyone would expect the labour market to do so. Demographic trends reported in the UK 1991 Census mean that the number of people aged 16–35 is likely to fall by about 10 per cent nationally in the 1990s. Once the economy recovers from recession, a relative shortage of skilled labour is generally expected, so the labour market is likely to affect preferred company locations in the UK.

Location and Property-Portfolio Strategies

Organisations' use of land and property as an input into the production process was explained in Chapter 2. In this chapter the spatial implications of property use are investigated more fully.

Organisations employ inputs of the factors of production – capital, labour and land – to contribute to the production of their output. Economists view labour both as a flow of services and as a stock of (human) capital. Similarly, organisations view property both as an operational facility contributing a flow of property services and as a stock of capital representing investment in an asset. Property as an asset is discussed in this section; the spatial effects of operational property management are considered in the section below.

Some organisations' approach to property management is becoming primarily proactive rather than primarily reactive due to a sharper focus upon the costs of property as an operational input. The main catalyst for change in recent years has been the instability associated with the asset value of property, especially in the UK.

Since 1986 the cyclical fluctuation experienced by the property market has been more volatile than that experienced by the economy as a whole. Property values also varied spatially across the economy's regions. In the late 1980s property became a scarce and expensive commodity and property values rose, in particular in certain locations, such as central London. This increased the gap between property values in the South East of England and other regions. In the early 1990s the reverse occurred: supply exceeded demand and property values fell in the South East in real terms.

The effects of this volatility in property values has fed through into organisations' balance sheets. One response has been to separate the management of the property portfolio from the management of the organisation's main activity.

This has two advantages. First, it facilitates measurement of the performance of each operational site on a comparable basis, for example, through the use of actual or imputed rent as a cost. Second, the asset value and investment performance of the properties can be measured on a basis that allows comparison among sites. In that both of these measurements are subject to consistent spatial differences, there are effects upon the regional distribution of location.

Location and investment portfolio strategies

A multisite organisation will seek to maximise the revenue earned from its property. To do this effectively it needs a strategy for the active management of its property portfolio. This strategy should be expressed relative to identifiable criteria. In turn these criteria should be related to, and consistent with, the organisation's overall business plan. Criteria should be expressed as measurable targets, for example, in the case of a retail multiple, the type and number of stores and the desired type of location.

As well as its existing locations, an organisation seeking to expand will need to identify locations in which it would like to be represented. These should then be included in the targets for the business-plan period.

For an organisation with an identifiable and measurable output, potential locations can be identified. Market analyses can be used, drawing upon such variables as the type, physical size and location characteristics of the site as well as the demographic characteristics, income levels and consumption patterns of the target population. The performance of existing locations may be measured by comparison with similar locations in relation to, for instance, levels of sales turnover. While this approach was briefly explained above in relation to retail location, analogous models can be developed for location decisions in other sectors of economic activity.

A portfolio strategy can therefore be developed using marketing analysis to identify suitable locations. By use of clustering techniques, locations with common characteristics can then be identified to enable comparison with similar locations where the organisation currently has sites. These criteria for site identification help to ensure consistency with the overall business plan in terms of sites, their location and their size.

An appraisal of a proposed location may be carried out against specific criteria before a location or relocation decision is taken. Questions the organisation might ask about potential location(s) include:

- Does the site meet with such benchmark criteria as forecast profitability? These benchmarks may be established by analysing the profit record of new locations in the past and their comparable performance.
- After assessing expected total costs against projected total revenue, will the site meet such investment criteria as target net present value?
- Does the new location support the organisation's overall business plan, that is, is this specific location suitable relative to the overall location pattern of the organisation's activities?
- Are the costs of the proposed relocation acceptable?

Consideration of these aspects of the organisation's property-portfolio decision-taking processes again indicates that regional and spatial variations in property costs and variations in the expected profitability of different locations will affect the actual pattern of location of economic activity across the regions of the economy.

Property Management and the Location Decision

The material discussed in these paragraphs draws upon *Property Management Performance Monitoring* (Avis *et al.*, 1993). The Property Management Performance Monitoring project looked in detail at three organisations from different service industries viz banking, retailing and distribution. All three are fully national across the English economy, with little if any regional bias in the sense of regional underrepresentation. All three organise property management through a central unit backed up by regional organisation, and all three regard property management as integral to their decision-making processes. Study of these three organisations was backed by a less detailed investigation of property management in other organisations, including organisations from central and local government as well as the private manufacturing and service sectors.

In organisations with a well-defined property-management strategy, this strategy clearly has implications for the location of their activity. Property has become more than the passive 'place of business': it is expected to make an active contribution to the balance sheet, or at least not to detract from the balance sheet.

In principle an organisation can measure the performance of its property-related activities separately from its other activities. The contribution to costs and revenues made by the land and property in which the production process takes place can therefore be measured independently of the other costs and revenues associated with that process. To take an illustration, retailers can measure the balance-sheet contribution of their retail space independently of the costs and revenue of their overall retail activity. If a manufacturing or retailing organisation finds that the operation of one site is proving more costly than the operation of other comparable sites, that extra cost will enter into the decision as to whether or not to continue to operate the relatively expensive site.

Where property-operating costs and/or property-asset values vary consistently across the different regions and areas of the economy, then there will be an effect upon the regional and spatial distribution of economic activity. Regions with relatively low property-operating costs will be preferred to regions and locations with relatively high property-operating costs. However where the organisation owns, rather than rents, the property it uses, regional differences in property values will affect the yield associated with property as an investment. This regional variation in property values will affect location driven by portfolio-investment considerations.

THE REGIONAL LOCATION OF PUBLIC-SECTOR ACTIVITY

The framework for property management explained above is relevant to the location of public-sector activities in the 1990s. For example, public-sector location in the UK economy is subject to 'value-for-money' financial scrutiny by the National Audit Office:

> In the last ten years there have been significant changes in the way departments and agencies manage land and property. These changes have stemmed from Government initiatives to make managers more aware of and more responsible for the costs of assets (National Audit Office, 1992, p. 13).

Most UK government departments and agencies are now responsible for their own property management. The emphasis is therefore upon maximising competition with the aim of minimising costs. In economic terms the emphasis is upon the attainment of productive or technical efficiency, as defined in Chapter 3 in relation to minimum costs.

In the UK, the past decade has been characterised by the political view that the public sector should become more akin to the private sector, and not only in relation to its property resources. The objective has been to enhance accountability and efficiency in the use of public sector resources. There have been several approaches towards this objective, ranging from privatisation of the main utilities such as gas and electricity to the regulation of public-sector activity and the introduction of private-sector management techniques into the public sector.

One limitation of seeking to compare public-sector management to the private sector in this way is the absence of an effective bankruptcy constraint upon the financial and economic performance of the public sector. On the other hand, it may be argued that management efficiency is unrelated to the public ownership/private ownership divide. The argument is potentially important given the extent of public-sector involvement in all the EC economies. It is also important with regard to the development of joint private–public-sector organisations, especially in countries such as France and the Netherlands.

In the UK the stock of government property is valued at over £50 billion. New acquisition of property by the government departments and agencies is valued at over £5 billion per annum. The value of construction and refurbishment works is over £3.5 billion per annum, and most of this work is contracted out to the private sector (National Audit Office, 1992, p. 13).

The extent of these government property resources and the value of the construction and property-maintenance works carried out in respect of them indicate that location of government property may be associated with significant positive local multiplier impacts. These local multiplier effects may benefit the local construction industry as well as those directly employed inside the buildings.

The presence of public-sector employment may also help to cushion a region against the cyclical effects of recession. An example is the Northern Ireland economy, where unemployment would probably be even higher in the absence of an unusually large proportion of public-sector employment in the region. The potential for public-sector location to serve as an effective instrument of regional policy is developed further in Chapter 8.

References and Further Reading

Armstrong, H. and J. Taylor (1993) *Regional Economics and Policy*, 2nd edn (Brighton: Harvester Wheatsheaf).
Avis, M. *et al.* (1993) *Property Management Performance Monitoring* (Wallingford: GTI Publishers/School of Real Estate Management, Oxford Brookes University).
Balchin, P. N., J. L. Kieve and G. H. Bull (1988) *Urban Land Economics and Public Policy*, 4th edn (London: Macmillan).
Bateman, Michael (1985) *Office Development: A Geographical Analysis* (Beckenham: Croom Helm).
Daniels, P. W. (ed.) (1979) *Spatial Patterns of Office Growth and Location* (Chichester: Wiley).
McGoldrick, P. (1990) *Retail Marketing* (London: McGraw-Hill).
National Audit Office (1992) *Annual Report* (London: HMSO).
Office of Population Census Statistics (1991) *1991 Provisional Figures*.
School of Real Estate Management (1993) unpublished reports (Oxford: Oxford Brookes University).
Smith, David (1994) *North and South*, 2nd edn (London: Penguin), ch. 10.
Townroe, P. M. (1969) 'Locational choice and the individual firm', *Regional Studies*, vol. 3, pp. 15–24.

6 Regional Growth

THE SPATIAL PATTERN OF GROWTH

We have seen earlier in the text that the interregional pattern of activity within the EC economies is spatially uneven. This unevenness is reflected in differences between the levels of income and output of different regions. Within England there are wide variations among regions in levels of income: the South East is one of the richest regions in the EC, while Merseyside in the North West is among the poorest localities in the EC.

The North West of England exhibits the symptoms typical of a region facing economic problems.

> Population and employment are declining, unemployment is high, incomes are low and the region's residents have poor health (Clarke, Gibbs, Brime and Law, 1992, p. 76).

The decline in population in the region in the 1980s was particularly marked in the main cities of Manchester and Liverpool. Many of the government's policy measures have been targeted at these urban areas, as we shall see in Chapter 7. However the region as a whole is experiencing long-term economic difficulties due to the long-term decline in traditional industries such as textiles. The share of service employment in the region has not increased in line with the national average for the UK, leaving the region relatively dependent upon manufacturing employment.

In their survey of the North West region's economic prospects for the 1990s, Clarke *et al.* (ibid.) suggest that the region is in danger of becoming a branch-plant economy, dominated by low-skilled, low-paid employment. The economic difficulties associated with this employment structure are exacerbated by the poor image of the region caused by the dereliction resulting from the decline of its traditional manufacturing base. The concern for the 1990s must be that the region's distance from the south of England and the European mainland will result in further economic decline as the EC becomes more integrated. It is this concern that is the focus of this chapter: will greater European economic integration bring about greater convergence or greater divergence in the growth experience of the EC's different regions?

Figure 6.1 shows that the degree of divergence among the EC economies lies between Greece at 47 per cent of the EC average GDP and Luxembourg, where per capita GDP in 1990 was 23.7 per cent above the EC average. The extent of regional divergence within the EC is even greater.

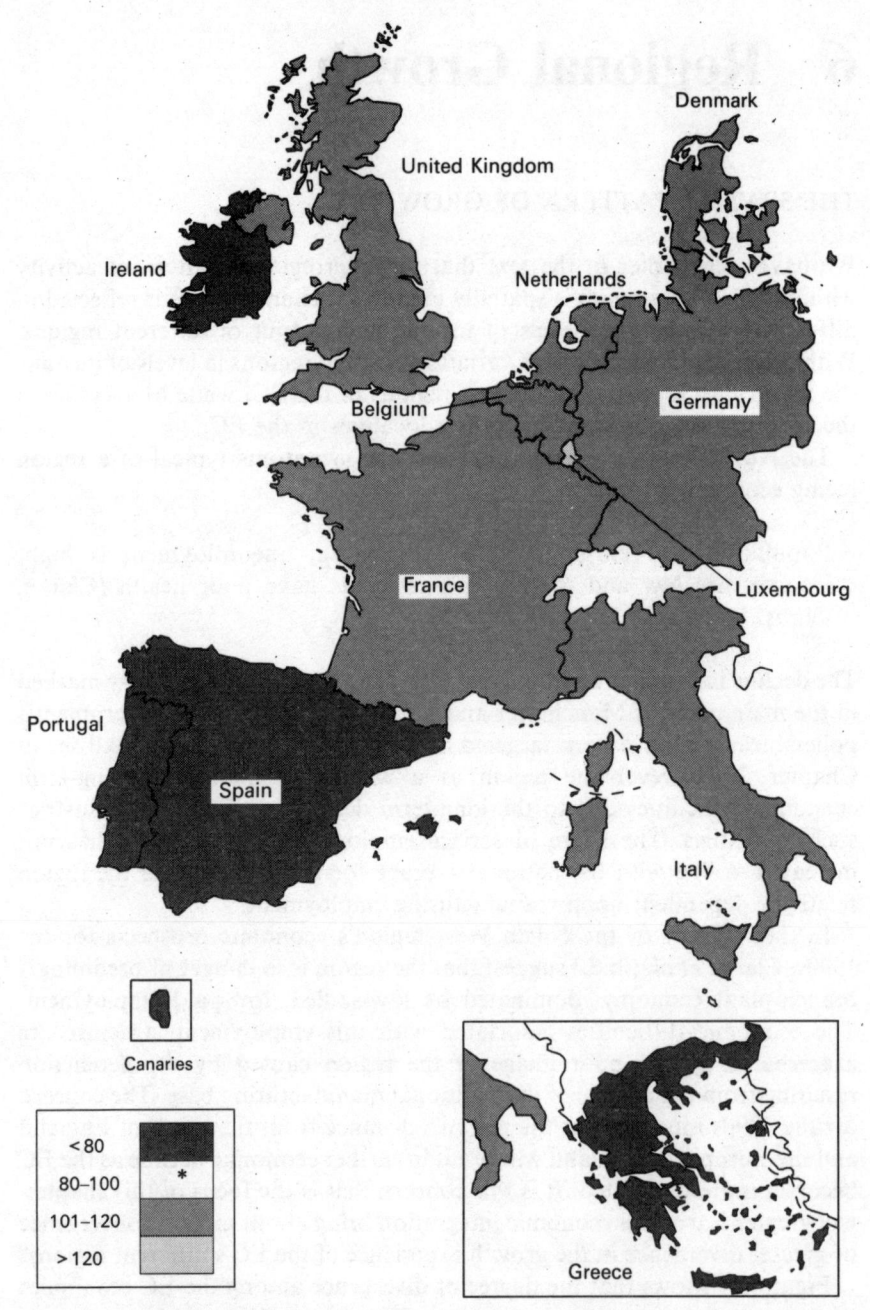

Figure 6.1 GDP per capita, EC economies, 1990, relative to EC average = 100.
*No observations.
Source of data: UK CSO, *Regional Trends* (1993), table 2.1.

There is little difference at the lower income level between regions and economies of the EC because the economies of Greece and Portugal contain little interregional variation. However three regions within the EC have GDP levels more than 50 per cent in excess of the average. These are the regions of Hamburg in Germany, the Ile de France in France and Brussels in Belgium. This type of upward variation in income in regions located in different EC economies has encouraged the concept of 'supranational' EC growth zones, which are discussed later.

To investigate the question of European convergence or divergence more fully, this chapter draws upon the explanation of regional import and export relationships in Chapter 3. It also builds upon the coverage of growth in Chapter 4, applying this specifically to the context of the debate around regional convergence and divergence. The final section of the chapter discusses the extent to which the institutional framework of the housing market may act as a particular constraint upon the growth potential of the constituent regions of the UK economy.

Interregional Trading Linkages

Economic linkages and interaction between different regions and areas occur in a variety of ways. Here we are particularly interested in three. First, there is trade in goods and services, the 'real' exchange of products between regional economies. Second, there are the financial flows generated by this trade, the equivalent of the current-account items in a national balance of payments. This category also includes the 'accommodating' flows of government transfer payments, such as unemployment benefit, which help to correct the interregional payment imbalances discussed earlier. Third, there are investment, or capital, flows: the equivalent of the capital-account items on a national balance of payments. These will be relatively high when a high proportion of the region's capital assets are owned outside the region.

Interregional investment flows help to determine the future structure of output and employment within both the giving and the receiving regions. It is through such flows of investment that best-practice technologies may be disseminated across regions within, for example, the EC. The creation of an internal free-trade area, extended to the much wider concept of a single internal market, is therefore crucial to the future of the economic development of the constituent regions of the EC. The single internal market should encourage greater freedom of movement for capital and investment within the EC boundaries. This should be reflected in increased economic interaction among all countries and regions within the EC.

As stated above, the central concern of this chapter is to look more closely at the likely effects of these stronger linkages upon the growth prospects of the regions within the economies of the EC. It is important to ask whether it matters that these regions were not initially identical in terms of their output and employment structure at the time of the implementation of the single internal market at the beginning of 1993.

Will the likely increase in the level of interregional trade and economic interaction tend to improve the growth rate of the less-well-off regions in the EC, helping to ensure their convergence towards an EC average? Or are these less-well-off regions likely to be left further behind their more prosperous competitors and diverge from the EC average unless serious efforts are made by governments to avoid such an outcome?

What effect may the enlargement of the twelve-member EC to encompass Scandinavia and/or Eastern Europe have upon the answers to these questions?

How may the result of this process be influenced by the predominantly agricultural nature of the economies of some of the less-well-off regions such as Southern Italy and Southern Ireland?

These are all important questions, and they underlie the discussion of the spatial pattern of regional growth in this chapter. They are also highly pertinent to the evaluation of regional policy in Chapter 9. First, the next section discusses the prospects of a region achieving growth through interregional trade, in relation to those EC regions which are predominantly agricultural and have per capita GDP below the EC average.

If a regional economy is predominantly agricultural, it has two main directions in which to proceed in search of future growth. One is to increase the productivity of the existing agricultural sector, so as to raise output and exports of agricultural produce. The alternative is to seek to diversify away from agriculture into other areas of production, that is, into manufacturing or into services such as tourism.

Both these strategies are looked at here: first we consider the possibilities of diversification and then the possible effects of continued agricultural specialisation in the region.

Diversification of the regional agricultural economy

Where the aim is that of diversification away from a predominantly agricultural base, investment will be needed in the capital equipment, buildings and infrastructure required by the new industry. It may be possible to undertake this investment within the region, or the new investment may have to be attracted into the region from outside. Either way the investment will require finance which will have to be resourced.

There are three possible sources for such investment: domestic savings, inward investment from outside the region or public-sector investment. Where domestic savings in either the private or the local-government sector are not readily forthcoming, the region will need to attract inward investment through either private companies or government agencies.

Inward investment has the advantage of contributing to the amount of effective savings upon which the regional economy can draw to finance its growth. Where private-sector firms invest, and later follow their initial investment with further injections of investment expenditure, the benefits will continue and increase in the longer term.

Two disadvantages of such inward investment should be offset against these potential benefits. First, the funds invested may be financed by a loan that is subject to interest payments that flow out of the region. The potential disadvantages of such interest-bearing debt are discussed below. Second, economic activity financed from outside the regional economy may also be effectively controlled from outside that economy, creating the branch-plant regional economic dependence identified in regions such as the North West of England and Scotland.

External control of the regional economy may be perceived as problematic for either economic and/or political reasons. In the case of a region receiving substantial inward investment, such as the investment into the Scottish oil industry, some would question whether the Scottish economy has benefited from stronger links to the investing economy, for example England. The critical view is that the investing economy exploits the host economy by increasing its economic control over the host economy and subordinating its welfare to that of the investing economy. The result is a regional economy that may find itself unduly dependent upon another region for its continued prosperity.

This view that partnership in economic relationships is fundamentally unequal may be stronger where the less-equal partner is particularly vulnerable during periods of recession. As we have already seen, regional economies typified by a large number of branches, rather than headquarters, of organisations may experience above-average vulnerability to unemployment and cutbacks. Equally, a region that is heavily dependent upon the export earnings from a single primary product, whether this is agricultural or an energy resource such as oil, may find that its export revenues are cyclically vulnerable.

The effects of inward investment If external investment into a region is not self-evidently beneficial to the region receiving the investment, what are the main potential costs and benefits that the receiving region should consider?

The present advantages of the initial inflow of funds to the region will have to be balanced against the potential future outward stream of profits to private companies, or interest payments and tax receipts to government and public-sector agencies. This means that the terms upon which inward investment is available will be crucial to its long-term value to the receiving region. Upon what conditions is the incoming finance being offered? For example, will the flow of interest payments out of the regional economy be unduly high? If the investment is subject to strict conditions, the likelihood of the region becoming increasingly economically dependent upon the donor region is increased.

In some circumstances a high level of imports may be needed in the short term to achieve the planned diversification of the economy in the longer term. For example, the making of cars requires plant and machinery which may have to be imported into the region where the car assembly is to take place. If this is so, the impact of these short-term increased imports upon the overall level of economic activity that can be sustained in the region will have to be considered.

If the inward investment is being financed by the private sector, is it likely to be stable in the longer term? Or will private investors withdraw their investment in the face of a short-term lack of profitability during a cyclical recession? In other words, will a new factory or office be a subsidiary branch liable to closure under recessionary conditions? The region anticipating receipt of inward investment should assess whether the investor believes that it provides an attractive long-term location or just a short-term financial expedient.

Continued regional agricultural specialisation

This strategy implies the building up of an existing base, such as agriculture, so may be less resource-intensive in the short term than that of immediate diversification. In this case investment will be needed to finance the new capital equipment required to generate higher levels of productivity and output. Strategies may also be needed to encourage the restructuring of land holdings into larger, more cost-effective units of agricultural production. The overall aim will be to increase agricultural output, and therefore to produce a greater tradeable surplus of agricultural output for export.

Increased exports of the main agricultural product or products should then provide earnings from which to finance increased investment in agriculture, or in a different sector. The revenue earned from exports will be critical as a source of additional finance and income to the regional economy. The extent of this revenue will depend not only upon the quantity of agricultural output produced and sold, but also upon the *value* at which it can be sold in the export market.

As was suggested above, one disadvantage of building economic development upon the expansion of agriculture or another primary-sector industry such as oil, is the potential instability of primary-product prices. Primary products typically have relatively inelastic conditions of both demand and supply, as illustrated in Figure 6.2.

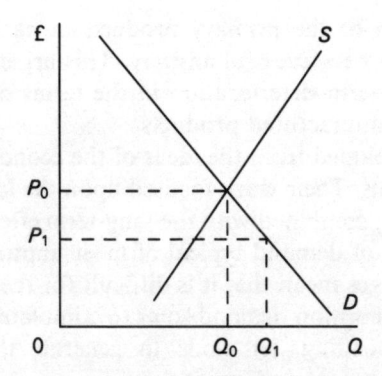

Figure 6.2 Characteristic market conditions for a primary product

The combination of the inelastic demand and inelastic supply conditions that are characteristic of the market for many primary products means that any change in price has little short-term effect upon the quantity demanded or supplied. The market adjusts mainly through changes in price, therefore, and experiences relatively little change in the quantity traded. Where the product is exported, the result may be fluctuating export revenues for the exporting economy in the face of unstable prices for its key export commodity.

In addition to its effect upon revenue earnings, this instability makes it difficult for producers to plan ahead. In turn this uncertainty may act as a deterrent to investment in the primary-product industry affected and so reduce overall investment in the economy.

The economic effects of such potential price and revenue instability may be countered by government-operated price-stabilisation schemes and/or income-support schemes for agricultural producers. Schemes such as the EC's Common Agricultural Policy help to reduce uncertainty for farmers and act as a further mechanism for resource transfer into some of the EC's poorer regions. Price- and income-support schemes, however, do not in themselves serve to offset the tendency for many areas of agriculture to produce in conditions of relatively low income and low value-added, possibly with limited prospects of enhanced growth. These limited growth prospects may be further restricted by the underlying trends in the terms of trade discussed below.

Regional Growth and the Terms of Trade

We have seen above that the price at which the regional economy's main export(s) can be sold is important due to its influence upon the region's export earnings. Some economists would argue that a development strategy based upon expansion of the primary product, in particular agricultural products is unlikely to be successful anyway. This argument is justified by observation of a long-term deterioration in the terms of trade of primary products relative to manufactured products.

This hypothesis developed from the ideas of the economists Prebisch and Singer in the early 1950s. Their work focused upon the low wages typical of agricultural economies, combined with the long-term effects of the relatively low income elasticities of demand typical of most unprocessed foodstuffs.

Low agricultural wages mean that it is difficult for the agricultural sector to generate extra consumption demand so as to stimulate the local economy through additional spending, let alone to generate the surplus income needed to finance investment and expansion.

If we assume that the income elasticity of demand for agricultural produce in general is low, what will happen to the demand for agricultural produce as incomes increase?

Low income elasticity of demand means that, as incomes in general rise, the demand for agricultural produce will fail to match that rate of expansion. So an economy that plans to expand through the medium of its agricultural sector is not likely to succeed.

This view is further supported by the observation that most of the expansion of international and interregional trade within the EC in recent decades has been in manufactured goods. This trade expansion has been demand led as producers have supplied an increasing variety of similar but differentiated manufactured goods in response to the increasing sophistication of consumer demands. The expansion of trade in cars among the main economies of the EC offers a useful example of this trend: the basic product is often similar, but individual models are carefully differentiated by the producers.

The Prebisch–Singer argument was propounded primarily with regard to international trading relationships between the less developed economies and the rest of the world. However it also indicates some pitfalls to be avoided by the regional economy attempting to expand within the EC. It must be noted that some regions in Europe have successfully developed a high-income, high-productivity agricultural sector, for example East Anglia in England. Those economies with low-income farm sectors may need to restructure their agricultural sector so as to encourage and make possible its transformation into the highly capital intensive agricultural production that is associated with high-value-added, high-income agricultural output.

The expansion of the EC

The economic restructuring described above was assisted in the EC during the 1970s and 1980s by financial support from the EC budget, especially through the European Regional Development Fund (ERDF). While the operation of the ERDF is discussed more fully below and in Chapter 8, it is worth noting here that the unification of Germany significantly affected the EC balance sheet for the 1990s.

In the late 1980s the ERDF was well-supported financially by West Germany as part of that country's encouragement of economic and monetary union across the EC. However since unification there has been less room for manoeuvre in the German economy. The German authorities are having difficulty in keeping overall public expenditure under control. The need to control internal government expenditure and to finance the internal development of the former East Germany is reflected in a less expansive attitude towards supplying funds for regional development to the other EC economies.

The geography of the EC may well alter further in the second half of the 1990s as Austria, Finland, Norway and Sweden are all considering membership. The existing EC members have also made a commitment to open their markets more fully to Eastern European output, and to consider extending membership in the longer term to include Bulgaria, the Czech Republic, Hungary, Poland, Romania and Slovakia. Such an extension north and east may affect the processes of spatial growth and development in the EC that are the focus of this chapter.

CONVERGENCE AND DIVERGENCE

Core and Periphery in the EC Regions

The increasing internationalisation of the European capital market was noted in Chapter 2. London's role as an international financial centre has encouraged the continuing involvement of British firms in the development of industrial and commercial activity in Western Europe, a trend accelerated by the lack of market opportunities in the UK economy during the 1990–2 recession. The role of Paris and Frankfurt in the European financial capital markets has had a similar effect. This provides just one example of the ways in which economic ties have been increasing and strengthening within the member economies of the EC. And it must be remembered that this heightened level of economic interaction is now taking place within the context of a potentially wider single market than that implied by the boundaries of the twelve member states of the EC.

What implications does this have for the spatial pattern of economic development, and so for the regions in the UK and Europe, in the 1990s? We need to consider whether there are pressures for equality that will ensure the convergence of levels of economic activity and income within the constituent regions of the EC. The strength of these convergent pressures must be weighed against pressures that may favour some areas at the expense of others, so that the EC experiences greater *divergence* in the economic experience of the regions within its boundaries. The peripheral regions of the UK such as Northern Ireland, Scotland, Wales and the South West of England, are concerned that their location on the edge of the EC will result in relative economic decline in the absence of positive policy action to prevent such a trend. Figure 6.3 shows those peripheral regions that are in receipt of support from the EC Regional Development Fund under Objective 1 funding. While policy initiatives such as this are considered in Chapter 8, this chapter asks: how realistic are concerns about the 'peripheralisation' of the regions that happen to be located around the edge of the EC?

Regional Convergence

The European Regional Development Fund (ERDF)

Before considering the market forces that could contribute to interregional convergence in the EC, these paragraphs will briefly introduce the role of EC regional policy, primarily administered through the European Regional Development Fund (ERDF).

The harmonisation of taxes, and of the level and direction of government subsidies to industry, will contribute to the harmonisation of costs of production and income levels throughout the different regions of the EC. In the harmonisation process, the member economies should move in a convergent direction with respect to these costs. A further important influence contributing to convergence in the income of the regions of the EC is the ERDF.

The ERDF was created in 1975 and expanded during the 1980s, especially after 1988. By the end of the decade it was recognised as having an important role to play in partnership with members' national and regional political authorities in the funding of projects designed to help overcome structural regional economic imbalance.

Regional policy expenditure administered through the ERDF now forms a major component of overall EC expenditure. ERDF grants are a major source of finance for the provision of the improved infrastructure needed to facilitate the development and growth of the small peripheral EC economies such as Greece, the Republic of Ireland and Portugal. By collecting tax revenue from the richer regions of the EC and using the revenue to fund expenditure in its poorer regions, the central EC budget may serve to increase equality in income between the component regions of the member states.

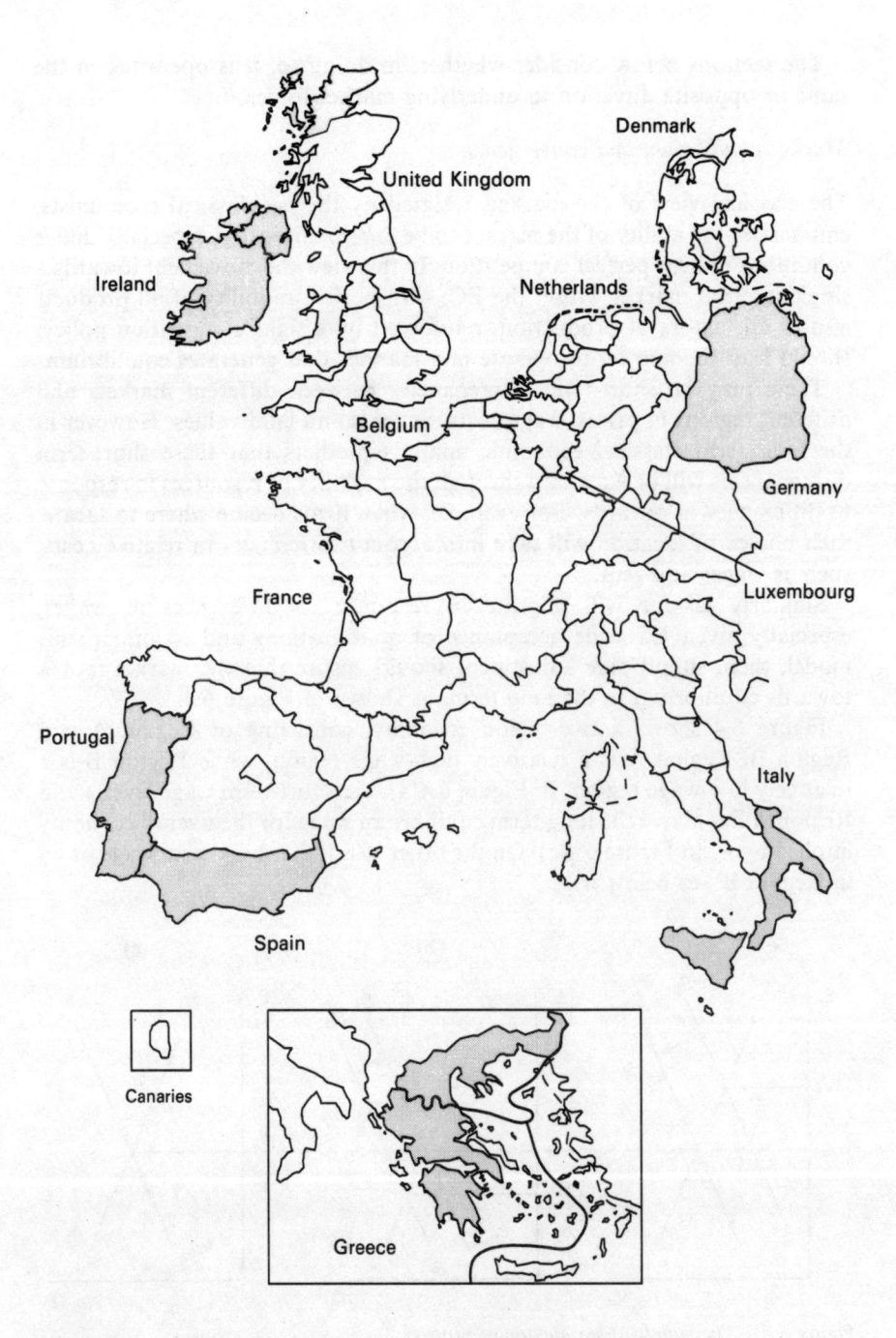

Figure 6.3 Peripheral regions in receipt of EC Objective Funding, 1993

The sections below consider whether, in doing so, it is operating in the same or opposite direction to underlying market forces.

Market equilibrium and convergence

The classical view of the market, restated by the neoclassical economists, emphasises the ability of the market to be *self-equilibrating*, especially under conditions of near perfect competition. In this view the movement towards a single internal market within the EC, with perfect mobility of all products and of all factors of production, reinforced by a tight competition policy, should lead the market to operate in a manner that generates equilibrium.

There may be short-term discrepancies between different markets and different regions in prices, wage costs, or rents and land values. However in the long term classical economic analysis predicts that these short-term discrepancies will be equalised through the mobility of resources in response to differences in rewards. For example, when firms decide where to locate, their choice of location will take into account differences in relative costs, such as wages and rent.

Similarly labour will migrate in response to differences in wages, especially given EC wide acceptance of qualifications and so on. In this model, then, supply-side adjustment should ensure that the market moves towards equilibrium in the long term, as shown in Figure 6.4.

Figure 6.4 shows a two-region economy, consisting of Region A and Region B. Region A is a relatively high-wage region, while Region B is a relatively low-wage region. In Figure 6.4(a), the short-term wage level, w_1 in Region A lies above the long-term equilibrium wage for the overall economy implied by w_e in Figure 6.4(c). On the other hand, the short-term wage of w_2 in Region B lies below w_e.

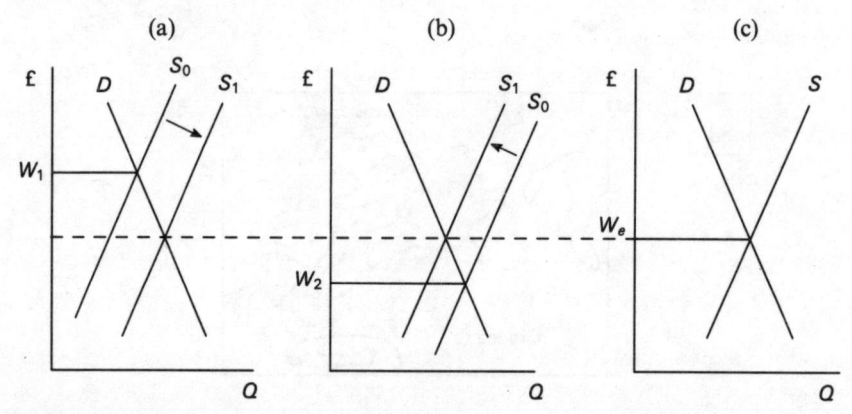

Figure 6.4 The supply-side adjustment process:
(a) short term, Region A; (b) short term, Region B; (c) long term

For the long-term equilibrium wage, of w_e, to be attained, certain assumptions must hold. First, the labour market for the economy as a whole must operate in such a way that information about these interregional differentials is readily available to labour in both regions. Second, labour must be homogeneous between the regions, so that the employer has no reason to prefer labour from one to labour from the other region. Third, labour must be mobile between the two regions.

Once these conditions are satisfied, the higher wage, w_1, in Region A will attract migrants from Region B. Labour supply into the high-wage Region A will increase, so depressing the equilibrium market wage in that region. Conversely labour will emigrate from Region B in search of higher wages in Region A, so reducing labour supply in Region B. The interregional migration of labour is important in the process of interregional economic adjustment, so is explained more fully in a later section of this chapter. For the present we can note that, if adjustment does occur in the long term, the equilibrium in Figure 6.4(c) will be attained for both regions.

Regional Divergence

The section above considered the possibility that interregional disequilibrium would be self-correcting in such a way that convergent wages, and prices, would be established between different regions. However the market may fail to adjust in this way, as evidenced by the persistence of such regional differences as the north–south divides of the UK and Italian economies.

The analysis in the section above assumed, among other things, that the factors of production, that is, land, labour and capital, were homogeneous between regions in the economy. It practice, they may actually be heterogeneous and not homogeneous, or they may be *perceived* to be heterogeneous and not homogeneous, as explained in earlier chapters. This section explores the main effect of such actual or perceived factor heterogeneity on a region's growth potential.

Perceived risk

Managers are professionals employed to generate profits: most are consequently risk-averse in their decision-taking behaviour. Where management decisions involve investment in property and/or land, most professional managers will look to locations characterised by current or expected growth and expansion, as explained in Chapter 5. As a result locations that are known to be 'safe' are likely to be favoured over unknown, 'unsafe' locations due to the higher level of risk associated with the latter. In the EC economies, locations in the Republic of Ireland, Greece or former East Germany may be rejected in favour of established centres such as former West Germany, Northern Italy or the UK.

Some regions are likely to benefit from this risk-minimising approach by management and may receive cumulative inward investment and expansion. Conversely other regions may lose and these disadvantaged regions may experience cumulative loss of investment and expansion.

Stigmatised locations

In reality, individual units of the factors of production, including labour, are neither actually nor perceived to be homogeneous but are heterogeneous, as explained earlier. In other words, their *quality* is actually and/or perceived to be variable.

One result of this is that locations and regions may be distinguished as 'attractive' or 'unattractive' to employers of these factors of production, their relative attraction depending upon both the common perception and the actual quality of the labour, land and capital available there.

In Chapter 4 we discussed the effects of differential labour productivity between regions upon relative wages and employment. We draw here upon this earlier explanation to explore the effects of differences in the quality of the available factors of production upon the region deemed to be attractive and that deemed to be unattractive.

One initial effect, illustrated in Figure 6.5, is that the attractive region benefits from new investment. This new investment raises the marginal value product (mvp) of the capital employed in the region from $\text{mvp}k_e$, the average for the whole economy, to $\text{mvp}k_a$. This higher capital productivity enhances the financial return to capital, shown by both the upward movement from e_e to e_a along the vertical axis and the amount of capital that can be profitably employed, shown by the movement from q_1 to q_2 along the horizontal axis. The relative extent of these effects upon the earnings of the factor of production and upon the quantity of the factor employed will be determined by the relative elasticities of the demand and supply curves.

One important outcome of this analysis affects the factors of production employed in conjunction with the more productive capital in the attractive region. The production process involves combining inputs of capital, labour and land to produce output. As a result, more productive capital is also likely to raise the potential productivity of labour. The enhanced mvp of capital shown in Figure 6.5 is therefore likely to be accompanied by a similar increase in the mvp of labour, which should be reflected in increased wages in the region. The effects of this on the two regions are outlined below.

Regional Growth

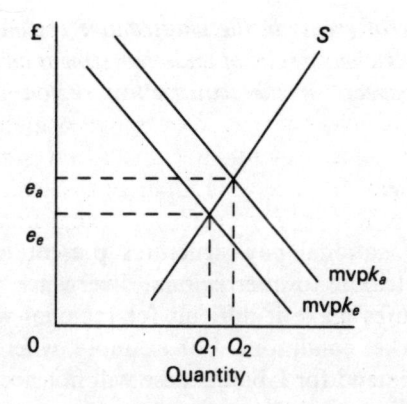

Figure 6.5 Investment-led expansion in the attractive region

Attractive region	Unattractive region
New investment:	*Lack of investment:*
– higher marginal value product of factors of production;	– lower marginal value product of factors of production;
– higher income;	– lower income;
– higher expenditure;	– lower expenditure;
– higher profits;	– lower profits;
– new investment;	– lack of investment;
– 'virtuous circle'.	– 'vicious circle'.

This sequence demonstrates the cumulative nature of the benefit to the attractive region, which experiences a virtuous circle of investment-led growth and expansion. New investment raises the mvp of capital in the region. This has beneficial spillover effects on the mvp of complementary production factors.

So there is the potential for higher income. Higher income brings potentially higher expenditure in the region, subject to the regional 'leakage' effects of such influences as expenditure on items imported into the region. (We saw in Chapter 3 that these leakages reduce the value of the regional multiplier to a value less than that we would expect for a national economy.)

Higher expenditure within the region will generate a positive multiplier effect upon the regional economy, so enhancing the profitability of firms in the region. Higher profitability provides the finance and the confidence upon which managements base their investment decisions. This means that there is likely to be further new investment in the attractive region and the virtuous circle continues.

Note the sequence of events in the unattractive region and make sure you understand how a 'vicious circle' of underinvestment can continue to depress the economic prospects of the unattractive region that fails to attract investment.

National pay structures

The predominantly national pay structures present in many of the EC economies also contribute to interregional divergence. This arises because national pay structures make it difficult for regional wage rates to reflect regional labour-market conditions. For example, where there are regional differences in the demand for labour, these will not necessarily be reflected in regional wage differentials if wages are set at a common national level.

The effect of such rigidity between regional labour markets due to national pay structures may be exacerbated by the wage-bargaining process. Let us take the example of a hypothetical national economy consisting of two regions. Region A has near-full employment of resources, best-practice technologies in production and high productivity. Region B has industries characterised by older technology, lower productivity and higher unemployment than those in Region A.

The wage-bargaining structure is primarily national, based upon collective bargaining between nationally organised trades unions and nationally organised employers' organisations. The unions' negotiating position is strengthened in the national collective bargaining forum by the near-full employment in Region A. Employers in this region are likely to be experiencing shortages of labour with certain skills and to be having difficulty in attracting and retaining some groups of labour. Their concerns with regard to potential labour shortages help the trades unions to negotiate wage rates reflecting the high productivity in Region A.

The national collective bargaining agreement also applies to Region B, although the newly agreed wage rates may be in excess of those suggested by its regional labour market conditions. The cost competitiveness of Region B is adversely affected by this process. In this example the national pay structure prevents the regional labour market from equilibrating at the lower wage rate needed to move towards regional convergence through the market.

The transmission of Region A's relatively high wages to Region B highlights the problems caused by extensive interregional disparities where there is national pay determination. The potential inflationary cost pressures generated by such interregional disparities underlines the undesirability of persistent interregional inequality for the overall performance of the labour market and the economy.

The above simplified example perhaps exaggerates reality. In some instances the nationally negotiated rate becomes an effective minimum, with bonus productivity payments creating local differences in wage rates to reflect local labour-market conditions. Nor are all the labour force covered by collective bargaining agreements.

However one major group of workers covered by national collective bargaining in most of the European economies are those in the public sector. Public-sector pay is usually negotiated nationally with comparatively inflexible pay structures. In the UK for example, the only major variation on national civil-service wage rates designed to reflect local labour market conditions has been the additional London 'weighting' or allowance. Consequently a civil-service office moving from London is able to reduce its existing wage bill. However a similar move from the South West of England to the North or Scotland may yield few labour-cost savings, as we shall see in the relevant section of Chapter 8.

Economies of scale

Economies of scale may be internal or external: both are important sources of potential growth, and both tend to have a cumulative effect upon the generation of output.

Internal economies help to generate expansion of the individual organisation through the reduction in unit costs obtained as the scale of output is increased. Internal economies of scale occur in relation to such costs as those associated with finance and marketing as well as the production process used by the firm.

External economies help accelerate the expansion of particular locations and regions, as is explained elsewhere in this book. External, or agglomeration, economies associated with particular regions or urban centres will encourage a cumulative growth process. The processes of invention and innovation are often associated with agglomeration economies.

The contribution of internal and external economies of scale to growth may increase the concentration or polarisation of growth and economic expansion into certain areas, or growth zones, and away from disadvantaged regions. Potential disadvantaged regions and potential growth zones in the EC are discussed more fully in the following sections of this chapter.

Growth Zones and the Periphery

Growth zones

One possible outcome of the process of divergence in the spatial pattern of growth within the EC is the creation of a supranational growth zone within the EC. One favoured area for such a supranational European growth zone is known as *La Dorsale*. *La Dorsale*, the spine, runs from London through

Frankfurt to Rome, as shown on Figure 6.6. If external, or agglomeration, economies of scale are generated in this core of the EC and the zone does become the favoured location for future growth and economic development, then the divergence of the EC into core and periphery could become extreme.

The growth-zone model emphasising *La Dorsale* is more popular with the Germans than the French for reasons of geography (Figure 6.6). The French prefer the concept of east–west supranational growth zones across the EC: a northern zone from Paris to Frankfurt to Berlin, and a southern zone from Barcelona to Marseilles to Rome, as shown on Figure 6.7, sometimes referred to as the *Arc Mediterranean*.

The periphery

If the core of the EC does generate significant agglomeration economies of scale and an above-average rate of economic growth, then the question arises as to the future of the regions in the EC that represent the periphery at maximum distance from the core. This periphery includes such regions as southern Italy, much of Greece, southern Spain, the Republic of Ireland and much of Scotland.

This section looks in more detail at the recent experience of one of these peripheral areas, namely the Republic of Ireland. The discussion is related to the question of alternative growth strategies through the agricultural sector or through structural economic diversification that was raised in the opening section of this chapter.

The Republic of Ireland is a good example of an EC area that is frequently perceived as peripheral. It also has its own strong cultural identity, history and language. Within the country there is a clear regional division between the area around the capital city, Dublin, and the remaining areas of the country.

The Republic of Ireland is the poorest economy in the northern part of the EC and has been identified as suffering from a combination of structural economic weaknesses. Walsh (1992, p. 127) summarises the main problems of the Republic of Ireland economy as follows:

- Locational disadvantage due to its lying on the periphery of the EC.
- Too centralised an economy with over a third of the population living in and around the capital city, Dublin, and little decentralisation of political and economic control away from Dublin.
- Too fast an increase in the labour supply relative to the demand for labour, resulting in relatively high unemployment in spite of high rates of emigration.
- Inadequate indigenous investment in industry.

175

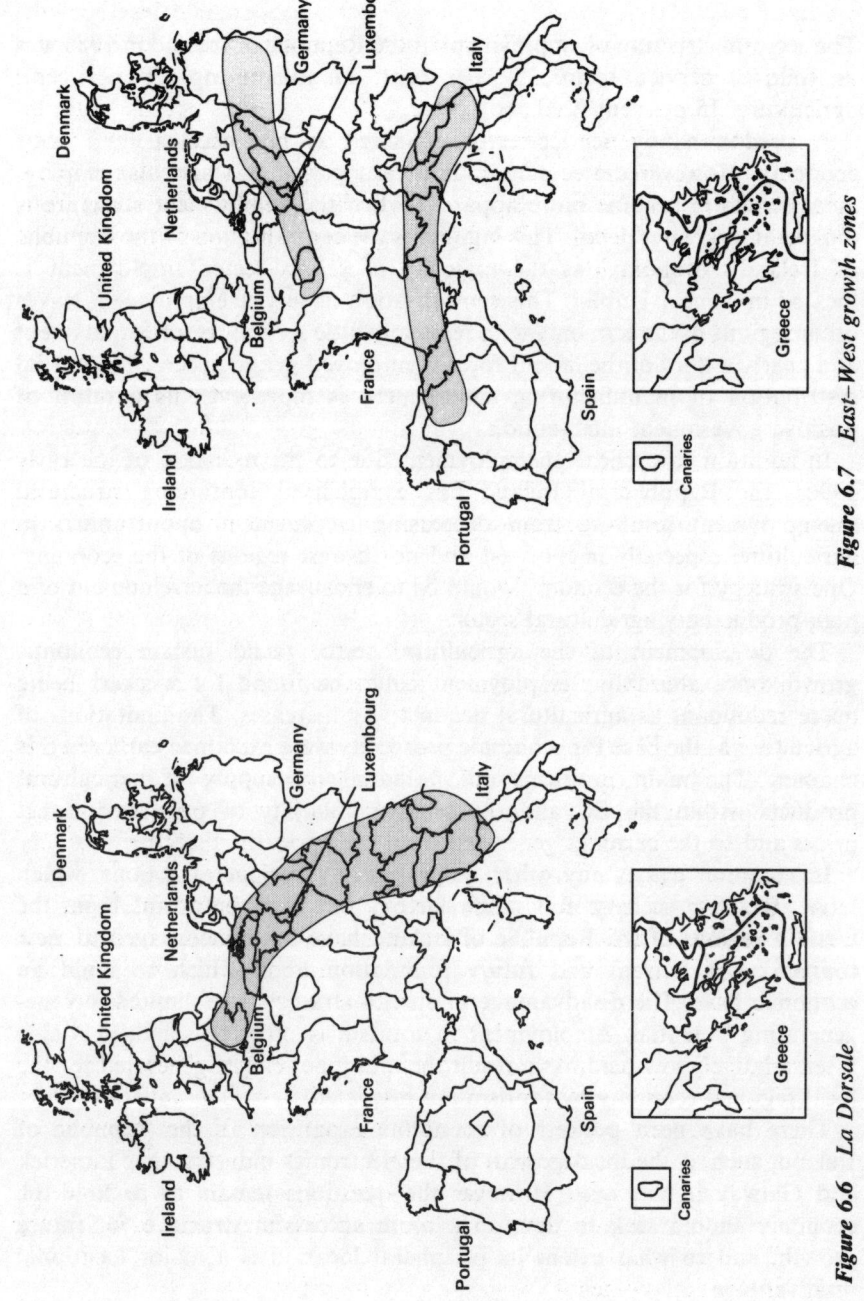

Figure 6.7 East–West growth zones

Figure 6.6 La Dorsale

❏ High domestic government expenditure relative to tax revenue resulting in government indebtedness.

The sectoral structure of employment in the Republic of Ireland in 1988 was as follows: service sector, 57 per cent; manufacturing, 28 per cent; agriculture, 15 per cent (ibid., p. 128).

A predominantly service-sector economy is not necessarily a poor economy. However the economic disadvantages of this paticular employment structure become more apparent when the employment structure is looked at in greater detail. This highlights the centralisation of the Republic of Ireland's economy, as the majority of service-sector employment is located in or near Dublin. This centralisation of service employment leaves other regions of the economy with relatively little service-sector employment and nearly a third of the labour force is employed in agriculture. The spatial distribution of manufacturing employment is more even as a result of positive government intervention.

In addition to cyclical unemployment due to the recession of the early 1990s, the Republic of Ireland has experienced continuing structural unemployment resulting from decreasing employment opportunities in agriculture, especially in the west and north-west regions of the economy. One strategy for the economy would be to encourage the development of a high-productivity agricultural sector.

The development of the agricultural sector could sustain economic growth once alternative employment could be found for workers being made redundant as agricultural productivity increases. The limitations of agriculture as the base for economic prosperity were explained earlier in this chapter. The main problems are potential oversupply of agricultural products within the EC and the relative volatility of primary product prices and so the earnings generated from the agricultural sector.

In common with many other geographically peripheral regions, which have attractive scenery and much history but little industrial base, the western regions of the Republic of Ireland have been encouraged to view tourism as a current and future foundation upon which to build an economic base. The disadvantage of such a strategy is its limited income-generating potential. Employment in tourism is often seasonal; it is also often relatively low paid. As a result the multiplier effects generated for the local regional economy by tourism are restricted.

There have been pockets of economic expansion in the Republic of Ireland, such as the local growth of the electronics industry near Limerick and Galway in the west. However the questions remain as to how the economy should seek to develop a more successful structure for future growth, and to what extent its peripheral location is a major locational disadvantage.

GROWTH AND THE REGIONAL LABOUR MARKET

Labour Mobility

This section develops further the earlier analysis of the regional labour market. Chapter 2 introduced the basic analysis of the regional labour market. In Chapter 4 the emphasis was upon the mechanisms of price adjustment in the regional labour market to restore equilibrium in the face of structural imbalance in the market. This section addresses the role of interregional labour mobility as a means of achieving interregional labour-market adjustment through changes in the labour supply, that is, the quantity rather than the price of labour. Later, in Chapter 9, the relative merits of regional policy measures designed to encourage interregional labour mobility are considered.

There are a number of different ideas contributing to our understanding of patterns of labour mobility through interregional migration. These are considered below as a prelude to looking at migration patterns in the UK and the particular impact of the housing market upon interregional migration in this economy compared with similar European economies.

Explaining interregional labour migration

The classical view In the classical labour-market model the regional labour market is self-equilibrating. This means that interregional differences in wage rates provide the incentive to interregional flows of migrants to restore market equilibrium. In other words, the appearance of premium, high wage rates in one region will attract inmigrants. This increases the supply of labour in that region, so depressing the wage rate until equilibrium is restored.

This model assumes perfect competition in the regional labour market if the market adjustment process is to function effectively. It therefore predicts that there will be more migration the more closely the regional labour market does corresponds to the perfect-competition model.

What assumptions would need to be satisfied for these conditions of perfect competition (and maximum labour mobility) to be achieved in the regional labour market?

We can identify five main assumptions:

❑ That the supply of labour to the market is perfectly elastic.
❑ That there are no costs attached to interregional mobility (neither financial nor social).

- ❑ That there are no other barriers to entry into and exit from regional labour markets.
- ❑ That wages are flexible so that interregional wage differences reflect relative conditions of demand and supply for labour.
- ❑ That perfect information is available to both migrant labour and employers.

These conditions are not fulfilled in practice: for instance labour is not perfectly elastic in supply, nor is information perfect. Interregional migration does not therefore operate as a perfect market-clearing mechanism. This means that, while the classical view of the labour market helps to illuminate a view of interregional migration, it does not provide us with a complete picture.

Human capital and interregional migration In the classical view, the decision whether or not to migrate is taken in response to information concerning immediate relative interregional wage rates. In contrast the human-capital view sees interregional migration as a labour market investment decision, rather than a labour-market consumption decision.

The benefits of migration in terms of enhanced income accrue over time, rather than immediately, and so the rational migration decision maker will evaluate these benefits over time in deciding whether or not to migrate. Migration may yield benefits in terms of enhanced income, but it also involves costs. Some of these costs are financial, such as the cost of housing, considered separately in a later section. Another important cost, especially to the first-time migrant, is the social cost of leaving family and friends.

The rational interregional migration decision then becomes analogous to other human-capital investment decisions. The objective is to maximise the present discounted value of the lifetime earnings stream. The decision maker should assess the expected costs and benefits associated with the migration decision over the appropriate time-horizon. If the discounted value of the stream of expected benefits is positive, the migration should be undertaken.

The decision maker in this context may be an individual or a household. While the number of single-person households is increasing, migration decisions in households with two or more earners may be the outcome of a joint decision-making process. This will be particularly true where more than one earner has relatively specific labour-market skills.

Migration and employment opportunities So far this discussion has considered interregional migration flows as a response to interregional wage and earning differentials. Interregional migration also occurs in response to differential regional employment opportunities. In other words, if jobs are readily available in a region migrants will be attracted there. If jobs are not readily available and unemployment is high, migrants will not be attracted there.

This last point offers a straightforward explanation for observed cyclical variations in interregional migration. In times of cyclical recession migrants do not leave depressed regions in large numbers to go to the usually prosperous regions. As the latter are also relatively depressed and lacking in job opportunites there is no incentive to migrate. Once the level of economic activity increases and employment opportunities improve, interregional migration will increase to take advantage of the improved supply of jobs in the buoyant region.

Migration and the life cycle Individuals' migration activity may also be affected by the stage in their life cycle. A very simplistic three stage model will help to outline the main points in this context.

In the first stage young people are seeking their first job, or a better job. Their decision to migrate is likely to be heavily influenced by interregional wage differentials and differential employment opportunities and job prospects.

In the second stage interregional migration may be the result of employer direction. The extent to which employers move labour between regions will depend upon staffing and promotion policies, but will also be influenced by the level of economic activity. Such moves are more likely in a time of expansion than in a period of recession.

In the third stage migrants may be retiring and seeking to return either to their region of origin or to one formerly resided in. This preference for a known region reflects a combination of the lower information costs associated with such knowledge and the benefits of familiarity with the area of destination.

Interregional labour migration in the UK in the 1980s

The UK 1991 Census indicated a significant decrease in the population of industrial conurbations, especially Merseyside, Greater Manchester and the West Midlands. The population of Greater London had also decreased by about 32 000 per annum. While this represents a decline in the population of Greater London of about 5 per cent, this was much lower than the 10 per cent outmigration recorded for the 1970s by the 1981 Census.

This depopulation of traditional urban centres in the UK reflects the 'urban–rural shift' of population and employment discussed in Chapter 2. It also provides an important part of the explanation for the priority accorded by government to the urban policies considered in Chapter 7.

Two types of town experienced above-average population increases in the UK during the 1980s. The first group were the new towns, such as Milton

Keynes. The second group mainly consists of the towns along the south coast of Hampshire and Dorset that attract retirement-age groups.

We saw above that the rate of migration varies directly with the level of economic activity. The rate of migration within the UK remained relatively stable during the first half of the 1980s. However it increased along with the level of economic activity in the mid-1980s, peaking at nearly two million moves in 1987–8.

While we saw above that the population of Greater London decreased during the 1980s, the population of the rest of the South East region increased (although by only about half the rate at which people were leaving London). The other main receiving region was the South West.

When the pattern of UK migration is broke down into age group, 16–24 year-olds were the most mobile age group during the 1980s. This age group also tended to be attracted to the South East. However, while the population of Wales increased during the 1980s, except in the South Wales industrial areas of Gwent and Glamorgan, 16–24 year-olds tended to emigrate from the principality.

The interregional migration pattern revealed by the 1991 Census yields some interesting results. The largest flow of outmigrants was from the South East of England. The main destination region was the South West, with relatively small flows to the UK outer regions. The same pattern applies to migration into the South East, which was mainly from the South West. Migration to the South East from the outer regions was also relatively small, in spite of the potential attraction of better employment opportunities.

Most other interregional migration occurred between neighbouring regions, with equivalent inward and outward flows. For example, migration from the North West to Yorkshire and Humberside was at a similar level to migration from Yorkshire and Humberside to the North West. This preference for migration to a neighbouring region illustrates the point made earlier with respect to the information costs of migration. Knowledge of an area is likely to decrease as distance increases, and so there is an information bias in favour of migration to a neighbouring region. (All migration data quoted in this section of the book is from 1991 UK Census materials.)

The effects of interregional migration The classical model's static competitive-labour-market analysis predicts that interregional migration will help to bring about regional labour-market equilibrium. Inter-regional labour migration acts as a supply-side adjustment mechanism, as explained earlier in this chapter in relation to Figure 6.4.

As explained earlier, a key assumption of the classical view is that of labour homogeneity. If we relax this assumption and allow for labour heterogeneity, the convergence mechanisms predicted by the classical model cease to operate in a self-equilibrating manner.

Heterogeneity of labour means that interregional labour migration may contribute to regional divergence and help to widen interregional disparities. Such an increase in divergence may arise where those with skills in short-supply and/or with high-income earning capacity emigrate from a depressed region. If professional, managerial and skilled labour is over-represented in outmigration from a relatively depressed region, the stock of human capital of that region will be depleted.

The data on the regional occupational distribution of labour in the UK shown in Table 2.3 suggests that such disequilibrating interregional migration may have occurred among the UK regions. The divergent effects of such migration patterns will have a cumulative positive impact upon the benefiting region and a cumulative negative impact upon the losing region due to the income multiplier effects of gaining/losing high-earning individuals. The regions of the UK are far from unique in experiencing such disequilibrating interregional migration, which is present in most contemporary economies, as skilled and highly qualified labour moves in response to interregional differentials in earning and employment opportunities.

Where the UK may be unique is in relation to the impact of the institutional framework of its housing market upon interregional labour mobility. It has been suggested that migration among UK regional labour markets is inhibited by the housing market, and the next section considers this in more detail.

Migration and the Housing Market

The pattern of house ownership

By European standards the UK has an unusually high rate of owner-occupation. This has occurred largely during the past forty years and was the outcome of rising incomes, political policies that actively encouraged owner-occupation as the predominant form of housing provision, and the effects of subsidised mortgage rates though various types of mortgage-interest tax relief. Throughout the 1970s the real rate of interest – that is, the interest rate after allowing for the effects of inflation – on borrowing to finance house purchase was negative once tax incentives are taken into account.

Households responded rationally to the relative price structure on offer: mortgage borrowing was a relatively attractive means by which to build up asset values over a lifetime, and so household saving was concentrated into mortgage debt and house purchase, rather than into other asset purchases.

Other European economies have a different housing structure, not least because building societies, the financial institutions that specialise in the provision of housing finance in the UK, are absent from these other countries. Here the cost of borrowing to finance house purchase is typically higher in real terms, with the result that the level of home ownership is lower and the private rented sector of the market is larger than in the UK. For example, in spite of their relative affluence, fewer than half of West German households owned their own homes at the time of German unification.

In the UK the real cost of borrowing has been relatively low and the extent of borrowing against house purchase has been unusually high. A large proportion of the overall purchase price may be borrowed by the mortgagee, which again encourages house purchase at both lower-income levels and at a younger average age than in comparable European economies.

The British tax system also encourages owner-occupation through aspects of the tax structure other than mortgage interest tax relief. In particular, capital gains realised by the owner upon the sale of a house in owner-occupation are tax exempt. In contrast a similar capital gain realised upon the sale of a house that the owner had rented out would be liable for capital-gains taxation.

As a result owner-occupation represents the predominant form of housing in the UK, as shown in Figure 6.8. By 1981 over two-thirds of households had become owner-occupiers.

The regional housing market in the UK

While over two thirds of UK households are owner-occupiers, the interregional distribution of the owner occupied and private rented sectors of the housing market is not spatially even, as demonstrated by Figure 6.8.

What would you identify as the main interregional differences in the UK pattern of owner-occupied and rented housing?

The South West of England and the South East outside London have the highest proportion of owner-occupied housing in the UK. In these regions, owner-occupation accounts for approximately 75 per cent of all households, and only approximately 25 per cent are in rented accommodation. Greater London and the North of England are the only areas in England where owner-occupation is below the UK average. The pattern of housing in Scotland is different from the rest of the UK, with rented housing representing a more important part of the housing market in the region.

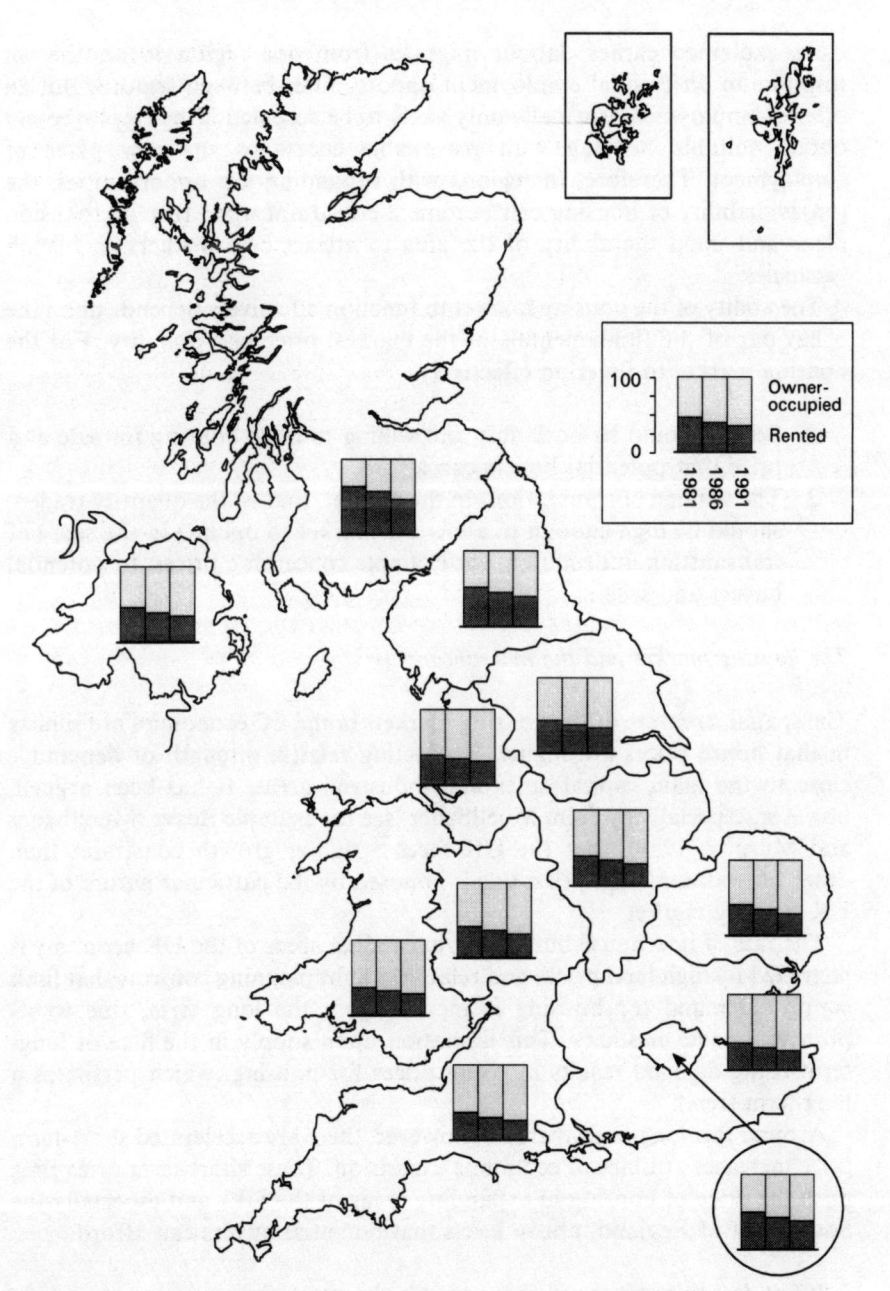

Figure 6.8 Regional distribution of owner-occupied and rented* housing, percentages, 1981–91
* Rented from local authority, private owner or housing association.
Source: data calculated from UK CSO, *Regional Trends*, vol. 28 (1993), table 4.2.

As explained earlier, labour migrates from one region to another in response to differential employment opportunities between regions. But an offer of employment is usually only likely to be accepted if the employee can obtain suitable housing with reasonable access to the new place of employment. Therefore, in regions with expanding job opportunities, the (un)availability of housing can become a constraint upon firm's expansion plans and upon the ability of the area to attract new workers to fill job vacancies.

The ability of the housing market to function effectively depends upon the behaviour of the fundamentals of the market: price and quantity. For the housing market to function effectively:

- Sellers should be both able and willing to offer housing for sale at a price that potential buyers can afford.
- The volume of transactions in the market, that is, the quantity traded, should be high enough to allow the market to operate in the sense of transmitting information, for example concerning prices, to potential buyers and sellers.

The housing market and the macroeconomy

The spatial structure of the housing markets in the EC economies are similar in that house prices are higher – reflecting relative strength of demand – close to the main capital cities and industrial areas. It has been argued, however, especially by John Muellbauer (see for example Bover, Muellbauer and Murphy, 1989), that the UK faces a tighter growth constraint than other EC economies and that this is imposed by the particular nature of the UK housing market.

The rate of new house building in expanding areas of the UK economy is restricted by high land prices and relatively tight planning controls that limit supply. Demand for housing is increasing in the long term, due to its positive income elasticity. This limitation upon supply in the face of long-term rising demand results in rising prices for housing, which persist as a long-term trend.

Around this long-term increase, however, there are accelerated short-term price increases at times of economic expansion. These short-term price rises push the price of housing in expanding areas of the UK, and especially the South East of England, above levels that potential buyers can afford.

What do you think may happen in this situation? Consider the example of an expanding organisation that wants to attract skilled labour, but is unable to do so because potential recruits cannot afford housing in the area where the organisation is situated.

There are three possible outcomes:

- The vacancy remains unfilled, restraining the expansion of the organisation for the present. This will add to pressures upon the firm to increase its wage offers in future to attract the labour it requires.
- The vacancy is filled, the recruited labour being offered either a higher wage than would otherwise have been the case; or being offered some form of subsidised housing by the employer. Again the result is an increase in the wage costs of the organisation.
- The firm will decide that labour shortages are restraining its activities to such a degree that it is worth considering relocation to a site where labour is expected to be more readily available. As we saw in Chapter 5, however, relocation is a major decision that a firm is unlikely to undertake lightly. So this outcome is only probable in the long term.

In the short-term, therefore, it seems likely that high house prices in a region receiving migrants are likely to exert an upward pressure upon wage costs. These rising nominal wage costs may be detrimental to the economic expansion of the region and the economy of which it forms a part.

This may be particularly true when we remember that the skilled managerial and professional occupational groups are those who are most likely to be owner-occupiers. From the organisation's viewpoint, these are also the groups that are likely to be in relatively inelastic supply at a time of expansion, compared with say, unskilled workers.

The interregional house-price gap

To what extent do high house prices exist, and to what extent are they a problem in regions receiving a net flow of immigrants? The south–north gap in the price of residential property in England has been the subject of much research and is monitored regularly by the main UK building societies.

While the presence of a south–north property-price gap is a long-term phenomenon in the UK economy, the size of the gap has been subject to sharp short-term fluctuations. For example, Forrest (1991) quotes Halifax Building Society figures that demonstrate that the average property-price gap between the South East and the North West of England was 72.1 per cent in the last quarter of 1988 but had shrunk to 37.5 per cent in the first quarter of 1990.

This short-term fluctuation in interregional house-price differentials in England is important for two reasons. First, the 72 per cent differential in late 1988 occurred when the national economy was expanding, so employment opportunities were appearing in the growing regions of the economy. However this size of differential makes it more difficult for workers to move in response to employment opportunities.

Second, the extent of these short-term fluctuations suggests that it may well be the volatile and unpredictable nature of the interregional housing market that curbs migration as much as the presence of a long-term gap in the price of residential property. No market operates effectively in uncertain and unstable conditions, and the housing market is no exception.

Why do you think that we find such price volatility in the UK housing market? What are the supply characteristics that contribute to this price instability?

In the short-term the housing stock is relatively fixed in supply because it takes time to build new houses and to rehabilitate existing dwellings. Short-term supply with respect to the price of housing is therefore relatively inelastic.

After a period such as 1990–1, when new housing stocks were at a very low level, supply will not expand rapidly once there is an upturn in demand for housing. The supply side of the market will respond, but there will be a significant time lag before more houses are available for purchase.

In the 1990–2 recession labour mobility within the owner-occupied sector of the UK housing market was also hindered by the low number of market transactions. The market did not operate effectively because of an absence of buyers relative to sellers. Lowered prices did not activate the market, which was effectively caught in a trap that hindered interregional and intra-regional movement of households.

In Figure 6.9, the initial market equilibrium before the onset of the recession is shown by p_0, q_0. We assume a relatively inelastic supply curve for housing. The recession brings a fall in sales at the prevailing level of house prices p_0. To stimulate sales, sellers cut prices to p_1. Basic market analysis suggests that, at the lower price of p_1, demand will be oq_1. However lack of transactions in the UK housing market in 1991–2 indicates that falling prices did not stimulate higher demand. At best the demand curve was inelastic – a constrained demand curve – as shown by AB in Figure 6.9.

Figure 6.9 suggests that demand for housing at prices above p_0 is normal and responds to changes in price, as we would expect, so the demand curve DA slopes as we would expect. However once the housing market becomes cyclically depressed and prices fall below p_0, demand fails to respond to any further fall in price, say to p_1. It could be argued that this constrained demand characterised the housing market in many areas of the South of England during much of 1990–2. Reductions in price failed to generate a positive response from buyers. The housing market in this region was therefore unable to regain equilibrium through price flexibility.

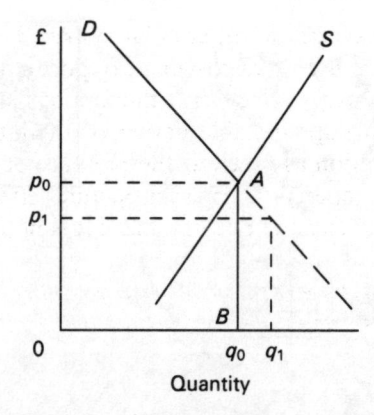

Figure 6.9 The housing trap

In this way, sellers in the housing market were caught in a 'housing trap' in which there was no demand for their house, however much they lowered the asking price. This housing trap inhibited migration between regions during the recession and did nothing to help the national economy return to equilibrium.

Regional differences in the quality of housing stock

While the south–north gap in residential property prices partly reflects differences in demand pressures, it also reflects differences in the nature of the housing stock on offer in different regions of the economy.

In that the housing stock is significantly different between, for example, the South East and the North West of England, then comparison of the average transaction price between these two regions yields limited information. There may be more smaller, older, less well-equipped houses in the housing stock in the North West, which would contribute to the apparent gap in house prices. When we refer to the south–north gap in house prices are we comparing like with like?

A house is a complex commodity. When you buy food you purchase a simple commodity designed to fulfill the function of being eaten. The purchase of a house is more complicated. Such a purchase is a very large-scale financial transaction for most buyers. It is also a purchase with both a consumption component – the benefit or utility derived from living in the house – and an investment component – the increase in the real value of the property that the buyer hopes to realise in the future (Figure 6.10).

According to this measure, housing prices in the South East appear less inflated compared with the rest of the UK. Allowing for the type of housing available in the region, the North West and the West Midlands become

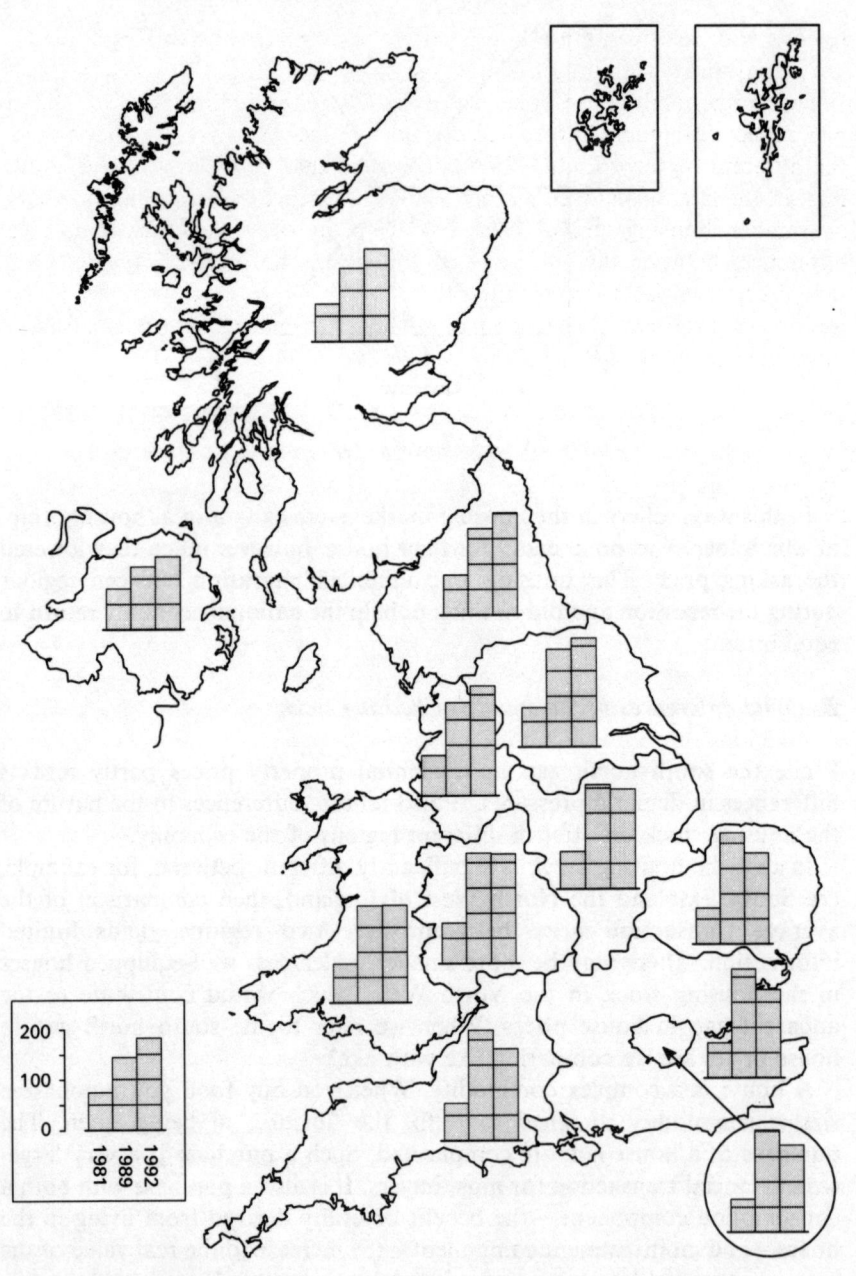

Figure 6.10 *Regional variations in house prices, 1981–92* (1985 = 100)*
* House-price index adjusted for regional differences in the housing stock, for example house size, age and so on.
Source of data: UK CSO, *Regional Trends*, vol. 28 (1993), table 4.7.

regions with relatively high house prices, while prices in Northern Ireland are significantly below the UK average.

The south–north house-price gap in the UK in the 1980s, therefore, did in part reflect differences in the characteristics of the housing stock available in the different regions. Evans (1989) suggested that new starts in the South East in the late 1980s were mainly geared towards increasing the provision of smaller housing units. This may help to even out the qualitative differences between the south and the north. However such an effect will take time to work its way through the market. As we have seen before, the housing market can only respond to changes in market conditions with a significant time lag.

Housing as a constraint on growth

The time lags referred to in the previous paragraph may continue to add to the unstable and potentially destabilising nature of the housing market relative to the macroeconomic performance of the UK and its component regions. It could be argued that positive action by central government is needed to counter such destabilising supply-side pressures upon the economy.

Within a region, local areas may have problems associated with disequilibrium in the housing market. These local problems may persist into the long term. For example, economic decline in an area may well lead to an excess supply of housing for a number of years. Examples are localities that experienced the closure of steelworks or coalmines in the 1980s and 1990s. Where the steelworks or the coalmine has been the main local source of employment, its closure is likely to lead to significant outmigration unless alternative employment opportunities become rapidly available. Such emigration may mean that many houses are put onto the market at a time when there is little reason to expect any significant inmigration into the locality.

On the other hand a locality experiencing rapid growth is likely to experience excess demand for housing, with a consequent increase in the price of available housing in the absence of new construction to supply the higher level of demand.

The UK has two thirds of its households in owner-occupation, that is, within the private sector and owned by those who live in the house. This section of the chapter has shown how such a high level of owner-occupation, by European standards, may contribute to constraints upon growth and expansion through, for example, upward pressure upon firm's nominal wage costs. This constraint may be particularly tight in regions such as the South East of England, where the rate of owner-occupation is above the national average.

The difficulties arising from the UK housing market in regions such as the South East of England centre upon the volatility of the market, which was discussed above. In other European economies interregional variations in house prices also exist. For example, the price of both rented and owner occupied housing in the Netherlands is higher in and around Utrecht than it is in the Rotterdam area. This is partly explained by differences in the regional housing stocks, but also by spatial variation. However, in contrast to the UK experience, these spatial variations have been relatively stable in recent decades. That housing market therefore is more certain than its UK counterpart.

If a greater proportion of housing in the UK was supplied through the public sector, these problems would not necessarily be solved. Public-sector housing can be associated with long waiting lists for occupancy and transfers. The market for publicly owned housing may be rationed by quantity rather than by price, but excess demand and market imbalances can exist in this sector of the housing market too.

The hypothesis that the housing market does act as a constraint upon economic growth in the UK, and especially in certain regions of England, such as the South East, during expansionary periods, cannot be dismissed. The institutional structure of the housing market in the 1990s and its effects upon interregional migration flows are therefore a consideration that should be taken into account in the formulation of government policies towards both the regions and the housing market.

References and Further Reading

Bover, O., J. Muellbauer and A. Murphy (1989) 'Housing, wages and UK labour markets', *Oxford Bulletin of Economic Statistics* vol. 51, pp. 97–136.

Catherwood, Fred (1991) 'European Integration:Political Union and Economic and Monetary Union', *National Westminster Bank Quarterly Review*, May, p. 45.

Ceccini, Paulo (ed.) (1988) *The European Challenge 1992* (London: Gower and Wildwood House).

Clarke, M., D. Gibbs, E. K. Brime and C. M. Law (1992) 'The North West' in Townroe and Martin (1992).

Evans, Alan (1989) 'South East England in the Eighties: explanations for a house price explosion', in M. Breheny and P. Congdon (eds) *Growth and Change in a Core Region*, London Papers in Regional Science, vol. 20 (London: Pion).

Forrest, David (1991) 'An analysis of house price differentials between English regions', *Regional Studies*, vol. 25, pp. 231–8.

Muellbauer, John and A. Murphy (1991) 'Regional Economic Disparities: the role of housing', in A. Brown and K. Mayhew (eds) *Reducing Regional Inequalities* (London: Kogan Page).

Office of Population Censuses and Surveys (1991, 1992) *Population Trends* (London: HMSO).

Singer, Hans W. (1950) 'The division of the gains between investing and receiving countries', *American Economic Review*, vol. 40, pp. 473–85.
Smith, David (1994) *North and South*, 2nd edn (London: Penguin).
Swann, Dennis (1988) *The Economics of the Common Market*, 6th edn (London: Penguin).
Townroe, P. and R. Martin (eds) (1992) *Regional Development in the 1990s* (London: Jessica Kingsley Publishers/Regional Studies Association).
United Kingdom Central Statistical Office (1993) *Regional Trends*, vol. 28 (London: HMSO).
Walsh, J. (1992) 'The Republic of Ireland', in Townroe and Martin (1992).

7 Urban Policies

Political power exists in a vacuum if it is not supported by the powers of expenditure and revenue-raising. The economic experience of regions in this context depends upon the patterns of expenditure and revenue-raising by central, regional and local government. That by central government affects the region from above: that by local government affects the region from below. Chapters 8 and 9 consider the regional implications of central-government expenditure and revenue-raising. This chapter focuses upon local-government finance, and upon local and central-government expenditure on urban policy measures.

In the UK there is currently no regional level of political power, that is, there is no regional political subsidiarity. This is in direct contrast to some other European countries, such as the Netherlands and Germany, where regional government is a well-established part of the political system. For example, in the Netherlands central government acts as the source of finance to regional and local government and defines the functions of these tiers of government. Regional government acts to support, help coordinate and supervise the implementation of functions such as urban policy by local town and city government.

This chapter looks beneath the regional economy at some of the subregional and urban problems that form integral components of the regional economy. In all the UK regions there are subregional variations in prosperity. The South West of England is a microcosm of the core and periphery discussed in the last chapter. The city of Bristol at the eastern side of the South West region is adjacent to the South East and a main motorway artery, so benefits from growth in the South East of England. At the western side of the region, Devon and Cornwall are on the periphery of the country so locationally are relatively disadvantaged.

As noted at the beginning of Chapter 6, Merseyside in the North West of England represents one of the poorest urban areas in the EC. In contrast, towns such as Clitheroe and Lancaster in the North West are relatively affluent.

Think about contrasts between relatively prosperous and relatively poor localities in the region in which you live and note the reasons why you think this variation has arisen.

The first section of this chapter considers the ways in which tax revenue can be raised in the local and regional economy and the ways in which it often is raised. Changes in local property taxation in the UK during the 1990s are used to illustrate these principles.

The second main component of the chapter deals with urban policies. The comparative experience of the Netherlands and the UK is discussed in developing urban policies, especially in relation to joint initiatives between the public and private sectors. Discussion of policy instruments focuses upon the UK during the 1980s and 1990s, details of UK policy being presented in the appendix to this chapter.

The structure adopted for this and the subsequent chapters, which deal with regional policy, reflects the consideration that, while policy analysis is common to the different EC economies, details of policy and their implementation are not. Also, the analysis of policy becomes out of date less quickly than does the detail of specific policy measures. Therefore coverage of specific policy measures is mainly confined to the UK economy and to the chapter appendix.

TAXATION IN THE LOCAL AND REGIONAL ECONOMY

The Local Tax Base

The two key principles of taxation relate to the fundamental economic principles of efficiency and equity, introduced earlier in this book.

Efficiency

Taxation should be efficient in the sense of fiscal neutrality. (Fiscal neutrality means that taxes should not distort the pattern of market prices so as to make relative prices less reflective of relative marginal costs of production and relative marginal utilities of consumption.)

A lump-sum tax levied upon everyone, such as the short-lived poll tax adopted briefly in the UK, has the initial attraction of not affecting the pattern of resource allocation unduly as all taxpayers are equally affected in absolute terms. However a £500 lump-sum payment is not entirely neutral in its effects. A wealthy person can better afford to pay £500 than a poor person. The wealthy person's pattern of consumption will be affected differently from the poor person's. The economic effect of the lump-sum tax is therefore not neutral.

This example indicates the relative price effects of the poll tax, or community charge, while it was in force in the UK. The demand patterns of those whose budgets were significantly affected by the need to pay the lump-sum tax did feed through into the pattern of relative prices in the economy. The regional effects of this were quite marked: expenditure patterns being affected more strongly in the lower-income than the higher-income regions of the economy.

If expenditure rather than income is to be taxed, then fiscal neutrality indicates that a low tax rate across a wide range of goods and services will be more efficient than a higher tax rate across a narrower range of goods and services. It is less distortionary to the prevailing pattern of relative prices to tax 100 goods at 10 per cent than to tax 10 goods at 50 per cent. The broad base of value added tax in most EC economies offers a good example of a relatively neutral tax. In contrast the 10 per cent car tax, abolished in the UK in 1992, was an example of a distortionary tax – unless we believe that there are other environmental grounds for taxing the purchase of cars.

Equity

As well as efficient, local and regional taxation should be equitable in relation to both horizontal and vertical equity. Horizontal equity means that individuals in the same circumstances should have the same tax burden, that is, the same tax liability. Vertical equity means that taxation should reflect the taxpayer's ability to pay.

This brief outline of the principles of efficiency and equity regarding taxation provide an initial framework for the discussion of local taxation that follows.

The tax base

The overall structure of taxation should be such that the individual taxes together form a coherent whole. Local and regional taxation should therefore be structured so that it complements the other elements in the overall tax structure of the economy.

Like other taxes, local and regional taxes may be either direct or indirect. Direct taxes are taxes levied directly on income and may be progressive, proportional or regressive. A progressive tax takes a higher proportion of the individual's income as that income increases. For example, the UK council tax is intended to contain some element of progressivity. A proportional tax takes the same proportion of an individual's income irrespective of the absolute amount of that income. A regressive tax takes a smaller proportion of the individual's income as income increases. The community charge, implemented in England between 1990 and 1993, was regressive and so did not reflect ability to pay.

What should be taxed? In other words, what should form the basis upon which taxation is levied?

Income is usually accepted as a key component of the tax base, especially as it directly reflects the principle of ability to pay. A local income tax would therefore have the advantage of incorporating this principle into the local tax base. The limitation of income as the base for tax raising in the region or the local area is that poorer regions generate less revenue.

Ownership of capital goods that yield a flow of services to the owner may also be argued to reflect ability to pay. The most valuable capital good owned by most people is their house and so it can be argued that home ownership should be included in the tax base. For traditional reasons, taxation of housing has been associated with local rather than national taxation and the UK council tax continues this historical connection.

Expenditure is also usually accepted as part of the tax base, reflected in sales taxes such as VAT. Again, expenditure may reflect ability to pay, although it is now accepted that this relationship is regressive. The regression of expenditure taxes arises from the diminishing marginal propensity to consume, outlined in Chapter 3. Expenditure taxes therefore affect the poor with a high marginal propensity to consume rather than the rich with a low marginal propensity to consume. Expenditure taxes are favoured because they are productive in terms of revenue raised. However use of a local sales tax to supplement national sales taxes such as VAT is not favoured in the UK because of its regressive effect.

People derive benefit from the consumption of publicly provided goods and services, so one argument is that the local tax base should reflect the benefit received by the individual from local services. This benefit principle was one factor underlying the introduction of the community charge. As all in the community benefited from the provision of services by their local authority, so it was argued that all in the community should pay a charge towards the cost of providing those services.

The benefit principle can be applied to essentially 'private' goods and services that happen to be provided by local government but which could just as easily be provided by private enterprise. Examples are museums and leisure services. But even these are not wholly private goods. It could be argued that museums have an educational value, which places their provision and consumption in the public, and not the private domain. The provision and consumption of leisure facilities such as sports centres help maintain health and fitness and so affect the public's health, which is a public and not a private good.

As the limitations of these examples demonstrate, there are few goods and services provided by the public sector to which the benefit principle can readily be applied, as most contain an element of public-good provision. As benefit received will not necessarily be connected to ability to pay, the merits of the benefit principle as a rationale for taxation are limited.

Property Taxes and their Regional Impact

Property has traditionally been the main source of locally raised tax revenue in the UK. The sources of finance for local government may be categorised as follows:

- ❏ The domestic household tax base.
- ❏ The business tax base.
- ❏ Grants from central government.

The last twenty years have been characterised by a constant battle between UK central and local government with regard to local-authority finance. Where central government reduced grants to local authorities to control their level of expenditure, local authorities responded by raising rates in both the domestic and business sectors.

The outcome has been increased central-government control and reduced local autonomy and democracy. For domestic payers, the level of council tax is strictly controlled by central government; for the business sector, the level of rates payable is now nationally determined. There has also been increased central control of property ownership since the early 1970s. Far more nondomestic property is now owned by national rather than local organisations, including the main financial institutions, than was the case in the past.

Over 75 per cent of local-government revenue is now provided by central government through its grants to local government which includes redistributed revenues from locally collected nondomestic rates. This leaves a residual of less than a quarter to be met from local revenue sources, of which the main one is the domestic tax base. The financial implications of these proportions are important. Should the local authority wish to spend over and above the level that central government thinks is required, then the local authority must raise all of the extra income from the local domestic tax base. In other words, a 5 per cent increase in local-authority expenditure requires at least a 20 per cent increase in revenue from the domestic tax base.

In the early 1990s local-government finance was also adversely affected by the same economic influences as industry and the private sector. High real rates of interest made debt servicing expensive, and the poor property market constrained attempts by local government to raise revenue through the sale of land and property.

Central government's justification for its tighter control over local-government finance is essentially twofold. First, central control protects local taxpayers from exploitation by an overspending local government that lacks local accountability to its electorate. Second, central government needs to control the overall economy – the macroeconomy – in order to fulfil macroeconomic objectives. Without tight control over the activities of local government, local government could implement policies contrary to the needs of macroeconomic policy.

In terms of spatial equity among regions, the current UK domestic council tax may be argued to reflect regional ability to pay to a greater extent than did the community charge that preceded it. A greater proportion of the total tax liability will be born by owners of higher-value properties in London and the South East than was the case with the community charge. Under the latter, the bulk of the revenue-raising burden fell on residents in the North of England living in lower-valued properties, and so the regressive nature of the tax was regionally inequitable. To this extent its implementation will help ensure that the overall tax structure better reflects ability to pay and contributes towards interregional equity.

The regional impact of the uniform business rate

The UK Local Government Finance Act (1988) restructured business rates so that control effectively passed from the local authority to central government. Instead of locally determined levels of rates, all businesses were to be assessed in relation to a national uniform business rate. The locally collected revenue from this national business rate is now collected by the local authority on behalf of central government. Revenues are forwarded to central government and redistributed from central back to local government on the basis of central-government estimates of local spending needs.

The business rate is a tax levied upon the occupier of property in nondomestic use. Unlike the domestic council tax, the nondomestic rate continues to be based on rental, and not sale, value. The 1988 Local Government Finance Act provided for five-yearly revaluations of nondomestic properties for rating purposes, that is, 1990, 1995 and so on. Each year the secretary of state for the environment sets the nondomestic rating multiplier, the rate payable then becoming rateable value x nondomestic rating multiplier.

In 1990 the nondomestic rating multiplier was set at 34.8p for England and 36.8p for Wales with the promise that the future annual rate of increase would be at, or less than, the annual rate of inflation.

The revaluation of all nondomestic properties, conducted for the implementation of the uniform business rate (UBR) in 1990, had an interesting interregional impact. The revaluation undoubtedly created gainers and losers, being far from spatially neutral in its impact. There were exceptions but, as a general rule the gainers were located in northern England and the losers in the south. This makes the revaluation resulting from the implementation of the UBR an interesting, although probably unintended, instrument of regional policy in the early 1990s.

A typical financial beneficiary from the property revaluation was an owner of industrial property in northern England, because the increase in its rateable value was likely to be less than the rate of inflation during the intervening years. A generally neutral zone, where property owners felt little financial effect from the revaluation, lies across England through Norwich and Leicester. The financial losers from the revaluation were located predominantly in London and the south, where rateable values rose by more than the rate of inflation during the 1980s.

This spatial dispersion reflected the rental-value base for the rateable value of nondomestic properties. Rental values rose faster in the south than in most areas of the north during the 1980s, and so the new rateable values took this difference into account.

Rental values for different types of property also rose differently during the decade, and this too was reflected in the new valuations. For example, the rental values of retail property generally rose by more than the average for the nondomestic property sector, and so rateable values were correspondingly higher. Industrial-property rental values increased by less than the average, and so rateable values for industrial property generally increased by less than retail property.

While this difference helped to cushion an otherwise even greater adverse impact upon industry in the recession of the early 1990s, it was reflected in the large numbers of empty shops in many towns and cities in southern England in these years.

This section has illustrated some of the principles that underpin a tax system that seeks to raise revenue, be it at national, regional or local level. The general explanation has been illustrated by reference to local taxation in the UK. However it is noticeable that local sources of revenue in the UK are insignificant compared with the scale of the central-government fiscal system. Nor is there any provision for a regional tier of fiscal activity.

This is important because it implies a highly centralised system of political control of the regions and their subregional component economies. The advantages of such centralisation are administrative economies of scale and a coherent single set of policy decisions. However the disadvantages stem from lack of local democratic control and lack of local accountability for the future of the regional economy.

URBAN POLICIES

Regional policies aim to alleviate disparities in the allocation and distribution of economic resources between the different spatial areas of an economy. Regions in the European economies usually have at least one major urban centre associated with them. The growth and development, or lack of growth and development, of that urban centre is therefore integral to the economic experience of the surrounding region.

In the UK in the 1980s expenditure on regional policy by central government decreased in real terms, while that on urban initiatives increased. This emphasis upon urban policy as a major component of UK regional policy is continuing in the 1990s. Consideration of urban policy in this section is accordingly a useful precursor to the discussion of other aspects of regional policy in Chapters 8 and 9.

The need for urban economic policies arises because urban areas suffer from economic problems that experience has shown the market does not solve unaided. Market forces fail to solve the problems of urban change and evolution largely due to imperfections in the property and finance markets, and because the social effects of urban problems are not readily integrated into the price mechanism. As the scale of urbanisation in the European economies has increased, so has the scale of the urban problem, creating a need for policy intervention at this spatial level.

Historically towns became of more or less importance over time: harbours and waterways dried up; changes in the political map were reflected in changes in the economic map. Towns were semiabandoned and new sites and towns developed.

In the present century, however, the effects of the natural changes in urban development have become more problematic for three reasons. Firstly, more structures are 'built to last' than was the case in the past. Natural processes of fire and decay fail to cure today's visual dereliction. Secondly, the scale of urbanisation is greater than in the past and the scale of dereliction is correspondingly greater. Thirdly, traditional inner-city areas have experienced the negative effect of the urban–rural shift discussed in Chapter 2.

This section therefore complements the discussion of regional policy that follows in Chapters 8 and 9 by investigating the urban problem and the main policy responses to it. In particular we ask:

- What is the nature of the urban problem?
- What urban policies have been attempted?
- What role is there for the private sector, the public sector and joint private/public-sector partnerships in urban regeneration?
- What urban policies are likely to be successful in the future?

The Need for Urban Policy

The need for urban policy intervention arises from the otherwise intractable nature of urban decline.

What would you identify as some of the characteristics of an inner urban area in a state of decline?

While you may have thought of others, in the present discussion we shall focus upon four main characteristics of an urban area experiencing economic decline. These are a declining industrial base, extensive derelict sites, poor housing provision and a negative image.

Industrial decline

Typically, the declining urban area is characterised by the presence of declining industrial sectors and so declining employment opportunities and derelict industrial sites. Both London Docklands in England and the Amsterdam Waterfront Embankment scheme, considered more fully below, represent derelict dock areas.

Other typical declining industrial sectors that have caused urban decline and dereliction throughout much of contemporary Europe are shipbuilding, steel and metal-working. The question arises as to why their decline has resulted in urban decay: why has the market not independently generated change and renewed prosperity for towns that were host to traditional heavy industry?

Industrial decline is accompanied by declining employment prospects and lack of job opportunities. This has been exacerbated in those cases where redevelopment has resulted in demand for skilled and clerical labour, offering little by way of employment opportunities to the unskilled manual workforce resident in the locality.

It is interesting to consider whether this shortfall in local labour-market opportunities has been greater in areas where redevelopment has been extensively redirected by the public sector, as in the case of the activities of the UK urban development corporations during the 1980s. The experience of the London Docklands development area has generated criticism in this respect. Local residents claim to have been overlooked especially during the early years of the development corporation's activities. Few employment opportunities were then created that were relevant to the local skill base.

An interesting contrast is offered by another example that discussed in more detail below, that of the IJ waterfront project in Amsterdam. Here the need for better schooling in the locality and improved training provision for local residents was seen as a precondition for a successful regeneration programme.

Site dereliction

Where a shipyard, dock or steelworks closes, a derelict site is left behind. This site is usually extensive, with outdated infrastructure and outdated industrial and warehouse buildings, and sometimes pockets of land contaminated by waste from industrial activities that took place on the site.

Reuse of the site for contemporary commercial purposes therefore involves relatively high development costs in relation to site clearance and cleansing, in addition to the modernisation of infrastructure and the construction of modern buildings. Without financial incentives to offset these additional costs, developers will normally prefer a 'greenfield', lower-cost site. Planning restrictions, such as those relating to 'green-belt' provision in the UK, limit the availability of such sites however, so that restriction is in terms of quantity as well as cost.

Several of the schemes outlined below, such as city grants, are accordingly designed to recompense the developer for the extra costs of reusing a secondhand site compared with new development on a site previously unused for commercial or industrial activities. The existence of grants and fiscal incentives to encourage private-sector property investment of this kind is currently greater in the UK than in most other comparable European economies.

Housing provision

As is noted below in relation to new-town policies, housing provision is sometimes inadequate in the sense of there not being enough housing in an urban area for all in need of accommodation. In times of urban population growth, therefore, there is often pressure for urban policies designed to increase the supply of housing available.

Urban areas in need of regeneration are typically characterised by poor housing provision. Older property becomes run down due to lack of maintenance and interest in its upkeep. Recent property tends to be dominated by postwar public-sector developments, at worst high-rise concrete-built accommodation with high maintenance costs and low fitness for habitation. Action to improve housing conditions, such as the City Challenge projects outlined briefly in the Appendix, are not directly relevant to our economic analysis, but are important to improve the social fabric of the urban area.

Poor-quality housing is reflected in low rental and market values, which in turn are reflected in a low-income population. This means that local government is faced with a correspondingly low local property tax base. This will mean little buoyancy in terms of local revenue-generating capacity. This lack of revenue will occur independently of whether the local tax base is related to sales, income or property.

Image

Abandoned and derelict sites create a poor visual appearance and therefore a poor image for the affected urban area. Such a negative image makes it difficult for the local authority or other agencies to attract inward investment and interest. The derelict area becomes stereotyped and stigmatised, making it increasingly difficult to generate the very demand that is a necessary condition for the removal of the dereliction.

Positive action is necessary to counter such negative images. One such type of positive action may be emphasis upon high-quality architectural design, as in the Amsterdam waterfront area where the regeneration programme seeks to reinforce Amsterdam's image 'as the spiritual capital of Europe' (Witbraad and Jorna, 1993, p. 235).

The Evolution of Urban Policies

1950s–70s growth centres and new towns

In countries such as the UK and the Netherlands, where rural land is valued as a scarce commodity and pressures on land use are significant, it is currently seen as essential to recycle urban land in order to minimise encroachment on greenfield sites. In both countries, urban policy has undergone an abrupt about-face in this respect. Between the late 1950s and the late 1970s both countries had an active policy of creating new urban communities on greenfield sites, referred to as 'growth centres' in the Netherlands and 'new towns' in the UK.

These new communities were planned to provide balanced communities, with housing, employment and leisure provided within the town. Expansion of both housing and employment provision was envisaged as rapid. In the Netherlands, for example:

> A growth centre is described as a subsidiary centre within a city region. A designated growth centre is supposed to gain at least 6,000 dwellings within ten years (Needham *et al.*, 1993, p. 36).

Fifteen growth centres were established in the Netherlands, including towns such as Almere and Helmond. Four growth cities, including Groningen, were also designated with the aim of establishing city regions in spatial areas lacking an existing urban focus.

In the UK new towns were similarly subsidiary centres designed both to accommodate overspill from existing cities and to generate new growth in their own right. They were located in the wider regions around the major conurbations, such as London and Liverpool/Manchester. New towns such as Harlow and Milton Keynes were successfully established as satellites of London, while new towns such as Skelmersdale and Runcorn were established as satellites to Merseyside.

In the UK those new towns in buoyant regions such as the South East thrived more easily than those established in other regions. In the

Netherlands the growth-centre policy was reinforced in the 1970s through generous financial incentives and subsidies from central government.

However in the early 1980s the direction of urban policy in both countries underwent a major change of emphasis against such new developments and towards the regeneration of existing urban areas. The recession experienced by both economies in those years meant that economic growth was inadequate to support both existing and new urban centres. Location preference for greenfield sites meant that established urban areas suffered seriously from the dereliction and unemployment explained earlier in this chapter as the symptoms of urban decline. Urban policies designed to accelerate the regeneration of declining urban areas were adopted and refined during the 1980s and continue to be the current direction of urban policy in both the Netherlands and the UK.

Urban regeneration policies in the 1980s and 1990s

This section looks at ways in which both local and central government can facilitate urban regeneration and development through the implementation of urban policies. The detail of UK urban policies in these years is outlined in the appendix to this chapter. In explaining the main direction and instruments of urban policy, the changing responsibilities of local government with respect to urban redevelopment are considered.

City Grants: subsidising private investment City Grants aim to turn commercially unprofitable projects into projects that a private developer would be prepared to undertake as a result of an injection of grant finance. The lack of commercial appeal of these projects usually arises from the high costs of site preparation and infrastructure provision on urban sites. The normal guideline for the allocation of city grants is that the developer should provide £4 of investment capital for every £1 of city grant allocation. The £1 city grant acts as a subsidy to recompense the private developer for the initial costs of site redevelopment.

In assessing projects for city-grant funding, the urban regeneration agency considers the following four criteria:

- ❑ The number of jobs to be created by the project.
- ❑ The degree of dereliction of the site to be developed.
- ❑ The visual impact of the proposed development.
- ❑ The likelihood of further investment being stimulated as a result of the project.

City grants have encouraged the regeneration of sites containing old industrial and warehouse buildings that might not otherwise have been redeveloped. However the figures in Table 7.3 in the appendix demonstrate that, at a crude estimate, the average cost to the taxpayer of each job directly created was about £6849 between 1988 and 1992. In 1988–9 the comparable cost per job was £5164.

Policy expenditure on city grants would have been more cost-effective than these initial figures suggest, due to secondary multiplier effects. It is interesting that the amount of expenditure required per job created was higher in the longer time period, which covers a period of recession. This is consistent with the expectation that it is more difficult to secure additional job creation in a depressed than in a buoyant economic environment.

In terms of the interregional distribution of city-grant expenditure, the West Midlands benefited most. This is true whether benefit is measured by the number of jobs created or by the amount of investment.

The local authority as entrepreneur and developer: development agencies and local enterprise initiatives   Development agencies and companies set up by local government, such as the Leeds Development Company, manage the functions carried out in Scotland by Scottish Enterprise (formerly the Scottish Development Agency) as regards the promotion of 'their' area and the attraction of inward investment by both the private and public sectors.

Local government is also often a major landowner in its urban area. This provides the advantage of its being able to redevelop its own property in the way it sees as best for the local community. Through their development agencies local authorities are able to act directly in a property-development role.

However the sale of property assets by local authorities to finance redevelopment and change was hampered in the early 1990s by the collapse of demand in the English property market. In the UK in recent years, falling property values and the difficulty of selling property at any price have adversely affected the redevelopment programmes of many local authorities.

Many UK local authorities have established local enterprise initiatives. These are not coordinated through central government and so their terms of reference and effectiveness vary from area to area. The relatively successful local enterprise initiatives, such as those in Lancashire and the West Midlands, demonstrate the potential role for local action in providing a well coordinated economic development service that brings together interested parties from local authorities, central-government departments and agencies, and private-sector business organisations.

Although accountable to the local authority, local enterprise agencies are separate entities, providing a focal point of contact for local business. They carry out a number of support functions for industry, including training and provision of expert support in relation to, for example, new production techniques and technologies, including information technology.

Enterprise zones: job creation or job diversion? Enterprise zones allow local government to accelerate redevelopment over the rate that would have applied in their absence.

Enterprise zoning does seem to have generated more activity within the designated areas than would otherwise have occurred. This means that redevelopment and refurbishment has greatly enhanced the visual appearance and the general image of the zoned areas. The government view seems to be that enterprise zones are effective as an instrument of urban and regional policy.

In terms of the creation of new output and employment the success of the enterprise zones is not wholly certain. It is always difficult to judge the extent to which *new* output and employment has been created by such a scheme. At least some of the output and employment generated inside the enterprise zones during the 1980s would probably have been generated outside the zones in their absence.

Enterprise zones are very clearly defined localities within subregions that are experiencing economic problems. As a result, designating an enterprise zone area within the subregional economy acts as an incentive to firms to relocate within the zone from other locations in the same subregion. Where this occurs, existing employment and output in the regional economy are *diverted*: no additional jobs or output are necessarily *created*.

A further limitation of the enterprise zone policy is that it does not necessarily directly address the heart of the regional problem: the presence of above-average unemployment. Enterprise zone status helps to provide the funding needed to regenerate derelict land. However this land regeneration does not necessarily lead to job creation. For example, the Tyneside enterprise zone provided the site for the MetroCentre shopping development. While highly successful as a retail development, critics would argue that the employment it provides offers little to those made redundant from the area's traditional manufacturing industries.

The success of enterprise zones therefore primarily depends upon the extent to which they have created new jobs and output rather than diverted existing jobs and output. Job diversion into otherwise derelict areas does bring some secondary benefit by reducing the extent of the dereliction.

As Table 7.2 in the appendix demonstrates, the life of most of the enterprise zones schemes initially spanned the 1980s. In general, government policy has been to terminate the schemes as planned. Only a few enterprise zone schemes have had their life extended into the 1990s, such as those for Inverclyde and Sunderland. In these cases it was felt that extension of the incentives was the best means of continuing to address the local urban problem.

Table 7.2 shows that many of the enterprise zones lost their status in the early 1990s. Why may the withdrawal of enterprise zone status in these years have caused economic difficulties in the affected areas?

With industry in recession in the early 1990s, the timing of the ending of enterprise zone status was unfortunate. Unemployment in the UK was still increasing at that time. In addition many firms faced liquidity problems, as explained in Chapter 2. This necessarily raises the question of the long-term viability of many of the organisations that became established in the enterprise zones during the 1980s. The success of the zones will be ephemeral if many of these organisations close down soon after the withdrawal of such enterprise zone incentives as nonliability for the uniform business rate.

Simplified planning zones A simplified planning zone (SPZ) is an area covered by an SPZ scheme drawn up by the local planning authority. As with the enterprise zones, there is no need for individual developers to obtain separate planning permission once their proposal lies within the planning brief specified by the SPZ scheme.

In view of the low initial take-up of the SPZ scheme by local planning authorities, the government made their implementation easier, if less democratic, by removing the requirement that a public enquiry be held into SPZ-scheme proposals should this be requested by a member of the public. While SPZs have normally been drawn up by the local authority, a small number of private developers, such as Slough Estates in Slough, Berkshire, have drawn up SPZ schemes for land owned by them.

The provision for SPZ schemes has not met with an overwhelmingly positive response from local planning authorities. Simplified administrative procedures alone are not enough to generate a response in the absence of accompanying financial incentives. Local authorities also have little incentive to support the creation of schemes that reduce their own control as planning authorities.

Centralisation: the urban development areas (UDAs) and corporations (UDCs) The UDC's main role was to create confidence in their UDA and improve the area's image to the extent that, when the UDC moved out, regeneration was secured in that private and local development would continue without further central-government aid. Details of the UDC programme are contained in the appendix to this chapter. The UDA/UDC programme absorbed the largest proportion of central-government finance in terms of total urban/local programme aid during the 1980s.

The regional impact of this expenditure has not been uniformly in favour of the UK's less-well-off regions, as London Docklands has dominated this expenditure programme. For this reason the experience of London Docklands is investigated in more detail later in this chapter.

Overall, the UDA/UDC programme has been generally counted a success. However there have been a number of criticisms of the programme. First, some of the UDCs have lacked local accountability and the programme has transferred responsibilities for local economic regeneration from local government to central government. Second, the new employment that has been generated has rarely utilised old skills, resulting in a severe skills mismatch between supply and demand in some local labour markets. Third, as noted above in the discussion of enterprise zones, it is difficult to estimate the extent to which new economic activity has been created, as distinct from existing economic activity diverted into the assisted area from unassisted areas in the same region.

Policy integration: English Partnership The urban regeneration agency, English Partnership, launched in 1993–4, was designed as the next generation of government agencies, and was intended to overcome the weaknesses and build upon the strengths of predecessors such as the UDCs.

The consultative paper relating to the urban regeneration agency was launched in July 1992. The government recognised the need to retain the strengths of its existing urban policy agencies, such as the UDCs described above. However the need to address the weaknesses of a multifaceted or, arguably, piecemeal approach to policy had been made more urgent by the prolonged recession and its negative effect upon the prospects for private-sector investment in derelict urban areas.

The government's consultative document for the proposed urban regeneration agency provided it with a wider brief than that of the UDCs:

- To enable regeneration by promoting private-sector development and liaising with local authorities and other agencies involved in urban renewal.
- To intervene in the operation of the private sector to the minimum extent necessary to enable a flexible and fast-moving programme of urban regeneration.
- To act as a single unifying central agency for urban land regeneration and for promoting relevant expertise.
- To work within the statutory framework of the planning system.

As well as taking over from the UDCs, the agency became an umbrella organisation for urban policy by taking over the administration of the city grants, and the work of English Estates and the urban programme. Like

English Estates and the UDCs, it is directly accountable to the Department of the Environment. It therefore does *not* represent a shift of urban policy initiatives back from central government control back to the local authorities.

Given the designation of UDA to areas with progressively lower levels of dereliction during the 1980s, it will be interesting to see what criteria are adopted for an urban area to come under the auspices of English Partnership. It will also be interesting to see over what time period the agency is intended to achieve self-sustainable development in its designated urban areas. Given the concerns over the planning powers of SPZs, the planning powers vested in the agency will also be a matter of note. On the positive side, it is to be hoped that the bringing together under the single agency umbrella of the different urban policy agencies of the 1980s will facilitate a more coherent and cohesive urban policy for the UK in the late 1990s.

Urban Regeneration: Public/Private Partnership

> The relations between the city and the national authorities, as well as those with business and capital in the private sector, shape the opportunities enabling the city to advance, develop and grow (Kohnstamm, 1993, p. 220).

Partnership schemes between the private and public sectors aim to stimulate private-sector investment in conjunction with publicly financed investment in urban areas that would otherwise be unattractive to private-sector investment. Public/private-sector partnership schemes have become increasingly important in the UK as well as in France and the Netherlands in recent years. The relative merits of such a partnership approach to urban policy and its implications for other regional policy initiatives are evaluated later in the chapter.

In the case of England in particular, urban policies in the 1980s were both diverse and diversified. Critics argue that the policy was too diverse and fragmented to have much chance of success in its first decade of operation. It is to be hoped that the lesson has been learnt, and that the increasing cohesion and coordination of urban policy in the 1990s will generate improved results.

The UK government's policy aim with respect to urban areas is:

> to improve the quality of life ... through economic, social and environmental regeneration. To this end, the government works in partnership with business, community and voluntary groups and local authorities (Department of the Environment, 1993, p. 53).

In the 1980s, as we have noted earlier in this chapter, political control in the UK became increasingly centralised from local to national government authorities. During the same decade the ownership of property became increasingly national and international rather than local. This trend towards increasing national ownership of local property was therefore mirrored by increasingly strong national control of local finance and planning initiatives.

Urban regeneration in the UK and the Netherlands

This section takes the form of a brief comparative case study between the London Docklands development area in the UK and the IJ Amsterdam waterfront project in the Netherlands, focusing upon the relationship between the public and private sectors in the two countries.

London Docklands development area Docklands is being developed as London's third commercial centre. It represents large-scale new provision of commercial space for the 1990s, so in principle should be able to attract plenty of demand for its modern, well-appointed buildings. It dominates government expenditure on the urban development corporations, accounting for nearly £294 million of an expected £621 million budget in 1992–93 (Department of the Environment, 1993, p. 63).

One problem facing Docklands was the low overall level of demand for commerical property in the early 1990s due to the combined effects of recession and an over-supply of new commercial building in London. But it also faced the problem of inadequate transport provision and so inadequate access to the development. Inadequate access rendered journeys to work difficult, making the area unattractive to workers. In turn this deterred the firms that employ them from locating in the area. The problem will be worsened if workers continue to perceive the area as being inaccessible and/or if skill shortages persuade employers to place a high premium upon the attraction and retention of staff.

While large-scale development of the road network is being undertaken as an integral part of the Docklands development, it has been undertaken relatively late compared with the initial building-construction phases of the project. Much criticism has been levelled at the inadequacy of publictransport provision. Until the mid-1990s the Docklands Light Railway will provide the main rail access, and it was not designed to carry the anticipated number of commuters who will wish to use it if Docklands prospers. The extension that will link the main London Underground system to Docklands is not scheduled for completion until late in the 1990s.

The pattern of accessibility to Docklands has implications both for whom will be employed and for local employment prospects. It seems likely that workers will be attracted to Docklands from East rather than West London.

This will affect employment levels in different areas of and around the capital city and local housing markets.

London may have enough overall growth in the 1990s and beyond to accommodate expansion in several key centres and in different directions. However if the city's total expansion is limited it may be that, for instance, the western end of London and Docklands will not both be able to thrive. In this case the expansion of one area of the city will take place at the expense of another.

The London Docklands development area is administered by the London Docklands Development Corporation (LDDC), which has been operational since 1981. The main aim of the LDDC has been to establish a local economy that will generate income and employment for the future. Its starting point was the attraction of private-sector commercial, residential and amenity development into Docklands. The LDDC targeted high-technology industry and later commercial offices, in marked contrast with the earlier dock-related use of the land in the area.

To complement the new employment venue, relatively expensive housing developments were encouraged, many of which have been highly successful. A marina has added to the image sought by the LDDC sought in transforming the derelict dock area.

As well as the problems of infrastructure and accessibility discussed above, one of the main limitations of the LDDC's programme concerns the impact of the development upon the local residents. The relatively high levels of local unemployment which existed in the early 1980s continued into the early 1990s. It may be argued that the LDDC should have made a greater effort to provide employment more suited to the local labour supply. Nor has the local resident population seen much improvement in housing or infrastructure provision during the time of the LDDC. The LDDC has therefore been accused of not only neglecting the needs but also harming the local community within its area.

As explained above, another problem that has arisen within the LDDC boundary is to the timing of such developments as offices and housing relative to the provision of infrastructure. The development of offices and housing in advance of some of the main access roads has resulted in both severe congestion of the existing road network and in noise and disturbance to residents and workers during construction. It might be argued that for an area such as Docklands, as for a region or the economy as a whole, the provision of infrastructure should be a prerequisite for development.

The IJ Embankments Project: the Amsterdam waterfront The IJ Embankments project on the Amsterdam waterfront represents a large-scale programme of regeneration for a derelict dockland area comparable in extent to London Docklands and Liverpool Merseyside. All three locations shared the common problem of redundant and therefore derelict land and buildings due to the decline in use of their port facilities. All three sites have potentially convenient access to their respective city centres, so making them potentially viable locations for a variety of uses, such as the provision of water-based leisure activities, new office space and waterfront housing.

The IJ waterfront project was initiated in 1982, more or less the same time that the London Docklands and Merseyside Development Corporations were set up in England. There however the comparison ends, in that agreement as to the form that the redevelopment of the IJ waterfront should take was not agreed until 1991. So the planning and gestation process took much longer in the Netherlands than it had in England.

The Amsterdam project was seen as having two distinct but clearly related aims: the regeneration of the waterfront area and its reintegration with the city centre. It is the latter which distinguishes the Amsterdam waterfront approach from that of at least some phases of the London Docklands development. Docklands was seen to a greater extent as a separate entity and competitor to the existing City of London. Like Merseyside, Amsterdam sought to enhance and complement the existing pattern of activity in the urban core.

Developments in the Merseyside development area sought to enhance its standing as a prestige location at primarily regional but also national level. London Docklands and the Amsterdam waterfront both reflect their capital-city association by directly aiming for an image of European and international status. Both therefore aim for the image and accessibility appropriate to a major international urban business centre.

As mentioned above, plans for the regeneration of the Amsterdam waterfront were tentative and subject to continuing discussion throughout most of the 1980s. In the late 1980s more substantive progress began to be made following the creation of a joint venture between the Amsterdam local authority and the private-sector Internationale Nederlanden Groep, a major financial institution with banking and insurance interests.

The proposed structure of the redevelopment builds upon the existing 'island' structure of the waterfront, and aims to establish an international reputation through the provision of high-quality architecture and a high-quality environment, including generous public areas. The main phase of the development is expected to take place between 1995 and 2010, with planned flexibility so that development can be tailored to meet contemporary demand in the future. Nearly one third of the total regeneration costs are expected to be spent upon infrastructure and nearly two thirds upon buildings.

The size of the project is such that it will have positive income- and employment-generating multiplier effects upon both the local and the national economies. Ideally, the planners seek to anticipate the social costs that will arise from the development project, so that they can be recognised, acted upon and minimised. The redevelopment is also intended to maximise social gain through provision of training and employment for local residents as well as provision of social and cultural facilities for the city's population as a whole. It is hoped that the participation of all local community groups at the early stage of the planning process will ensure the maximum benefit to all the community once the project is in progress.

In principle, the patient and long-term approach to the regeneration of the waterfront in Amsterdam may result in a scheme less brash and blatantly capitalist than some phases of the London Docklands redevelopment have been, especially in the heady days of the late 1980s. But this will only become clear in the future. While some aspects of the London Docklands redevelopment have entailed high social and financial costs, Docklands will have been largely redeveloped and will be generating income years ahead of the Amsterdam redevelopment. There is not yet any simple single answer to the question of how best to regenerate derelict dock and other large-sale redundant areas of industrial wasteland at strategic locations in terms of the local, regional and national economy.

Future Directions for Urban Policy

The development of a significant national urban policy as a component of regional policy has only occurred in the UK since the early 1980s and active urban policy in other European economies, such as the Netherlands, is even more recent. However several issues important to the formulation of effective urban policies have emerged, and these are discussed here.

Increased centralisation

In the UK, the 1978 legislation aimed to provide finance from central government to aid local government in its attempts at removing urban dereliction. During the 1980s, there was growing centralisation of local-government finance and increasing political tension between a series of national Conservative governments and Labour-controlled local government in many of the main urban areas. This was accompanied by a move away from the granting of central-government financial aid to local government, and since 1985 the value of central-government financing of local-government urban initiatives has fallen in real terms.

Public/private-sector partnership schemes (PPPs)

As the European economies become increasingly urbanised and the pace of structural economic change quickens, so the scale of both regional and urban structural change increases. As the above discussion of the London Docklands and Amsterdam IJ waterfront projects demonstrated, many major urban programmes are already large scale and this trend is likely to continue. Such large-scale urban schemes necessarily encompass a wide range of land use, from the construction of offices and warehouses to shops, housing, leisure facilities and infrastructure. Some of these, such as office development, are traditionally undertaken by the private sector; others such as infrastructure provision are traditionally undertaken by the public sector.

In the mid-1970s to early 1980s there was increasing recognition that the successful regeneration of urban areas yielded benefits to both private and public sectors. In economic terms, urban regeneration yielded potential private benefits, as a more attractive urban centre with good infrastructure was an urban centre in which private financial capital could invest and reap profits. Equally there are clearly social benefits from urban regeneration if it helps to create additional and/or improved employment opportunities and an improved image for the urban centre.

The corollary of the combination of private and social benefits was seen to be that *both* the private sector and the public sector should contribute to the cost of urban-improvement programmes. Public/private-sector partnership schemes therefore came to be seen as a suitable instrument by which the objective of urban improvement might be attained.

An additional advantage of such partnership schemes was seen to be the ability to draw upon the existing property-development expertise in the private sector, and to inject the public sector with a dose of private-sector management and profit-oriented motivation.

In principle, PPP schemes encourage the public sector to provide land-use and planning expertise, infrastructure and social assets such as museums. In return the public sector and by implication the taxpayer, benefits from an accelerated rate of urban redevelopment at a lower financial cost than would otherwise have been the case.

The private sector is encouraged to provide risk-bearing finance, marketing and management expertise. In return the private sector and its shareholders benefit from an accelerated rate of urban improvement leading to a greater potential profitability than existed in the absence of the PPP scheme.

The cynical observer might also perceive an additional underlying rationale for PPP schemes as being the desire of central government to reduce its own expenditure in the 1980s and 1990s.

Since the mid-1980s financial help has been targeted primarily at the private sector, either independently or in partnership with local-authority and government agencies in several of the European countries with active urban programmes. In the UK the UDC programme has been strengthened during these years. As a result, in the financial year 1990–1, the £575 million spent by central-government on UDCs was more than twice the £250 million funding received by local government under the urban programme (Department of the Environment, 1993).

In the Netherlands PPP schemes have been underway since the early 1980s in five major cities, namely Amsterdam, The Hague, Maastricht, Rotterdam and Utrecht.

The cyclical availability of private-sector financial capital

The growing importance of major institutional investors, such as insurance companies and pension funds, as property owners in several European countries during the 1970s and 1980s was noted earlier. One objective of PPP schemes is to harness these institutional funds into the process of urban regeneration, in addition to attracting financial capital from more traditional sources such as private-sector property developers.

This redirection of urban policy towards the provision of financial support for private-sector investment might have been successful. However the recession at the beginning of the 1990s slowed down, if not halted, most private-sector property development in the UK. As we have seen, the property industry was particularly badly hit by this recession, and so the redevelopment of urban areas slowed down and/or stopped. The experience of the UK in the early 1990s emphasises the point that the concept of attracting private-sector investment to reinforce public policy objectives can only be useful when there is potential private-sector capital to be attracted.

One lesson from the experience of European urban regeneration during the 1980s is that such programmes take decades, rather than years, to achieve their objectives. This means that private capital will only be provided to the extent that it is available over such a lengthy period, and to the extent that the expected return is perceived to compensate for the risks involved in the investment.

At present in the UK lack of development activity in urban regeneration schemes due to lack of private capital in the property sector seems to be reinforced by lack of confidence in its relationship with government, for reasons outlined in the section below.

Here we concentrate on the implications of cyclical variations in the availability of private-sector capital to long-term urban regeneration schemes that may span several business cycles. It would seem sensible for the public sector to be prepared to 'pump-prime' private finance in a countercyclical manner. Urban regeneration schemes in the 1980s and early 1990s suffered from recessionary stagnation due to the withdrawal of private-sector financial support in both the UK and the Netherlands. The existence of a – not wholly predictable – business cycle does affect the relative yield obtainable from property as an investment. Institutional investors will respond to variations over time among the yields of different prospective investments and so cannot be seen as a source of *constant* funding over the time scale of an urban regeneration programme.

For this reason public-sector funding is needed both to keep the programme moving at times when private-sector funding is not forthcoming and to act in a Keynesian countercyclical manner during periods of recession.

The private and social costs and benefits of regeneration

There is potential conflict between the roles of the public and private sectors in urban redevelopment. This arises mainly from the difficulty of quantifying the extent of the relative private and social costs and benefits generated from redevelopment.

We can illustrate this point by referring back to the section on 'externalities' in Chapter 3, which explained the distinction between private and social costs and benefits.

One problem often faced by developers in the context of urban site redevelopment is that of contaminated land where all or part of the site has been polluted by contaminants.

Figure 3.8 demonstrated the economic analysis of pollution in terms of private and social costs. Using Figure 3.8 and the related explanation, revise your understanding of these ideas before reading on.

Contaminated land is a form of pollution and so the contaminator is imposing social costs upon society in excess of the private costs of production, as shown in Figure 3.8. Where grants such as the UK government's Derelict Land Grant are given to developers to compensate for the costs of decontaminating a site, the payment of such a grant may be justified in terms of compensation for these extra social costs of clearing pollution.

The example of infrastructure provision is the opposite to this example of pollution. The presence of pollution as a by-product of the production process means that society wishes to see *less* of the polluting product produced than does the private producer.

As the provision of infrastructure such as roads yields benefits to both the private developer and society, this provides an example where society often wishes to see *more* of the infrastructure produced than does the private producer. This is shown in Figure 7.1 where the social quantity produced Q_s is greater than the private quantity produced, Q_p.

The potential for conflict between the public and private sectors arises from their differing estimates of the positions of the social supply, S_s and

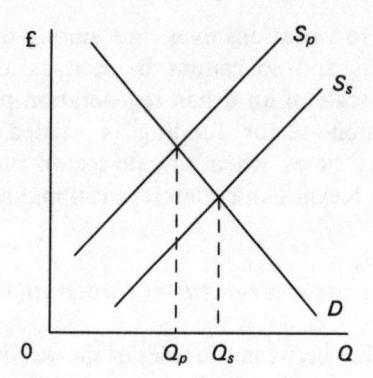

Figure 7.1 The positive externalities of infrastructure provision

private supply, S_p curves. Only if both parties agree the relative positions of these supply curves will an amicable cooperative arrangement be likely.

The use of this approach to the analysis of externalities in relation to urban regeneration and development is increasingly apposite in the 1990s. This reflects the increasing concern with raising the quality of the urban environment in respect of new development and regeneration schemes. Traffic-calming and reducing schemes, greater safety for cyclists and pedestrians and more open space are examples of social and environmental objectives being included in urban policies in the 1990s.

Disagreement between the public and private sectors with regard to the positions of the social supply, S_s, and private supply, S_p, curves in the diagram arises because, for instance, on the one hand the private sector will not fund development in the absence of reasonable infrastructure provision by the public sector. On the other hand the public sector does not wish to provide profits to the private sector by providing infrastructure while reaping only limited benefit from the expenditure of taxpayers' money.

Where the two sides fail to agree, the losers are urban areas and those who would benefit from their regeneration. Agreement requires cooperation and mutual understanding, rather than conflict, between the private and public sectors. Conflict frequently does arise, both because of different public- and private-sector approaches to the concept of profit and because of distrust between the parties involved.

To avoid or at least minimise such conflict, a clearly outlined plan for the overall regeneration scheme should be negotiated between all the concerned parties at the outset of the programme. The experience of 1980s urban development corporations and of analogous initiatives in France and the Netherlands suggest the merit of including residents and existing local employees as interested parties.

Once the programme is in operation, an independent third party to whom disputes could be referred could help alleviate ill feeling and defuse conflict before it reaches the stage of litigation, as happened between the Docklands residents and the developers.

The future direction of urban policy

The experience of UK urban policy in the 1980s was, as we have seen, of many different programmes and initiatives. In spite of the creation of groups with coordinating roles, such as the city action teams, the perception was of many different bodies implementing different aspects of urban policy. Greater cohesion and focus might have yielded greater success.

1980s experience in the UK and in comparable European economies demonstrated that urban regeneration is a process that takes time and is measured in decades rather than years. Urban policy in the Netherlands increasingly accepts a twenty-year time horizon as the realistic minimum for a successful urban programme. The extensions granted to many of the initial ten-year urban development corporations in the UK indicate that a similar conclusion is being drawn. Such a long timescale implies the need for both realistic expectations regarding the likely role of private capital and for a flexible programme of regeneration that is capable of being adapted to meet altering needs and requirements.

Urban policy in its present form is relatively recent. There is little experience upon which to build the foundations of successful urban regeneration programmes. The experience of the 1980s is therefore especially valuable as a source of successes and failures from which precedents for more successful future urban programmes can be developed.

If joint public/private-sector partnership schemes are to evolve into a successful blueprint for future urban revitalisation, the different management approaches of the two sectors will need to develop strategies to enable positive cooperation to occur. In the absence of such strategies, it seems likely that the pattern of urban growth will either be subject to the whim and short-term cyclical instability of the private sector, or will need to be comprehensively – and perhaps inflexibly – planned by the public sector. A pattern of cooperation rather than conflict is much more firmly established in France and the Netherlands than it is in the UK. For instance, in the Netherlands the 'negotiating culture' means that:

> plans are implemented not only by . . . formal instruments available under . . . law, but also by persuading many of the parties involved to enter into commitments to implement the plan (Needham *et al.*, 1993, p. 87).

It seems certain that the need for urban policy is unlikely to vanish in a changing industrial society: as new industries grow while old industries shrink, there will be corresponding changes in the pattern of land use. In the absence of policy intervention, it will be cheaper to develop greenfield sites to meet new demands.

Policy intervention will therefore continue to be necessary both to minimise the extent of derelict land in the European economies and to ensure the urban dynamism essential to the economic development of the region within which the urban area lies. Whether the current emphasis upon urban policy out of the regional context, which appears to dominate UK government strategy, is the most effective policy format is a matter for debate. Rather than appearing to be separate, an effective urban-policy strategy should be implemented in the context of the regional economic environment and the wider regional-policy issues discussed in the following chapters.

APPENDIX: URBAN POLICY IN THE UK: 1969-93

1969: *The Local Government (Social Need) Act* sought to direct central government resources towards city areas of 'special social need'. In 1977 its remit was extended to cover industrial and environmental as well as social responsibilities, and administration was transferred from the Home Office to the Department of the Environment.

The urban programme funding under this Act was the main source of finance received by local authorities from central government to fund urban regeneration programmes during the 1980s and it benefited 57 local authority areas. In the 1992-3 financial year the programme only provided the finance needed to complete existing projects. No new commitments were made under this scheme as its role was taken over by English Partnership (see below).

1978: *The Inner Urban Areas Act* With this legislation, central government recognised the problem of urban decline in the industrial English cities. Action focused upon the clearance of derelict sites and the provision of modern infrastructure. The aim was to help cleared inner-city sites to compete with greenfield sites in attracting commercial development.

1981: *Urban development areas/corporations* The urban development area (UDA) was introduced in 1980 with the aim of creating conditions to attract private investment to unattractive urban areas that were patently failing to attract private investment. For each UDA a corresponding urban development corporation (UDC) was established, to implement action to create more favourable conditions for investment. It is noteworthy that the board members of the UDCs were accountable to the secretary of state at the Department of the Environment and not to the local authority.

The UDCs had extensive powers, the main ones being (1) the right to compulsorily purchase, hold, manage, reclaim and sell land; (2) to provide infrastructure within the UDA; and (3) to carry out the construction of buildings within the UDA.

These powers meant that quite extensive decision-taking responsibilities were removed from the local authorities affected and transferred to these central government agencies. With decision-making control went control of finance: the UDCs received government money that could have been provided direct to the local authority.

Table 7.1 Urban Development Corporations in England

UDC	Date established	Area (hects)	Previous main use	Pop. size	Grant 1988–9 (net £m)
Merseyside*	March 81	350*	Docks	450*	21.0
London, Docklands	July 81	2070	Docks	40000	116.4
Trafford, Manchester	Feb. 87	1267	Industry	40	15.5
Teeside	May 87	4565	Steel, chemicals	950	21.0
Tyne & Wear	May 87	2375	Shipyards	4000	24.0
Black Country	May 87	2598	Metal ind.	35000	23.0
Manchester	June 88	187	Mixed ind.	250	2.5
Leeds	June 88	540	Mixed ind.	7500	2.7
Sheffield	June 88	900	Steel	300	8.0
Bristol	Jan. 89	360	Mixed ind.	1500	0.3

* In November 1988 the area of the Merseyside UDC was increased to 960 hectares, extending the size of the resident population inside the UDC to 7000.
Source: Department of the Environment, *Annual Reports*, 1989–93.

Figure 7.2 shows the geographic spread of urban development areas in England. As is clear from Table 7.1, urban development areas were designated in three phases. The first two, designated in 1981, Liverpool's and London's dockland areas, were both dock sites and were estimated to have over 80 per cent and 40 per cent dereliction, respectively, within their boundaries. This derelict land had been lying idle for years with little sign of interest from the private sector.

In 1987 a further four areas of land – each with major tracts of dereliction following the closure of industrial sites – were designated for positive action under the UDA programme.

220   *Regional Economics*

Task forces

Existing
1. South Tyneside
2. Bradford
3. Hull
4. Liverpool
5. Manchester
6. Wirral
7. Nottingham
8. Derby
9. East Birmingham
10. Hackney
11. Deptford
12. North Peckham

To close during 1993
13. Middlesbrough
14. Coventry
15. Bristol
16. West London

To open during 1993
17. Stockton
18. Ladywood
19. Tottenham
20. Plymouth

City Action Teams
1. Tyne and Wear
2. Cleveland
3. Leeds/Bradford
4. Manchester/Salford
5. Liverpool
6. Derby/Nottingham/Leicester
7. Birmingham
8. London

Urban Development Corporations
1. London Docklands
2. Merseyside
3. Trafford Park
4. Teesside
5. Tyne and Wear
6. Black Country
7. Bristol
8. Central Manchester
9. Leeds
10. Sheffield
11. Birmingham Heartlands

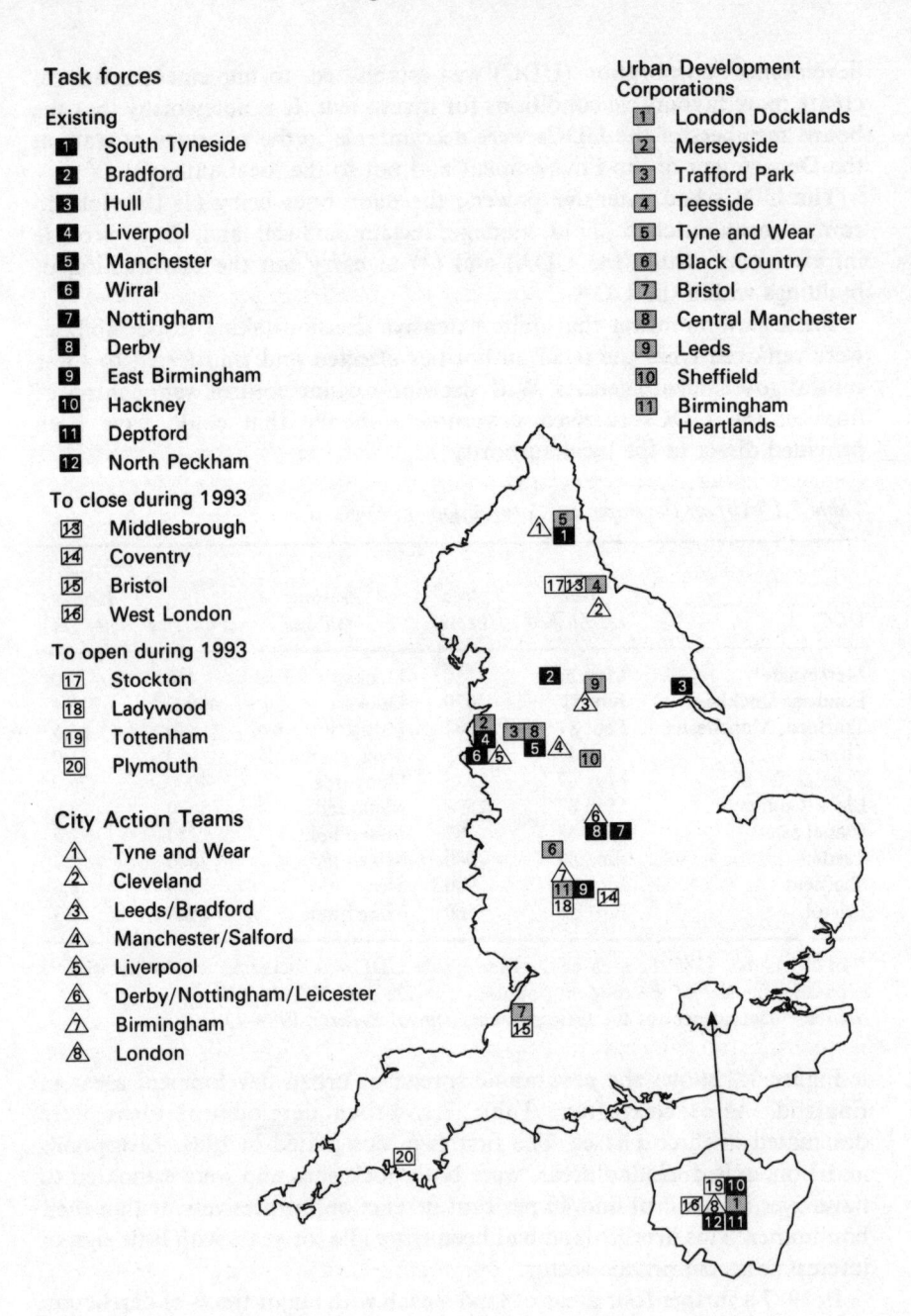

Figure 7.2   UDCs, Inner City Task Forces and City Action Teams, England, 1993
Source: Department of the Environment (1993) *Annual Report*, figure 63, p. 66.

The third phase was announced in 1988–9 and covered four more areas with derelict sites. However it is worth noting that the percentage of derelict land within the boundaries of two of these UDAs, Leeds and Bristol, was between 20 per cent and 25 per cent of the total land area. All areas previously designated as UDAs had had over 30 per cent dereliction inside the designated area.

The fourth designations were Birmingham Heartlands in 1992 and Plymouth in 1993, for an expected period of about five to seven years.

In practice the operation of individual UDCs varied within the overall framework established by the legislation. The life of the UDC was expected to vary from five years to more than ten years depending upon the scale and intractability of the dereliction problem in the individual UDA. The life of the UDA/UDC could be extended if the Department of the Environment believed that such an extension would be beneficial.

The UDCs were primarily financed by grants from central government, although revenue could also be earned by the UDCs through the sale of land and properties held by them and they were permitted to borrow small amounts from the National Loans Fund. City Grants were still available, usually on a partnership basis, for private-sector-led projects inside a UDA. Partnership is often such that the UDC retains ownership of the land while development is in the hands of the private sector.

1981: Enterprise zones The first enterprise zone was designated in Swansea in 1981. By 1990, 27 zones had been designated: 18 in England, four in Scotland, three in Wales and two in Northern Ireland. As Table 7.2 shows, the majority of the zones were initially designated for a decade in the early 1980s, so were due to expire in the early 1990s. In practice this timing had its difficulties as it meant that enterprise zone status ran out during time of general economic malaise – not the best time to be withdrawing government subsidies and incentives to develop derelict areas.

The main incentives available to the zones are (1) exemption from the payment of rates on industrial and commercial property for the period of designation; (2) 100 per cent tax allowance against capital expenditure on industrial and commercial buildings; and (3) a simplified planning system so that certain uses do not need to obtain individual planning permission in order to proceed. In English enterprise zones the requirement for individual planning permission is waived except for certain identified types of development. In Welsh enterprise zones only certain identified types of development can proceed without obtaining individual planning permission.

1982: Urban development grants/derelict land grants/urban regeneration grants were provided to inner-city areas to finance new developments. All these grants are now under the auspices of English Partnership.

Table 7.2 Enterprise zones in the UK

Zone	Expiry date	Area in acres
Belfast, Northern Ireland	1991	190
Clydebank, Strathclyde	1991	568
Corby, Northants	1991	280
Delyn, Clywd, Wales	1993	291
Dudley, West Midlands	1991	540
Glanford, Humberside	1994	124
Hartlepool, Cleveland	1991	270
Inverclyde, Strathclyde	1999	110
Invergordon, Highland	1993	148
Isle of Dogs, London Docks	1992	363
Londonderry, Northern Ireland	1993	270
Lower Swansea Valley, S. Wales	1991	736
Middlesbrough, Cleveland	1993	195
Milford Haven, Dyfed, Wales	1994	361
North East Lancashire	1993	282
North West Kent	1993	375
Rotherham, South Yorks	1993	259
Salford, Manchester	1991	869
Scunthorpe, Humberside	1993	259
Speke, Merseyside	1991	195
Sunderland, Tyne & Wear	2000	150
Tayside, Scotland	1994	296
Telford, Shropshire	1994	279
Tyneside, Tyne & Wear	1991	1121
Wakefield, West Yorks	1993	223
Wellingborough	1993	133
Workington, Cumbria	1993	215

Source: Department of the Environment, 1993.

1984: Freeports. Six freeports, including Merseyside, were designated as being outside the UK customs area with the objective of revitalising useage of the designated ports.

1985: City action teams. The limitations of an uncoordinated response to urban problems by central-government agencies was recognised. Eight city action teams were established to formally liaise between the Departments of the Environment, Trade and Industry, and Employment in the English cities shown (in Figure 7.2).

1986: Inner-city task forces. Sixteen of these were created to extend the intra central-government liaison of the city action teams to liaison in the city between central government, the local community and the private sector. A further four task forces were designated in 1993, as shown in Figure 7.2. They usually have a life-span of two or three years, being designed to encourage the a short-term, positive involvement of the local community in urban regeneration.

1988: City grants. These replaced the previous systems of urban development grants and so on. The aim was to simplify the grant system and offer grants for a wider range of urban-development schemes than had been previously possible. Responsibility for the type of property funding carried out under the grant scheme was effectively transferred from the local authorities (under the previous scheme) to the Department of the Environment in line with the trend towards centralisation of financial control as regards urban-policy initiatives in these years.

City grants are administered through English Partnership to fund capital-investment projects within priority areas. City grants were available on similar terms to Urban Development Areas under urban development corporation control before the establishment of the URA. Until 1991–2, the Grants were available for projects valued above £200 000; in 1991–2 the limit was raised to £500 000, except in 'City-Challenge' areas, where it remains at £200 000.

Table 7.3 City Grants, May 1988–November 1992

Region	No. of schemes approved	Approved total city grant plus private-sector investment	New jobs
W Mid	56	347	11 154
E Mid	36	124	4868
N West	64	323	5663
North	51	126	2215
London	20	116	3137
Y & Humb	36	179	5125
Mersey	31	168	4460
S West	6	47	2364
Total	300	1430*	38 986

* of which £1163 million from the private sector and £267 million from the government
Source: Department of the Environment, 1993.

1992: Capital partnership programme. This programme enables local government to draw upon its receipts from the previous sale of capital assets, such as council housing, in order to fund urban development in partnership with private enterprise. Under this programme 46 inner-city councils share a £20 million urban partnership fund to finance 81 projects. The value of the fund is notably smaller than the funds available to English Partnership.

1992: City challenge. Aims to finance regeneration of the inner city and its housing. Eleven programmes were selected for assistance in 1992, and a further 20 in 1993. Allocation is on a competitive-bid basis.

1992: Coalfield areas fund. Aims to finance regeneration of local communities and economies adversely affected by local mine closures. A relatively short-term programme of approximately £2 million funding in 1992–3 and 1993–4.

1993: English Partnership. Formed as an umbrella organisation responsible to the secretary of state for the Environment and charged with facilitating urban regeneration, primarily through action on property. It absorbed the roles of English Estates and the UDCs, and the administration of city grants and derelict land grants. It has planning and compulsory-purchase powers.

References and Further Reading

College of Estate Management (1990) *Urban Regeneration, Planning and Financial Incentives* (Reading: C.E.M).
Department of the Environment (1988) *Planning Policy Guidance Note 5, Simplified Planning Zones* (London: HMSO).
Department of the Environment (1989a) *Action for Cities* (London: HMSO).
Department of the Environment (1989b) *Urban Regeneration and Economic Development – the Local Government Dimension* (London: HMSO).
Department of the Environment (1992a) *The Urban Regeneration Agency* (Consultation Paper) (London: HMSO).
Department of the Environment (1992b) *Council Tax* (London: HMSO).
Department of the Environment (1993) *Annual Report* (London: HMSO).
Kohnstamm, P.P. (1993) 'Urban renewal and public–private partnership in The Netherlands,' in J. Berry, S. McGreal and B. Deddis (eds) (1993) *Urban Regeneration* (London: E. and F.N. Spon), pp. 220–9.
Needham, Barrie *et al.* (1993) *Urban Land and Property Markets in the Netherlands* (London: University College London Press).
Prestwich, Roger and Peter Taylor (1990) *Introduction to Regional and Urban Policy in the United Kingdom* (London: Longman).
Steel, John (1992) 'Urban Regeneration, Urban Development Corporations, and the new Urban Regeneration Agency', *Property Review*, October, pp. 45–7.
Witbraad, F. and P. Jorna (1993) 'Waterfront Regeneration: the IJ Embankments Project in Amsterdam', in J. Berry, S. McGreal and B. Deddis (eds) *Urban Regeneration* (London: E. and F.N. Spon), pp. 230–9.

8 Regional Economic Policy

AN INTRODUCTION TO REGIONAL POLICY

Regional Policy Aims and Objectives

The aim of regional policy is the attainment of a more efficient and/or equitable interregional distribution of economic activity. As demonstrated earlier in this book, the UK during the past 15 years has experienced an underlying widening, and not narrowing, of disparities in the interregional distribution of economic activity as measured by, for example, output and employment. On the surface, recent UK regional policy appears to have been a failure rather than a success. This view is taken by several regional economists, including Townroe and Martin whose view is that,

> arguably never well specified or targeted, regional policy had failed to keep pace with the changing nature and pattern of the regional problem (Townroe and Martin, 1992, p. 20).

This and the following chapter accordingly provide a detailed discussion of regional policy, with particular reference to policy in the UK since 1977. Following a period of active regional policy between about 1963 and around 1976, UK regional policy has been less marked since 1977. In the absence of a strong, overt regional policy, therefore, the government's policy response to interregional disparities merits detailed consideration.

This chapter opens with an explanation of regional policy in the wider economic policy environment. The policy instruments available to government are then introduced, and actual regional policy measures are explained. These are listed in detail in the appendix to this chapter. The final section of the main text of the chapter places UK regional policy in the wider context of EC regional and economic policies.

The aims of regional policy may be translated into more specific objectives, many of which are capable of measurement. For example, the attainment of a reduction in above-average regional rates of unemployment represents a quantifiable policy objective. We can see that this objective reflects its macroeconomic counterpart of attaining full employment: the primary objective of much macroeconomic policy between 1950 and 1979.

The replacement of full employment by price stability as the prime UK macroeconomic policy objective during the 1980s and early 1990s coincides with the period during which central government perceived active regional policies to be less important. Does this mean that regions and regional policy are perceived by the decision makers to be irrelevant in the context of antiinflation policy? This seems to be the likely explanation, although arguably a misguided and myopic view, as demonstrated by the discussion of inflation in the regional context in Chapter 4. So a second valid objective for an active and effective regional policy should be the containment of inflationary pressures in the regional economy.

Economic growth is an accepted macroeconomic policy objective that has been translated into regional and intraregional policy objectives especially in the context of growth zones, discussed in Chapter 6, and urban-regeneration policies, discussed in Chapter 7. In the UK, however, the fourth macroeconomic policy objective, that of balance-of-payments equilibrium, has not been translated from the macroeconomic to the regional sphere. As with inflation, there is no a priori reason why this should be the case. Regional balance-of-payments constraints and the difficulties that arise from them are recognised by US economists in the analysis of their internal economy. Similarly, regional payments imbalances have implications for the UK regions, as discussed earlier.

Concepts of regional equity are inherent in the importance given to the alleviation of regional unemployment discrepancies. Employment is the main source of personal income in the economy, and so regional discrepancies in unemployment imply regional discrepancies in income-earning potential. However this objective remains implicit rather than explicit in the political processes of policy formulation and implementation.

The Policy Framework

The political perception of the need for and the importance of regional policy has been subject to significant variation during recent decades. The 1960s and 1970s were decades of active regional policy in the UK, the focus being upon taking jobs to the workers. In contrast the 1980s saw an overall change in the political direction of economic policy, reflected in a halving of the real level of regional policy expenditure by the UK government. Given this recent pattern of contrasting experiences, it will be interesting to see what degree of political priority is accorded to regional policy during the second half of the 1990s.

The difficulty of reconciling conflicting government macroeconomic policy objectives also impinges upon regional policy. There may be a conflict between the encouragement of national economic growth and economic growth at the regional level. The interactions between growth at the two different levels of spatial aggregation, and therefore the relative extent to which resources should be channelled towards each other, are not well understood.

It may also be argued that neglect of regional policy results in greater inflationary pressures within the economy than would occur in the presence of a strong regional policy that successfully reduces regional disparities.

The central problem of the *assignment* of policy instruments to policy objectives applies as much to regional economic policy as to national economic policy. In other words, at the regional level the problem remains that there are likely to be more policy objectives than policy instruments with which to reach those objectives.

Individual policies are also interdependent in their effect. Their primary effect may be accurately identifiable and so an individual policy instrument assignable to the attainment of a specified objective. However secondary effects mean that policies in this area of policy making, as in others, must be complementary and not conflicting if they are to be successful.

An additional problem with policy implementation at the regional level is the higher level of leakages from the regional than from the national economy. We have seen that regional multipliers are typically lower than the multipliers for the national economy. This reduces the leverage a given change in regional policy may have upon the regional economy compared with the leverage a comparable amount of macroeconomic policy would be likely to exert upon the macroeconomy. This lower leverage reduces the effectiveness of any given level of regional policy expenditure, unless that expenditure is carefully targeted to avoid any major leakage. Regional policy expenditure therefore needs to be carefully designed, implemented and monitored to be effective.

The effectiveness of regional policy is considered more fully in Chapter 9. Meanwhile this section has looked at *what* aims and objectives regional policy seeks to achieve within the environment of other government economic policies. The following section considers *how* these objectives may be achieved by looking at the main instruments of regional policy.

POLICY INSTRUMENTS

Macroeconomic and Regional Policy Instruments

It is interesting to consider which of the policy instruments available for government macroeconomic management are available to the policy maker for use in the regional economy. Monetary policy is traditionally determined solely at the macroeconomic level, with no attempt to vary interest rates directly at the regional level. As we have seen, the region is a price taker in relation to the supply of financial capital.

The money market is not an active medium for the implementation of regional policy. In fact many monetarists would argue that regional policy is irrelevant at best. In their view, markets are self-equilibrating and so there is no need for policy intervention. Such intervention may be seen as positively harmful where it prevents the attainment of free-market equilibrium, or where the government sector crowds out potentially profitable private-sector activities.

Regional policy has been implemented in the UK primarily through fiscal policy rather than monetary policy. The money market may not be of prime importance to regional policy, nor may the markets for goods and services. It is the markets for the factors of production – labour, land and capital – that hold the key to understanding traditional regional policies in the UK. Policies have accordingly aimed to influence the patterns of spatial activity in the factor markets so as to encourage activity in those regions perceived to be in need of assistance.

This aim has been sought through various policy measures that are intended to affect the demand-side of the economy, the supply-side or both. Demand for factors of production in these regions has been enhanced through such measures as investment grants towards the cost of expenditure on capital. The quality of the supply of labour has been enhanced through training programmes. The cost of factors of production to the employer has been subsidised, for example, through selective depreciation tax allowances. The instruments available to the policy makers and their application in the context of UK regional policy in recent decades are considered in greater detail below.

As well as specific regional policies, other macroeconomic policies implemented by both the UK and the EC authorities impact upon the regional economy. Earlier in this book we explained the differential regional effects of fiscal policy. Taxation affects the economies of different regions differently, as do such categories of expenditure as unemployment benefit and expenditure on roads and health care.

A further example of central-government policy indirectly affecting the region is planning legislation. Supply-side controls such as planning restrictions may have a spatially uneven effect upon different regions of the economy, influencing the location of economic activity.

Supply-side employment policies affect the region through the provision of training and education. In some economies the regional distribution of higher-education expenditure is very uneven. The UK is no exception, with the highest proportion of school leavers entering higher education and the highest proportion of graduates being located in the South East, the lowest proportion being in the North of England (see Figure 2.15).

These examples illustrate that, in addition to direct regional policy, other government economic policies have differential interregional effects.

Regional Policy Incentives and Constraints

How could the spatial distribution of economic activity be improved? Should policy instruments seek to mitigate regional disparities through the operation of the private market? Or should there be more active government intervention in the operation of the regional economy?

Regional policy incentives

Private-sector economic activity can be encouraged to locate in regions in need of assistance by such policy measures as regionally discriminatory tax incentives. Such incentives have often been referred to as 'carrots', in the literature of regional economics, as they are designed to attract economic activity to locations where it is otherwise unwilling to be led.

An example of such a regional policy carrot is the regional development grant (RDG), which was available as a subsidy to manufacturing investment in plant, machinery and buildings in designated development areas in the UK between 1972 and 1984.

Industry subsidies have been a useful instrument of regional policy in several European economies in recent decades. However their extent and form has been subject to tighter controls in recent years than was the case in the 1960s and early 1970s. This is because such subsidies now have to be designed to avoid conflict with the EC's competition policies. While reliable statistics are difficult to obtain, OECD figures for 1988 estimated that the value of West German government subsidies to West German industry was the equivalent of about 2.3 percentage of GDP. For the same year UK government subsidies to UK industry were worth about 1.3 per cent of GDP.

On this basis West German industry would appear to have been at a competitive advantage relative to UK industry because it received higher subsidies from its domestic government. It is this sort of consideration that has led to scrutiny of regional subsidies to industry by domestic governments, to try to ensure their compatibility with the EC's concept of a single internal market.

Regional policy constraints

The corollary of carrots to attract the unwilling to regions perceived to be in need of increased economic activity is that of constraints, or 'sticks', to prevent the willing from being economically overactive in already prosperous areas. There are examples of such policies being implemented in recent decades in the UK, but they are infrequent. UK regional policy has emphasised the use of carrots rather than sticks.

What will be the effect upon the quantity supplied to an urban or regional market of a control such as tight planning controls on the quantity of new office development in London?

Tighter controls upon any market will, if reasonably effective, have the effect of restricting the level of supply below that which would otherwise be forthcoming. The general effect of controls therefore is to restrict supply, the effect of the stick being to redirect activity elsewhere.

While there have been fewer examples of sticks operating in the UK in recent years, the supply of office buildings London was strictly controlled by the requirement for office development permits in the 1970s. The consequent limitation of the supply of offices in London resulted in increased rents, as would be expected. These higher London rents acted as an incentive to organisations to seek offices outside, rather than inside, London and the South East of England. The initial restriction on the quantity of offices was reinforced by the further restriction of higher prices in the form of premium rents.

The private sector's energies may also be harnessed jointly with those of the public sector. Joint private/public-sector action has been undertaken in France for many years but is more recent in the UK. As we saw in Chapter 7, this concept underlies many current urban policy initiatives.

The government itself controls the spatial distribution of its own expenditures and activities and this may act as an effective instrument of regional policy. Some major components of direct, general, government consumption expenditure, such as wages and salaries in the defence sector, have a marked regional impact. One region to have benefited from relatively high levels of expenditure from the government's defence budget is the South West of England.

This aspect of regional policy is discussed more fully below and might be identified as the 'broccoli' component of regional policy. It is nutritionally valuable to the receiving region, unattractive to donkeys, and an inherent ingredient in the range of vegetables used by government to implement regional policy.

To be effective, regional policy requires an integrated overall approach that coordinates individual policy measures. These measures are discussed more fully in the next section.

REGIONAL POLICY MEASURES

The Evolution of UK Regional Policy

Active regional policy in the UK can be traced back through sixty years to the Special Areas (Development and Improvement) Act of 1934. The motivation for this first piece of regionally oriented legislation was the scale of interregional discrepancies in unemployment. For example, while unemployment in London and the South East was approximately 14 per cent, in the North West, Scotland and the North East it was over 25 per cent and in Wales over 36 per cent.

These levels of unemployment were reflected in the regional location of the four areas designated as 'special' by the legislation: central Scotland, the North East coast, west Cumberland and South Wales. Two million pounds of government expenditure was allocated for infrastructure improvements to assist these special areas.

The upheaval associated with the prolonged depression of the 1930s and its uneven regional impact upon those regions that had been the heartlands of nineteenth-century industrial activity led to the establishment of a Royal Commission on the Geographical Distribution of the Industrial Population. The commission's report – the Barlow Report – was produced in 1940 and provided the framework for regional policy both in the immediate postwar years and during the 1960s. It might be argued that the 1990s follow-up to the Barlow Report is now overdue!

It was the Barlow Report that established the stick and carrot framework within which many regional policies have since been constructed. The sticks have attempted to restrict further economic development in areas of above-average economic activity and growth, while the carrots have tempted economic activity into the relatively depressed areas of the economy. In practice the balance of regional policy over the years has favoured the use of carrots rather than sticks.

1945–51: From factories to finance

The 1945 Distribution of Industry Act extended the boundaries of the special areas and renamed them 'Development Areas'. Policy intervention was extended from the provision of infrastructure to the reclamation of derelict land and provision of factories in the development areas. Factory development elsewhere was discouraged through the introduction of the requirement to obtain a building licence for developments in excess of 10 000 square feet. This was the forerunner of the Industrial Development Certificate, the main stick of UK regional policy.

The location of economic activity was subject to increasingly tight local control following the 1947 Town and Country Planning Act, which resulted in clearer specification and prescription of land use. The areas covered by regional assistance were extended so that by 1948 about 20 per cent of the UK population lived in development areas.

Further legislation in 1950 and 1951 extended the range of regional policy from provision of factories and infrastructure to direct financial assistance to relocate firms and their key workers. The financial incentives needed for a potentially effective regional policy were now in place.

1960–6: Change and continuity

In 1959 unemployment was low by modern standards, averaging 2.2 per cent. However regional disparities remained, with the South East at 1.3 per cent and Scotland at 4.4 per cent. These continuing disparities underlay the definition of the assisted areas in 1960 in terms of areas with actual or expected rates of unemployment in excess of 4.5 per cent. The result was a patchwork of pockets of assistance across the country. This lasted until the development areas were redefined as five larger assisted areas in 1966, viz Merseyside, the North, the South West, Scotland, and Wales.

Policy measures continued to emphasise the provision of financial assistance to relocate key workers and help towards the cost of buildings, plant and machinery in the assisted areas. Building, investment grants and depreciation allowances became increasingly generous in the face of persisting regional unemployment disparities.

In 1963 the Hailsham Report recommended for the first time that assistance be targeted towards growth poles or growth zones within the assisted areas, rather than spread thinly throughout these areas.

Meanwhile the structure of the economy had been undergoing major change. The service sector was expanding rapidly, but only in certain locations. By 1965 half of the office space in the UK was located in London and the South East. In that year Industrial Development Certificates were complemented by the introduction of Office Development Permits (ODPs) for all office development in excess of 5000 square feet in London, the South East, East Anglia and the Midlands.

The object of ODPs was to try to ensure that the growing service sector became more evenly distributed across the economy, rather than being concentrated in the already relatively prosperous regions. This was seen to be particularly important as, at this time, the expansion of output in the service sector was significantly more labour intensive than was the expansion of output in the manufacturing sector. In principle the service sector accordingly had greater potential for the alleviation of unemployment than did the manufacturing sector.

1966–71: Widening the scope of regional policy

By the mid-1960s there were two main concerns about the form of regional policy.

Firstly, there was concern that the money spent on regional policy was encouraging recipient firms to employ capital-intensive production processes and was therefore not well directed towards the overriding policy objective of reducing unemployment in the assisted areas. Consequently, in the later 1960s the existing financial incentives were further augmented by direct labour subsidies designed to encourage greater employment of labour.

Secondly, there was a view that dividing the national economy into assisted areas and nonassisted areas was too narrow and simplistic an approach to the problem of uneven regional economic development. In response, the late 1960s saw the emergence of a more complex categorisation of regions in the context of policy.

The key concept of development areas was retained. However this was supplemented by the identification of special development areas to receive more generous financial assistance in such locations as West Cumberland, where unemployment was seen to be particularly acute.

Intermediate areas, where unemployment was not as serious as in the development areas but where regional economic potential was seen to be lacking, were also identified. These too became eligible for financial assistance, although on a lesser scale than the development areas.

1972–9: The persistence of regional disparities

Against a backdrop of rising national unemployment and the continuation of above-average rates of unemployment in the assisted areas despite the 1960s regional policy measures, the 1972 Industry Act sought to establish the basis for regional policy in the 1970s. The assisted areas established under the Act are shown in Figure 8.3 in the appendix to this chapter. The key details of the Act are also enumerated in the appendix. Two points are especially relevant here:

> The Act sought to 'encourage any developments which might contribute to national economic growth since it was believed that this, in turn, would have "spread" or "trickle down" benefits for the less prosperous regions' (Prestwich and Taylor, 1990, p. 145).

The designation of intermediate areas was also extended so that over half of the UK became assisted areas. The following year the range of financial assistance was extended to attract the service as well as the manufacturing industry to the assisted areas. This extension of policy was crucial in light of the growing economic importance of the service sector to the national economy.

Also in 1973, the Hardman Report recommended the decentralisation of Civil-Service jobs from London. These recommendations were made on grounds of both government efficiency and regional policy and formed the precursor to the current public-sector relocation policies that are discussed more fully later in this chapter.

1973 also saw the entry of the UK into the EC and hence the availability of assistance from the European Regional Development Fund to regions in the UK. This added a new dimension to the provision of regional assistance in the UK, which we consider later.

By the end of the 1970s regional policy had been in active operation for over 25 years, had cost the public purse large sums of money, and yet familiar regional disparities in unemployment persisted. A few controls had been applied, but their use had been cautious in view of the danger of preventing economic growth. Many regional financial incentives had been applied, but none seemed to have solved the regional problem.

For these reasons it is perhaps unsurprising that disillusionment with regional policy expenditure, which became clear after 1979, seems to have begun in a small way earlier. An increasing emphasis upon industrial rather than regional policy initiatives began in 1975, and accelerated during the 1980s.

1979–93: No sticks and fewer carrots

The election of the Conservative government in 1979 signalled a change in the philosophy of government intervention in the UK economy. The philosophy for the 1980s represented the encouragement of market forces and the discouraging of government intervention, which was seen as interference. The 'invisible hand' of the market was perceived as benign and was to be encouraged to untangle economic problems. The government's underlying monetarist ethos meant that active regional policies were seen as unduly interventionist. In this context the revision and reduction of regional policy expenditure that characterised the 1980s is hardly surprising.

The sticks of Office Development Permits and Industrial Development Certificates were abolished, creating a 'carrots only' policy approach. The carrots were to be found in fewer fields, however, as the assisted areas were successively reduced in scope in 1979, 1982 and 1984 to those shown in Figure 8.5 in the appendix.

The idea of targeting regional development into fewer, more precisely defined geographical areas was reflected in the new emphasis upon urban rather than traditional regional policy (considered in detail in Chapter 7).

In Scotland the roles given to Scottish Enterprise, Highlands and Islands Enterprise, and the local enterprise companies also meant that control was primarily with Scottish Enterprise and the UK government rather than with local government in Scotland. The role played by the Scottish local authorities in regional and local economic development has been reduced. Instead the private sector has been encouraged to play a more active role through involvement with local enterprise trusts and initiatives under the auspices of Scottish Enterprise.

Scottish Enterprise also has responsibility for the implementation of urban policy in Scotland. Scottish Enterprise is responsible to the UK government in London. This pattern of responsibility for the implementation of regional and urban policies in Scotland means that the situation there mirrors the increased centralisation of regional and urban policy control in England during the 1980s.

In 1984 the government announced its intention of reducing regional policy expenditure by half between 1983 and 1987. To achieve this, in 1984 regional selective assistance and regional development grants were linked more directly to employment creation with the aim of making regional policy more cost-effective. Figure 8.1 shows that overall UK expenditure did not fall by half in the second half of the 1980s, although it did fall by half in the English regions.

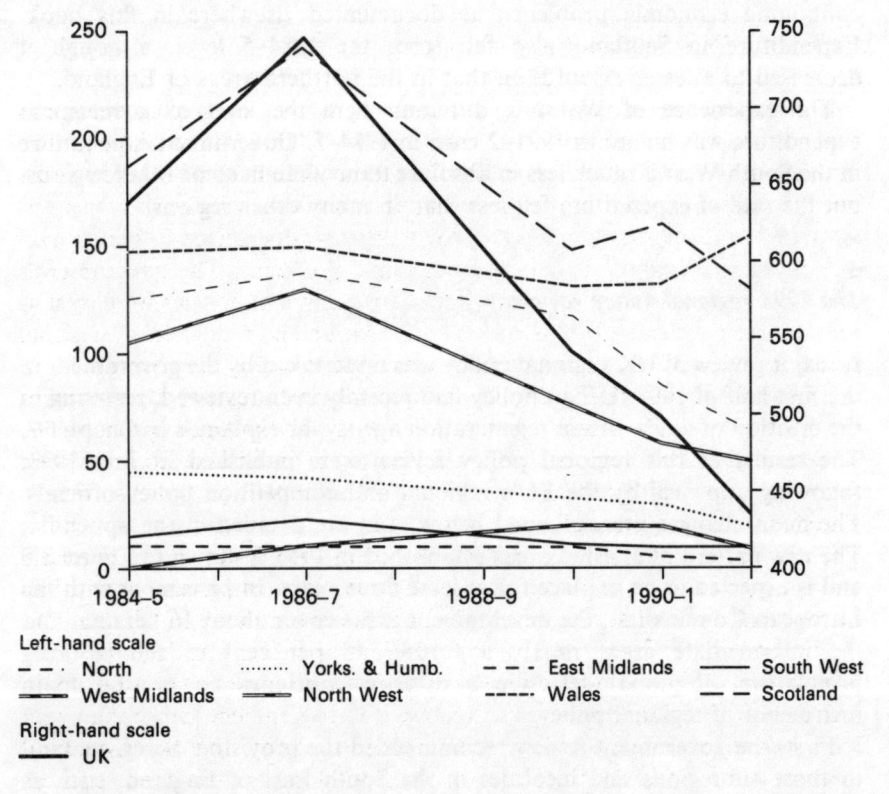

Figure 8.1 Government expenditure on regional preferential assistance to industry in the assisted areas, £ million, 1984–5 to 1991–2

Source of data: UK CSO, *Regional Trends*, vol. 28 (1993), table 13.7.

In 1988 regional development grants were abolished and replaced by regional enterprise grants, available on a discretionary basis as outlined in the appendix to this chapter. The 1988 enterprise initiative for industry generally indicated a further tightening of the conditions under which industry could obtain grants for capital expenditure, resulting in emphasis upon job creation within existing firms rather than encouraging the creation of new firms.

What were the main changes in the regional distribution of industrial assistance between 1984 and 1992 according to the data in Figure 8.1?

The expenditure on industrial assistance received by individual UK regions varied widely among regions, as shown by Figure 8.1. Expenditure received by the North and North West of England halved during these years, in spite of these regions' relatively poor economic performance and continuing economic problems, as documented elsewhere in this book. Expenditure in Scotland also fell from the 1984–5 level, although it decreased to a lesser extent than that in the northern areas of England.

The experience of Wales is different: here the level of government expenditure was higher in 1991–2 than in 1984–5. Government expenditure in the South West is much less in absolute terms than in some other regions, but the rate of expenditure fell less than in many other regions.

The 1993 regional policy review

A major review of UK regional policy was undertaken by the government in the first half of 1993. Urban policy had recently been reviewed, resulting in the creation of a new urban regeneration agency, as explained in Chapter 7. The results of this regional policy review were published in July 1993, following approval by the EC's regional and competition policy officials. The main changes are explained below, and are detailed in the appendix. The new pattern of assisted areas established in 1993 is shown in Figure 8.8 and is expected to be in place for at least three years. In agreement with the European Commission, the development areas cover about 16 per cent and the intermediate areas nearly a further 18 per cent of the working population. Regional selective assistance continues to be the main instrument of regional policy.

First, the government review recommended the provision of regional aid to those subregions and localities in the South East of England, such as Thanet and Dover in east Kent, that experienced high increases in unemployment during the 1990–92 recession. The granting of assisted-area status to these locations indicated government acceptance of the view that their local unemployment reflected underlying structural long-term unemployment and not solely short-term cyclical unemployment. The mid-1993 unemployment figures demonstrated that the South East and South West of England were recovering from the 1990–2 recession much faster than the outer regions of the UK. However these localities were granted assisted-area status in the belief that they would not benefit from regional economic recovery in the South East without such aid.

Second, the government review responded to the impact of reduced defence expenditure in selected locations in the South West and North West, for example, Barrow in Furness. The effect of accelerated closure of coalmines upon the subregions most affected, such as the mining area of Derbyshire, was also recognised. Here, towns such as Chesterfield and Mansfield were granted assisted-area status for the first time.

The effect of mine closures upon the local labour market has therefore influenced the spatial distribution of government assistance resulting from the review. The need for wider help to affected mining communities has also been recognised through the creation of the Coalfield Areas Fund for 1992–4 as outlined in the appendix to Chapter 7.

While the evaluation of regional policy in general is discussed in Chapter 9, some specific points regarding the UK 1993 policy review are considered in the following paragraphs as the 1993 policy review is of great interest to all those concerned about the widening regional disparities of the 1980s.

There may well be a case for granting regional assistance for local travel to work areas in the South East and South West of England that demonstrably have economic difficulties. However an alternative source of support to these localities might be through the medium of county and regional planning to facilitate their involvement in the economic expansion already present at the regional level.

In view of the continuing spatial economic disparities in the UK, it is unfortunate that assistance to these localities in the South East and South West appears to be *instead of* and not *in addition to* assistance designed to meet the needs of other regions. Towns adversely affected by the past closure of steelworks such, as Scunthorpe in the Yorkshire and Humberside region, and Shotton and Port Talbot in North and South Wales respectively, have had their regional assistance status downgraded. The assumption that their local economies have become self-sustaining seems optimistic.

The overall effect of the 1993 policy changes appears to favour the south of England to the detriment of the North of England, Wales and Scotland. It would therefore appear to respond to the medium-term difficulties created by the recession of the early 1990s and not to the endemic long-term problems inherited from the 1980s which, as we have seen, persist in several regions of the UK.

UK regional policy continues to be oriented very strongly towards unemployment as a measure of regional health. The following criteria were taken into account by the Department of Trade and Industry in identifying the 1993 Assisted Areas:

- ❏ current unemployment (measured as the average over the past twelve months to eliminate seasonal variations).
- ❏ structural unemployment (measured by the persistent incidence of unemployment over the past five years).
- ❏ the duration of unemployment
- ❏ future employment prospects
- ❏ economic activity rates
- ❏ urban problems
- ❏ peripherality
- ❏ major impending closures likely to adversely affect employment. (Department of Trade and Industry, 1993, p. 6)

The major criteria used are the first two, that is, current and structural unemployment, the others also being taken into account. To categorise areas by unemployment as the main measure of their need for assistance has the merits of consistency, comparability and comprehension.

However such an approach has its limitations. First, the resulting patchwork pattern of assisted areas is likely to encourage spatial diversion of economic activity at the regional and subregional level. To this extent the problem is moved around rather than solved.

Second, unemployment rates offer a superficially comparable measure between regions and subregions. However we saw earlier that other measures of labour-market activity, such as activity rates, are subject to interregional variation. For example, actual unemployment in some areas of Wales may be underrecorded by the unemployment data if some of the economically inactive would become economically active in a more buoyant labour market.

Third, while the use of unemployment as the main criterion has the advantage of simplicity, it provides a one-dimensional view of a multi-dimensional problem. The basis of policy may accordingly be undesirably narrow.

UK regional policy continues to rely on the carrots of selective regional assistance to industry. Will these carrots prove tempting enough to attract industry to the undergrazed areas of the outer regions and away from perceived and actual growth zones such as the M4 corridor in the south of England?

The Regional Impact of Public-Sector Location

This section considers the potential spatial effects of government policy initiatives with regard to the location and relocation of public-sector activity. Gripaios and Bishop observed that in the 1980s in the South West of England:

> a 'hidden' regional policy has effectively operated through the regional impact of defence spending. The south west has been a major beneficiary of defence spending because of the location of many important defence contractors and defence bases in the region (Gripaios and Bishop, 1992, p. 45).

The importance of this 'hidden' regional policy is demonstrated by the fact that government expenditure on regional assistance per head of population in the South West in 1988–9 was £3.20, while government expenditure on defence equipment per head of population in the South West in 1988–9 was £242.00. (ibid.) Table 2.3.2, p. 45.

Public property and public policy

The principles underlying location decision making by central government were introduced in Chapter 5. As explained then, organisations hold their portfolio of property for a combination of operational and investment purposes. As property has a spatial location, the choice of location affects regional economies.

In the case of central government, its extensive properties may be held for policy purposes as well as for operational and investment purposes. The management of public-sector property may accordingly seek to integrate the requirements of policy into the management process. This means that, in the case of government property, the need for effective property management to reconcile multiple roles and objectives is further complicated by the requirements associated with policy implementation. Effective reconciliation and integration of these different roles and objectives is necessary to yield enhanced efficiency in the allocation and utilisation of public-sector property resources.

An important question is whether the political and social agendas relating to regional policy location initiatives and their implementation can and/or should be embedded in the management objectives of public property. It is necessary to focus first upon what *is* happening before the question as to whether this *should* be happening can be addressed.

In relation to public property, the National Audit Office sees:

> a sharper focus to capital values, operational costs and performance measurement, and a move from reactive to proactive asset management. This in turn should lead to better value for money (NAO, 1992, p. 17).

This statement suggests a predominantly cost-driven view of public-sector location. We return at the end of this discussion to the question of whether this 'value-for-money' emphasis includes at least some consideration of social benefits and spatial equity.

Public-sector location and regional policy

> The Employment Secretary's . . . plan is to relocate many of our armed forces to the North of England . . . although we have 420,000 service personnel, only 20,000 . . . are stationed in the north. . . . And . . . virtually *all* unemployment is in the north . . . if we move 300,000 servicemen . . . to the north we will create masses of civilian jobs: clerks . . . builders . . . 300,000 extra pay packets to be spent in the shops (Lynn and Jay, 1987, p. 9).

While the extract above is fictional, it aptly conveys the point that relocating public-sector activity to regions in need of assistance will produce beneficial multiplier expansionary effects in the receiving region. Such relocation can therefore act as an effective instrument of regional policy.

Government regional policy alters rather more frequently than does the location of public-sector activity. This mismatch means that location decisions taken in the past may not always contribute effectively to the fulfillment of today's regional policy objectives. However, in spite of the frequency of alteration to the shape of the policy framework, some underlying policy objectives can be identified as continuing in the longer term.

For example, one underlying objective has been that of decentralising government activity and employment from London. Such decentralisation is seen as a means of generating greater employment in areas experiencing rates of unemployment above the national average.

At times when London and the South East are experiencing property costs in excess of the national average, such as in 1986–7, decentralisation is associated with reduced property costs. However in 1992 the excess supply of office space in London reduced rents to levels highly competitive with those in major regional centres such as Birmingham and Manchester. The – rejected – proposal put forward in summer 1992 to relocate a major portion of central London Civil-Service employment to Canary Wharf in Docklands reflected this altered pattern of regional rental and property costs. London office-space rent levels are likely to remain relatively low in the next few years – but relocation decisions have to be made over a longer time span.

Current Treasury guidance states that any proposal requiring longer than 20 years to produce a positive net present value 'will need particularly careful scrutiny' (HM Treasury, 1991, p. 4) indicating a very long time horizon. For a large-scale move involving hundreds rather than tens of employees, planning and implementation could also take years rather than months.

For example, a typical time scale for a major relocation by the public sector could span seven years as follows:

Early/mid year 1	Commence relocation study.
Late year 2	Decide in principle to relocate.
Early/mid year 3	Decide where to relocate.
Late year 3	Commission construction work and so on.
Mid year 5	New site ready for occupation.
Early year 7	Relocation complete.

While this example will vary depending upon the scale of the relocation and whether the move is to existing or new, purpose-built accommodation, it does serve to demonstrate that short-term cyclical movements in the labour and property markets should not be given undue weight when making location decisions.

The initial costs associated with relocation are relatively high, and it takes several years before the benefits stemming from the relocation cover these costs. For example, Ashcroft *et al.* (1988) studied the relocation of the Overseas Development Agency from central London to East Kilbride in Scotland. They found that although the initial costs of relocation were high, these were covered within six years. This further emphasises the long-term nature of relocation activity.

Government relocation since 1988

The government has control over the location of its own activities, and has used this control to further its regional policy objectives in some periods during the last forty years. Marshall *et al.* (1991) suggest that this has not been such a high priority since 1988. In their view 'traditional' regional policy considerations were less dominant between 1988 and 1990, being replaced by a 'market-oriented' approach to the location of government activity.

As Marshall *et al.* point out, the overall cost advantages of relocating public-sector activities away from London and the South East were greater in the 1980s than in earlier decades. This is explained by the greater regional differences in labour and property costs in the 1980s. Actual relocation and decentralisation was, however, hindered by the perceived distance attributed by employees to regions further from London than the Midlands and Yorkshire.

How would you expect the lower rents and higher unemployment in London in the early 1990s to have affected the cost disadvantages of being located in the capital city?

Higher unemployment both reduced upward pressure upon London wage costs and reduced rates of staff turnover. In addition, the slack property market in these years reduced the cost of London property. In other words, the recessionary slackening of the labour and property markets in the South East markedly diminished the English regions' 1980s comparative cost advantage. Further, it seems plausible that increasing awareness of European influences will reinforce perceptions of the South East as a preferred location.

It appears that the recession of the early 1990s led to some reappraisal of government objectives in this area of decision making. While the 1988 Treasury guidelines for Civil-Service relocation emphasised the National Audit Office 'value-for-money' approach, the revised guidelines issued in December 1991 gave greater recognition to the need for public-sector employment location to reinforce regional and urban policy initiatives. The weak labour market of 1991 strengthened the ability of the government as an employer to relocate employees away from the South East without the risk of unduly high turnover.

As Figure 8.2 shows, the main destination regions are the South West and the North West. It is intended that fewer than 1000 jobs be moved to East Anglia, while fewer than two thousand are planned for Scotland, Wales and Northern Ireland.

It should be noted that the figure for the South West is primarily made up of 4230 posts being moved by the Ministry of Defence.

Government relocation of activity away from London and the South East region is a response to regional variations in the labour market as well as the property market. Earlier in this book it was noted that demographic trends indicate that organisations, including those in the public sector, may meet a labour-supply constraint. This may result in rising real wages and tighter availability of labour in the South East in the mid-1990s.

If it had been implemented, the 1992 proposal to move civil servants to London Dockland's Canary Wharf would not have contributed to well-understood regional policy objectives such as enhanced employment opportunities in regions experiencing above-average unemployment. Nor

Regional Economic Policy 243

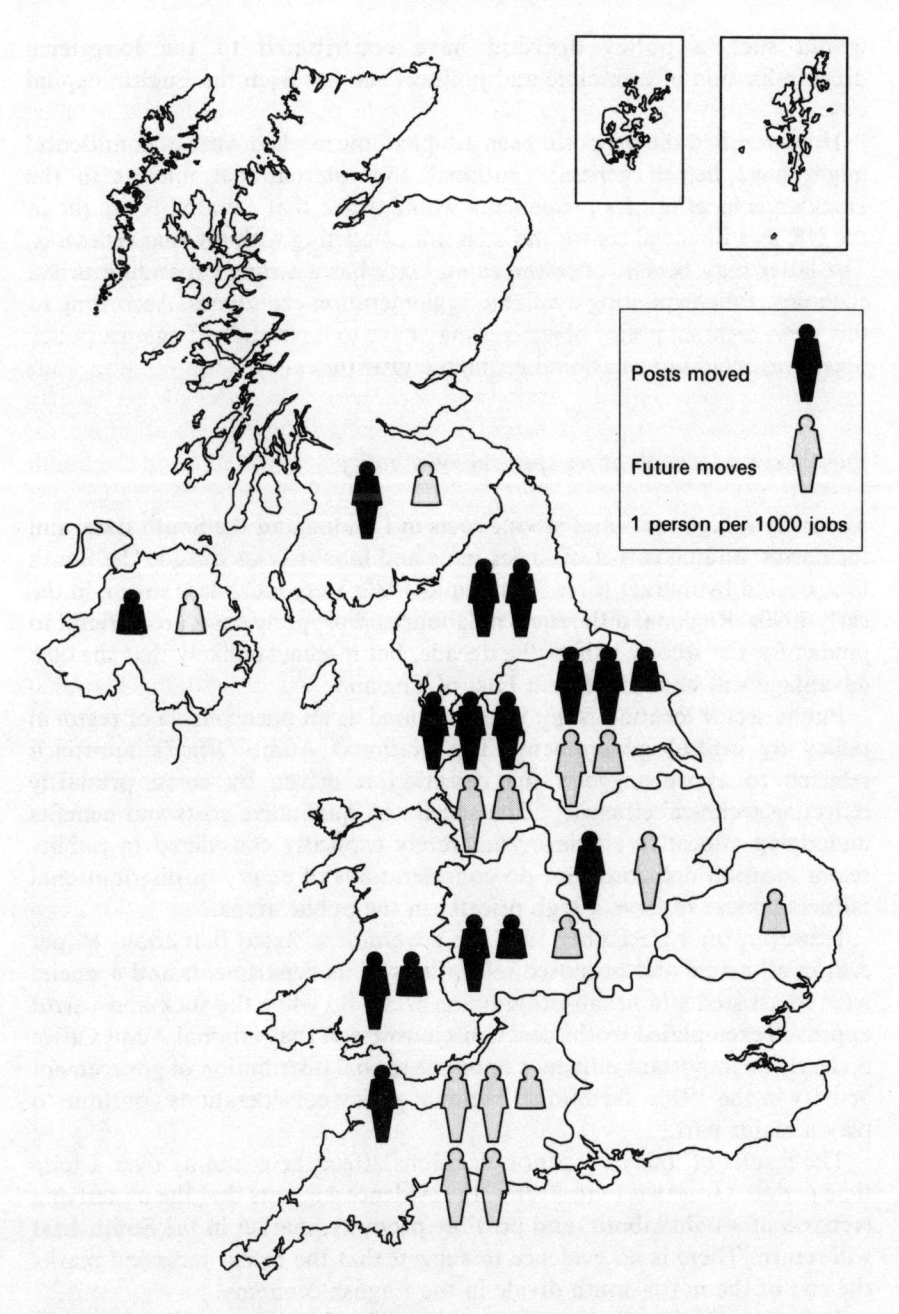

Figure 8.2 *New locations and relocations of government departments and agencies from the South East since March 1988*
Source of data: Hansard, 17 December 1992.

would such a policy decision have contributed to the long-term decentralisation of economic and political activity from the English capital city.

However, had the proposal been adopted, the implied 'vote of confidence' might have helped generate national and international interest in the Docklands location. Its proponents would argue that London is unique in the UK as a financial centre and so is not competing with provincial centres. The latter may benefit once the capital city has a strong expanding urban economy, fully exploiting available agglomeration economies. According to this view, regional policy objectives may have to be traded off against policy objectives relating to national economic growth.

Public-sector location as an open regional policy

The stick of high rents and labour costs in London and the South East, and the corresponding carrot of lower rents and labour costs outside the South East caused by market forces in the mid-1980s were much less strong in the early 1990s. Regional differences in labour and property costs are difficult to predict for the second half of the decade, but it seems unlikely that the cost advantage will be in the South East of England.

Public-sector location is not currently used as an open vehicle of regional policy by central government. The National Audit Office's approach referred to above suggests that location is driven by costs, primarily reflecting technical efficiency. The social and qualitative costs and benefits underlying allocative efficiency are rarely explicitly considered in public-sector location decisions, nor do considerations of equity or distributional fairness appear to have a high priority in the public arena.

However, on 4 December 1991 the government stated that about 80 per cent of all actual and proposed relocations of its departments and agencies were to assisted and urban-programme areas. So while the stick-and-carrot approach exemplified by the cost consciousness of the National Audit Office is clearly an important influence upon the spatial distribution of government activity in the 1990s, traditional regional-policy considerations continue to play a major part.

The results of today's location decisions affect the economy over a long time period. Over that longer term, the evidence suggests that the underlying scenario of a tight labour, and possibly property, market in the South East will return. There is no evidence to suggest that the recent recession marks the end of the north–south divide in the English economy.

Therefore the location and relocation of public-sector activities could effectively contribute to the attainment of long-term regional policy objectives. However this relationship should be open, rather than hidden as described by Gripaios and Bishop (1992). The planning and implementation of property management and associated location decisions in the public sector could and should be designed so as to dovetail with government decisions relating to its wider regional policies.

REGIONAL POLICY AND THE EUROPEAN COMMUNITY

Chapter 6 considered the theoretical aspects of the debate as to whether the EC can expect to see relative convergence or relative divergence in the economic prosperity of its member economies. This section looks at the main regional policy issues created by the present spatial divergence in economic prosperity among the members of the EC and their constituent regions.

Active regional policy measures designed to draw their economies towards economic convergence are an essential prerequisite if the long-term goal of a community with a unified economy and single currency is to be attainable. The single internal market cannot operate as effectively in the face of widely disparate economies as it could given an economically cohesive grouping. The real and monetary aspects of the economy both need to move in the same direction if greater economic unity is to be achieved in the EC. Similarly, political and economic unity are interdependent, and so greater political cohesion is dependent upon greater economic convergence.

It is against this backdrop of the aim for greater economic and political unity that the regional policies of the EC need to be considered.

The Policy Framework

Chapter 6 demonstrated that, if there is to be convergence in income levels within the EC, major net financial transfers will be required from the richer core regions in parts of France, western Germany and northern Italy to the poorer peripheral regions, such as eastern Germany, southern Italy, Greece, Spain, Portugal, the Republic of Ireland and Northern Ireland.

These financial transfers occur through a number of EC funds. These are primarily the regional and social funds, and the cohesion fund. The latter is a special fund designed to support local areas and regions that are competitively disadvantaged as a result of the implementation of the EC's single-market provisions. EC regional policy initiatives administered through the European Regional Development Fund (ERDF) significantly benefited some regions and localities of the UK during the 1980s. As we saw above, the UK government's regional policy expenditure fell in terms of its real value during the 1980s. In contrast, the real value of receipts by the UK from the ERDF rose during the decade.

The expansion of the EC to include such poorer economies as Greece, and the unification of former East Germany with the richer West Germany, significantly affected the spatial pattern of income in the Community for the 1990s. One result is that most of the UK regions cannot realistically expect to receive as much support from the EC after the mid-1990s as they did during the 1980s.

During the 1980s the benefiting regions of the UK fell into two main categories: those receiving agricultural support, and those receiving support for developing their infrastructure. The Highlands and Islands of Scotland, Wales, Northern Ireland and the South West of England were beneficiaries of EC agricultural-policy support. These predominantly rural areas had not derived so great a benefit from the industrial orientation of traditional UK regional policy measures.

EC assistance to Birmingham and Coventry in the West Midlands of England also provides an example of a subregion receiving assistance from the EC before it was recognised as an area in need of assistance by the national UK government. In this case EC assistance came through funding to support improvements in the provision of local infrastructure, which was forthcoming throughout the 1980s.

EC funding for infrastructure development was also important in the 1980s for localities affected by the closure of steelworks, such as Corby in the East Midlands and the Cleveland area of the North East of England. Other infrastructure projects in the North East to benefit from EC funding were the construction of the Kielder Reservoir and the Newcastle Metro underground train system. These examples demonstrate that EC funding underpinned a variety of projects in a wide variety of locations in the UK during the 1980s.

The scale of this expenditure flow into the UK should be remembered when considering the need for the domestic government to seek approval from the EC for its national regional policies. There has been criticism that the UK has sought to cut back on its own policy provision in the hope that EC funding will fill the gap. Cooperation to achieve a coordinated and complementary set of policies between national governments and the EC is clearly important.

The EC has a strong policy in favour of competition as it wishes to avoid market distortions within the single internal market. For this reason too, national policy measures designed to subsidise domestic industry are subject to scrutiny by the EC before receiving approval. Regional policy measures in this category must therefore satisfy the EC that they are designed to raise the assisted industry to the average level of competition in the single internal market and are not designed to raise it above this level.

The EC Regional Fund

An individual country's contribution to the EC's budget is based upon a combination of a percentage of VAT receipts and a sum weighted by the value of domestic GDP. The main net contributors to the EC budget in the 1970s and 1980s were therefore the richer member countries, such as Belgium, France and especially West Germany.

The main beneficiary economy during these years was the Republic of Ireland. The ways in which EC funding assisted the Republic of Ireland's economy are discussed more fully below. The early 1990s saw the expansion of the EC to include other economies in need of as much assistance as the Republic of Ireland. EC funding will play a vital role in financing the provision of the improved infrastructure that will be needed to facilitate the development and growth of the small peripheral EC economies such as Greece, the Republic of Ireland and Portugal, and the eastern regions of the German economy.

In the late 1980s the EC budget was well supported financially by West Germany as part of that country's encouragement of economic and monetary union. However there has been less room for fiscal manoeuvre in the German economy since unification. The German government has experienced difficulty in keeping its public expenditure effectively under control given the expenditure needs of the eastern regions of the economy. This heightened need to control internal government expenditure in Germany is reflected in a less-expansive attitude towards supplying funds for the regional development of other EC economies.

It is therefore within this framework of probable increased need relative to available finance in the second half of the 1990s that EC regional policy is discussed below in more detail.

Assistance to the EC Periphery

The section in Chapter 6 covering growth zones and the periphery in relation to the spatial pattern of growth and economic development across the EC looked briefly at the experience of the Republic of Ireland. Here we build upon that earlier section to consider *how* the economy of the Republic of Ireland has benefited from EC assistance to one of its poorest peripheral member states. The relative extent of EC financial support to the Republic of Ireland's economy has been substantial. In 1993 the Republic of Ireland had about 1 per cent of the total EC population but received over 13 per cent of the total allocation of structural funds.

As we saw earlier, the south and western regions of the Republic of Ireland's economy were, and still are, heavily dependent upon agriculture, much of which is dominated by very small farm units. One result of this has been large-scale outmigration from these regions and unemployment, as agricultural productivity has risen and the number of workers employed in agriculture has fallen.

The decline in employment in agriculture would have been more marked in the absence of the EC's agricultural price support. In contrast to the UK, which is a substantial net contributor to the Common Agricultural Policy price-support fund, the Republic of Ireland has been a substantial beneficiary. This reflects the contrast between the high average productivity of the agricultural sector in the UK economy and the dominance of low-productivity small farming in the Republic of Ireland.

Agricultural price support has been accompanied by EC financial support for structural measures designed to raise agricultural productivity and promote the economic development of rural areas through the EC's Objective 5 funding. In addition to farming, horticulture and forestry and tourism have been encouraged in rural regions. As noted in Chapter 6, the potential disadvantage of this strategy is its limited potential for generating a high-productivity, high-income regional economy.

In view of this limitation, the contribution of other measures to complement agricultural support is crucial. It is therefore important that EC support to the Republic of Ireland under its other policy objectives has also benefited its manufacturing and service sectors.

For example, funding under Objectives 3 and 4 has helped provide improved training of the labour force. Innovation by industry has been encouraged, as well as direct assistance towards the cost of capital investment. Although it is too early to judge their long-term success, a number of business parks, such as Galway, have been developed near to universities in the hope of encouraging closer links between the academic research community and organisations in the region.

The poor domestic budget situation faced by successive governments in the Republic of Ireland in the 1980s and early 1990s meant that EC funding of regional assistance, and assistance to the economy as a whole, was particularly important. In this setting the concern of the Republic as to the future scale of assistance it may receive in an enlarged EC can be understood. As a result of the expansion of the EC, it seems unlikely that the Republic of Ireland will continue to be in receipt of over 10 per cent of all EC structural funds after the mid-1990s for reasons explained in the following section.

EC Regional Policy in the 1990s

In the second half of the 1990s it is likely that some rural areas of the UK, such as the Highlands and Islands of Scotland, will continue to benefit from

EC regional assistance. However other rural areas such as much of Wales and the South West of England, are in competition for regional funding with even poorer areas of the EC, such as rural Greece and eastern Germany.

The EC agreed a budget of approximately £132 billion in 1992 to finance economic restructuring and development in its member states during the 1990s. Approximately two thirds of this total budget is to be allocated to Objective 1 funding for the EC's poorest regions, as measured by per capita GDP.

In the UK, Northern Ireland, the Highlands and Islands of Scotland and Merseyside in the North West of England satisfy this criterion. As shown on Figure 8.4, the other EC regions satisfying the criterion for Objective 1 assistance with effect from 1993 are the whole of Greece, the Republic of Ireland and Portugal; and southern Italy, southern Spain and Cantabria, former East Germany and the Hainault region in Belgium. The Objective 1 areas prior to the 1993 revision are shown on Figure 8.3. As can be seen, the main 1993 changes were the inclusion of the whole of former East Germany and the exclusion of parts of northern Italy and Spain.

Finance from the EC's Regional Fund is also available to regions less poor than those listed above, but adversely affected by the decline of their traditional industrial base. In the UK, Scotland, Wales and parts of the North and Midlands of England fall into this category of Objective 2 funding. Assistance under Objective 3 is also available to regions and areas experiencing above-average rates of long-term unemployment due to fundamental structural change. Retraining programmes may also attract EC funding under Objective 4.

The final objective, Objective 5 funding, aims to accelerate and help the economic development of rural and agricultural areas, such as those in the Republic of Ireland outlined above.

To summarise, EC policy funds three main categories of regional need:

- The needs of the poorest regions in the EC.
- The needs of relatively poor regions adversely affected by industrial change.
- The needs of those regions whose agriculture is characterised by low income and low productivity.

APPENDIX: REGIONAL POLICY IN THE UK, 1972–93

For a detailed listing of UK regional policy prior to 1972, the reader is referred to alternative sources, such as Armstrong and Taylor, 1993.

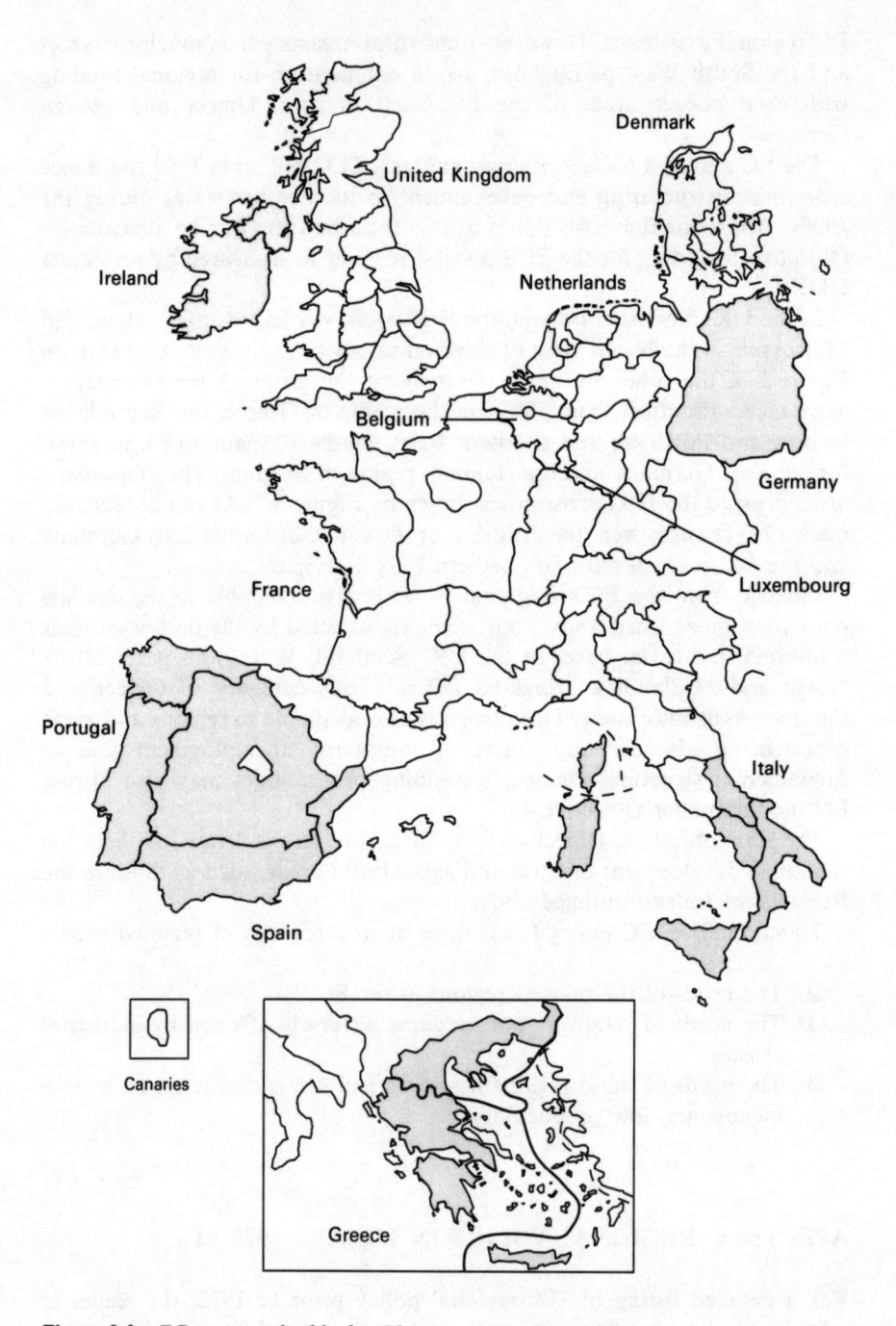

Figure 8.3 EC regions eligible for Objective 1 Funding, 1989–93

Regional Economic Policy 251

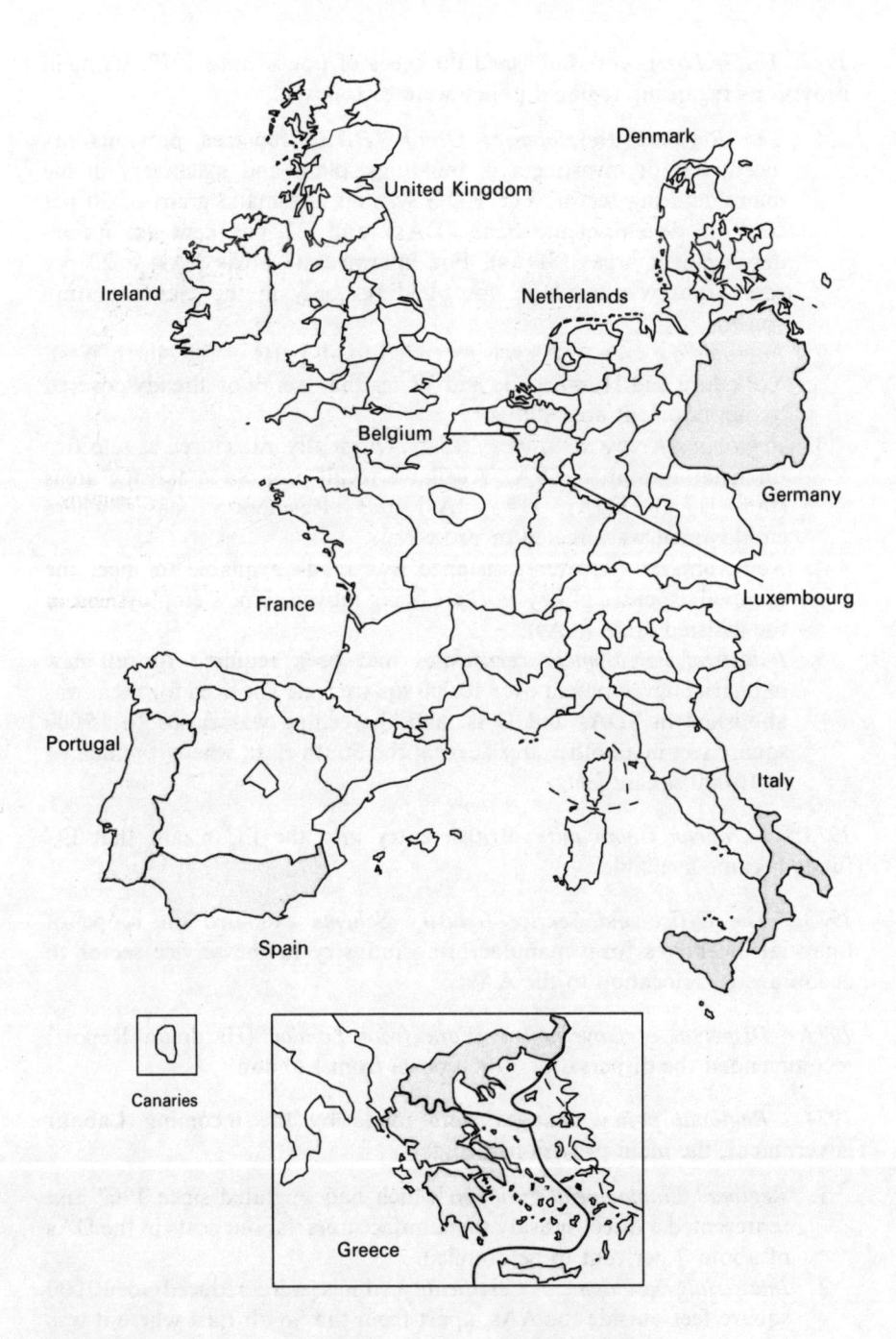

Figure 8.4 EC regions eligible for Objective 1 Funding, 1993

1972: The Industry Act established the basis of policy until 1979. Its main provisions regarding regional policy were as follows.

1. *The Regional Development Grant (RDG)* replaced previous tax incentives for investment in buildings, plant and machinery in the manufacturing sector. The RDG was an automatic grant of 20 per cent in development areas (DAs) and 22 per cent in special development areas (SDAs). For intermediate areas (IAs) a 20 per cent grant was available for buildings only in the manufacturing sector.
2. *Intermediate area* status was extended to all parts of the North West, Yorkshire and Humberside and Wales that were not already covered by development area status.
3. *Regional selective assistance (RSA)*. Originally introduced as selective financial assistance (SFA). Available to all projects in assisted areas (that is, all SDAs, DAs, IAs) and elsewhere in cases where employment was created or protected.
4. *Key workers* – greater assistance was made available to meet the removal expenses of key workers being moved to new employment in the assisted areas (AAs).
5. *Industrial development certificates* had been required for all new industrial development over 10 000 square feet. The need for them was abolished in SDAs and DAs, and the ceiling was raised to 15 000 square feet in all other areas except the South East, where it remained at 10 000 square feet.

1973: European Community. British entry into the EC meant that EC funds became available.

1973: The Office and Service Industry Scheme extended the scope of financial incentives from manufacturing industry to the service sector to encourage its relocation to the AAs.

1973: Dispersal of Government Work from London (Hardman Report) recommended the dispersal of 30 000 posts from London.

1974: Regional policy changes were made by the incoming Labour government, the main provisions being:

1. *Regional Employment Premium* which had operated since 1967 and represented a direct subsidy to manufacturers' labour costs in the DAs of about 7 per cent to be doubled.
2. *Industrial Development Certificate* ceilings were reduced to 10 000 square feet outside the AAs, apart from the South East where it was reduced to 5000.

3. *Development Area* status was extended to Edinburgh and Cardiff.
4. *Special DA* status was extended to Merseyside and parts of North Wales.
5. *Factory provision* was instigated in the AAs through a programme of small advanced factory construction schemes.

1975: The Industry Act provided for an intensification of industrial as distinct from regional policy support.

1975: The European Regional Development Fund (ERDF) was set up to provide funds on a quota basis to assist regional development in EC member states. Funding was mainly for investment grants and interest rebates on loans for approved projects.

1975: Scottish Enterprise was established as the Scottish Development Agency, but was redefined in 1989 and renamed Scottish Enterprise. It acts as agent for the UK government in Scotland with respect to industrial development. Its main functions are:

1. The administration of the provision of loans, grants and investment capital to incoming business organisations.
2. Marketing and promotion of Scotland as a location for footloose investment in both the UK and internationally.
3. To undertake area renewal programmes in rundown areas such as Glasgow.
4. To oversee the activities of the twenty Scottish local enterprise companies (LECs), which are mainly involved in local employment and training initiatives.
5. To act as the agent through which European Regional Development Fund grants are administered in Scotland.

1976: The Welsh Development Agency was established to act as agent for the UK government in Wales with respect to industrial development. Its main functions are:

1. The administration of the provision of loans, grants and investment capital to incoming business organisations.
2. Marketing and promotion of Wales as a location for footloose investment in both the UK and internationally.
3. To act as the agent through which European Regional Development Fund grants are administered in Wales.
4. To promote industrial property development in the Principality, especially in partnership with private enterprise.

1977: Regional Employment Premium abolished.

1979–83: Regional policy changes were made by the incoming Conservative government, the main changes being:

1. *Regional development grant* – maintained at 22 per cent in SDAs but reduced to 15 per cent in DAs and abolished in IAs.
2. *Industrial Development Certificates* – abolished.
3. *Regional selective assistance* (RSA) – to be allocated under more stringent conditions respecting employment creation and maintenance in the AAs.
4. *Assisted area* (AA) – coverage reduced.

1981: English Estates' responsibilities extended beyond the boundaries of the assisted areas to other industrial development initiatives such as Chatham Dockyard in Kent. English Estates had been established in 1960 as the industrial development section of the Department of Trade and Industry. Until 1981 its primary responsibility was for the government's programme of building factories in the assisted areas in England. In 1993 its role was absorbed by English Partnership.

1984: European Regional Development Fund (ERDF) reformed so that finance is allocated among the regions of the member states on the basis of approved programmes, rather than in line with a predetermined quota.

1984: Industrial Development and Cooperative Development Agency Act aimed to make regional policy more cost effective and responsive to social rather than economic disparities between the regions.

The main regional policy provisions of the Act were:

1. *Regional development grant* to be reformed to *RDGN*;
   Available as a grant of £3000 for each new full-time job created (subject to EC regulations); or as 15 per cent grant towards eligible expenditure on new capital, with a ceiling of £10 000 per job created for firms with over 200 employees, or a ceiling of £75 000. Availability extended from manufacturing only to some service industries, but tied specifically to job creation.
2. *Regional selective assistance (RSA)* available only where new jobs created. Availability extended from manufacturing only to some service industries.
3. *Assisted areas* – boundaries redrawn. SDA status abolished, while DA and IA areas redefined.

4. *Regional policy* cost to be halved from £617 million per annum in 1983 to under £300 million per annum in 1987–8.

1988: Amendments to regional policy aimed at increasing industrial competitiveness, encouraging innovation and improving training and skills, especially in the assisted areas and the inner cities. The main provisions were:

1. *Regional development grant* abolished and replaced by:
2. *Regional enterprise grant* (REG) – available on a discretionary basis as follows: firms with fewer than 25 employees can apply for a once-off 15 per cent investment grant of up to £15 000 towards the fixed asset cost of a qualifying project; firms with 25–50 employees can apply for a 50 per cent innovation grant of up to £5 0000 towards the cost of developing new products or processes.

1989: *European Structural Funds*, including the European Regional Development Fund (ERDF), were altered so that their allocation is related to following objectives:

Objective 1: targets the poorest regions in the EC.
Objective 2: aids regions experiencing industrial decline.
 The UK has received more funding under this, than under the other objectives.
Objective 3: assists regions experiencing long-term unemployment.
Objective 4: funds training and retraining programmes.
Objective 5: promotes the development of rural and agricultural regions.

In addition to the ERDF, the main structural funds are the Social Fund and the Cohesion Fund. The latter is directed towards providing help for areas and regions suffering a competitive disadvantage due to implementation of the EC single-market provisions. In July 1993 the EC agreed a package of regional aid that will bring about £2 billion into the UK between 1994 and 1999.

1993: *Regional policy review* resulted in a revised assisted-areas map covering 125 travel-to-work areas and about one third of the working population. The first major revision of the assisted areas since 1984 provides for both development areas and intermediate areas. Twenty-nine travel-to-work areas gained assisted-area status for the first time; 16 areas lost their assisted-area status. The main policy instruments remain the regional selective assistance scheme, with a £193 million budget for 1993–4, and the regional enterprise grant.

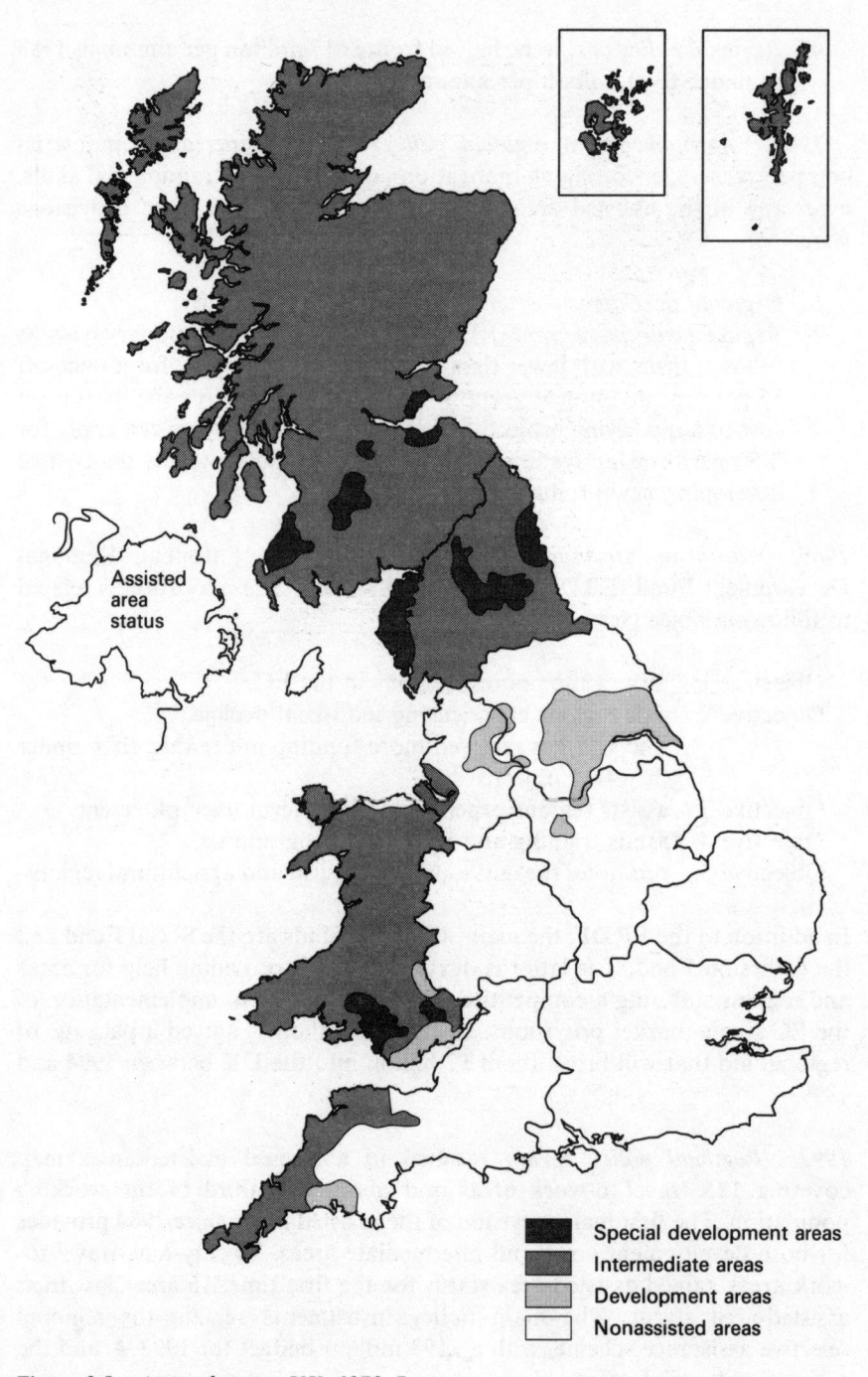

Figure 8.5 Assisted areas, UK, 1972–7

Regional Economic Policy 257

Special development areas
Intermediate areas
Development areas
Nonassisted areas

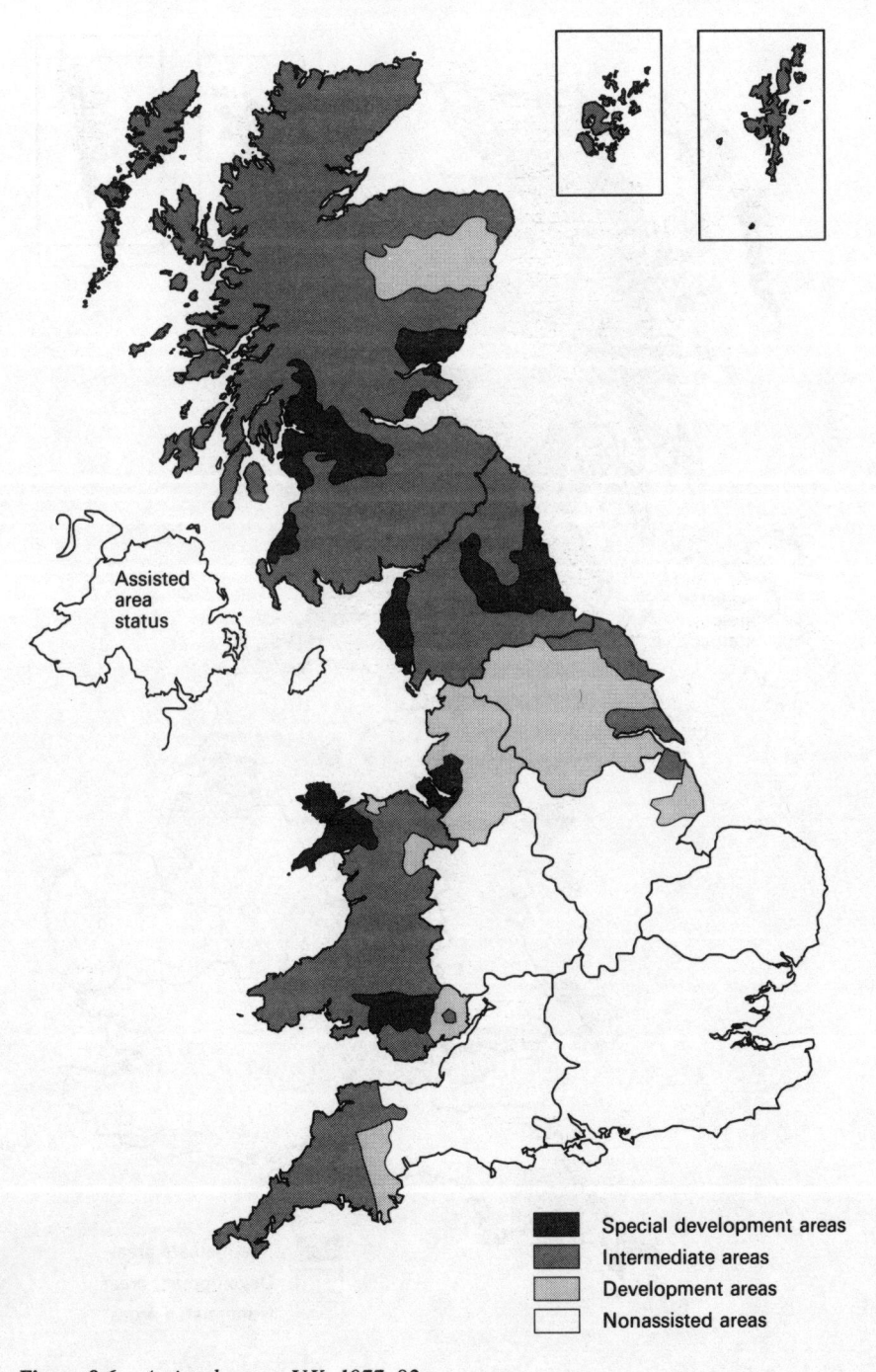

Figure 8.6 Assisted areas, UK, 1977–82

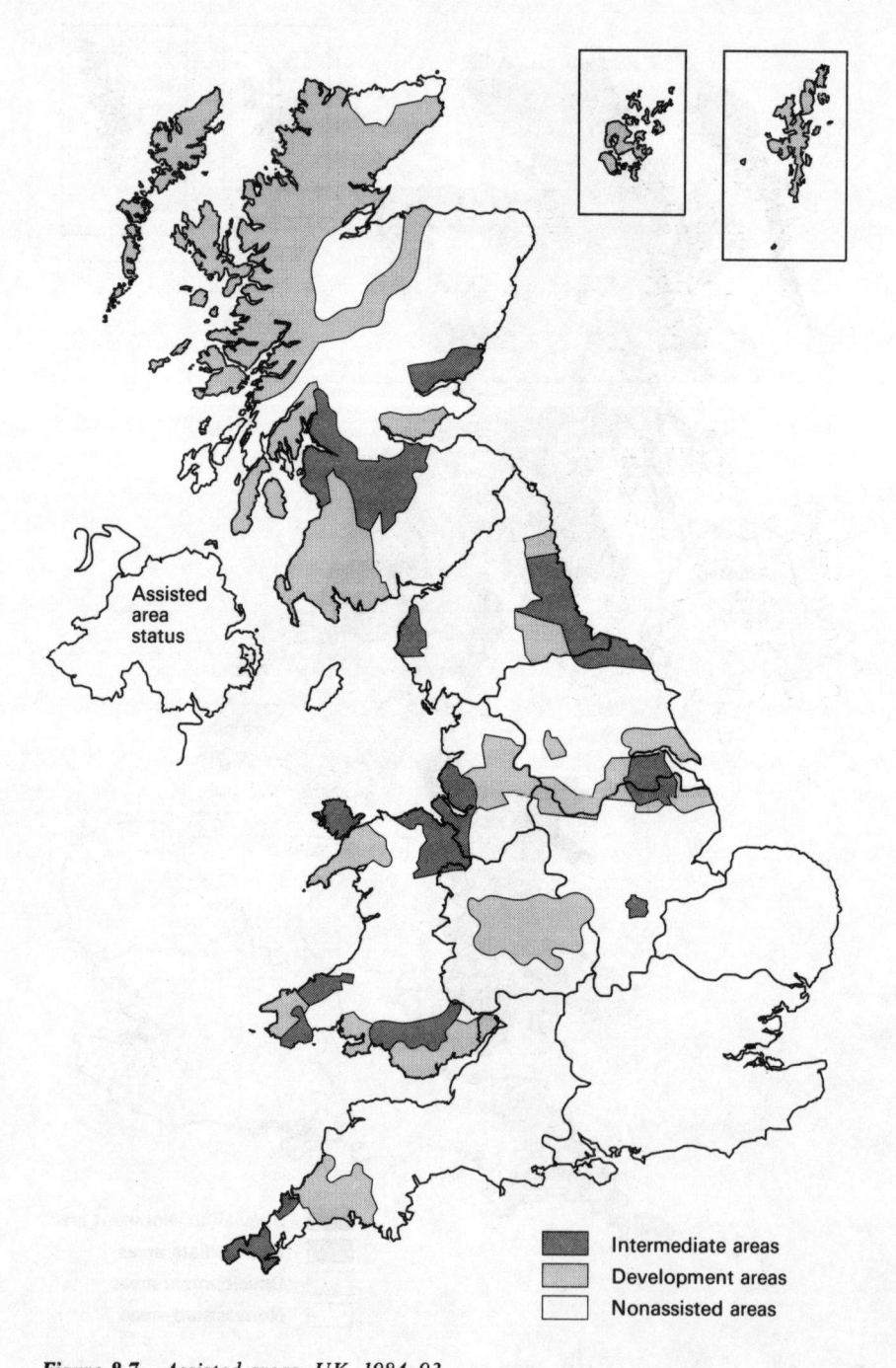

Figure 8.7 Assisted areas, UK, 1984–93

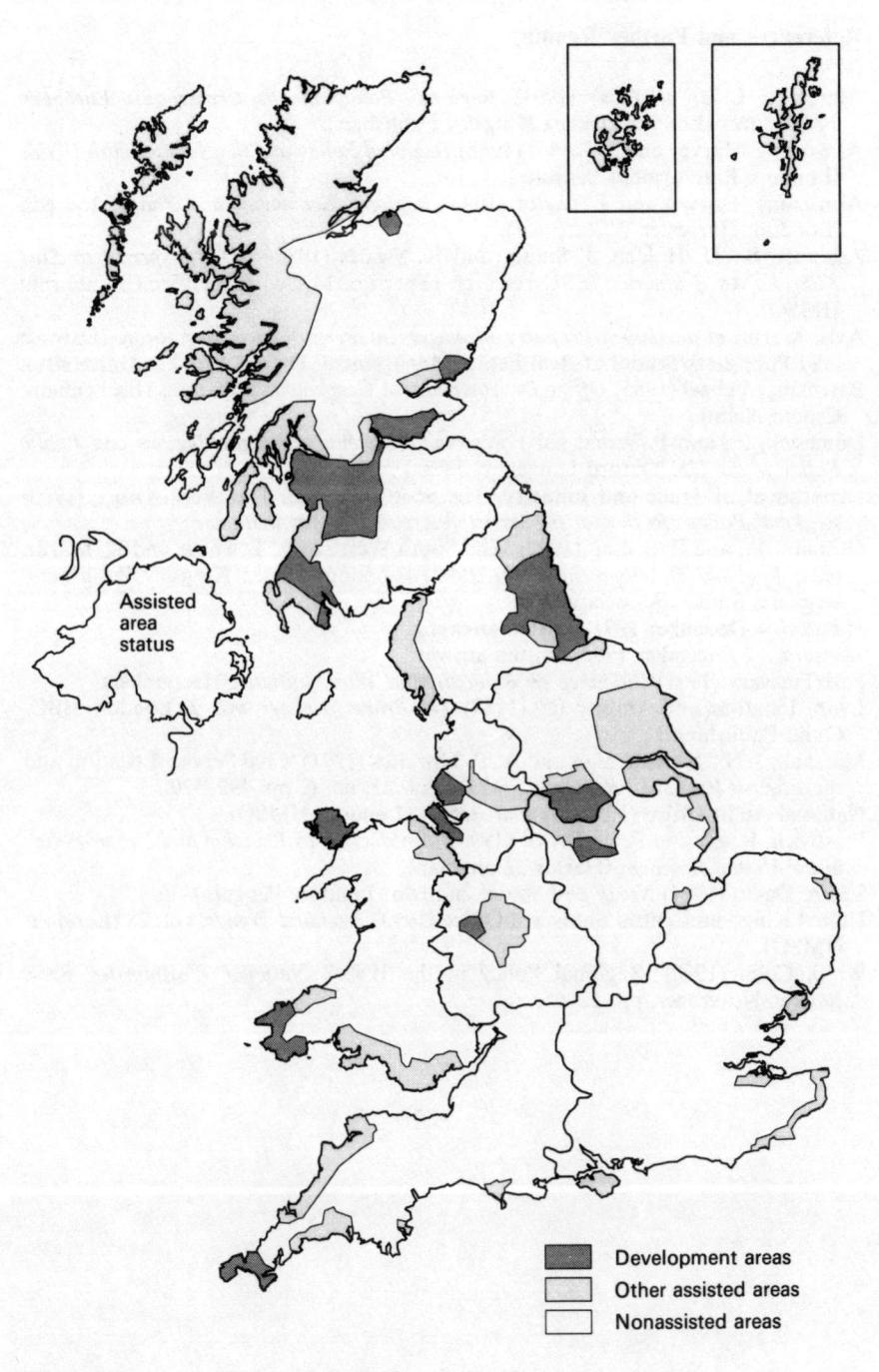

Figure 8.8 Assisted areas, UK, 1993

References and Further Reading

Albrechts, L. *et al.* (eds) (1991) *Regional Policy at the Crossroads: European Perspectives* (London: Jessica Kingsley Publishers).
Armstrong, Harvey and J. Taylor (1988) *Regional Policy and the North–South Divide* (London: Employment Institute).
Armstrong, Harvey and J. Taylor (1993) *Regional Economics and Policy*, 2nd edn (London: Harvester Wheatsheaf).
Ashcroft, B., D. Holden, J. Smith, and K. Swales (1988) *ODA Dispersal to East Kilbride: An Evaluation*, ESU research paper no. 14, Scottish Office (Edinburgh: HMSO).
Avis, Martin *et al.* (1993) *Property Management Performance Monitoring* (Oxford: GTI Publishers/School of Real Estate Management, Oxford Brookes University).
Bateman, Michael (1985) *Office Development: A Geographical Analysis* (Beckenham: Croom Helm).
Damesick, P., and P. Wood (eds) *Regional Problems, Problem Regions and Public Policy in the UK* (Oxford University Press).
Department of Trade and Industry, The Scottish Office, The Welsh Office (1993) *Regional Policy: Review of the Assisted Areas of Great Britain*.
Gripaios, P., and P. Bishop (1992) 'The South West', in P. Townroe and R. Martin (eds) *Regional Development in the 1990s* (London: Jessica Kingsley Publishers/ Regional Studies Association).
Hansard, 4 December 1991, written answer.
Hansard, 17 December 1992, written answer.
HM Treasury (1991) *Guidance on Relocation at Work Initiative* (December).
Lynn, Jonathan and Antony Jay (1987) *Yes Prime Minister*, vol. 2 (London: BBC/ Guild Publishing).
Marshall, J. N., N. Alderman and A. T. Thwaites (1991) 'Civil Service Location and the English Regions', *Regional Studies*, vol. 25, no. 6, pp. 499–510.
National Audit Office (1992) *Annual Report* (London: HMSO).
Prestwich, Roger and Peter Taylor (1990) *Introduction to Regional and Urban Policy in the United Kingdom* (Harlow: Longman).
Smith, David (1994) *North and South*, 2nd edn (London: Penguin).
United Kingdom Central Statistical Office (1993) *Regional Trends*, vol. 28 (London: HMSO).
Wren, Colin (1990) 'Regional Policy in the 1980s', *National Westminster Bank Review*, November, pp. 52–65.

9 An Effective Regional Policy?

THE IMPLEMENTATION OF REGIONAL POLICY

The Targeting of Policy Measures: (1) The Focus of Regional Policy

With the benefit of hindsight it is relatively easy to criticise early regional policy initiatives in the UK for being too broad-based and therefore not highly cost effective in the attainment of their primary objective of reducing interregional economic and social disparities. Some of the changes made to the direction of regional policy since the early 1970s have therefore represented the focusing of regional policy upon narrower objectives.

We saw in Chapter 8 that there was a degree of disillusionment with traditional regional policy measures in the second half of the 1970s. These paragraphs consider in more depth the reasons for that disillusionment, and the subsequent change of direction of regional policy in the UK.

In terms of the direct creation of new employment, much of UK regional policy in the 1960s and 1970s was relatively ineffective in that the majority of government expenditure went to finance subsidies to investment by large, capital-intensive firms in such industries as chemicals. Investment grants to capital-intensive industries generate little direct new employment. Whether there is a positive employment effect from such policy expenditure mainly depends upon the indirect, secondary-expenditure-generating effects of the policy.

For example, if the investment grant results in the recipient firm becoming more profitable and paying higher wages, then a positive multiplier effect upon regional income and expenditure can be predicted. It is this multiplier effect, not the initial investment grant, that generates the new employment in the region. However, this example of benefit to the regional economy is based upon three assumptions.

If you think back to the earlier coverage in this book of regional multiplier effects, can you suggest what at least one of these assumptions might be?

First, it assumes that the investment grant does raise the receiving firm's profitability. Second, it is assumed that this profit is converted into increased payments to the factors of production hired by the firm, for instance wages, and that these payments stay *within* the region. If this extra income is paid outside the region, the region does not benefit. Third, that this extra income is used to finance extra expenditure *within* the region. If the extra income is spent on goods imported into the region, for example, the regional economy does not benefit from a positive multiplier.

If the objective of regional policy is defined narrowly in terms of employment creation, the above explanation indicates that policy instruments such as investment grants are not a very cost-effective means of attaining this objective. The potential for leakage of the policy expenditure out of the regional economy is so great that the leverage of this policy instrument is restricted.

Much of the rationale for the redirection of regional policy after the mid-1970s rested upon this restricted leverage of many traditional regional policy measures upon the regional labour market.

While the point is difficult to establish quantitatively, it was also felt that traditional regional policy measures before the mid-1970s tended to divert existing expansion from one (unassisted) region of the UK to another (assisted) region. This meant that the effect of regional policy was to divert existing economic activity rather than create additional economic activity.

A sizeable proportion of regional policy expenditure was received by large firms taking advantage of regional incentives to minimise the location costs of their operations, especially of subsidiary branch plants. In extreme cases, large firms set up branch plants using government finance, then closed them and relocated as soon as the regional assistance map altered. The result was instability for the regions affected and a lack of long-term employment from these uncommitted employers.

A further disadvantage of these subsidiary branch plants was their cyclical vulnerability. An organisation would use government incentives to fund expansion and establish an additional branch plant during the boom phase of the economic cycle. Once the cycle reached recession and the organisation's overall profitability fell, these branch plants were highly susceptible to closure. This also added to the unstable nature of jobs created in the regions in the 1960s and 1970s.

For the reasons outlined above, the 1980s saw government regional financial assistance being increasingly focused upon the creation of new jobs within existing small firms. By targeting firms already operating in the region, it was hoped policy expenditure would be more effectively directed towards creating additional employment rather than diverting existing employment.

Small locally owned firms were also perceived to be more committed to a location within their region of origin. They were therefore thought less likely to relocate out of the region in response to changes in the pattern of regional financial incentives. It was also hoped that indigenous small firms would be less prone to closure in times of recession. This meant that the disadvantages felt by the branch-plant dominated regional economy in the downturn of the economic cycle would be minimised if not altogether avoided.

Chapter 8 noted that the 1980s were the decade in which real UK government expenditure on regional policies fell by nearly a half. This was partly due to disillusionment with regional policy, underscored by the prevailing monetarist ethos of government. However, in the same decade, there was an increase in EC expenditure on UK regions in need of economic assistance.

The suspicion, shared by some EC observers, was that the UK government hoped to save its own resources by relying upon EC intervention. Perhaps unsurprisingly, experience led to the drafting of EC policy expenditure criteria in terms requiring at least some input of resources from the recipient government. These terms resulted in wrangling between the EC and individual member governments over a number of issues, not solely those concerned with the UK government and its contributions to expenditure upon regional policy.

The Targeting of Policy Measures: (2) Policy Interdependence

Government policy does not occur in a vacuum, but is dependent upon and influences current political priorities. One aspect of government policy is similarly related to other government policies. For example, regional policy is not separate from, or independent of, other aspects of government macroeconomic policy. While regional policies may affect other government policies, they may also be affected, or sometimes swamped, by goverment policy.

A deflationary policy strategy of economic management at national level may completely negate local or regional policy measures designed to encourage expansion in a locally depressed economy. For example, a policy of maintaining high real interest rates to control monetary expansion in the macroeconomy may well prove detrimental to the survival of small businesses in a depressed local economy.

If these conflicts are to be minimised, policy makers must be conscious of the potential difficulties in designing policy instruments that target the economy effectively at one level of spatial aggregation without having undue unwanted economic side-effects at other levels of the spatial hierarchy. Readers familiar with the problem of the assignment of macroeconomic policy instruments to macroeconomic policy objectives will recognise the dilemma. Effective spatial policies require a similar assignment of policy instruments to local and/or urban policy objectives; to policy objectives in the regional economy; and to policy objectives in the national economy. Arguably, given the extent of policy interaction with the EC in the 1990s, policy assignment is pertinent in this context too.

There are clearly not enough policy instruments available to allow an allocation of one instrument for each policy objective at each relevant level of the economic spatial hierarchy. However, for spatially targeted policies to be effective, they must have significant leverage.

Our example above could have referred to an investment grant given to a firm in the north of England. The money could have been used to buy machinery imported from Switzerland. The extra profits generated by the additional output produced by the new machinery could have been distributed to shareholders, the vast majority of whom lived in the south of England. The net benefit of the investment grant to the north of England has been largely diminished through leakages outside its regional economy. For a regional policy to be effectively targeted upon a region, it must minimise these leakages.

There is no room for a 'one-policy-instrument, one-policy-objective' approach to policy making. However policies should be targeted in such a way as to ensure their maximum efficacy through their direct impact upon the part of the economy they are designed to affect.

Policy Implementation

The implementation of regional policy is subject to difficulties and constraints analogous to those experienced by other areas of economic policy. The main constraints considered in this section are those arising from the presence of uncertainty, time lags and the nature of the political environment.

Time lags

Time lags are notably difficult to predict in the context of economic policy, and regional policies are no exception. The presence of time lags generates inherent problems in the effective implementation of economic policy in four different ways:

- Identification of the problem to be addressed by the policy.
- Design and implementation of the appropriate policy.
- Initial effect of the policy upon the regional economy.
- Multiplier secondary effects upon the regional economy.

The effect of these time lags upon the implementation of regional policy can be illustrated by a training scheme for labour. The first stage is to identify the problem to be addressed by the policy. In our example, it becomes clear that employers in a particular region are consistently experiencing a shortage of labour with a specific skill, such as electricians.

Having identified the problem, the policy response is to design and implement a policy that provides more local training schemes to train electricians. This policy response takes time, not least as trainers and potential trainees both have to be recruited. The implementation of the training process takes time too.

Only after this may the initial effect of the policy upon the regional economy be felt in the form of an increased availability of electricians to local employers. Positive multiplier secondary effects upon the regional economy should then follow, after a further time delay.

The cynical view of the policy-making process is that by the time the new electricians have been trained, local and national economic circumstances will have changed to the extent that there is no longer a demand for more electricians in the local labour market.

Uncertainty

The difficulties created by uncertainty as to the future course of events is well illustrated by the above example. We do not know what the demand for electricians will be in three years' time. Such uncertainty permeates the processes integral to the conduct of public policy. Policy makers necessarily have only imperfect knowledge of the future, and their ability to forecast the future path of the economy is imperfect. Consequently policy responses are also imperfect.

However, in spite of the difficulties that uncertainty causes for public policy, some positive policy response is preferable to an entirely laisser faire approach to economic problems, including those of the regional economy.

The political environment

Regional policy, like other economic policy, is implemented in the context of wider political goals and objectives. As a priority of government policy, regional issues clearly slipped down the political agenda in the UK during the 1980s and the first half of the 1990s.

It was suggested earlier that this was a direct outcome of the wider adoption of anti-inflation policies as the government's primary macroeconomic policy objective in place of the earlier long-term macroeconomic policy commitment to full employment. A narrow view of 'the regional problem' views it as a problem of interregional disparities in unemployment. If national unemployment is seen as politically less sensitive, then regional unemployment also becomes correspondingly less of a political issue.

It was also suggested earlier that the view that regional policies are irrelevant to an anti-inflation-oriented macroeconomic policy is misguided. The greater the extent of interregional disparities across the economy, the sooner the macroeconomy is likely to encounter supply-side constraints in expansionary phases of the economic cycle. For this reason the subsuming of regional policy during past 15 years in the UK has damaged the economy as a whole.

Another view is that the downgrading of regional policy during these years represents a simplistic political response to prevalent spatial voting patterns. If the inhabitants of Scotland and the north of England are voting Labour to such an extent that Conservative candidates have no realistic chance of being elected, there may be little incentive for the Conservative government to spend money on financial assistance to Scotland and the North of England. Spending the money on the more prosperous regions may at least retain the political loyalty of Conservative voters.

Whether or not this voting-based explanation for the relative lack of importance shown to regional policy is accurate, the extent to which regional issues have been overlooked has clearly not helped, and has very probably hindered, the economic progress of the economy as a whole during these years.

THE MEASUREMENT OF THE EFFECTS OF REGIONAL POLICY

To measure the effects of regional policy, a quantifiable framework is required that facilitates a comparison of the costs of the policy with the results of the policy. The most straightforward approach adopted to such measurement has been the appraisal of regional policy instruments in terms of the number of jobs created for a given sum of policy expenditure. The cost of implementing the policy is known to the government so is reasonably easy to estimate. Where the regional policy expenditure is directed primarily at training labour or subsidising the location of firms, the number of jobs directly created by the regional policy can be reasonably estimated.

The task of measuring the effects of regional policy, however, can quickly become more complicated. First, it may be felt that the effects of regional policy are wider than is implied by the simple measure of jobs created. Second, the initial regional policy expenditure may have positive multiplier effects upon the recipient regional economy, and this should also be taken into account. Some of the main difficulties associated with measuring the effects of regional policy are discussed later in this section.

The Costs and Benefits of Regional Policy

One approach to constructing a measure of the effect of policy that is wider than just that of jobs created is through the use of cost–benefit analysis. A framework for such a cost–benefit approach, which is similar to that suggested by Armstrong and Taylor (1993) is shown in Table 9.1.

Table 9.1 Main social costs and benefits of regional policy

Benefits (B)		Costs (C)	
B1	Extra output, income and employment generated from increased economic activity.	C1	Output, income and employment lost due to diversion of resources from earlier productive use.
B2	Fewer migrants mean lower costs to public sector in provision of services and infrastructure.	C2	Infrastructure costs generated by effects of regional policy on the pattern of economic activity.
B3	Fewer migrants mean lower private costs of migration.	C3	Costs of moving to a new location.
B4	Reduced externalities of, for example, pollution in congested areas.	C4	Increased externalities, for example, environmental damage.
B5	Equity benefits.	C5	Administrative costs.
B6	Political benefits.	C6	Political costs.

Source: adapted from Armstrong and Taylor (1993), table 14.15.

To explain the points made in Table 9.1 more fully, we shall consider the benefits and then the costs associated with regional policy.

The benefits of regional policy

The first benefit, identified in Table 9.1 as B1, is that of the extra output, income and employment which is generated as a result of the policy expenditure. As suggested earlier, this has two components. First, there is the immediate direct effect upon the level of economic activity in the receiving region as a result of the policy expenditure. Second, this initial expenditure will generate secondary, indirect, multiplier beneficial effects upon the region's level of economic activity. Here the value of the relevant regional economic multiplier will be crucial in determining the cost-effectiveness of the policy expenditure. As was explained earlier, the greater the value of the multiplier, the greater the total positive effect of the regional policy expenditure upon the regional economy.

If the regional policy expenditure succeeds in reducing the extent of interregional disparities in employment opportunities and income levels across the economy, then the second and third beneficial policy results, B2 and B3 in the table, arise from the likelihood of less interregional migration. Where income and employment opportunities are markedly better in one region than another, more migrants are likely to leave the disadvantaged region in favour of the advantaged region.

Migration imposes costs both upon the migrant (the private costs of migration) and on society (the social costs of migration). A reduction in interregional migration flows therefore benefits the economy by reducing both the private and social costs of migration. The private costs of migration are the financial costs of moving home, and the wider costs of leaving social ties, such as family and friends. The social costs of migration arise from the need to provide more houses, schools and hospitals in the receiving region, and to support underused facilities in the losing region.

The next benefit of regional policy arises from the more even spatial distribution of negative externalities such as pollution. If it is assumed that pollution has a cumulative effect upon the environment, then to spread pollutants more evenly across the economy reduces the prevalence of blackspots where there are concentrations of pollution.

B5 in Table 9.1 identifies the equity benefits that stem from regional policy. An active regional policy should reduce the extent of interregional disparities in income, and therefore help to produce a greater degree of spatial equality in the distribution of income. Concentrating the economy's income into a spatial subsection of the economy is inequitable. While the presence of policies such as progressive income tax help to reduce such interregional disparities in income, they do not overcome them. Interregional disparities in income also usually reflect other sources of spatial inequity, such as differences in regional access to well-paid employment, and sometimes to services such as education and health care.

Finally, an active regional policy yields political benefits. Interregional disparities threaten the political cohesion of the nation. For example, in Italy the northern regions became politically disenchanted in the early 1990s partly, although not wholly, because of the high cost, through taxation, of supporting the much poorer southern regions of the country. In the UK interregional disparities contribute to the outer regions' feelings of distance and disenfranchisement from the centre of political authority in London. Economic unity across the nation is likely to contribute to political unity. In this way regional policies yield political benefits as well as economic and social benefits.

The costs of regional policy

Often regional policy results in the employment of resources that would otherwise have been unemployed. In this case additional economic activity takes place that would not have occurred on the absence of the policy intervention. The creation of this additional activity brings economic and social benefits at very little cost.

However, in circumstances where resources are diverted from one economic activity to another, regional policy does involve an opportunity cost, as indicated by C1 in Table 9.1. The policy benefit is then the net gain attributable to the increase in economic activity due to the diversion of resources from less productive to more productive uses. Of course, if regional policy is formulated so that resources are diverted from more productive to less productive uses, the policy actually imposes a net cost upon society rather than a net benefit.

The second category of costs identified in the table are those associated with the provision of infrastructure. We saw in Chapter 8 that a proportion of national and EC expenditure on regional policy finances the provision of infrastructure in regions where it is currently inadequate. In some predominantly rural areas, infrastructure such as roads may not exist. In some established industrial areas, the problem may be one of outdated infrastructure in need of replacement.

Where an organisation relocates in response to financial incentives offered as a component of regional policy, it will experience relocation costs.

What do you think will be the main costs facing an organisation that is relocating from one region to another?

Relocation costs include the costs of moving key workers to the new location, to the extent that these costs are not covered by the regional policy incentives. There will also be the costs associated with staff turnover, as some of the existing labour force are likely to refuse to move to the new location. The organisation will also have to bear the cost of recruiting and training new staff at the new location.

In addition there will be the cost of constructing new buildings for use by the relocating organisation, or the refurbishment of existing buildings. The firm will also face short-term administrative costs associated with alterations to such activities as its working practices, distribution and transport patterns.

These relocation costs are all costs associated with an active regional policy in that the organisation would not necessarily have relocated in the absence of the policy.

C4 draws attention to the potential environmental impact of regional policy upon the benefiting region. These costs are likely to be low, or negative, where relocation involves reutilisation of existing industrial sites that are currently underused or derelict. However, where greenfield development is involved, there may be costs to the local environment and pressures upon, for example, rural land use.

C5 draws attention to the administrative costs associated with implementing regional policy. In the absence of the policy, these costs would not exist.

Finally there are political costs associated with an active regional policy. We saw above that some voters in regions of northern Italy were politically disenchanted with paying taxes to support government expenditure in the poorer regions in the south of the country.

More generally, expenditure on regional policy may prove attractive to voters in the regions benefiting from the policy measures. However more expenditure on regional policy implies that fewer funds will be available for another type of government expenditure. This lower expenditure may discourage those voters who believe they are being adversely affected by supporting the political party in government.

This summary demonstrates that regional policy is not costless. In particular, it is important that policy measures are targeted so as to assist in the creation of additional economic activity rather than the diversion of existing activity. It is also important that money spent upon regional policy measures is directed effectively so as to maximise the benefit to the regional economy in question.

Some Problems of Measurement

This section considers some of the main problems of measuring the effects of regional policy. First, the limitations of measuring the private and social costs and benefits associated with regional policy are considered. Second, the main difficulties of isolating the effects of regional policy from the effects of other events are explained. Finally, the difficulty of measuring the effects of regional policy are discussed in relation to a brief overview of the recent experience of Northern Ireland, which has received more regional financial assistance than any other UK region.

The limitations of a cost–benefit approach to measurement

The advantage of using a cost–benefit framework for the measurement of the effects of regional policy is that it allows these costs and benefits to be expressed in directly comparable financial terms. In principle, it is possible to state that £10 000 in expenditure costs has yielded £15 000 benefit to the regional economy.

However this straightforward monetary comparison obscures the difficulties of estimating these relative costs and benefits accurately in terms of the underlying economic tenets of efficiency and equity. In Chapter 3 the main limitations of the prices created through the unfettered action of the market were discussed. That section of this book demonstrated that the prices resulting from the private market do not necessarily yield a price structure that accurately promotes economic welfare.

Can you remember some of the influences that result in market prices that do not yield a result that maximises economic welfare?

One major practical consideration that results in distorted market prices is the presence of monopoly in the product markets or monopsony in the markets for the factors of production. The price structure that reflects economic efficiency is that where *all* prices reflect marginal cost, and so measure the opportunity cost of that particular resource use. This price structure will only result where perfect competition exists in all markets, which is not the case in practice.

Another limitation associated with the use of market prices as a measure is their failure to include the effects of externalities, the social, as distinct from private, costs and benefits associated with economic activity. The outline of the costs and benefits of regional policy in the section above demonstrated the importance of social costs and social benefits in the context of measuring the effects of regional policy.

For example it was argued earlier that, while pragmatic, measuring a regional problem and its solution solely by reference to unemployment and job creation is unduly restrictive. A regional policy that succeeds in reducing interregional disparities in income, output and employment will also contribute to improving the quality of life in the benefitting regions. This limitation in relation to social costs and benefits is therefore an important constraint upon the usefulness of market prices as a measure in this respect.

The third main limitation of the use of market prices as a measure of the effects of regional policy concerns the time scale over which regional policy expenditure may be expected to affect the regional economy. The presence of time lags in the policy process was explained earlier in this chapter. In addition, Chapter 7 noted that experience increasingly suggests that effective urban regeneration programmes take 20 years rather than 10. Why should the process of regional regeneration be expected to be more rapid? The example of the Northern Ireland economy outlined later certainly suggests that it will not necessarily occur within any less a time scale than several decades.

If an effective regional policy is going to take decades rather than a few years, it becomes difficult to measure policy effects because many of them occur at a future date. Problems of uncertainty concerning the future then add to the problems of measuring policy effects over, for example a period of two years.

Isolating the effects of regional policy

Measuring the effects of regional policy can never be entirely successful. Attempts to undertake such measurement must overcome the universal problem of 'what if?' that is faced by all social scientists, including economists. Economists can never fully identify the precise extent to which a change in regional policy affects a particular regional economy. This is because other features of the economic environment will have changed while the regional policy was in effect.

For example, a 5 per cent increase in the value of investment grants available to firms in a region is accompanied by a 10 per cent increase in the amount of investment undertaken by firms in that region in the following two years. However the relevant two year period may have coincided with the recovery phase of an economic cycle in the national economy. This means that some increase in investment could have been expected in the absence of the extra investment grant. This provides one, relatively simple, example of the difficulty of isolating the effects of one policy, such as an increase in investment grants, from other influences on the regional economy during the same period. The magnitude of these difficulties is clear once the open nature of the regional economy is taken into account. Because of the high rate of economic interaction between the typical individual regional economy and the national and international economies of which it is a constituent part, the effects of regional policy are heavily dependent upon influences external to the regional economy.

Isolating the effects of regional policy is also complicated by the complex anatomy of the regional economy. The main features of this anatomy were built up in the early chapters of this book. To investigate the effects of regional policy, an economic model is required that can represent policy effects upon the individual components of the regional economy and account for the interaction among them. Contemporary sophisticated models of the UK and Scottish economies, such as that outlined briefly in Chapter 3, have the potential to improve our understanding of the operation of the regional economy and so of the impact of regional policies. However, the assumptions upon which they are constructed have to be taken carefully into account before their results can be applied without reservation.

Measuring the effects of regional policy is further complicated by the different aspects of these regional policies, as explained in Chapters 7 and 8. Some regional policy is implemented by national government, but some is effectively implemented at a more local level. In addition there are the policy initiatives of the EC that affect the regional economy. Isolating the effects of one aspect of these policies from those of the other economic policies operatiing at the same time is particularly difficult.

The effects of regional policy in Northern Ireland

This section concludes the present discussion of measuring the effects of regional policy by looking at a brief case study of the effects of regional policy expenditure in Northern Ireland. Northern Ireland is an apposite example for several reasons. First, it has a peripheral location relative to both the EC and the rest of the UK. Second, it has consistently experienced the highest rate of unemployment of all the UK regions since the 1950s. Third, the level of UK government expenditure upon regional policy assistance to Northern Ireland has been at least 50 per cent higher than that spent upon the other UK regions during the 1970s and 1980s.

Finally, the reduction in the real value of regional policy expenditure experienced by the other UK regions in the 1980s did not affect Northern Ireland, where the real value of UK regional financial assistance was maintained over the decade. For these reasons it is interesting to see what effect this relatively high level of regional policy expenditure has had upon the problems of the Northern Ireland economy.

UK government regional policy in Northern Ireland is implemented through the Northern Ireland Department of Economic Development. A major priority during the 1980s was the encouragement of new industrial employment in the region to take the place of declining employment in such traditional manufacturing industries as textiles, shipbuilding and engineering.

New employment was encouraged in the region in a number of ways. Large organisations in the private sector were approached to relocate into the region from outside, with the advantage of a wide range of financial incentives. Organisations already operating in the region were provided with assistance and encouraged to expand their activities within the region. The establishment of small businesses by local people was also positively encouraged. Finally, the public sector provided a growing source of employment within the region.

In terms of attracting existing firms into the region and assisting in the establishment of new firms, the Department of Economic Development has been relatively successful. The region's political problems cannot therefore entirely be blamed for its economic problems, as industry does not appear to have been unduly discouraged from operating in the region. However the region's problems as measured by the highest regional unemployment rate and lowest income level in the UK remain.

The reason for this appears to be the comparatively high rate of company failure experienced by small locally owned firms and of branch closure by larger firms in the region. This raises the question as to why these closures are occurring. This high closure rate is important both because it explains the persistence of the region's economic problems and because it appears to suggest that regional policy expenditure is not having a very significant positive effect upon the region's economy. How do economists try to establish the reasons for this apparent ineffectiveness of policy in the region?

One approach is through an investigation of the likely value of the relevant economic multipliers within the region. Such investigations highlight two problems.

The first is related to the relatively low domestic income level in the region compared with the UK as a whole. Figure 3.1 demonstrated that in 1991 income in Northern Ireland was about 86 per cent of the UK average. An unusually high proportion of the population is dependent upon government benefit payments as their major source of income. For example, government benefit payments accounted for about 16.5 per cent of income receipts in Northern Ireland in 1990–91 (Table 3.1).

Why is the low level of average income in Northern Ireland a cause for concern?

The region's low income and dependence upon government benefit income means that consumers in the region have relatively little money to spend. Spending is primarily on low-value goods and services. The region is accordingly trapped in a cycle of low income and low expenditure, which makes it difficult to sustain regional growth. The regional economy in Northern Ireland fits the case of the 'vicious circle' explained in Chapter 6, and has found it difficult to break out of this circle. The income levels provided through the fiscal transfer of government benefit payments to the region are not an adequate stimulus for the generation of significant economic growth.

The second problem related to the value of the multiplier effect of regional policy expenditure in Northern Ireland is the high degree of openness of the economy. One result of the region's limited domestic economic base is that firms import a comparatively high proportion of their inputs and intermediate goods. A relatively high proportion of regional policy expenditure therefore leaks out of the region, yielding limited long-term multiplier financial benefit to the region's economy.

Another approach to studying the effects of regional policy upon the Northern Ireland economy has been through the precise measurement of production charcteristics in the region and their comparison with similar characteristics in regions with superior records of economic growth. For example, 'matched-plant' comparisons have been undertaken between manufacturing plants in Northern Ireland and comparable plants in England and Germany.

These detailed comparisons have enabled many characteristics to be measured. They have established that a number of effects are not important determinants of the disappointing effects of regional policy expenditure in Northern Ireland. For example, differences in the structure of industry between Northern Ireland on the one hand and England and Germany on the other do not explain the difference in their economic performance.

The peripheral location of Northern Ireland suggests that transport costs might place firms operating in the region at a competitive disadvantage relative to other locations in the UK and Europe. However research suggests that transport costs represent such a small proportion of total costs for most organisations as to be unimportant.

Fothergill and Guy (1990) conducted a detailed case study of branch-plant closures in Northern Ireland between 1980 and 1986. Their conclusions reinforce the points made above that neither the region's political problems nor its locational peripherality offer the main explanation for the high closure rate experienced in the early 1980s recession.

Their study indicates that Northern Ireland experienced the worst of the potential problems of the branch-plant economy. (The analysis of the benefits and problems deriving from branch-plant location in the regional economy are discussed in Chapter 2.) The majority of branch plants closed in the region were shut down either because their size was no longer adequate for the parent organisation's needs, or because their product line had become outdated. Recession and the accompanying squeeze on company liquidity and profitability meant that the parent organisation chose closure of these branch plants rather than reinvestment.

This experience of Northern Ireland in the 1980s recession underlines the concern of several regional economists that the peripheral and/or branch-plant regions are becoming the source of 'reserve' economic resources. In other words, the presence of a sizeable pool of unemployed resources at the end of the recession attracts firms to open new branches there in the economic boom years of the cycle. The presence of government financial incentives adds to the attractiveness of such a strategy. However these branches are predominantly carrying out low-skill, low-order functions for the parent organisation. Their importance in the organisational hierarchy is minor: the onset of the next recession means that the organisation can then restore profitability by closing the branch with little organisational disruption to the parent company.

This analysis is not only relevant to Northern Ireland and other branch-plant regional economies in the UK. Elsewhere in Europe other regions are experiencing a similar cyclical vulnerability. Comparatively low wage costs by European standards may make a region especially likely to attract branch-plant investment. The European periphery, as decribed earlier, is accordingly vulnerable to this effect, as are the low-cost economies of Eastern Europe.

The studies outlined in the above paragraphs do not suggest easy solutions to the problem of designing a regional policy that will effectively remove the economies of Northern Ireland and similarly placed regions from the 'vicious circle' that has left them with high unemployment and low income relative to the rest of the EC. However these studies demonstrate the importance of trying to understand the effects of regional policy upon the regional economy in spite of the limitations of such measurement. As knowledge of the effects of regional policy measures improves, so should the ability to formulate and implement effective regional policies.

AN EVALUATION OF REGIONAL POLICY

An evaluation of regional policy in the mid-1990s in the UK must take into account the increasing role played by urban policy since 1980. UK government expenditure upon urban policy initiatives is now as great as its expenditure on conventional regional policy instruments. UK regional policy has also been affected by the increased level of policy expenditure on the part of the EC's structural funds, including the Regional Development Fund.

These alterations to the policy framework mean that regional policy is now in some respects a more complex topic than was formerly the case. An evaluation of regional policy must consider traditional national regional policy measures, but also the recent emphasis upon urban policies and the role of the EC.

The Private Sector, the Public Sector and the Welfare of the Region

The amendments to UK regional policy introduced in 1988 aimed to encourage enterprise in the regions as a vehicle for accelerating economic development. This enterprise was expected to be largely forthcoming from the private sector, either independently or in partnership with the public sector. Some regional economists have criticised the philosophy underlying these policy changes as representing the privatisation of regional policy.

The role of the private sector in partnership with the public sector (PPP) was discussed in some detail in Chapter 7 in relation to urban policy in both the UK and the Netherlands. In the UK such PPP schemes have been tried out more fully in the context of urban rather than traditional regional policy. Looking back at the coverage of PPP in Chapter 7, some lessons can be learnt that help to evaluate the potential contribution of PPP to regional policy. Three conclusions of particular relevance to the present discussion can be drawn.

First, that it is sensible for policy makers to seek means by which the entrepreneurial energy and financial capital of the private sector can be harnessed to further the attainment of spatial policy goals, whether at urban, subregional or regional level.

Second, that private-sector enterprise and finance will only be available in response to profit incentives. Private-sector finance is also available only when organisations have confidence and liquidity. It is unrealistic to expect private-sector venture finance to be forthcoming in times of recession, such as in 1990–2. There is accordingly an essential role for the public sector as a countercyclical source of development finance in the regional economy.

Third, as noted above, private enterprise responds to the incentive of profit. However, in the same way that 'the regional problem' involves rather more than unemployment statistics that are worse than the nation's average, a region's development involves rather more than the provision of enhanced profitability to employers located within it.

The welfare of the region is about more than maximising the profit of private-sector organisations, most of whom operate in market conditions that anyway fail to satisfy the assumptions of the perfect-competition model. The limitations of the market as a vehicle for maximising welfare were explained in Chapter 3. The central issue for the present discussion is that policy makers should make clear their acceptance of the view that the goal of regional policy is to improve the welfare of the regional economy, not only to improve the profitability of some of the private organisations located within the region.

As outlined in Chapter 3, the Pareto optimal view of welfare is such that general welfare can only be improved in circumstances where it is possible to make one person, or a group of people, better off without making another person, or group of people, worse off. Much regional policy fails to satisfy this criterion. If an organisation relocates from London to Newcastle, the North East region of England is presumably better off but the South East is likely to be worse off.

However it was noted in Chapter 3 that this Pareto criterion is often regarded as too restrictive. According to a less restrictive version, such as the Hicks–Kaldor, regional policy may be justified in terms of general welfare once the welfare gain resulting from the policy exceeds the welfare loss resulting from the policy. In the above example, the policy satisfies these conditions once the benefit to the North East exceeds the loss to the South East.

Whether this is the case can be ascertained. If, in principle, the beneficiaries in the North East could pay compensation to the losers in the South East and remain better off, then general welfare has improved as a result of the policy. If regional policy is evaluated using this criterion, it can be predicted that a greater degree of policy intervention may contribute to overall welfare than where the more restrictive Pareto criterion is adopted.

Competition or Complementarity?

One potential problem with the multiplication of policy initiatives implied by the addition of urban and EC policies to the traditional national regional policy is that of greater competition for funding from these different sources on the part of those regions in need of assistance. Instead of concentrating their efforts upon one source of policy intervention, they may now concentrate on several different sources.

The different policy structures may also generate competing or conflicting outcomes. EC funding may be received by Town A in a region, while urban policy favours the regeneration of Town B. Other towns in the same region find that economic activity is diverted away from them in search of the financial incentives available in towns A and B. Towns A and B are competing for economic activity in the region; so are Towns C and D, who feel left out by the policy structure.

> over the past decade, government initiatives in Yorkshire and Humberside have been many and varied, resulting in an increasing number of overlapping activities which ... in some cases have led to competition and rivalry at the local level (Leigh and Stillwell, 1992, p. 74).

This aptly illustrates the problems that arise when policy leads to competition between different locations within the same region. Given current policy structures, such competition may arise. The absence of a regional planning and political structure in the UK leaves a corresponding gap in the policy structure.

In the absence of a regional framework within which policy can be effectively coordinated, it is difficult to avoid the conclusion that a proportion of economic activity is currently diverted to different locations within a region. The emphasis of policy, as we have seen, should be upon the creation of new economic activity rather than the diversion of existing economic activity, especially where that diversion occurs from one deserving location to another equally deserving location in policy terms.

The Need for Subsidiarity

Regional policy in the UK has, for the most part, been controlled from London since the Second World War. The increasing role of urban policy noted above has been accompanied by increased centralisation of control of urban policy expenditure away from local authorities and to central government, as was explained in Chapter 7.

This overall centralisation of UK spatial policy has the advantage, in principle, of allowing for greater uniformity in the policy process. However the advantage of local government's local experience and knowledge of its own local economy has been diluted if not lost. Policy centralisation has brought with it a potential loss of local democracy and local involvement in the future of the local economy.

The result is a need for a recognition of the importance of subsidiarity to allow regional and local economies to play an active role in taking decisions that affect their future. An irony of the regional policies of the UK in the 1980s and early 1990s was emphasis upon the development of growth lying *inside* the region but control of policy and the region's economy lying *outside* the region, in London.

It was noted earlier that the nation regions of Scotland and Wales have a greater cultural and political identity than the UK regions in England. This separate cultural identity should be reflected in greater subsidiarity and devolution of responsibility to the nation regions.

The relationship between the UK and the EC in terms of regional policy is analogous to that between the UK national government and its constituent regions. The need is for cooperation and coordination rather than competition and conflict.

The relationship between the national government and the EC is important with respect to regional policy. Both tiers of government have a role to play with respect to policy intervention in the UK regions. The enlargement of the EC means that some UK regions are relatively disadvantaged compared with other more prosperous domestic regions, but are themselves prosperous compared with many less-well-off regions in the larger Community. In their case, national policy initiatives are required to even out interregional disparities. Only the most disadvantaged of the UK regions can expect significant policy assistance from the EC.

The coverage of UK regional policy also has to take into account the dynamics of future growth and development inside the market of the larger EC. While the UK economy as a whole may benefit from the growth generated by the community market, it is not clear that policy to date has explicitly sought to protect those areas of the UK economy that are losers rather than gainers from this process.

The Effects of Deindustrialisation

The data discussed in this book have made clear the extent to which the regions of the UK have experienced decline in their traditional manufacturing base since the early 1980s. In addition the UK economy as a whole, in common with similar economies within the EC, is experiencing a shift in economic structure. The manufacturing sector of the economy is declining in importance, while the service sector is increasing. Employment in the public sector represents a high proportion of the total, and this is likely to continue.

Such changes in the industrial and employment structure bring concomitant changes in the location and variety of economic activity. The ethos of much government economic policy, including regional policy, during the 1980s was that these changes would be primarily accommodated by the operation of the market. The increasing divergence of regional disparities through the 1980s demonstrates that the market did not operate to equilibrate the spatial imbalances within it. On the contrary, these imbalances became more exagerrated.

A positive regional policy should respond to these structural changes in the economy. The potential gain to regional development from the relocation of organisations in the manufacturing sector is now limited by the limited size of the manufacturing sector. The location of the service sector, in both the private and public spheres, is crucial to future regional growth.

For this reason the considerations that underlie location decisions in the service sector were discussed in some detail in Chapter 5. A greater understanding of these aspects of the location and relocation of economic activity is needed if future regional policies are to affect location at minimum cost and maximum benefit.

Regional policy must also take account of the contemporary operation of the markets for the factors of production in the economy, as explained in the early chapters of this book. For example, the incidence and duration of unemployment in the disadvantaged regions indicates a need for stronger policy initiatives to encourage retraining and reemployment for those out of work in these regions.

AN EFFECTIVE REGIONAL POLICY?

The Need for a Regional Policy

> Nowadays we've got a craze
> To follow clever Keynesian ways
> And computers measure economic growth.
> We've got experts milling round
> Writing theories on the pound
> Caring little whether we can buy a loaf
> And I'm standing at the door, at the same old ... door,
> Waiting for the pay-out like me father did before.
> (Plater, 1969, pp. 49–50)

Alan Plater's play *Close the Coalhouse Door* was written 25 years ago as a comment on the effects on life in the North East of England of conditions in the coalmining industry and the restructuring of that industry that was then taking place. It is therefore equally relevant to the UK in the 1990s, when the coalmining industry is again being 'restructured'. The son of the redundant miner of 1969 may well be redundant in another coalfield in 1994.

As the above extract suggests, the restructuring of the coalmining industry is not the only recurrent theme linking 1994 to a generation earlier. The perceived lack of interest of the political rulers in London for the plight of the unemployed and the poor in the outer regions continues, perhaps more so in 1994 than in 1969.

The presence of relative poverty in these regions is also a continuing theme of the UK economy. Interregional disparities have shown little sign of long-term convergence in the past, and particularly since the recession of the early 1980s.

The Keynesian analysis that helps explain why the economy may be in equilibrium without guaranteeing full employment (see Chapter 3) seems to have progressed little closer to helping reduce the incidence of unemployment in general, and of long-term regional unemployment in particular.

Nor do the decades of regional policy expenditure outlined in Chapter 8 seem to have achieved much progress towards greater interregional equality and self-sustaining growth in the disadvantaged regions. The UK government's response to this lack of progress appears to have been to divert resources away from traditional regional policy into other policy areas, notably urban policy.

It is therefore important to consider whether regional policy is a waste of resources that could be directed to more productive use elsewhere, as many monetarists would argue, or whether it is possible to construct an effective regional policy.

Conditions for an Effective Regional Policy

It is not easy to catalogue all the conditions that would be sufficient for the implementation of an effective regional policy. This is true not least because of the problem of predicting the effects of changes in the external economic and political environment upon the individual regional economy and its component subregions and localities. It would also form rather a lengthy catalogue. This section accordingly discusses a selection of some of the main conditions that would facilitate the formulation and implementation of an effective regional policy.

One condition is the political will needed to ensure a successful regional policy. While this is present in many European countries, in the UK the political determination to advance regional equality seems to have evaporated since the mid-1970s. As a result the UK has experienced widening interregional disparities, apart from a brief period during the early 1990s recession. A contemporary version of the 1930s Barlow Report, referred to in Chapter 8, may be needed to restore political urgency to regional policy in the UK.

There is much useful academic research being done on a wide variety of particular aspects of the regional economy, much of it beyond the scope of this book. The results of this research mean that the operation of the regional economy is understood better in the mid-1990s than was the case ten years earlier. Effective regional policies will build upon this understanding to identify the causes of the weaknesses in the regional economy and help in the formulation of policies to alleviate them.

An effective regional policy needs to be directed so that the stimulus provided by the policy expenditure remains inside the region at which it is targeted. The openness of the regional economy, and the tendency for public policy assistance to leak out of it, was commented upon earlier. Policy expenditure should aim to exercise effective economic leverage upon the receiving region, through targeting expenditure where it can lead to significant local and regional multiplier effects.

Regional policy expenditure that subsidises the relocation and establishment of firms and plants that close down within five years is not cost-effective. While some failures are inevitable, an effective regional policy requires an understanding of location costs and conditions in the different regions and the different employment sectors of the economy. This knowledge can then inform financial incentives to subsidise the relocation and establishment costs of organisations that are reasonably likely to thrive in the receiving region. As we have seen, it is important that these organisations have strong linkages with the local and regional economy if they are to help foster sustainable growth in the region.

The component local and subregional economies of the region need to be identified if regional policy is to be effective. Local areas can act as growth poles, but are more effective if new economic activity is encouraged within them rather than existing activities being diverted around the region.

The need to ensure cooperation rather than competition among the localities in a region indicates the need for some regional planning framework. The same framework could be responsible for integrating public- and private-sector initiatives and encouraging the positive use of private/public-sector partnership in regional development.

In the 1960s UK regional policy was criticised for being short-term in outlook and subject to such frequent change that organisations could not treat regional financial assistance with any degree of certainty. A further condition for an effective regional policy is therefore continuity rather than radical change. The persistence of the UK's regional economic problems, and the decades it is taking for urban regeneration, indicate that regional regeneration will also take decades.

This is especially true after the experience of the 1980s recession. The outer regions of the UK economy were weak when they entered the recession, but they emerged significantly weaker, as evidenced earlier in this book and did not advance to any great extent during the expansionary years at the end of the 1980s. Their regeneration will take even more effort than before the 1980s.

The 1990s recession affected the more prosperous regions of the UK, but less severely. This view is supported by the ability of regions such as the South East to pull out of recession during 1993 at a faster rate than regions such as the North East of England. Positive regional policy will therefore be needed to reduce the extent of interregional economic disparities in the UK in the second half of the 1990s.

There has been increased London centralisation of control of the processes of UK spatial policy since the mid-1970s. This raises at least two issues. The first is whether it is sensible for the mainstream urban and regional policy processes to be controlled from a location in one of the better-off regions of the economy. The second is whether local government, and local partnerships between the public and private sectors would not be as, if not more, effective at generating local economic prosperity in their areas.

Control of spatial policy could be decentralised in a reversal of the centralised model of the early 1990s. In the same way as the EC is recognising the need for subsidiarity in its relationship with its member states, the nation state could recognise the value of subsidiarity in its relationship with the regions of the economy.

However it would then be necessary to create an administrative structure to ensure the coordination and integration of different local initiatives. Such an administrative function might be carried out by a regional development corporation with responsibility for coordinating the activities of the local and regional bodies in both the private and public sectors in its region. These regional development corporations could act as an umbrella organisation to coordinate policy across all the regions and liaise with other bodies such as the European Commission. Similar regional tiers exist in several other European countries, such as Germany and the Netherlands.

Whether or not a regional administrative structure exists for regional and urban policy administration, a key to an effective set of spatial policies is that both individual policies and individual areas at which those policies are directed should be complementary and not conflicting.

References and Further Reading

Armstrong, Harvey and J. Taylor (1993) *Regional Economics and Policy*, 2nd edn (London: Harvester Wheatsheaf).
Batemen, Michael (1985) *Office Development: A Geographical Analysis* (Beckenham: Croom Helm).
Fothergill, S. and N. Guy (1990) *Retreat from the Regions* (London: Jessica Kingsley Publishers/Regional Studies Association).

Leigh, C. and J. Stillwell (1992) 'Yorkshire and Humberside', in Townroe and Martin (1992).
Plater, Alan (1969) *Close the Coalhouse Door* (London: Methuen).
Townroe, P. and R. Martin (eds) (1992) *Regional Development in the 1990s* (London: Jessica Kingsley Publishers/Regional Studies Association).

Conclusion

Whatever the future pace of formal economic and monetary integration among the economies of the EC, informal economic integration has already occurred to an extent that ensures that the regional economies within the EC are interdependent. The role of the EC as a budgetary and policy-making body which seeks to actively even out interregional disparities in income and growth is therefore crucial.

A central problem for the EC members and their constituent nations and regions is that of securing the benefits of economies of scale and greater centralisation – but without unduly weakening the economies of those regions least likely to benefit directly from the processes of market-led growth and development in the near future. For the local and regional economy to prosper, the concept of economic and political subsidiarity may offer a crucial route towards maintaining and encouraging local interest in and influence upon the local and regional components of larger economic and political units such as the nation state and the EC.

There is wide variation in the economic structure of the member economies of the EC, and this diversity may increase as membership expands further. For the regions of such economies as Greece and Portugal, policy intervention is required to prevent the effects of the transition from a predominantly agricultural to a more industrial economy from being too destabilising and inequitable.

Other member states have regional economies affected by the deindustrialisation process and the underlying structural changes associated with it. For the UK economy, these changes are yielding a spatial distribution of economic activity that is neither more efficient nor more equitable than that of the 1970s. The relatively low priority accorded to regional issues since the mid-1970s needs to be altered if the spatial operation of the economy is to improve in the near future.

The emergence of the service sector also has implications for the regional economy. In general, a smaller proportion of service output is exported from the region than is the case with manufacturing output. Nor do all service-sector activities generate high value-added or high income. In general, producer services are more valuable to the regional economy than are consumer services. However consumer services such as hairdressing tend to be spatially more evenly spread across the economy than producer services such as marketing. A high proportion of service activities in the European economies, such as education, health and defence, are within the public sector. This raises questions regarding the direct use of the location of such public-sector activities as an instrument of regional policy.

These underlying structural changes in the regional economy bring with them concomitant changes in the structure of employment. The inherent skill content of employment is increasing over time, and the nature of employable skills is altering. Both these changes are resulting in unemployment: of the unskilled and of those with redundant skills.

Regional disparities in unemployment are an important indicator of the presence of a regional problem. The human cost of unemployment adds a further dimension to the truism that unemployment means irretrievably lost potential output and income for the affected economy. The emphasis given to local and subregional unemployment as the yardstick against which the UK government measures the need for policy intervention has further added to its importance.

Interregional variations in economic-activity rates suggest that regional unemployment is not necessarily easily capable of objective measurement. The labour force in different regions is neither actually homogeneous nor perceived to be homogeneous by potential employers.

When an organisation has to scrap an item of physical capital, or when the value of its property declines, this fall in value is reflected in the balance sheet. The interregional heterogeneity of labour and the impact of both redundancy and training might be made more transparent were labour to be similarly treated. Redundancy involves the scrapping of a human capital asset, so should be reflected as a debit item on the balance sheet. Training should enhance the value to the employer of human capital, so could be reflected as a credit item.

However, as the EC's approach to regional policy indicates, the political economy of a region concerns more than the unemployment of labour as a factor of production. This book has accordingly also discussed the role of the markets for financial capital and land or real estate in the operation and future potential of the regional economy.

One important point to be reiterated here with regard to these markets in the second half of the 1990s concerns the likely degree of risk-aversion that may affect the market behaviour of the relevant decision-takers. The experience of the early 1990s recession may render such decision-takers more cautious than they were in the late 1980s.

If so, the preference for 'safe' locations could have major implications for changes in the European and national spatial location of economic activity if market forces are left to operate unhindered. Alternative locations are not perceived as homogeneous, so preferences develop. These preferences are likely to reinforce existing pressures for interregional divergence, both nationally and across the EC.

One result may be an increasing tendency to interregional divergence within the EC. Market forces may tend to concentrate economic activity and growth in limited zones rather than yield a more even spatial spread across the community. For this reason, public policy intervention in the regional economy is likely to continue to be of importance to mitigate both the inefficiencies of congestion and the inequities of spatial disparity.

The European markets for financial capital and property are becoming more centralised and international. For example, in the UK the increased number of mergers between local and regional building societies since the early 1980s has resulted in a national framework for these previously subnational financial institutions. Many larger finance and property organisations have also widened their sphere of operations to become more European or international than national.

Increasing centralisation of the ownership of organisations at national and supranational level and the reduction in local ownership of economic activities makes it more likely that location decisions are correspondingly made on a national and supranational scale. Regional and local economies are increasingly opened up to competition with alternative locations: there is little local loyalty in the absence of local ownership.

The increasing importance of the EC's regional policy intervention is a sign of increasing centralisation in this respect too. In the UK, political centralisation has also occurred in the national context, although this is not the case for all European countries.

In the case of the UK, the current lack of priority and cohesion in respect of regional policy highlights a gap in the country's politico–economic structure. The geographic map of assisted areas, effective from 1993, as shown in Chapter 8, may indicate a rather piecemeal approach to regional policy. The increasing importance given to urban policy since the early 1980s has not contributed to a coherent regional strategy. The persistence of interregional disparities does not support the view that, once local policies are implemented, the region will look after itself. Urban policies need to be coordinated with regional policies in the same way as regional policy should be coordinated with national macroeconomic policy and the latter with EC policy.

There is increasing interest in joint cooperation between private and public sector in urban and regional initiatives in, for example, France, the Netherlands and the UK. For this reason, the role of private and public-sector partnership was investigated in some detail in Chapter 7. This discussion pointed to the cyclical variability in the supply of private-sector finance. In other words, for private/public-sector partnership schemes to be viable in the long term, the public sector's participation may need to be overtly countercyclical in its timing.

This suggests that policy intervention should be framed in the context of long-term strategy, spanning short-term variations in the level of economic activity. This proposition is underlined by the persistence of regional problems over recent decades in most of the European economies. The proposed future expansion of the EC is likely to bring further pressures in association with fundamental developmental shifts in the regional economies of its member states. The issues central to the regional economy discussed in this book are accordingly likely to remain highly relevant to the European economies in the coming years.

Select Bibliography

Albrechts, Louis, Frank Moulaert, Peter Roberts, and Erik Swyngedouw (eds) (1991) *Regional Policy at the Crossroads: European Perspectives* (London: Jessica Kingsley Publishers).
Alexander, Ian (1979) *Office Location and Public Policy* (Suffolk: Longman).
Allen, K., H. M. Begg, S. McDowall and G. Walker (1988) *Regional Incentives and the Investment Decision of the Firm* (London: DTI, HMSO).
Armstrong, Harvey and Jim Taylor (1988) *Regional Policy and the North–South Divide* (London: Employment Institute).
Armstrong, H. and J. Taylor (1993) *Regional Economics and Policy*, 2nd edn (Brighton: Harvester Wheatsheaf).
Ashcroft, B., D. Holden, J. Smith and K. Swales (1988) *ODA Dispersal to East Kilbride: An Evaluation*, ESU research paper no. 14, Scottish Office (Edinburgh: HMSO).
Avis, Martin, Robert Braham, Neil Crosby, David Gane, Marion Temple, and Alexandra Whitman (1993) *Property Management Performance Monitoring* (Wallingford: GTI Publishers/School of Real Estate Management, Oxford Brookes University).
Balchin, Paul N. and G. H. Bull (1987) *Regional and Urban Economics* (London: Harper and Row).
Balchin, P. N., J. L. Kieve and G. H. Bull (1988) *Urban Land Economics and Public Policy* 4th edn, Macmillan Building and Surveying Series (London: Macmillan).
Balchin, Paul N. (1990) *Regional Policy in Britain: the north–south divide* (London: Paul Chapman).
Baldwin, Richard (1989) 'The Growth Effects of 1992', *Economic Policy*, no. 9.
Barnekov, T., R. Boyle and R. Rich (1989) *Privatism and Urban Policy in Britain and the United States* (Oxford University Press).
Barnett, R. R., R. Levaggi, and P. Smith (1990) 'An assessment of the regional impact of the introduction of the Community Charge in England', *Regional Studies*, vol. 24.
Bateman, Michael (1985) *Office Development: A Geographical Analysis* (Beckenham: Croom Helm).
Benko, Georges and M. Dunford (eds) (1991) *Industrial Change and Regional Development* (London: Belhaven Press).
Berry, Brian and John Parr (eds) (1992) *Market Centers and Retail Locations* (New Jersey: Prentice Hall).
Berry J., S. McGreal and B. Deddis (eds) (1993) *Urban Regeneration* (London: E. and F. N. Spon).
Bover, O., J. Muellbauer and A. Murphy (1989) 'Housing, wages and UK labour markets', *Oxford Bulletin of Economic Statistics*, vol. 51, pp. 97–136.
Bowen, A. and K. Mayhew (eds) (1991) *Reducing Regional Inequalities*, Policy Issues Series, National Economic Development Office (London: Kogan Page).
Breheny, M. and P. Congdon (eds) (1989) 'Growth and Change in a Core Region', *London Papers in Regional Science*, vol. 20 (London: Pion).

Brownill, Sue (1990) *Developing London's Dockland* (London: Paul Chapman).
Cameron, Gordon, B. Moore, D. Nicholls, J. Rhodes, and P. Tyler (1991) *Cambridge Regional Economic Review* (Cambridge, PA Cambridge Economic Consultants/ Department of Land Economy, University of Cambridge).
Campbell, Mike (1991) 'Trends and prospects in the regional labour market', *The Regional Review*, vol. 1, no. 2, pp. 16, 17.
Catherwood, Fred (1991) 'European Integration: Political Union and Economic and Monetary Union', *National Westminster Bank Quarterly Review*, May, pp. 35–46.
Ceccini, Paulo (ed.) (1988) *The European Challenge 1992* (London: Gower and Wildwood House).
Champion, A. G., A. E. Green, D. Owen, D. J. Ellin and M. G. Coombes (1987) *Changing Places: Britain's Demographic, Economic and Social Complexion* (London: Edward Arnold).
Champion, A. G. and A. R. Townsend (1990) *Contemporary Britain: A Geographical Perspective* (Sevenoaks: Edward Arnold).
Cheshire, Paul (1990) 'Explaining the Recent Performance of the European Community's Major Urban Regions', *Urban Studies*, vol. 27, pp. 311–33.
Cheshire, Paul and D. Hay (1989) *Urban Problems in Western Europe:an Economic Analysis* (London: Unwin Hyman).
Cheshire, Paul and A. Evans (1991) *Urban and Regional Economics* (Cheltenham: Edward Elgar).
Chisholm, Michael and P. Kivell (1987) *Inner City Wasteland: an Assessment of Government and Market Failure in Land Development*, Hobart Paper no. 108 (London: IEA).
College of Estate Management (1990) *Urban Regeneration, Planning and Financial Incentives* (Reading: CEM).
Cooke, P. (ed.) (1989) *Localities: The Changing Face of Urban Britain* (London: Unwin Hyman).
Cullingworth, J. B. (1988) *Town and Country Planning in Britain*, 10th edn (London: Unwin Hyman).
Damesick, P., and P. Wood (eds) (1987) *Regional Problems, Problem Regions and Public Policy in the UK* (Oxford University Press).
Daniels, P. W. (ed.) (1979) *Spatial Patterns of Office Growth and Location* (Chichester: Wiley).
Day, Graham and G. Rees (1989) *Contemporary Wales: an annual review of economic and social research* (Cardiff: University of Wales).
Debbage, K. and J. Rees (1991) 'Company Perceptions of Comparative Advantage by Region', *Regional Studies*, vol. 25, no. 3, pp. 199–206.
Diamond, D. R. and N. A. Spence (1983) *Regional Policy Evaluation: A methodological review and the Scottish example* (London: Gower).
Dudley, James W. (1989) *1992: Strategies for the Single Market* (London: CIMA).
El-Agraa, Ali M. (ed.) (1990) *The Economics of the European Community*, 3rd edn (London: Philip Allen).
Emerson, Michael, M. Aujean, M. Catinet, P. Goybet, and A. Jaquemin (1988) *The Economics of 1992* (Oxford University Press).
Evans, Alan W. (1990) 'A house price based regional policy', *Regional Studies*, vol. 24, pp. 559–67
Evans, Alan W. and G. Crampton (1989) 'Myth, Reality and Employment in Central London', *Journal of Transport Economics and Policy*, no. 23, pp. 89–108.
Evans, Alan W. and D. E. C. Eversley (eds) (1980) *The Inner City: Employment and Industry* (London: Heinemann).

Forrest, David (1991) 'An analysis of house price differentials between English regions', *Regional Studies*, vol. 25, pp. 231–8.

Fothergill, S. and G. Gudgin (1982) *Unequal Growth: Urban and Regional Employment Change in the UK* (London: Heinemann).

Fothergill, S. and N. Guy (1990) *Retreat from the Regions* (London: Jessica Kingsley Publishers/Regional Studies Association).

Fujita, M. (1989) *Urban Economic Theory – Land Use and City Size* (Cambridge: Cambridge University Press).

Goddard, J.B. and A.G. Champion (eds) (1983) *The Urban and Regional Transformation of Britain* (London: Methuen).

Goddard, J.B. and M.G. Coombes (1987) *The north–south divide: local perspectives* (Centre for Urban and Regional Development Studies, University of Newcastle on Tyne).

Gordon, Ian R. (1985) 'The cyclical sensitivity of regional employment and unemployment differentials', *Regional Studies*, vol. 19, pp. 95–110.

Gore, Charles (1984) *Regions in question: space, development theory and regional policy* (London: Methuen).

Gudgin, Graham, B. Moore and J. Rhodes (1982) 'Employment Problems in the Cities and Regions of the UK: Prospects for the 1980s', *Cambridge Economic Policy Review*, vol. 8, no. 12.

Hamnett, Chris (1988) 'Regional variations in house prices and house price inflation in Britain 1969–1988', *Royal Bank of Scotland Review*, no. 159, pp. 29–40.

Harloe, Michael; Christopher Pickvance and John Urry (eds) (1990) *Place, Policy and Politics: Do Localities Matter?* (London: Unwin Hyman).

Harris, R.I.D. (1988) 'Market structure and external control in the regional economies of Great Britain', *Scottish Journal of Political Economy*, vol. 35, pp. 335–60.

Hart, M. and R. Harrison (eds) (1992) *Spatial Policy in a Divided Nation* (London: Jessica Kingsley).

Harvey, Jack (1992) *Urban Land Economics*, 3rd edn (Basingstoke: Macmillan).

Healey, Michael J. and B.W. Ilbery (1990) *Location and Change* (Oxford University Press).

Henley Centre for Forecasting (1990) *Local Futures: The Geography of British Prosperity 1990–1995* (London: Henley Centre).

Herington, John (1990) *Beyond green belts: managing urban growth in the 21st century* (London: Kingsley).

Hodges, Michael and W. Wallace (eds) (1981) *Economic divergence in the European Community* (London: Allen and Unwin).

Hudson, R. and J.R. Lewis (eds) (1982) *Regional Planning in Europe* (London: Pion).

Hughes, G. and B. McCormick (1987) 'Housing markets, unemployment and labour market flexibility in the UK', *European Economic Review*, no. 31, pp. 615–41.

Kaldor, N. (1970) 'The case for regional policies', *Scottish Journal of Political Economy*, vol. 17, pp. 337–48.

Keating, Michael and B. Jones (1985) *Regions in the European Community* (Oxford: Clarendon).

Keeble, David (1982) *The influence of peripheral and central locations on the relative development of regions* (Cambridge: Department of Geography, University of Cambridge).

Lewis, J. and A. Townsend (eds) (1989) *The North–South Divide: Regional Change in Britain in the 1980s* (London: Paul Chapman).

Love, J. H. (1989) 'External takeover and regional economic development', *Regional Studies* vol. 23, pp. 417–29.
Marshall, J. N., N. Alderman and A. T. Thwaites (1991) 'Civil Service Location and the English Regions', *Regional Studies* vol. 25, no. 6, pp. 499–510.
Martin, Ron (1989) 'The growth and geographical anatomy of venture capital in the UK', *Regional Studies*, vol. 23, no. 5, pp. 389–403.
Martin, Ron and B. Rowthorn (eds) (1986) *The Geography of Deindustrialisation* (Basingstoke: Macmillan).
Martin, Ron and P. Townroe (eds) (1992) *Regional Development in the 1990s* (London: Jessica Kingsley Publishers/Regional Studies Association).
McGoldrick, P. (1990) *Retail Marketing* (London: McGraw-Hill).
McWilliams, Douglas (1992) *Commercial Property and Company Borrowing* (London: Royal Institute of Chartered Surveyors).
Molle, Willem (1980) *Regional disparity and economic development in the European Community* (Farnborough: Saxon House).
Moore, Barry and J. Rhodes (1973) 'Evaluating the effects of British regional economic policy', *Economic Journal*, vol. 83, no. 329, pp. 87–110.
Moore, Barry, J. Rhodes and P. Tyler (1982) *The interaction of regional and urban policy in the United Kingdom*, Cambridge, Department of Land Economy discussion paper no. 4 (University of Cambridge).
Moore, Barry, J. Rhodes and P. Tyler (1984) *The co-ordination of urban and regional policies*, Cambridge, Department of Land Economy discussion paper no. 11 (University of Cambridge).
Moore, Barry, J. Rhodes and P. Tyler (1987) *The Effect of Government Regional Economic Policy* (London: HMSO).
Needham, Barrie, B. Kruijt and P. Koenders (1993) *Urban Land and Property Markets in The Netherlands* (London: University College London Press).
Nevin, Edward (1990) *The Economics of Europe* (Basingstoke: Macmillan).
Pinder, David (1983) *Regional Economic Development and Policy: theory and practice in the European Community*, Studies on Contemporary Europe, no. 5 (London: Allen and Unwin).
Pissarides, C. and J. Wadsworth (1989) 'Unemployment and the inter-regional mobility of labour', *Economic Journal*, vol. 99, pp. 739–55.
Prestwich, Roger and Peter Taylor (1990) *Introduction to Regional and Urban Policy in the United Kingdom* (Harlow: Longman).
Royal Town Planning Institute (1988) *Strategic Planning at National and Regional Levels* (London: RTPI).
Schofield, J. A. (1989) *Cost–Benefit Analysis in Urban and Regional Planning* (London: Unwin Hyman).
Seers, Dudley and K. Ostrom (eds) (1983) *The Crises of the European Regions* (London: Macmillan).
Seers, Dudley and C. Vaitsos (eds) (1980) *Integration and unequal development: the experience of the EEC* (London: Macmillan).
Smith, David (1994) *North and South*, 2nd edn (London: Penguin).
Steel, John (1992) 'Urban Regeneration, Urban Development Corporations, and the new Urban Regeneration Agency', *Property Review*, October, pp. 45–47.
Stewart, Murray (1990) *Regional development trends*, Bristol, School for Advanced Urban Studies, working paper no. 29 (University of Bristol).
Swann, Dennis (1988) *The Economics of the Common Market*, 6th edn (London: Penguin).

Townroe, P. M. (1969) 'Locational choice and the individual firm', *Regional Studies*, vol. 3, pp. 15–24.
Twomey, J. and J. Taylor (1985) 'Regional Policy and the inter-regional movement of manufacturing industry in Great Britain', *Scottish Journal of Political Economy*, vol. 32, pp. 257–77.
Wilkinson, David (1992) 'Has the north–south divide come to an end?', *National Institute Economic Review*, November, pp. 88–98.
Wren, Colin (1990) 'Regional Policy in the 1980s', *National Westminster Bank Review*, November, pp. 52–65.
Wrigley, N. (1988) *Store Choice, Store Location and Market Analysis* (New York: Routledge).
Yuill, Douglas *et al.* (eds) (1990) *European regional incentives* (London: Bowker-Saur).

Government Publications and Official Reports

Commission of the European Communities (1986) *The contribution of infrastructure to regional development*, final report by the Infrastructure Study Group (Luxembourg).
Commission of the European Communities (1990) *The Regions in the 1990s* (Luxembourg).
Department of Employment (1990, 1992, 1993), *Gazette* (London: HMSO).
Department of the Environment (1988) *Planning Policy Guidance Note 5, Simplified Planning Zones* (London: HMSO).
Department of the Environment (1989a) *Action for Cities* (London: HMSO).
Department of the Environment (1989b) *Urban Regeneration and Economic Development – the Local Government Dimension* (London: HMSO).
Department of the Environment (1990) *Indicators of comparative regional/local economic performance and prospects: final report* (London: HMSO).
Department of the Environment (1992a) *The Urban Regeneration Agency* (Consultation Paper) (London: HMSO).
Department of the Environment (1992b) *Council Tax* (London: HMSO).
Department of the Environment (1993) *Annual Report* (London: HMSO).
Department of Trade and Industry, The Scottish Office, The Welsh Office (1993) *Regional Policy: Review of the Assisted Areas of Great Britain.*
Hansard (4 December 1991) written answer.
Hansard (17 December 1992) written answer.
National Audit Office (1992) *Annual Report* (London: HMSO).
National Economic Development Office (1985) *Investment in the Public Sector Built Infrastructure* (London: HMSO).
National Institute for Economic and Social Research (1992) *Review*, February.
Office of Population Censuses and Surveys (1991, 1992) *Population Trends* (London: HMSO).
Rural Development Commission (1989) *Promoting Jobs and Communities in Rural England* (London: RDC).
United Kingdom Central Statistical Office (1990) *Social Trends* (London: HMSO).
United Kingdom Treasury (1990) *Economic Briefing* number 1.

Index

ability to pay 196
accelerator 116
accommodating flows 159
activity rates 50, 238
   in UK regions, 1992 50
additionality 205, 267
age structure of population 48
agglomeration economies *see*
   economies of scale, external
aggregate demand 80-83
   economic cycles 114
   full-employment equilibrium 83, 127
   regional growth 110
aggregate supply 107
   economic cycles 115
   elasticity 107
agriculture
   policy support 246-8
   specialisation 160-2, 176
Amsterdam Waterfront 210
Arc Mediterranean 174
Armstrong, H. and Taylor, J. 65, 118, 249, 266
Ashcroft, B. 39, 241
assignment of policies 227, 263
assisted areas 230-8, 252-9
   current designation 238
average input cost
   of labour 51
   of land 65

balance of payments, interregional 90
   expenditure-changing policies 91
   expenditure-switching policies 90
Barlow Report 231
Bateman, M. 141, 148
behavioural theory 55
Belgium
   EC funding 249
   gross domestic product 159
Benelux
   gross domestic product 104
   service-sector employment 14

black economy 33
branch plant 39, 40, 262, 273-5
   benefits to region 39
   branch plant closures 40, 275
   costs to region 40
   and Northern Ireland 273-5
Brussels 159
built-in policy stabilisers 92, 117

capital expenditure, in UK
   regions 108, 109
capital intensity, of manufacturing
   sector 30
capital/output ratio 111
capital productivity 129
capital supply, economic growth 108
catchment areas 140, 150
central place theory 140
characteristics of the unemployed *see*
   unemployed, characteristics
Christaller, W. 140, 141
City Action Teams 222
city grant 203, 207, 223
   job-creation effects 204
   regional distribution 223
   in West Midlands 204
civil service decentralisation 240-2
   Hardman Report 233
classical unemployment 125-9
coalfield areas fund 224, 237
collective bargaining 172
compensation principle 101, 277
complementarity, of inputs 170
conditionality, of investment 162
conflicts in policy aims 263
constraints on policy 264-71
   political priorities 265
   time lags 264, 271
   uncertainty 265, 271
consumption expenditure 79-81
   consumption function 80
contaminated land 215
convergence 168, 245
core regions, in the EC 166, 174, 245

cost–benefit evaluation 144, 266, 270
  of regional policy 266
cost-effectiveness evaluation 143, 267
council tax 195
creation of employment 204
cycles
  and branch plants 262, 275
  causes 114
  in the housing market 186
  and interregional migration 179
  in the property market 152
  in the regional economy 111, 118
  in the UK economy 111
  and urban regeneration 214

Daniels, W.W. 139
defence expenditure 237, 239, 242
  and current regional policy 237
  in South West region 239, 242
deindustrialisation 12, 16, 26–34
  full-time male employment 33
  and location 145
  long-term trend in the UK 12
  manufacturing employment 16
  manufacturing output 27
  regional inequality 28, 29
  regional unemployment 33, 119
Denmark, service-sector
  employment 14
dependency, economic 3
derelict land grant 215, 221, 224
development areas 229–36, 252–5
diminishing returns 52
discouraged workers 50
discrimination, in the labour
  market 48, 56, 123
disparities, interregional, in the
  UK 11, 106
displacement effects *see* diversion
disposable income
  regional distribution 71
  subregional distribution 72
Distribution of Industry Act 231
divergence 20, 169, 181, 245
  attractive/unattractive regions 170
  and market failure 169
  and migration 181
  in the UK 20
diversion of activity 205, 268, 278
Dublin 174, 176
duration of unemployment 35, 123
  by gender 120

East Anglia
  civil service relocation 242
  gross domestic product 106
  occupational distribution 62
  population change 48
East Midlands of England
  labour force qualifications 59
  manufacturing employment 16
  occupational distribution 62
  primary-sector employment 30
economic dependence 161
economic rent 58
economies of scale
  external economies 65, 109, 141,
    147, 173
  internal economies 109, 173
efficiency 93–8, 142
  and public-sector location 155, 244
  in regional policy 277
  in taxation 193
  welfare 93–8, 101, 270
employers' organisations 172
employment, sectoral distribution *see*
  sectoral distribution of employment
English Estates 207, 224, 254
English Partnership 207, 223, 236, 254
enterprise initiative 236
enterprise zone 205, 221
  job-creation effects 205
  financial incentives 221
equity
  benefit principle 195
  horizontal equity 194
  and public-sector location 244
  in taxation 193
  vertical equity 194
equity, interregional 40, 97, 144, 196,
    240, 268
  effects of branch plants 40
  regional policy effects 268
European Regional Development
  Fund 165, 234, 245, 253–5
  net beneficiaries 247
  net contributors 247
Evans, A. 189
evaluation of regional policy 276–80
export revenue, to the region 162
externalities 98–101, 215, 268–71
  effects of branch plants 40
  consumption externalities 98, 99
  production externalities 98, 99
  property rights 100

externalities (*cont.*)
  in regional policy 268–71
  in urban regeneration 215
external ownership 40

feedback effects *see* multiplier
female employment, part-time *see* part-time employment
financial capital 38–46
  demand for financial capital 45
  mobility 41, 42
  supply of financial capital 42–5, 170, 213
financial institutions 41
fiscal neutrality 193
Forrest, D. 185
Fothergill, S. and Gudgin, N. 37
Fothergill, S. and Guy, N. 39, 40, 275
France
  gross domestic product 104, 159
  office location 147
full employment 127

geographical mobility *see* mobility of labour
Germany
  city states 9
  and EC regional policy 245–9
  gross domestic product 104, 159
  housing market 182
  labour supply 128
  regional labour markets 131–3
Greater London, long-term unemployment 120
Greece
  and EC regional policy 245–9
  gross domestic product 157
  peripheral location 174
  primary-sector employment 14
Gripaios, P. and Bishop, P. 76, 239
gross domestic product (GDP)
  in the EC economies 104, 158
  in the UK regions 11, 104, 105
growth poles 88, 202, 232
growth potential 107
growth rate 111
growth, regional 103–11
  cumulative nature of 171
  and the housing market 189
  supply constraints 106, 107
  underlying trend rate of growth 103

growth zone 104, 159, 173
  Arc Mediterranean 174
  La Dorsale 174
  supranational zones 159, 173
Gudgin, G. and Roper, S. 78

Hailsham Report 232
Hardman Report 233, 252
Hamburg, regional GDP 159
Harrod–Domar 111
Hicks–Kaldor criterion 101, 277
hidden unemployment 33
housing market 181–90
  in the economic cycle 186
  effect on growth 189
  effect on inflation 185
  income elasticity of demand 93
  house prices 186
  owner-occupied housing 181, 190
  quality of the housing stock 187
  regional price differentials 185–7
  rented housing 182
human capital 62, 178

Ile de France, regional GDP 159
implementation of policy 261–6
income differentials, reasons for 75
income, disposable
  intraregional variation 73
  subregional distribution, 1990 72
  UK regional distribution, 1991 71
income elasticity of demand 164
income sources *see* sources of income
income tax liability, regional distribution 92
industrial concentration 39
Industrial Development Certificates 231, 234, 252–4
industrial location 137, 145
Industry Act 231–3, 252
industry subsidies 229
  regional distribution 235
inflation, regional
  effects on regional growth 135
  house prices 135
  wage pressures 63, 134, 172, 185
infrastructure provision 209, 215, 246, 269
input–output 85–90
  role of linkages 88
institutional investors, role in urban regeneration 214

Index

interest rates 41, 46, 76
  effects on income 77
intermediate areas 233, 236, 252–5
international capital market 41
investment
  interregional distribution 108, 109, 159
  portfolio strategies 153
  regional growth 110
  sources of finance 160
investment appraisal 153
investment grants 228, 232, 253, 261, 272
  multiplier effects 261
  as a regional policy 272
involuntary unemployment 126
inward investment 38, 42, 141, 161
Italy
  EC funding 249
  gross domestic product 104
  labour market adjustment 133
  southern region 174

Keynesian unemployment 124–6
Kohnstamm, W. 208

La Dorsale 173
labour costs, non-wage labour costs 47
labour demand 52
  effect on unemployment 129
  elasticity of 53, 133
  employer preferences 55, 56
labour force
  occupational distribution *see* occupational distribution of labour
  qualifications 59
  skills 58, 61
labour heterogeneity 58, 124
labour markets, regional 48–56, 133, 168, 177
  adjustment 133, 134, 168, 178
  discrimination 48, 56
  imperfectly competitive 55
  migration 177
  perfectly competitive 53, 177
  segregated labour markets 55
  stigmatised labour market 55
labour mobility *see* mobility of labour
labour productivity 64, 129
labour subsidies 233

labour supply 48–51, 107, 129
  in economic growth 107
  elasticity of 51, 63, 130
land markets, regional
  demand for land 66
  supply of land 65, 67, 107
Leigh, C. and Stilwell, J. 278
leverage of policy 227
linkages 88
local government
  development agencies 204
  local enterprise 204
local income tax 194
location choice 153, 205, 240
  enterprise zones 205
  public sector 240
location decision 151, 241, 269
  relocation costs 269
  timescale 241
location disadvantage 174–6
location theory 138–54
  central place theory 140
  and economic efficiency 142
  management theories 138, 154
  and organisation objectives 143
  spheres of influence 140
locational hierarchy 139, 275
locational preferences 146, 169, 286
London
  housing market 182
  migration 179
London Docklands 209, 240
  accessibility 209
  negative externalities 100
  office development 148
long-term unemployment 59, 120–4
Luxembourg, gross domestic product 104, 157

Mackay, R.R. 34
manufacturing
  employment 16, 30
  location 145
  value added 108, 109
market failure 95–101
marginal input cost
  of labour 50
  of land 65, 67
marginal private benefit 98
marginal revenue product
  of labour 52
  of land 66

marginal social benefit 98
Marshall, A. 241
Martin, R. 43
Martin, R. and Townroe, P. 225
matched plant comparison 274
McGoldrick, W. 150
measurement of policy 266–76
Merseyside
  assisted area status 232
  disposable income 73
  EC funding 249
  long-term unemployment 121
  migration 179
migration, interregional 177–80
  costs associated with 267
  and employment opportunities 178
  and the housing market 187
  as an investment decision 178
  and labour market adjustment 177
  and the life cycle 179
  effect on regional skill levels 62
  UK pattern 179
migration flows 180
mobility of financial capital 41, 42
mobility of labour
  by age group 180
  geographical 108, 168
  occupational 108
Muellbauer, J. 184
multiplier 84, 88–90, 116, 204
  effect of city grants 204
  in the construction industry 156
  in the economic cycle 116
  employment multiplier 89
  income multiplier 78, 89, 274
  effect of investment grant 261
  marginal propensity to consume 84
  output multiplier 89
  of regional policy 227

National Audit Office 144, 155, 240–4
Needham, B. 202, 217
Netherlands
  Amsterdam Waterfront 211
  growth centres 202
  housing market 190
  PPP schemes 214
  subsidiarity 192
new towns in UK 202
North of England
  activity rates 50
  assisted area status 232, 236
  EC funding 246
  gross domestic product 11, 106
  housing market 182
  long-term unemployment 120
  as a manufacturing location 146
  manufacturing value added 109
  occupational distribution 62
  population change 48
  sources of income 74, 78
  unemployment rate 119
  uniform business rate 197
North/South divide 40
  in UK house prices 185–7
North West of England
  civil service relocation 242
  disposable income 73
  economic dependence 161
  house prices 187
  long-term unemployment 120, 123
  regional policy expenditure 236
  subregional unemployment 121
Northern Ireland
  civil service relocation 242
  EC funding 246, 249
  effects of outmigration 21
  employment by sector 16, 30–2, 156
  GDP relative to UK 11
  house prices 189
  income by source 72, 78
  labour force qualifications 59
  labour market adjustment 133
  manufacturing value added 109
  occupational distribution 62
  regional policy impact 272–4
  unemployment 119, 120

occupational distribution of labour
  in UK regions, 1992 61
occupational mobility see mobility of labour
office development 148
office development permits 230–4
office location 146–8
organisation of production 110
out-of-town retailing 149
outer region see peripheral region

Pareto criterion 95, 101, 144, 277
part-time employment, female employment 32
perceived risk, effect on regional investment 169

peripheral regions, 174, 274
  in the EC 166, 174–6, 238, 245
  EC funding 249
  relative per capita GDP 11
planning restrictions 228, 230
poles de croissance see growth poles
political centralisation 2, 278, 283
political costs of policy 269
political priority of policy 281
pollution *see* externalities
population
  age structure in UK regions 48
  regional change 48
  regional UK growth, 1961–91 49
population density 48
Portugal
  EC funding 249
  gross domestic product 159
Prebisch, W. and Singer, H.W. 164
Prestwich, R. and Taylor, P. 233
price system 93–101
  market adjustment 93
  market failure 95, 271
primary product prices 162
primary-sector employment 14, 16, 30–2
private/public-sector partnership schemes (PPPs) 208–14
  Amsterdam Waterfront 211
  in regional policy 276
  role in urban regeneration 212
privatisation of policy 276
producer services 28, 141
productive potential 63, 115
property management 154, 239
property market 141
property taxes 195
public-sector employment 156
public-sector location 143, 155, 240–4, 286
  efficiency of, 155, 244
  and regional policy 285, 286
  relocation 242
public-sector pay 173

qualifications of workforce 59, 60
  UK regional differences 60

recession, UK regional impact 119
regional development grant 229, 235, 252–5
regional employment premium 252–4

regional enterprise grant 236, 255
regional government 192, 283
regional policy, 1993 review 236–8, 255
regional selective assistance 235, 252–5
relative price effects 26
Republic of Ireland 174–6, 247–9
  EC funding 247
  peripheral location 174–6
  western region 176
retail location 140, 149, 150
Robinson, F. 38

sales taxes 195
savings rate 111
Scotland
  assisted area status 232
  civil service relocation 242
  EC funding 246–9
  effects of external ownership 40, 161
  employment by sector 30–2
  GDP relative to UK 11
  housing market 182
  income by source 71–3, 78
  as a nation region 5
  peripheral location 174
  population change 48
  regional policy expenditure 236
  subregional unemployment 121
Scottish Enterprise 204, 234, 253
sectoral distribution of employment
  in the EC economies, 1990 15
  male and female 32
  in the Republic of Ireland 176
  in UK regions 17, 31
service-sector employment 14, 16, 30–2
service-sector location 147, 280, 285
shadow prices 144
shift-share analysis 35–7
simplified planning zones 206
single internal market 159, 229, 245
  effect on investment 159
skill mismatch 33
skills, and unemployment 122
social security income 74
  UK regional distribution, 1990 77
sources of income 73–8, 274
  earned income 75
  investment income 76
  self-employment income 74
  transfer payments 74, 77, 274
  UK regional distribution, 1990 74
  unearned income 76

South East of England
  activity rates 50
  assisted area status 236
  civil service relocation 242
  effect of 1990s' recession 119
  employment by sector 30–2
  GDP relative to UK 11
  housing market 182, 187, 190
  income by source 72, 74
  income tax payments 92
  investment and value added 109
  labour force characteristics 48, 59, 62
  as a manufacturing location 146
  migration 180
  supply constraints 107
  unemployment rate 119
  uniform business rate 198
South/North divide *see* North/South divide
South West of England
  assisted area status 232
  civil service relocation 242
  defence expenditure 237
  EC funding 246
  employment by sector 16, 30–2
  housing market 182
  occupational distribution 62
  population age structure 48
  regional policy expenditure 236
  sources of income 72, 75
  subregional unemployment 121
Spain
  EC funding 249
  southern region 174
spatial equity *see* equity, interregional
special development areas 233, 253
speculative development 148
spheres of influence 140
stigmatised labour market 55
stigmatised locations 170
Structural Funds, EC 255
structural unemployment 124, 238
  EC policy 249
subregional unemployment 121
subsidiarity 9, 192, 278
supply-side 106, 168, 180, 228
  adjustment 168, 180
  economic growth 106

task forces 223
tax base 193–5

technical efficiency 244
technology transfer 39
terms of trade 164
time lags in policy process 264
tourism 176
trade, interregional 13, 159
trade unions 172

underemployment of labour 63
unemployed, characteristics
  age 35, 122
  industry 122
  skill level 122
  skill type 122
unemployment
  explanations of 124–7
  interregional labour market adjustment 131, 168, 178
  labour force characteristics 122
  regional labour market 127
  and regional policy criteria 238
unemployment rates 50, 118–21
  in EC in 1980s 34
  in selected UK subregions 121
  in the UK regions 118
uniform business rate 197
urban areas 199–202
  housing provision 201, 210
  image 201, 205, 210
  industrial decline 199
  site dereliction 200
urban development areas 206, 209, 218–21
urban development corporations 206, 209, 218–21
urban programme 207, 214, 218, 244
urban regeneration hgants 221
urban–rural shift 37, 145, 179

value added in manufacturing, in UK regions 108, 109
value of marginal product
  of capital 170
  of labour 52, 55, 129, 133
  of land 66
venture capital 43, 277
vicious circle 171, 274
virtuous circle 171
voluntary unemployment 125
voting patterns 9, 266

wage determination, national pay
    structures 172
wage differentials, interregional 46, 56,
    62, 172
  effects of national pay rates 132
Wales
  activity rates 50
  assisted area status 232, 237
  civil service relocation 242
  EC funding 246, 249
  employment by sector 30–2
  GDP relative to UK 11
  hidden unemployment 33
  income by source 72, 75, 78
  as a manufacturing location 146
  migration 180
  occupational distribution 62
  population, age structure 48
  regional policy expenditure 236
Walsh, R. 174

welfare 57, 93–98
welfare loss 57, 58, 63, 277
Welsh Development Agency 253
West Midlands of England
  city grants 204
  EC funding 246
  house prices 187
  impact of deindustrialisation 28
  income tax payment 92
  labour force qualifications 59
  long-term unemployment 120
  manufacturing employment 16, 30
  migration 179
Witbraad, F. and Jorna, P. 202

Yorkshire and Humberside
  assisted area status 237
  sectoral distribution of
    employment 32
  service-sector employment 30